Ideology, Mimesis, Fantasy

**UNC** | COLLEGE OF ARTS AND SCIENCES
Germanic and Slavic Languages and Literatures

From 1949 to 2004, UNC Press and the UNC Department of Germanic & Slavic Languages and Literatures published the UNC Studies in the Germanic Languages and Literatures series. Monographs, anthologies, and critical editions in the series covered an array of topics including medieval and modern literature, theater, linguistics, philology, onomastics, and the history of ideas. Through the generous support of the National Endowment for the Humanities and the Andrew W. Mellon Foundation, books in the series have been reissued in new paperback and open access digital editions. For a complete list of books visit www.uncpress.org.

# Ideology, Mimesis, Fantasy
Charles Sealsfield, Friedrich Gerstäcker, Karl May, and Other German Novelists of America

JEFFREY L. SAMMONS

UNC Studies in the Germanic Languages and Literatures
Number 121

Copyright © 1998

This work is licensed under a Creative Commons CC BY-NC-ND license. To view a copy of the license, visit http://creativecommons.org/licenses.

Suggested citation: Sammons, Jeffrey L. *Ideology, Mimesis, Fantasy: Charles Sealsfield, Friedrich Gerstäcker, Karl May, and Other German Novelists of America*. Chapel Hill: University of North Carolina Press, 1998. DOI: https://doi.org/10.5149/9781469656717_Sammons

Library of Congress Cataloging-in-Publication Data
Names: Sammons, Jeffrey L.
Title: Ideology, mimesis, fantasy : Charles Sealsfield, Friedrich Gerstäcker, Karl May, and other German novelists of America / by Jeffrey L. Sammons.
Other titles: University of North Carolina Studies in the Germanic Languages and Literatures ; no. 121.
Description: Chapel Hill : University of North Carolina Press, [1998] Series: University of North Carolina Studies in the Germanic Languages and Literatures. | Includes bibliographical references.
Identifiers: LCCN 97048282 | ISBN 978-1-4696-5670-0 (pbk: alk. paper) | ISBN 978-1-4696-5671-7 (ebook)
Subjects: German fiction — 19th century — History and criticism. | America — In literature.
Classification: LCC PT763 .S26 1998 | DCC 833/ .7093273

# Contents

Introduction ix

Abbreviations xiii

## Part I. Ideology: Charles Sealsfield

1. The Sealsfield Riddle 3

2. What Is an Austrian Jacksonian? Sealsfield's Political Evolution from *The Indian Chief* (1829) to *Der Legitime und die Republikaner* (1833) 23

3. Slavery, Race, and Nation: The Antebellum Southern Context 37

4. The Shape of Freedom in the Plantation Novels 59

5. *Die Deutsch-amerikanischen Wahlverwandtschaften*: An Attempt at a Social Novel 79

**Excursus I.** The Emergence of the German Western: Balduin Möllhausen and Friedrich Armand Strubberg 90

## Part II. Mimesis: Friedrich Gerstäcker

6. The Revealed Vocation 113

7. The Multicultural Bear Hunt: An Introduction to Gerstäcker's Narrative Devices 136

8. Gerstäcker's America: Social and Political Observations 151

9. The Immigration Trilogy: *Nach Amerika!*, *Gold!*, *In Amerika* 177

**Excursus II.** Anti-Americanism? Talvj, Ferdinand Kürnberger, Reinhold Solger 201

## Part III. Fantasy: Karl May

10. Germany's Americans: Old Shatterhand and Winnetou — 229

11. On the Absence of Germany's Americans in America — 246

Outlook — 257

Notes — 271

Bibliography — 303

Index — 337

# Introduction

This inquiry into German fiction about America in the nineteenth century had its origin in the United States Bicentennial of 1976. Those working in the German field at that time will recall that there was a considerable amount of commotion concerning German-American history and cultural relations, much of it sponsored by the West German and Austrian governments for policy reasons. In my relentless though not always successful pursuit of relevance, I endeavored to participate in the occasion with a graduate seminar on the nineteenth-century German novel about America. I regarded this topic as a segment in my ongoing inquiry into the nineteenth-century German novel, which, since my discovery that the much vaunted national dominance of the *Bildungsroman* is a mirage, has been focused on what I sometimes call the books people at the time actually read. I began to project a four-part treatise, of which the first volume, a period study, had appeared in this series as *Six Essays on the Young German Novel* in 1972. The second, an author study, *Wilhelm Raabe: The Fiction of the Alternative Community*, was published by Princeton University Press in 1987. The third, a thematic study, is the present volume. The fourth, a generic study of the social and political novel, remains inchoate for the time being.

A number of factors combined to cause this segment of the project to take much longer and require considerably more effort than I had supposed. At the outset I greatly underestimated the magnitude of the topic. I knew little about it and was acquainted with only a couple of authors' names. It was soon evident that I had found my way into a major discourse of nineteenth-century Germany, both fictional and expository. Becoming acquainted with even a fraction of it required years of reading. At the same time, there was relatively little in the way of helpful literary-historical and critical materials, and much of that was old. But in the meantime this aspect of the situation has changed dramatically. Partly impelled by the Bicentennial and perhaps also by the so-called German-American Tricentennial of 1983, studies have proliferated enormously. While at the beginning I was able to master the secondary literature without difficulty, today it is all but impossible to keep up with it, and I have had at some point to draw a line under it, approximately around the middle of 1995. This expansion has involved not only the field of literature but also those of history, political science, international relations, and certain kinds of cultural studies concerning such topics as the immigration, the German American experience, and the imaging of the West and of Indians. Some of this work, especially in regard to current affairs, and a certain amount of institutionalization of research have been impelled by an apprehension that, notwithstanding blue jeans, pop music, McDonald's, and the Internet, the German and American cultures are bifurcating and growing stranger to one another. From the perspective of my own field I fully share this perception. I feel that there is an obligation of Americans in all areas of German studies to address this development; with that purpose in mind, I have added a concluding conspectus of the America theme in German letters from the end of the nineteenth century to the present.

Another hindrance to the efficient execution of my project was a strong disinclination to deal with Karl May. On the one hand, the contour of my subject seemed to require his inclusion; on the other, I remained unproductively baffled that an author whom I found silly and tedious should be, by a gigantic margin, the best-selling fiction writer in his homeland and not only a favorite of children, as one might expect, but an object of veneration and solemn contemplation by many adults and even scholars. Few features of the German culture that is supposed to be my life's work have contributed so much to my sense of strangeness from it than the phenomenon of Karl May. But it occurred to me that, although I would never pretend to be a representative American, in this respect I am quite typical, for, although Karl May's international reputation is not inconsiderable elsewhere, he has never been able to obtain a footing in this country despite various initiatives. Since the reasons for this are not immediately obvious, I determined to address the reception problem as a way of relating May to the topic as a whole.

The not inconsiderable space given to questions of race in these pages may look like adaptation to current concerns, but in fact it is required by the material, for race issues were bound to preoccupy any serious observer of America in the nineteenth century. Although the institution of slavery was, in a sense, the distillate of racist presuppositions, I have placed somewhat more emphasis on race itself than on the depiction of slavery in the novels; the latter has been extensively discussed and there has been a sometimes self-serving German American appropriation of innocence in regard to the support of abolition and the Union cause in the Civil War. It is quite possible to be opposed to slavery and yet remain racist. A racist discourse in the broadest sense was all but universal in the nineteenth century; much of the time abolitionists were no less racist than slave owners, censorious German observers no less than insouciant Americans. Some attention to the nuances of the fictional discourse on race can be applied to test authors' acuity of vision.

That is a mimetic consideration, and by adducing it I may raise a different suspicion, that my undertaking is out of touch with certain mainstream conventions of literary scholarship. The approach here is not postanything. My instinct is to bring an initial respect to the integrity of texts and to authorial intention without fetishizing either. While the purview of my topic is clearly intergeneric, encompassing travel literature and a huge body of expository, informational, and hortatory writing, I do not hold with methods that would obliterate the boundary between fiction and nonfiction, because the fictive imagination, being less obliged to coherence, consistency, or the actual accomplishment of whatever program may have impelled it, captures more of the richness, ambiguity, irony, and irreducibility of reality than more disciplined exposition is normally able to encompass.

This formulation, too, contains a mimetic canon that may seem, in the current atmosphere, quixotically contrary. There has grown up in the field of comparative literature a subdiscipline known as "imagology," the study of the literary representation of foreign nations and peoples. Deeply infected by the epistemological skepticism that besets the humanities on all sides, imagologists tend to deny that the images can have anything to do with their putative referents, insisting that they are intelligible only within the mind-sets, interests, preoccupations, and ideologies of the culture that generates them, the implication being that the other is radically unknowable. In my opinion, the texts treated in this study illustrate the inadequacy of such a proposition, in part because it obscures quite manifest distinctions along a mimetic scale. In Charles Sealsfield we find a mimesis of discourse, reproduced with astonishing fidelity from the American South and Southwest; in Friedrich Gerstäcker, a mimesis of experience, a mimetic ethos grounded in a sense of obligation to the public; in Karl May, about as acute an absence of mimesis as can be achieved while making a pretense to it in order to dupe the reader. These are qualitative distinctions, and I am not hesitant to link mimesis with value. If this seems inconsiderate of dominant theoretical norms, I can only point to the texts.

Numerous people have been helpful with advice, encouragement, and materials, and in some cases in enabling me to grasp the dimensions of my many-sided ignorance of American literature and history. From among these I should like to thank particularly: Professor Irene Stocksieker Di Maio, Louisiana State University; Dr. Robert P. Forbes, Department of History, Yale University; Professor Walter Grünzweig, University of Dortmund; Dr. Erwin J. Haeberle, Berlin; Erich Heinemann, Hildesheim; Professor Rolf Max Kully, Director, Central Library,

Solothurn; the late Dr. Glen E. Lich, Kerrville, Texas; George A. Miles, Curator of Western Americana, Beinecke Rare Book and Manuscript Library, Yale University; Professor Helmut F. Pfanner, Vanderbilt University; Professor James L. Rolleston, Duke University; Dr. Alexander Ritter, University of Hamburg; Dr. Christa Sammons, Curator of the German Literature Collection, Beinecke Library; Dr. Jerry Schuchalter, University of Turku; Dr. Franz Schüppen, Herne; Dr. René Wagner, Director, Karl May Museum, Radebeul; Professor Martha Kaarsberg Wallach, Central Connecticut State University; Elisabeth Wohofsky, Vienna; and Joseph C. Zamenick, Belfast, Maine; as well as no fewer than three astronomers: Chris Dolan of the University of Wisconsin, and Bradley E. Schaefer and Paolo Coppi of Yale.

I am grateful to those who have allowed me to present my findings at symposia, to publish preliminary studies, and to reprint them here. The following segments of this book have or will have appeared elsewhere: chapter 2 as "An Austrian Jacksonian: Charles Sealsfield's Political Evolution, 1829–1833," in *Austrian Studies* 7 (1996): 3–16; chapter 4 as "The Shape of Freedom in Charles Sealsfield's Plantation Novels" in *Schatzkammer der deutschen Sprache, Dichtung und Geschichte* 21, nos. 1 and 2 (1995): 1–20; a version of chapter 5 as "Charles Sealsfields *Deutschamerikanische Wahlverwandtschaften*. Ein Versuch," in *Exotische Welt in populären Lektüren*, ed. Anselm Maler (Tübingen: Niemeyer, 1990), pp. 49–62; and a segment of excursus II as "The Nationalist Anti-Americanism of a Prussophile Austrian: Ferdinand Kürnberger's *Der Amerika-Müde* in the Context of his Career," in *History and Literature: Essays in Honor of Karl S. Guthke*, ed. William Collins Donahue and Scott D. Denham (Bern and Munich: Francke, 1998).

Finally, I am obliged to the Frederick W. Hilles Publication Fund of Yale University for assistance with publication costs.

Short titles in the notes refer to the bibliography, where materials relating to one of the authors discussed in this study are alphabetized under the author's name.

New Haven, Connecticut<br>
Spring 1998

# Abbreviations

| | |
|---|---|
| AA | Solger, *Anton in Amerika* |
| AH | Strubberg, *Alte und neue Heimath* |
| AJR | Strubberg, *Amerikanische Jagd- und Reiseabenteuer* |
| A-M | Kürnberger, *Der Amerika-Müde* |
| AmT | Gerstäcker, *Aus meinem Tagebuch* |
| AuD | May, *Ardistan und Dschinnistan*. Vols. 1–2 |
| AWS | Gerstäcker, *Amerikanische Wald- und Strombilder* |
| AzW | Gerstäcker, *Aus zwei Welttheilen* |
| Br. 1 | Gerstäcker, *Mein lieber Herzensfreund! Briefe an seinen Freund Adolph Hermann Schultz 1835–1854*, ed. Ostwald |
| Br. 2 | Gerstäcker, *Mein guter Herr von Cotta. Friedrich Gerstäckers Briefwechsel mit dem Stuttgarter Cotta Verlag*, ed. Roth |
| Briefe | Castle, *Der große Unbekannte. Das Leben . . . Briefe und Aktenstücke* |
| BW | Strubberg, *Bis in die Wildness* |
| Cost. Corr. | Gerstäcker, "Friedrich Gerstäckers Briefe an Hermann Costenoble," ed. McClain and Kurth-Voigt |
| DAFS | Gerstäcker, *Der deutschen Auswanderer Fahrten und Schicksale* |
| E | Talvj, *The Exiles* |
| Eck | Gerstäcker, *Im Eckfenster* |
| F | Strubberg, *Friedrichsburg* |
| Fl | Gerstäcker, *Der Flatbootmann* |
| Fp | Gerstäcker, *Die Flußpiraten des Mississippi* |
| FW | Gerstäcker, *Fritz Waldau's Abenteuer zu Wasser und zu Lande* |
| G | Gerstäcker, *Gold!* |
| Haz | Gerstäcker, *Die Hazardspieler in Kalifornien*, ed. Ostwald |
| Hi | Möllhausen, *Der Halbindianer* |
| IA | Gerstäcker, *In Amerika* |
| KENS | Gerstäcker, *Kleine Erzählungen und Nachgelassene Schriften* |
| LH | Kürnberger, *Literarische Herzenssachen* |
| MB | Gerstäcker, *Mississippi-Bilder* |
| Md | Möllhausen, *Der Mayordomo* |
| NA | Gerstäcker, *Nach Amerika!* |
| NR | Gerstäcker, *Neue Reisen durch die Vereinigten Staaten, Mexiko, Ecuador, Westindien und Venezuela* |
| OS | May, *Old Surehand*. Vols. 1–3 |

| | |
|---|---|
| PuS | Gerstäcker, *Pfarre und Schule* |
| PV | Gerstäcker, *Eine Parcerie-Vertrag* |
| R | Gerstäcker, *Reisen* |
| Reg | Gerstäcker, *Die Regulatoren in Arkansas* |
| RF | Möllhausen, *Reisen in die Felsengebirge* |
| SJ | Gerstäcker, *Streif- und Jagdzüge durch die vereinigten Staaten Nord-Amerikas* |
| SR | Kürnberger, *Siegelringe* |
| TR | Möllhausen, *Tagebuch einer Reise von Mississippi* |
| W | May, *Winnetou der Rote Gentleman*. Vols. 1–3. *Winnetou*. Vol. 4 |
| Wie? | Gerstäcker, *Wie ist es denn nun eigentlich in Amerika?* |
| Z1 | Gerstäcker, *Erzählungen für die "Fliegenden Blätter"* |
| Z2 | Gerstäcker, *Erzählungen für die "Hausblätter"* |
| Z3 | Gerstäcker, *Arbeiten für die "Gartenlaube"* |
| Z4 | Gerstäcker, *Arbeiten für das "Pfennig-Magazin"* |
| Z5 | Gerstäcker, *Arbeiten für das "Illustrirte Familienbuch"* (unpaginated; references are to original page numbers of articles) |
| Z6 | Gerstäcker, *Arbeiten für das "Buch der Welt"* (unpaginated) |
| Z7 | Gerstäcker, *Arbeiten für "Das Ausland"* |

# Part I. Ideology: Charles Sealsfield

# 1. The Sealsfield Riddle

The author of the first important body of German-language fiction about the United States was an escaped Moravian monk, Carl Postl (1793–1864), who called himself Charles Sealsfield. Having long languished on the periphery of literary history, he has more recently been a beneficiary of the expanded interest in German writing about America. Nevertheless, in some ways our understanding of him remains in a relatively primitive state. This deficit is owing not to a lack of energetic research and perceptive criticism, but rather to the recalcitrance of the author himself. Sealsfield is surely one of the most puzzling and, for the researcher and critic, frustrating figures in the history of German letters. His biography, despite laborious efforts to make sense of it, remains inexplicable. He lived a mysterious, masked life so successfully that he continues to elude us. Much of the little he had to say about himself is pure invention. Dogged research has unearthed a substantial amount of information, but the remaining puzzles have led to a good deal of sometimes dubiously founded speculation that gets copied from one account to another without examination. He is an interesting test case of the proposition that adequate literary understanding and assessment are independent of biographical context.

The main outlines of his life are well known. Carl Postl was born March 3, 1793, in the village of Poppitz near Znaim into a family of vintners and wine dealers. He attended the *Gymnasium* in Znaim and then became a student at the convent of the Order of the Holy Cross with the Red Star in Prague. There he encountered the teachings of the liberal, rational theologian and internationally recognized pioneer of mathematical logic, Bernard Bolzano, whose influence on him, much discussed in the critical literature, presents problems that I shall address in chapter 3. Postl joined the order in 1813 and took his first vows the following year; there is some evidence that he entered upon this clerical career at the urging of his mother. Being an exceptionally intelligent and competent, if perhaps also somewhat irritating and arrogant young man, in one more year he became secretary to the grand master of the order. But for some reason he became disaffected, and in 1823, practically from one day to the next, he simply vanished. The authorities combed Bohemia and Austria but could find no trace of him. For his family, friends, and enemies, that was the end of the history of Carl Postl for the next forty years.

4    *Ideology*

We know that he turned up later that year in New Orleans, apparently having passed through Switzerland; for the next three years he lived variously in Pittsburgh, New York, Philadelphia, and Kittanning in western Pennsylvania, spending his winters in Louisiana. He apparently acquired a passport, allegedly issued by Louisiana, under the name "Charles Sealsfield, Citizen of the United States, clergyman, native of Pennsylvania."¹ This document, of which we know only at second hand, is itself quite mysterious and may be part of his elaborate coverup; it has been speculated that he obtained it from a corrupt Louisiana official.² Since he became zealously hostile to the Catholic Church and certainly would not have wished to figure as a Roman cleric, but professed throughout his life a more general but consistent Christian belief, the document suggests to me that he might have become ordained in some American denomination, probably, given his antihierarchical attitudes, Congregationalist, or possibly Presbyterian, as there is in one of his plantation novels a highlighted scene of children in the backwoods singing Presbyterian hymns (15:347).³ But these are just guesses; there is no other evidence, except a report that in a Swiss census he listed himself as neither Catholic nor Reformed, but "einer anderen christlichen Konfession angehörig."⁴ In his general attack on the Catholic religion in his polemic against Austria, he contrasts it "with the simplicity and dignity of our Protestant worship" (3:200). In 1826 he returned to Europe, spending the next year and a half in France, Germany, and England. He opened his literary career with a two-volume expository work on America, published under the name of "C. Sidons, citizen of the United States of North America" in German by Cotta as *Die Vereinigten Staaten von Nordamerika* and anonymously in English by a London publisher as *The United States of America as They Are* and *The Americans as They Are*. He followed these by an assault on the despotism of the Metternichian regime, *Austria as It Is*, published also anonymously in London in 1828; perhaps to escape detection, Postl-Sealsfield-Sidons composed this book in the form of a clearly imaginary travel report.

In 1827 he returned to the United States. He is supposed to have owned and failed with a plantation on the Red River, but no trace of it has ever been found.⁵ During this time his sketches and stories began to appear in American and English journals. The bibliography of these ephemera is in an insecure state; many items have been tentatively ascribed to him, but only a few are certainly his. In 1829 he rather bravely published a novel, *Tokeah; or the White Rose*, in English; it appeared first in Philadelphia, then, somewhat revised, as *The Indian Chief; or, Tokeah and the White Rose*, in London; we shall return to it in chapter 2. For some months in 1830 he was associated with the *Courrier des Etats-Unis* in New York, a long-lived newspaper that at that time was owned by Joseph Bonaparte, the former king of Naples and of Spain, then resident in New Jersey.[6] Sealsfield apparently became a kind of agent for Joseph, running errands for him in Switzerland to Hortense, the former queen of Holland and mother of the future Napoleon III.

Later in 1830 Sealsfield returned to Europe, traveling in France and England; there is some evidence that he visited Sir Walter Scott, whom he regarded as a model. From December 1830 to January 1832 he wrote some sixty generally undistinguished articles on the aftermath of the French Revolution of 1830 and the evolution of the July Monarchy for the *Morning Courier* and the *New York Enquirer* (24:99–332).[7] Beginning in 1832, though he continued to be peripatetic, he became more evidently a resident of Switzerland, living in Arenenberg, Aarau, Stein, Baden, and Zurich. Here his literary career began in earnest. Lasting about a decade, it is remarkable not only for its extraordinary productivity within a brief space of time but also for the variety of his initiatives, as he left apparent failures behind and went on to the next challenge. He began with a German version of *Tokeah*, considerably expanded and revised under the title of *Der Legitime und die Republikaner* (1833). He then opened the central phase of his career with *Transatlantische Reiseskizzen und Christophorus Bärenhäuter* (1834), which contains the first of his stories set in what was then the Southwest, *George Howard's Esq. Brautfahrt*, the tale of a young man who becomes disgusted with the affected, fashionable belles of New York society and wanders to Louisiana in search of an unspoiled bride. This was followed in the following year by a novel of the chaotic political history of Mexico, *Der Virey und die Aristokraten oder Mexiko im Jahre 1812*, and in the same year *Die große Tour*, under the new collective title of *Lebensbilder aus beiden Hemisphären*. The development of these collective titles indicates that Sealsfield understood his project from an early stage as an extensive, interconnected, multivolume epic of American life.

*Die große Tour*, later called *Morton oder die große Tour*, is incomplete. Morton is a young American businessman driven to the brink of suicide by a shipwreck that bankrupts him; he is rescued by a prosperous elderly German, who introduces him to a powerful Philadelphia financier; the latter sends Morton on a mysterious mission to London, where the novel breaks off. The last part of the fragment contains a passage about a miserly moneylender lifted from Balzac's *Gobseck*; indeed, the whole endeavor may have suffered from Balzac's influence. Sealsfield seems to have taken Balzac's melodramatic demonization of money and commerce literally, and in his scenes of international capitalist con-

## 6  Ideology

spiracy in London he has left his mimetic ground; he no longer knows what he is talking about, as he so evidently does elsewhere, and the novel, which has been called "the most overtly ideological of Sealsfield's texts,"[8] may have foundered in implausibility. He claimed to have written the remainder but to have held it back "gewichtiger Gründe wegen" (11:XIII*). Assertions of this sort have contributed to the atmosphere of mystery and conspiracy that has been generated around him.

The remaining volumes of the *Lebensbilder* followed in quick succession, developing Sealsfield's characteristic structure: interlocking, overlapping stories hooked loosely together in a set of Chinese boxes of first-person narrations, a device that was noted in his time and even parodied in Karl Immermann's novel *Münchhausen*.[9] Linked to *George Howard's Esq. Brautfahrt* is *Ralph Doughby's Esq. Brautfahrt* in 1835, the story of a crude, wild Kentuckian who nevertheless is shown to be a positive character, for he develops into an activist Jacksonian politician. The fourth and fifth parts, *Pflanzerleben* and *Die Farbigen*, both in 1836, consist of sketches, stories, and conversations about society and politics in Louisiana. The "colored," incidentally, are not the blacks but dark-skinned Creoles suspected of being of mixed race and therefore dangerously sensual and morally suspect. Sealsfield's sexual representations are simultaneously moralistic and lascivious. His American characters are always chaste, a point of which he makes much, as did other visitors to America at the time, but a dangerous sensual magnetism can be generated by women of darker racial composition—a motif that would play an important role in his last novel. His view of the French in Louisiana, as of all non-Anglo-Saxon peoples in America, is condescending, but also amusedly tolerant of their childlike frivolity and European social notions. Both Doughby and Howard marry Creoles, thus symbolizing the amalgamation of the two cultures, but with the clear understanding that the American culture is superior and must establish the tone of social and political relations. I shall show later on that there is a progressive diminishment in the respect shown the Creoles in the plantation novels.

An assimilated Frenchman is the main narrator of the sixth part, *Nathan der Squatter-Regulator, oder Der erste Amerikaner in Texas* in 1837, a historical novel that takes the reader back to the time of the Spanish administration of the Louisiana Territory. In Nathan Strong one sees Sealsfield's ideal American leader, modeled after the notorious contraband trader on the Mexican border, Philip Nolan, and probably also Daniel Boone. He is invincible because he is an agent of the ineluctable spread of freedom. He is a creator of law and discipline, but he can bear no governance outside his own will, and, as the writ of the federal government makes itself increasingly felt after the Louisiana Purchase, he removes to ungoverned Texas to begin again and become extremely wealthy.

This is a prodigious output; but then Sealsfield turned to an ambitious social novel of contemporary New York, *Die Deutsch-amerikanischen Wahlverwandtschaften* (1839–40), to which we shall return in chapter 5; it is also a fragment, though a bulky one, and also bears a collective title, though one never used again: *Neue Land- und Seebilder*. This work seems to be in part a consequence of a short visit to the United States in 1837, when he experienced on his sea voyage the contrast of frightening storm and frustrating calm, most impressively rendered in the novel. His next effort, *Das Cajütenbuch* (1841), consists of three parts: *Die Prärie am Jacinto*, *Der Fluch Kishogues*, and *Der Kapitän*. The short story in the middle is an extended Irish joke, and *Der Kapitän*, an increasingly sentimental tale of love, courtship, and marriage, has been dismissed by some though not all critics as the weakest of his works.[10] But *Die Prärie am Jacinto* has become the best known of them, especially in the form canonized by Hugo von Hofmannsthal in his frequently reprinted *Deutsche Erzähler* of 1912 under the title of *Die Erzählung des Obersten Morse*. This abridged version stresses its adventure aspect, but one that is not without an ideological point: it is, as many readers will recall, the reminiscence of a colonel of the Texan Republic named Morse, who as a young man foolishly rides out alone into the trackless prairie, becomes hopelessly disoriented, and is dying of thirst when he is rescued by Bob Rock, a hallucinating murderer. Bob is reprieved from execution by the local law official, an American despite his Spanish title of "Alkalde," and this move turns out to be a wise one, for Bob's violent nature becomes an asset in the subsequent battle for Texan independence. The story is justly famous for its panoramic vision of nature and its symbolism. But this commonly known version has excised the frame, a running commentary, often skeptical and sometimes boorish, by a group of southern gentlemen and officers, and a long central section of some ideological importance.

The last novel, *Süden und Norden* (1842–43), tells of four Americans and a German who are on some vague statistical mission in what is now the Mexican state of Oaxaca but who are actually touring out of curiosity and love of adventure in the midst of the turmoil following Mexican independence in the 1820s, searching futilely, as it turns out, for a utopia of plenitude and gratification.[11] There has been some dispute as to whether Sealsfield ever actually visited Mexico,[12] though it does not much matter here, for this is the most fantastic of his works. The travelers are caught up in a complex, murky conflict of intrigue among the reactionary Catholic Church, the dispossessed aristocracy, and the republican government, a tangle that does not become altogether clear even when it is recapitulated in the third volume. The effect of the exotic environment is to derange the travelers; to bewitch and hypnotize them; and to arouse hallucinations, pathological states, and abrupt personality changes. At one point the narrator himself feels that he is in a fantastic novel (19:155–56). In the end the narrator is not sure whether his story is "Wahrheit" or "Dichtung" or "Träume einer krankhaften Phantasie" (20:490).

The effect seems to result in part from the variegated mountainous landscape, which at times appears as a paradise, a Garden of Eden painted in the most gorgeous imaginable colors, at others as a veritable hell in which fever-bearing mosquitoes attain demonic proportions. The travelers are put into a religious ecstasy by the sight of the Southern Cross (18:163–64, 173–74). It appears to them late at night high in the sky, although at the latitude of Oaxaca it would be visible only in the evening just above the horizon, an indication that the landscape is at least partly imaginary.[13] But the derangement is also caused by the overwhelming erotic allurement of the Indian girls, who are portrayed as though they were houris of the orientalist imagination. All the Americans are drawn into this web—the German is too pedantic to be distracted in this way. Three of them free themselves, but one causes an international incident by courting Mariquita, the daughter of a wealthy aristocrat; it is illegal for Mexicans to marry foreigners, and there is a widespread horror of the travelers, who are regarded as infidels and Jews because they are Protestant. In the end, two of the Americans and the German are saved by the United States Marines, while the other two and Mariquita are lost at sea. Much of the novel is driven by Sealsfield's violent anti-Catholicism and his scorn for Mexican immorality, perfidiousness, superstition, and political incompetence, but it has also been interpreted as a warning against American imperialism in Mexico.[14] In any case, it is, as he himself said, "ohne Zweifel das poetischste meiner Werke" (*Briefe*, 252), and some of its passages are truly remarkable in their resourcefulness of language and imagery. It seems virtually to require postmodern analysis.[15]

Just as his publishing career was ending, his reputation suddenly burgeoned in the United States. The boom was set off by a remark in Theodor Mundt's continuation of Friedrich Schlegel's history of literature to the effect that "Seatsfield" was a major American writer superior to Cooper and Washington Irving.[16] This claim led in 1844 to a flurry of discussion in American newspapers as to the identity of "Seatsfield," the second "Great Unknown" after Scott, and the question of what his nationality might be; some partisans of indigenous literature, among them Edgar Allan Poe, scoffed. An enterprising New York publisher, Winchester, brought out with great rapidity several translations, pirated, naturally, of "Seatsfield's" works.[17] Around the same time, in the mid-1840s, twenty adaptations of Sealsfield's stories and anecdotes appeared in translation in *Blackwood's Edinburgh Magazine*.[18] Although the uproar soon died down, for a long time pirated, excerpted, abridged, and rewritten texts appeared in both German and English, so that he continued to have a reading public after his few minutes of fame had faded away. Curiously, the flurry of American interest coincided with the end of his literary career, though he was barely fifty and had another twenty-one years to live.

It should be noted, however, that he did not conclude his writing career as abruptly as it may appear. In the 1840s he negotiated with Metzler in Stuttgart an edition of collected works, in which he rearranged his novel cycle somewhat. Since *Morton* was the only one of the *Lebensbilder* that takes place in the Eastern Hemisphere, he separated it out of the series and retitled the rest as *Lebensbilder aus der westlichen Hemisphäre*, beginning the cycle with *George Howard's Esq. Brautfahrt* from *Transatlantische Reiseskizzen*; this is the arrangement in which they have commonly been known to literary history. In an appendix to a contract with Metzler of July 1844, he offers a new three-volume novel, *Ost und West*; should he fail to complete it, he offers instead a three-volume work, *Kleinere Lebensbilder*, but should he fail to complete *that*, the remainder of the contract shall stand, and he promises to publish no other German-language work until the appended contract is fulfilled (*Briefe*, 186–87). In 1848, he claimed a new work, thought to be *Ost und West*, was ready to print (*Briefe*, 225). In 1845 he had spoken of writing what appears to be a *Bildungsroman*, *Ein Mann aus dem Volke*, that was to depict the mistreated, degraded, depraved German people; in 1849 he asserted it had been completed for eighteen months. But by the end of that year he is complaining that unforeseen political circumstances have undermined the premises of his work, and he repeatedly blames his publisher for obstructing him. In 1854 he continues to claim that he has two completed works that cannot appear because of the unsettled political situation (*Briefe*, 210–11, 228, 235, 246, 247–48). What this backing and filling means, no one knows; it is not clear why these works did not appear or why Sealsfield did not pursue publication more vigorously. He may have been writing for New York newspapers as late as 1856 or 1857.[19] In 1862 he thought about dictating his memoirs (*Briefe*, 330–31). By 1851 he was living in Schaffhausen; in 1853 he returned to the United States for the fourth time, traveling about in New York, Pennsylvania, and

Louisiana until 1858. On his return he settled in Solothurn, where he lived a rather lonely bachelor's existence until his death on May 26, 1864. He ordered carved on his gravestone the phrase "Bürger von Nord Amerika," along with the initials of his real name, "C. P." Bequests to family members in his will, similarly signed "Charles Sealsfield, Bürger der V S von Amerika," set in motion the inquiry that revealed his true identity.

It is quite difficult to make sense of this biography. It presents us with a number of enigmas and some genuine cruxes that so far have appeared insuperable; Sealsfield was quite successful in what we cannot doubt was his purpose of hiding himself. For example, though a refugee from Metternich's Austria and soon to be on record in violent opposition to it, in 1826 he wrote a letter in odd English to Metternich, offering himself as a spy; Metternich sent an agent, who was no fool and became instantly skeptical of the "se disant américain," noting his uncertain English and his German accent; Metternich's embassy in Paris was warned about him, and it was found that the American minister in Paris did not know of him as he claimed (*Briefe*, 109–13). This looks like a poor effort if serious; could it have just been political theater? But in 1837, though opposed to President Van Buren, he again offered his services as a spy through Joel Poinsett, Van Buren's secretary of war, with whom Sealsfield seems to have been acquainted (*Briefe*, 160–62). No one can explain such antics, unless they were driven by sheer need. The first incident also raises the question of Sealsfield's English. Why did a man who could write whole books in reasonably acceptable and certainly fluent English not write less awkward and faulty English in his personal letters?[20] The books must have been rather thoroughly edited in the publishing house; the contract for the English version of his expository work on America specifically reserves to the publisher the editing of the text (*Briefe*, 121).

But there are weightier puzzles. In the first place, we do not know why and under what circumstances he left the religious order. If Metternich's vaunted police state was unable to find out despite straining every resource, perhaps we shall not be able to do so, either. One reasonable guess has been that, like many other intellectuals in the Hapsburg Empire and the German states, he had come to rebel against that police state. His mentor Bolzano was removed from his teaching position and his writings were proscribed in 1819. Sealsfield's tract, *Austria as It Is*, confronts Metternichian despotism in the most uncompromising and contemptuous tones. It is a work that appears as a harbinger of the Young German movement of the next decade, with which he has sometimes been associated by literary historians. A character in the *Die Deutsch-amerikanischen Wahlverwandtschaften* defends the committed literature of the Young Germans (21:1, 52). At the time this was written, however, the Young German movement had been crushed; Sealsfield merely acknowledges it through his fictional figure from a distance. Furthermore, since he seems to have been a refractory, even disagreeable character, it is possible that abrasions with his colleagues and superior may have contributed to the breach. It is also noteworthy that in his writings he comes to be virulently anti-Catholic; he exhibits the zeal of the apostate. If this affect was not acquired from the American anti-Catholic atmosphere of the time, it may suggest a massive crisis of allegiance to the church while he was still in the convent. One minor puzzle is why he eventually settled in Solothurn, an almost ostentatiously Catholic city. He is buried by the wall of a Catholic church; however, the graveyard of the church, I learned upon a visit there, is ecumenical, serving the whole community. He did contribute three hundred francs to the building fund of the Reformed church in Solothurn and left another three hundred in his will (*Briefe*, 340, 349).

It has never been entirely clear why Sealsfield masked his identity to the end of his life; the best guesses seem to have been that he lived in fear of exposure and perhaps recapture by Austrian authorities and that, as a priest, he would not have been able to will his property to heirs other than the church. In a more psychological vein, it has been suggested that he lost track of his own self, "daß er während der langen Jahre des Exils sich selbst zu einer Abstraktion geworden war und über die Chiffre 'Charles Sealsfield—Der große Unbekannte' hinaus keinen rechten Begriff mehr von sich und seiner wahren Identität hatte."[21]

Our problem thus far is just a matter of not knowing the details. There is nothing intrinsically strange about flight from the Metternichian prison house; the numbers of emigrants from the German Confederation were already beginning to build. More of a riddle is what Sealsfield lived on. One does not, after all, travel from Prague to New Orleans and then dally for three years in the United States on pocket money. From beginning to end Sealsfield's finances are completely incomprehensible. Recent research suggests that he at first hoped to be an associate of Mathew Carey, whose economic theories and those of his son, Henry Charles Carey, the publisher of the English-language version of Sealsfield's first book on America and of *Tokeah*, strongly influenced him.[22] However that may be, it is clear that he did not succeed in finding an enduring footing in the United States. Among his relatively few preserved letters, a number are desperate appeals for support from publishers and, at times, governments that sound like the cries of a destitute man. Yet for years he is constantly on the move, around the United States, to England and France, within Germany and Switzerland.

In the last phase of his life, which is the best documented, he makes a rather prosperous impression. Of course, he was a single man of simple habits who doubtless did not need much; nevertheless, he seems to have been quite comfortable and was able to leave something to his heirs. At the end of his life he estimated himself in possession of $27,000 worth of property in New York and several thousand francs in Swiss investments (*Briefe*, 344). Evidently he acquired some American railroad stocks, probably good investments, but, unless he at some time hit the jackpot in the scorned, demonic capitalist system, it is difficult to understand where the initial funds came from. Some observers have thought they came from his earnings as a writer. We are not completely informed about what he was paid by his publishers, but the figures that appear in his preserved correspondence and contracts are quite modest, and anyone familiar with the economics of literature in the German-speaking lands of the mid-nineteenth century must doubt that he can have earned more than his immediate upkeep from that source; he received, of course, nothing for the American publications, for international copyright was not recognized in the United States at that time. Coupled with this problem is the question of what Sealsfield *did* when he was not writing. How, for example, did he fill his time during his sojourn in the United States from 1853 to 1858? Even a notorious miser, as he was reputed to have become, cannot spend day and night for six years attending to a handful of railroad stocks.

Unfortunately, the solution that was found for some of these problems turned out to be a cure worse than the disease. The biographer Eduard Castle, an indefatigable positivist of the old school, observed the frequency with which Freemasons turn up in Sealsfield's life, among them prominent ones like Joseph Bonaparte, the wealthy Philadelphia financier Stephen Girard, and the American diplomat Poinsett. Sealsfield's political hero Andrew Jackson was also a prominent and active Mason, while Jackson's and Sealsfield's bête noir John Quincy Adams allied himself for a time with the Antimasonic Party. In both the German and English versions of his descriptive book on America, Sealsfield notes in passing the presence of Masonic lodges in New Orleans—not in itself unusual, as Freemasonry had been establishing itself in every state at this time. There is some indirect evidence from acquaintances of the elderly Sealsfield that Masons may have helped him as a young man through Switzerland on his way to New Orleans. In his youth Freemasonry had been technically banned in the Hapsburg Empire, but it is likely that Masons maintained informal contacts with one another, sustaining Enlightenment and liberal religious traditions in the Metternichian atmosphere of obscurantism and bigotry. Why should they not have helped a lapsed monk in a crisis of faith and rebellion escape to America? Even if there is no real evidence for it, the supposition is plausible, especially, since *someone* must have helped him in a substantial and extensive way.

However, Castle, having become entangled in superstitions about an international Masonic conspiracy, constructed a virtually tragic scenario in which Sealsfield, in order to effect his escape, found he had made a Faustian bargain. When he endeavored to expose the international capitalist conspiracy in *Morton*—Stephen Girard is thought to be the model for the omnipotent financier Stephy in that novel—the Masons forced him to abandon the novel. Through their influence on the publishing industry they prevented the publication of his later works, totally losing interest in him. Bound by his fateful oath of silence, Sealsfield was condemned to permanent subjection, unable to divulge the evil he had uncovered about the Freemasons: "ihnen war es nicht zu tun, wie er gleich vielen anderen naiven Gemütern gewähnt hatte, um einen Bruderbund zu Beförderung der Menschlichkeit, Freiheit, Erwerb aller geistigen Güter, sondern um eine Weltverschwörung zu Ausübung von Macht, Herrschaft und Gewinn aller materiellen Güter."[23]

While this phantasm has not been without influence in some quarters, most serious Sealsfield scholars have recognized it as rubbish.[24] But it raises more serious questions. As is well known, the Masonic conspiracy is an element of the cynical populism of reactionary politics that flowed into fascism. Although it was conjoined to the international Jewish conspiracy at a relatively late date in the metamorphoses of the infinitely adaptable *Protocols of the Elders of Zion*,[25] the link was a constant of fascist doctrine and came to be particularly virulent in formerly Hapsburg lands such as Croatia. Although Castle's biography was not published until 1952, it is a product of researches that go back to the 1920s, a time rife with conspiracy theories, and was largely composed during the Nazi period. Castle has been certified as a victim of the Nazis, who are said to have removed him from his professorship and banned his books.[26] But, in regard to the Masonic conspiracy, I am fully in agreement with Friedrich Sengle's blunt charge: "Castles Biographie gehört, trotz der wahrscheinlichen Änderungen in der Nachkriegszeit, zur Geistesgeschichte des Dritten Reiches."[27] Sealsfield turned out to be a convenient writer for Nazi cultural politics,[28] and a failure to recognize clearly how that could be the case still leads to some obfuscation in Sealsfield studies.

Not altogether unconnected with the nationalist and regionalist components of the fascist image of Sealsfield, though ultimately independent of them, is a long-standing insecurity and, at times, dispute over his location in literary history. Still unsettled is the question of whether he is to be regarded as an American or German (i.e., Austrian, Swiss, European) writer. He obtains a place as easily in the *Oxford Companion to American Literature* as in the *Oxford Companion to German Literature*. One of the most important recent studies of him appeared in a series on "Anglo-Saxon Language and Literature" and strongly insists on regarding him as an American and, especially, a southern writer.[29] The Austrian Americanist Walter Grünzweig has objected to seeing him exclusively as a German-language and Austrian writer.[30] Conversely, Friedrich Sengle, after having placed him in his capacious category of *Biedermeier*, has implied that he was a Swiss writer,[31] and Günter Schnitzler's recent, ambitious study, which goes farther than any other in presenting him as having come to be passionately anti-American, portrays him as primarily Austrian and European.[32] His placement appears to be a matter of perspective. On the whole, German and Austrian Germanists tend to locate him as a Central European writer, while American Germanists along with German and Austrian Americanists regard him as an American writer. The problem, of course, was initially generated by Sealsfield himself, who actually spent only a few years of his literary career in the United States; published only one of his novels, and that an apprentice work, in English; lived most of his life in Europe, primarily in Switzerland; published all the rest of his novels in German there or in Stuttgart; and yet insisted to his dying day and even beyond it upon his American identity.

One way to approach the problem would be to attempt to contextualize him literarily. This turns out not to be very easy to do in the German literary context, in which Sealsfield himself shows relatively little interest. Among the *Biedermeier* authors with whom he might plausibly be compared, the most likely would be Jeremias Gotthelf.[33] Sealsfield's opinion of Gotthelf was mixed; in 1861 he found *Die Käserei in der Vehfreude* "zu viel pfarrerisch" (*Briefe*, 322). One might also think of Willibald Alexis.[34] However, Alexis draws us into the succession to Sir Walter Scott, and this leads to one of the most persistent misunderstandings in Sealsfield reception. It goes back to the author himself, who, in one of his very few comments on his self-understanding as a writer, the preface to *Morton*, praised Scott as the only writer who had raised the prestige of the novel and as much superior to Goethe "in sittlich-patriotischer Hinsicht" (10 [1]:6, 9). In an 1854 draft for an article in the Brockhaus encyclopedia, Sealsfield credits himself with having created "im nazionalen oder höherem VolksRomane" a form in which the whole people is the hero, a concept that seems to derive from Scott (*Briefe*, 291). But there are fundamental differences in narrative style. Scott, a patient, calm, stylistically even narrator, is close to the reader, whom he keeps with him at a distance, sometimes faintly ironical, from the narrated. Sealsfield is a high-strung, tonally varied narrator closely involved with the narrated and located at a didactic distance from the reader—thus his numerous first-person narrators, telling others in no uncertain terms how it is. Sealsfield can be comical, surreal, or sarcastic, but he has no irony, for he is too firmly persuaded of the singular rightness of his perspective. The allegiance to Scott is more of an ideological nature, as I shall try to show later on.

Things come no clearer if we turn to the Young Germans. With the exception of Heinrich Laube's *Die Krieger* and possibly Theodor Mundt's *Madonna*, Young German fiction is set in hardly any definable place or time, while Sealsfield's fiction has specific real-world settings. Young German political doctrine is, generally speaking, philosophical, the speculations of sedentary intellectuals; Sealsfield's perspective is again specific, drawn in every particular from an identifiable context of practical politics and explicitly hostile to bookish doctrine, especially of European provenance. The Young Germans were preoccupied with religious and sexual emancipation; Sealsfield constantly recurred to Christian principles and was quite prudish in sexual matters. In a private letter of 1860 he mounted a severe critique of Karl Gutzkow's *Ritter vom Geiste* as unpoetic, but by then the Young German movement was long defunct. In the same letter, incidentally, he discards Eugène Sue's immensely popular (and nearly twenty-year-old) *Mystères de Paris* as "ein Buch für den schweinischen Haufen" (*Briefe*, 314–15). In his next letter he adds that Gutzkow is one of the hollowest writers he knows; there is little hope for Germany if such literature reflects the national condition. Napoleon realized that the Germans were stupid when he read their literature, a donkey packed with learning—a non sequitur, one would think, as Gutzkow was two years old when Napoleon was driven from Germany (*Briefe*, 315–16).[35] Sealsfield's most prominent characteristics—the energy and violence of his writing, the political detail of his narrations, and their engagement with questions of liberty, property, monetary policy, banking and credit, mob rule, the rise of working-class agitation, and so forth—do not recall the Young Germans, not to speak of the *Biedermeier* in general. It is likely that he did not think literature could flourish under *Vormärz* oppression and censorship. In *Austria as*

*It Is* he gives a moving account of Franz Grillparzer as "neglected," "harassed," and "fettered": "What would have become of Shakspeare had he been doomed to live or write in Austria?" (3:209–10).

What, then, of the American literary context? The American writers of that time best known abroad are Washington Irving and James Fenimore Cooper, whose names have been adduced from time to time, though not with notable precision. It would not be easy to detect in Sealsfield any affinity with Irving, especially not in the work that takes place largely in Irving's Dutch New York landscape, *Die Deutschamerikanischen Wahlverwandtschaften*; Sealsfield, moreover, was quite hostile to Irving (10 [1]:86). While there are Cooperesque elements in Sealsfield's first novel, especially in its primitive English version, his pioneer ideology of manifest destiny comes to move quite far away from Cooper's elegiac resignation, and Sealsfield became quite critical of Cooper also (10 [1]:15). It turns out that the writers likely to be most relevant in Sealfield's environment—among them Timothy Flint, James Kirke Paulding, Anthony Ganilh, John Pendleton Kennedy, Catharine Maria Sedgewick, Lydia Maria Child, George Tucker, and William Gilmore Simms—are largely unknown except to specialists in American studies; with the possible exception of Simms, they have been decanonized and overshadowed by the protomodern masters Poe, Hawthorne, Melville, and Whitman, although some of them were well known at the time in German translation.[36] For many years there were limited, source-hunting excursions into this material. It has long been known that Sealsfield borrowed from Flint one tale of a village idiot and his fearsomely competent wife for the story *Christophorus Bärenhäuter* and another of a kidnapped child for the third chapter of *Pflanzerleben I*, from an anonymous Texan memoir elements of the perilous ride of Colonel Morse in *Das Cajütenbuch*, and from Samuel Lover an Irish anecdote for *Der Fluch Kishogues* in the same work, as well as other items.[37] Today, after initial probes by Franz Schüppen, we have an extensive and persuasive study by Walter Grünzweig.[38] Grünzweig has shown such a vast amount of echo and borrowing from the antebellum writers that there can be no doubt that Sealsfield read in them extensively.

However, in retracing Grünzweig's steps I have come to a somewhat different view.[39] Again, Sealsfield seems to me a quite different kind of writer. The literature in question is a product of a kind of American enlightenment and is, in a sense, preromantic, despite the occasional wildness of its setting. It precedes the journeys into myth and romance—into the twilight zone, so to speak—of Melville, Hawthorne, or Poe. But, while it varies in quality, most of it is well written and well formed. On the whole, narration is linear and free of notable complexities. It is true that John Pendleton Kennedy's *Swallow Barn* (1832), said to be the first plantation novel, presents itself as a kind of antinovel, narrated in a leisurely, apparently arbitrary manner that may owe something to the example of Fielding. But nowhere does one find Sealsfield's characteristic Chinese-box construction of encapsulated first-person narrations, nor his sheer sprawl, the sense that the texts are all middle without beginning or end. Timothy Flint's *Francis Berrian* (1826) is an encapsulated first-person narration, but well within the established conventions of frame stories. The inner narrator is a well-educated Harvard man on the Texan frontier. In the terms of Philip Rahv's famous metaphor of the polarization of American literature, Sealsfield, at least within his narrative personae, is a "redskin," not a "paleface." The paleface is "patrician," "highbrow," "tends toward a refined estrangement from reality. . . . At his highest level the paleface moves in an exquisite moral atmosphere; at his lowest he is genteel, snobbish, and pedantic." The redskin is "plebeian," "lowbrow," "accepts his environment, at times to the degree of fusion with it, even when rebelling against one or another of its manifestations. . . . In giving expression to the vitality and to the aspirations of the people, the redskin is at his best; but at his worst he is a vulgar intellectual, combining aggression with conformity and reverting to the crudest forms of frontier psychology."[40] Seen in this scheme, almost all the American writers who have been adduced as sources for or influences upon Sealsfield are palefaces.

The Americans write a middle style with a decorum tending to refinement, a drawing-room style; even when the matter is far away from domesticity, the point of view, on the whole, is not on the frontier, but at a point of observation distant from it. Sealsfield's rawness, his enthusiasm for violence, the loudness of his volume, are not modeled in the American texts, even in the places where one might expect to find it: not in Flint's extremely popular biography of Daniel Boone (1833), almost certainly known to Sealsfield, written in a dignified but unornamented middle style with graceful, rhythmic periods, nor even in Flint's edition of the hair-raising adventures of the hapless westerner James O. Pattie (1831), nor yet in Paulding's *Westward Ho!*, a tale of the most primeval Kentucky frontier. Something of Sealsfield's often rough, masculine tone, his delighted dilation on the vulgar and boorish, might be found in Simms, who, in fact, once charged Sealsfield with plagiarism.[41] But Simms presents chronological difficulties. He was thirteen years younger than Sealsfield, and the beginnings of his literary career are so closely contemporaneous with Sealsfield's writing decade that a direct influence seems unlikely, especially as he would have had to acquire at least some of Simms's works in Switzerland. Simms's own suspicion of plagiarism has been refuted partly on the grounds of chronology. There are also important ideological differences, especially in respect to slavery and racism, to which I shall return in chapter 3. We shall see there also that Sealsfield's contextual environment is not primarily literary at all.

This, in turn, raises another set of puzzles, perhaps the most recalcitrant of all. What was Sealsfield's attitude to literature and to his own vocation as a writer, and why did he break off his writing career so suddenly when he seemed to be at the height of his powers? His commentary on literature is scattered, for the most part occasional, and not infrequently banal; Alexander Ritter regards his mentions of authors as name-dropping.[42] Indeed, in his letters, Sealsfield is often such a philistine that it is hard to detect the artist at all. Once in a while, for example, in his haggling with Cotta, he sounds as though he were writing primarily for money; late in life, in 1861, when he was worried about his finances, he grumbled: "Wird es recht schlimm, so greifen wir wieder zur Feder" (*Briefe*, 148, 154–55, 323). Schuchalter has speculated that if Sealsfield had not gone bankrupt as a planter, he might never have become a writer.[43] Some of his comments seem to make no sense at all. For example, when describing *Tokeah* to Cotta, he said, "das ganze ist in einen *Roman* auf die Art wie *Corinna* eingekleidet" (*Briefe*, 144). Neither *Tokeah* nor any other Sealsfield novel bears any detectable resemblance to Madame de Staël's *Corinne*, except insofar as the fiction in the latter is a pretext for the communication of travel impressions and doctrine, and this may be, in fact, what he meant. To be sure, some literary antecedents were of some value to him, such as Bulwer-Lytton's *Pelham* for *Die Deutsch-amerikanischen Wahlverwandtschaften*, as we shall see in chapter 5. Furthermore, for a writer who seemed to take some pride in his creativity, he was remarkably inattentive; many of his texts give an appearance of haste in their repetitiousness, their stylistic and even grammatical carelessness, and their passages of dubious English and impossible Spanish. The misprints in the unattractively printed books suggest that he did not waste much time proofreading. In *Süden und Norden* one of the Americans is called "Whitely" in the first two volumes but "Withely" throughout the third.

There is good reason to think that Sealsfield regarded literature as just another resource of the phenomenal world, "clothing" reality and ideas, as he remarked of *Corinne*, in fictional guise. In 1847 he consulted some contemporary American novels to retain impressions and estimate conditions, "wenn sich auch aus denselben wenig oder gar nichts benützen läßt" (*Briefe*, 218). In the preface to *Morton*, he asserted that his tendency was higher than novelistic; it was historical, and his type of novel was designed to affect "die Bildung des Zeitalters" (10 [1]:18–19). For the Brockhaus article, he defined his purpose as depicting "die Republik der V. St. dem deutschen Publikum im Romangewande." The conventional materials of fiction—"Liebesszenen und Abentheuer"— were but a foil to the representation of the public and private life, past and future, of the American nation in order to provide a supplementary resource to history (*Briefe*, 291–92). While it is clear from the article that he did reflect on his formal devices and their differences from novelistic conventions, these utterances seem to be somewhat reticent in regard to his actual purposes. For his novels are not only reportorial and (allegedly) mimetic; they are intensely didactic in their propagation of the Jacksonian, agrarian-patriarchal, internally democratic but externally hostile and aggressive, internally disciplined but externally anarchic society of the South and the Southwest, with its values of life, liberty, and the pursuit of property as a new dispensation in human history, a utopia held up to forlorn contemplation by the backward, ossified, shackled societies of Europe.

Consequently, just about all modern authorities, though they may differ considerably in details and perspectives, are in agreement that, when historical developments made this vision of America untenable, he abandoned his literary career, thus explicitly or implicitly giving support to the view that, for him, artistic creativity was wholly subordinate to the figuration and transmission of ideology.[44] It would be fair to say, however, that it was not the Jacksonian movement that failed him, but that he was unable to live up to its potential of democracy— that strand traced out in Arthur Schlesinger's classic study that led to the widening of political participation, to the Locofocos, and to the administration of Martin Van Buren. It is true that any admirer of America might have been dismayed by the increasing crudity of political discourse and the shenanigans of the election campaign of 1836, memorably portrayed in *Die Deutsch-amerikanischen Wahlverwandtschaften*, but it is also true that Sealsfield was unable to show the working-class mobs—the Locofocos *were* the Jacksonians of the late 1830s—as much tolerance as he had shown to the boorishness of the Kentuckian Ralph Doughby in the *Lebensbilder*, and he became wholly hostile to Van Buren, who, despite his fastidious tastes, well understood and adapted himself to the extension of democracy. Thus, the novelist Sealsfield became a victim of his inflexibility, which strangled his creativity.

In itself this may not seem so remarkable. There are doubtless many cases in the history of letters where creativity subordinated to ideology fails when ideology, for one reason or another, is unable to sustain it. But the case becomes more curious if we find unusual literary quality in the writer. In the past, this was not much of an issue. Older critics did not think very highly of Sealsfield as an artist, finding him of interest for other reasons. He was regarded as slovenly in composition and macaronic if not rebarbative in style. But, since in modern times we no longer bring normative expectations to the novel, we are able to acknowledge Sealsfield's deviant mode, perhaps as an example of "authoritarian fiction," defined as "written in the realistic mode (that is, based on an aesthetic of verisimilitude and representation), which signals itself to the reader as primarily didactic in intent, seeking to demonstrate the validity of a political, philosophical, or religious doctrine."[45] But beyond this, an awareness has been growing of his literary excellence and power. A transitional view was held by Norbert Fuerst: "the strange thing is that, in spite of such primitive qualitative means, he achieves—in every volume—areas of sheer intensity, where his theme and his technique, his obsessions and his very shortcomings coalesce into a crude and boisterous fulfillment."[46] Ritter's study of Sealsfield's landscape depiction elevates him well above this level and makes strong claims for formal excellence.[47] Even stronger claims are made by Schnitzler, who brings Sealsfield primarily into connection with the visual arts, with the landscape painting of Salvator Rosa, Claude Lorrain, and the Hudson River School.[48] Schuchalter speaks of "the loftiness of Sealsfield's intention" as "the progenitor of a new kind of novel" and defends his attention to form.[49] I, too, hold with these views generally if not at every point; I regard him as a writer of formal ingenuity and incomparable vitality of tone. A certain formal insouciance turns qualitatively into a kind of experimentalism. Not only did he interlock first-person narratives; *Pflanzerleben I* suddenly takes the form of a diary, which can be somewhat tedious for the modern reader, since it brings the novel's action to a halt, but does meet the purpose of providing a *Lebensbild*. In *Pflanzerleben II*, the Frenchmen form an ensemble to reenact their first experiences in Louisiana; thus the collective narration takes on the form of drama. In both *Die Deutsch-amerikanischen Wahlverwandtschaften* and *Süden und Norden*, the author shifts into the second person, thus abruptly foreshortening the distance between narrator and reader.

It is thus all the more disconcerting that his literary career came to an abrupt end among clear signs that his last works, especially *Die Deutsch-amerikanischen Wahlverwandtschaften*, *Die Prärie am Jacinto*, and *Süden und Norden*, were growing stronger and more experimental. Yet this increase in artistic possibilities seems to have given no satisfaction; it could not compensate for the increasing untenability of the superintending ideological construct. He was caught in a paradox. His originality lay in his literary artistry, but he was not ambitious for a location in the order of literature; his intertextuality relates not to literature as such, but primarily to the ideological public discourse of the antebellum South, of which literature is only a part, and by no means the most privileged part. It is here that his intentionality was overtly centered, but also here where he is least original. Thus this innately gifted, mentally energetic, eccentrically innovative writer ultimately missed his vocation in two ways. He came to occupy a subordinate and eventually rather obscure place in the history of literature because he was unable or unwilling to invest in the artistry potentially at his command, and he lost the thread of his purpose as an enlightener and liberator because he allowed himself to become so ideologically frozen into a historical moment as to be unable to cope with its dynamic and dialectic. As Schuchalter observes, "in not believing in America, Sealsfield could not fully believe in himself. He thus became a fractured, fragmented personality."[50]

Finally, there is one more oddity, one that does not have directly to do with Sealsfield himself, but is a virtually occult reprise of his peculiar case, almost exactly one hundred years later. As Sealsfield is the major German-language writer of fiction about America in the second quarter of the nineteenth century, so the major German-language writer about America in the second quarter of the twentieth century is B. Traven. Sealsfield arrived in New Orleans, according to our best estimate, in the early fall of 1823, Traven in Mexico in the summer of 1924. Both went to great lengths to mask their true identities, in both cases probably initially out of fear of exposure, though later in Traven's case evidently also out of roguishness and as a public-relations stunt, and both complicated the search for their identities by insisting that they were Americans. Both were radically disaffected in politics and in flight from their homelands. The narrative tone in both cases was intensely ideological and homiletic. Both developed idiosyncratic German styles adulterated, in Sealsfield's case perhaps more intentionally than in Traven's, with American English. Both experienced phases of considerable notoriety in Europe and America, only to decline, on the whole, to objects of curiosity on the periphery of literary scholarship. Both concluded their writing careers many years before the end of their lives, Sealsfield never realizing any of his major projects after 1843, Traven writing nothing after 1940 except for revisions, translations, film treatments, minor prose, and the novel *Aslan Norval* of 1960, a work that no informed person seems to take seriously. For not wholly absurd reasons, critics of both have sometimes had difficulty believing that they were the authors of their books, for in both cases elaborate, major books appear with astonishing rapidity; there once was a rumor that Sealsfield had murdered the actual author of his works and appropriated them;[51] the Traven discussion has been bedeviled by the theory of the *Erlebnisträger*, the postulated supplier of experiences or even of texts that would account for the rapid appearance of his novels shortly after his arrival in Mexico. The reception history of both was subject to serious distortions, Sealsfield having come to be designated as an "ethnographic writer," as though it had been his intention to transmit Indian lore and the mores of backwoodsmen; Traven becoming more prominent from a film made of one of his novels than from the novels themselves. So striking are some of these parallels that one wonders if Traven might not have known of Sealsfield and modeled his career strategy after him.[52]

## 2. What Is an Austrian Jacksonian? Sealsfield's Political Evolution from *The Indian Chief* (1829) to *Der Legitime und die Republikaner* (1833)

Aside from the debated question of Sealsfield's placement in literary history as to whether he was an American or European writer, there is an extensive if imperfect consensus as to his purpose: that he meant to hold up to his German and Austrian readership a model of democracy, that he was thus a didactic political writer and to that extent related to the Young German movement and the politicized literature of the *Vormärz*. Sealsfield himself did not very explicitly indicate that this was his motivation. In his sporadic comments on his purposes, he tended to speak of his works as popular social novels striving for a true picture of America. In the dedication to the second edition of *Lebensbilder aus der westlichen Hemisphäre*, he came closest to defining a didactic political purpose: "Der zum Bewußtseyn ihrer Kraft und Würde erwachenden deutschen Nation sind diese Bilder des häuslichen und öffentlichen Lebens freier Bürger eines stammverwandten, weltgeschichtlich groß werdenden Staates als Spiegel zur Selbstbeschauung hochachtungsvoll gewidmet" (11:[5]).

Contemporary reviewers, hungry for any kind of democratic discourse, praised Sealsfield as an inspiration, although some doubted his relevance to German conditions.[1] In 1850, the first German history of the novel concluded with praise of Sealsfield for having introduced the democratic principle into the genre.[2] Some modern commentators have been more emphatic, arguing that his whole effort was directed toward confronting inhabitants of the timid and oppressed petty German states with a representation of the strong, free, and confident American people; that his fiction formed an explicit contrast to Europe; that his didactic purpose was to teach liberty to Europe; that the often articulated hostility to Mexico was in fact directed against the Holy Alliance and Austria; that the origins and aims of his work were rooted in "Austro-German culture"; that his narrated America always is a representation of Europe and particularly of Austrian conditions.[3] But when we look carefully at the texts, we may ask ourselves how they can be expected to have had these effects and whether they in fact did. Grünzweig has had occasion to observe that Sealsfield's conception of his audience remains largely unclear to us and that *Der Legitime und die Republikaner* continues to be one of the least accessible of his works for the European reader.[4]

As far as I know, Sealsfield is the only European author of German-language fiction about the United States to have located himself explicitly in an American political context. To be sure, some German authors, such as Berthold Auerbach in *Das Landhaus am Rhein* (1869), whose protagonist joins the Union side in the Civil War, exhibited solidarity with the movement to abolish slavery (as Sealsfield emphatically did not), but abolition was not strictly a party issue; it tended, rather, to divide parties. Other German or, more commonly, German American authors have been committed to socialism, which, however, has rarely been a significant element of American party politics. But, as is well known, Sealsfield allied himself from an early date with the Jacksonian movement. He arrived in the United States in the year before the controversial election of 1824, which, because the outcome had to be negotiated in the House of Representatives, was widely regarded by Andrew Jackson and his supporters as having been "stolen" by John Quincy Adams; the "corrupt bargain" of February 1825 remained the most crucial political experience in Jackson's mind for the remainder of his career, as a subversion of egalitarian and majoritarian principles.[5] The English-language version of Sealsfield's first book on America, *The United States of North America as They Are* (1828), has very much the appearance of a political tract, if not so much in Jackson's favor, then certainly against President Adams, who "if he had been sent by Metternich himself . . . , could not pursue more closely the principles of the Holy Alliance" (2:21).

The critical political allegiance did not go unnoticed in Europe. Sealsfield's English publisher, in order to distance himself from the odor of Jacksonianism, had an attack on the book printed in his own *Quarterly Review*, and a letter of evaluation on the German version elicited by the publisher Cotta castigated Sealsfield's blatant partisanship.[6] But Sealsfield's fiction is so intensely assimilated to the details, not just of the Jacksonian movement in general, a large, evolving, incoherent, and often opportunistic political phenomenon, but of its southern and southwestern agrarian and expansionist faction, that one wonders whether European readers, not notable in those times for their interest in the details of the American scene, would have found them fully intelligible. Subsequent scholars have sometimes not looked closely enough at the context and have contented themselves with generalities about freedom and democracy, concepts that have quite specific delineations in the Jacksonian context and consequently in Sealsfield's fiction. In my experience of reading about the Jacksonian era, Sealsfield seems ever more compactly and seamlessly located within its discourse. In an effort to shed some light on this question, I should like to look a little more closely at the alterations he made in his first novel from the English to the German version, in order to show that in this evolution from an American book to a German book he becomes not more European but more Jacksonian, thus, a fortiori, more American.

Sealsfield's first novel was written and anonymously published in English, as *Tokeah; or the White Rose* by Carey, Lea and Carey in Philadelphia in 1829, and later that year, in a slightly revised version, by Newman in London as *The Indian Chief; or, Tokeah and the White Rose*. The book was probably written largely during the presidential campaign of 1828, in which Jackson achieved the victory he believed had been denied him four years earlier. It opens when a band of Indians in Georgia, led by the Oconee chief Tokeah, bring a baby girl for safekeeping to a backwoods trader named Copeland. After seven years Tokeah, filled with bitterness against the whites, takes her back, moves the remnant of his tribe across the Sabine River into what he later realizes is the Mexican province of Texas, and raises the "White Rose" as a companion to his daughter Canondah, subsequently betrothed to the young, heroic Comanche chief El Sol. Again seven years later, a young English aristocrat, Arthur Graham, who had been taken captive by the pirate Jean Lafitte, turns up as a fugitive near the encampment, where he is badly wounded by an alligator and secretly tended by Canondah and Rosa. Restored to health, Arthur is helped to escape, but is recaptured by Tokeah, who is enraged at what he believes to be the treacherous harboring of a probable spy. But, because Arthur does not kill the Indian who attacks him, Tokeah realizes that he is not an enemy of the red men and allows him to seek to return to his people, extracting from him, however, his word of honor that he will not reveal the tribe's location. Tokeah, who has made an unwise alliance with Lafitte and promised Rosa to him as a wife, comes to fathom his true character and turns away from him, whereupon the pirate and his men attack the encampment. Owing largely to El Sol's battle skills, the pirates are defeated and captured but Canondah is killed. Arthur, meanwhile, has found his way to Opelousas, where he is detained as a British spy and collaborator with the Indians, for the British are about to invade New Orleans in a critical battle of the War of 1812. However, Copeland, now mellowed into a country squire and justice of the peace of rough-hewn wisdom, recognizes the lad's good qualities and puts him in the care of a prosperous Creole planter and state senator named Gentillon, who lectures the still benighted aristocrat on American principles of freedom and democracy, after which Copeland is obliged to bring him to Jackson's camp for examination. There Tokeah, who has been commanded in a dream to recover his father's bones in Georgia, appears with El Sol, Rosa, and the captured pirates; after several complications Tokeah releases Arthur from his word so he can clear himself. Tokeah does recover the bones but is killed in an attack by another Indian tribe on his way to an alliance with El Sol in Texas. Rosa is revealed to be the lost daughter of a Spanish aristocrat and in the last chapter she is shown living contentedly as Lady Graham with Arthur on his plantation in Jamaica.

It seems likely that, if it were not for Sealsfield's remarkable subsequent career, this book would be remembered, if it all, as no more than a bibliographical curiosity. The style, as has been pointed out with pedantic thoroughness by modern editors, is riddled with Germanisms and other off-center turns of phrase, though anyone who has written a book in a foreign language might feel some sympathy for what Sealsfield managed to achieve. But in structure, characterization, and sensibility it is notably inferior to the antebellum American fiction from which he drew. The close resemblance of Sealsfield's novel to Cooper's *Leather-Stocking Tales*, three of which had appeared, and especially to *The Last of the Mohicans* (1826), was remarked at once and has been much discussed since, though not always in complete recognition of Sealsfield's deviation from Cooper's model in his evaluation of the Indian fate and of westward expansion. American reviews were few, superficial, and very mixed (reprinted 24:1–13).

Although the story begins at the end of the eighteenth century and the main action occurs prior to the Battle of New Orleans in January 1815, at the narrative level the novel is clearly set in the Jacksonian context and, as has been rightly argued, is not to be understood without Jackson.[7] He himself is, for the most part, indirectly present—as in Scott's novels, the heroic historical figure is seen primarily in the middle distance and from below—though he makes one important appearance in a confrontation with the Indian chiefs Tokeah and El Sol. That the attitude toward the Indians is generally Jacksonian in spirit can be obscured for readers by a pervasive rhetoric of sympathy with the Indians' tragic fate, "these unfortunate Parias of the west" (5 [3]:131) and by the castigation of the pillaging by the whites. Nevertheless, the novel accepts that the Indians' cause is lost and that their removal from settled territory is a necessity. At the very outset Copeland is resentful of the Indians' agricultural settlements and hostile to the philanthropists who encourage them (4 [1]:21-23). While Sealsfield has been charged with a failure to represent Indian culture accurately,[8] nevertheless he caught the point that local pressures subverted federal government efforts to seek equitable solutions.[9] There is an odd but, for its time, characteristic incoherence between the ascription of Indian suffering and decadence to the greed and violence of the whites on the one hand and the clear implication on the other that Indian character and level of civilization improve by assimilation to white culture. The older the Indians, especially the women, the more savage and hideous they are, while the younger ones have benefited from contact with civilization. White influence, for example, has caused the Cherokees to treat their women better and has made Canondah and the other Oconee girls "well formed and graceful" (4 [1]:93-94, 96). If Tokeah had not been a savage, he would have been a hero or benefactor of men, but, as it is, he is morbidly suspicious (4 [1]:205-6); yet we are also told that he has been made more savage by persecution (4 [2]:65-66). El Sol, for his part, has, rather astonishingly, become less savage owing to his "warlike intercourse with the Spaniards" (4 [2]:97). Jackson is fairly severe toward Tokeah, whom he accuses of savage conduct in the past, but friendlier to El Sol, to whom he gives a medal, doubtless because he and his Comanches are at home where they are supposed to be, in the Far West outside the boundaries of the United States (5 [3]:158-65). Jackson tells the chiefs that the red men "should remember that we are as lawful possessors of the land as they are, and certainly the strongest. We could have made them slaves" (4 [3]:161). There can be no doubt that *The Indian Chief* is in consonance with the Jacksonian policy of Indian removal, counting but also accepting its cost in suffering and injustice.[10]

*The Indian Chief* contains much of Sealsfield's customary rhetoric in praise of American freedom, of the sovereign people, their energies, initiative, and public-spiritedness unshackled from European despotism and bureaucracy, in this case explicated largely by the Creole Gentillon to cure Arthur of his aristocratic prejudices. The doctrine as propagated here is marked by an insistence on property and its preservation, a Jacksonian obsession as it was for Sealsfield. It is always understood as landed property along with its exploitation through agriculture and trade. Wealth of any other kind and its pursuit are always represented pejoratively in Sealsfield's fiction. It is the acquisition and maintenance of property that is causing the backwoodsmen to become more civilized (4 [2]:179; 5 [3]:6-8). Jackson in his farewell address in 1837 stressed that the Constitution had "secured the rights of property."[11]

*Der Legitime* was published in 1833, in the first year of Jackson's second term. As a translation or adaptation it follows about half of *The*

*Indian Chief*, after which it deviates almost completely, employing only a couple of scenes of the earlier work.[12] The revision is a clear improvement, in the first instance stylistically, since the author was now writing in his own language, although, as in all of his subsequent works, the text is peppered with Americanisms of which it is often difficult to say how intentionally and consciously they are employed. Structurally the novel is better integrated. In *The Indian Chief*, Tokeah rather implausibly takes Lafitte and the pirates as prisoners to Jackson's headquarters. In *Der Legitime* they are released because the Indians believe that such nasty characters will do evil to white people. To Tokeah's shock and horror, they turn up as volunteers in Jackson's forces at the Battle of New Orleans, as was the case historically. Arthur Graham has been displaced by James Hodges, no longer a disdainful aristocrat but the son of a wealthy merchant. A British midshipman who had been captured by Lafitte while clamming, he is a rather impetuous and disrespectful lad, thus better suited for conversion to Americanism. At the same time his moral character is heightened. Unlike Arthur, James realizes that his flight from the Indian village has put Canondah in danger of her father's rage, and so he endeavors to return, swimming back across the Sabine before he is recaptured by the Indians (6 [1]:291). The sentimental, trivial love story is dispensed with; James is impervious to Rosa's charms and ignores Canondah's matchmaking hints. The ultimate discovery of Rosa's Spanish parentage is pushed into the background and Rosa herself disappears from the end of the novel; James marries one of Squire Copeland's daughters.

Sealsfield no longer has any use for Spanish and British aristocrats in his concluding idyll. However, it is no longer class consciousness that needs to be overcome, but national traits, the conditioned arrogance and false sense of superiority of an Englishman. In this as in many other details Sealsfield has elaborated the political and, one must say, nationalistic fabric of the work. *Der Legitime* deviates from *The Indian Chief* at the point where, in the latter, Copeland conducts Arthur to the Creole planter Gentillon for his instruction in American doctrine. Gentillon does not recur in the revision; his role is taken over by a wealthy American colonel and his wife, who, although suspected of "Tory" sentiments, nevertheless are true Americans who help James understand the rules of the democratic environment. (Actually they appear to hold Whig sentiments, but it was a rhetorical device of Jacksonian democracy to denote all opponents as "Tories" if not monarchists.) Evidently Sealsfield no longer wished to employ a Creole in such an ideologically foregrounded role; in *Der Legitime* the Creoles' courage and loyalty in the face of the British invasion are called into question (7 [2]:134–36), while

Copeland tells James that Jackson treats Creoles like Negroes (7 [2]: 170).[13] This shift parallels the deteriorating portrayal of the Creoles in the plantation novels, as we shall see in chapter 4.

The specifically Jacksonian aspect is intensified through a number of details. The War of 1812 is now defined in the American understanding as an imposed and necessary war of independence from Britain (6 [1]:156) and Jackson's role in it is more explicitly heroized. He is introduced descriptively much earlier in the novel (7 [2]:136); his debate with Tokeah and El Sol is expanded and is placed for greater emphasis closer to the end (7 [3]:271–93). Although the senior John Adams was fleetingly mentioned in *The Indian Chief* among the "great men" who founded the nation and came "from the people" (5 [3]:11, 13), he and his son now clearly represent the enemy faction. Copeland in the first episode of the novel wishes the elder Adams to the devil (6 [1]:30); the wealthy colonel is suspected of attachment to Adams's false doctrines (6 [3]:112). Sealsfield's pejorative vocabulary of Tories, monarchists, and the like is sometimes seen as evidence of an imposition of European political concepts on the American context but, in many places, appears quite consonant with American usage. When the opposition of the colonel's wife to free immigration exposes her as a crypto–"Tory" (7 [3]:132), that, too, exactly reflects a Jacksonian position of the time.[14] However, when large-scale immigration, especially of the Irish, was perceived as an economic threat, the movement became more nativist, and Sealsfield would loyally follow it in that direction. Sealsfield's depiction of John Quincy Adams, especially in *The United States*, as a monarchist seeking to establish a hereditary presidency in his family reads like overwrought campaign propaganda, but his biographer has observed: "he had been accustomed since youth to look upon that office as a family inheritance. In his tall pride he desired it to come to him as it had come to Washington: unsolicited, unconnived for, without commitments or bargains with any man, a prize for which he, the son of President John Adams and Abigail, would not lift a finger or make a nod. 'If my country wants my services, she must ask for them.'"[15]

There is one more motif that is quite minor here but appears significant in retrospect: the association of the southern yeomanry in its energy of expansion, land taking, and conquest with the Normans. Barely adumbrated in *The Indian Chief* (4 [1]:180), it appears more explicitly in *Der Legitime* (7 [3]:249), where Copeland describes the inhabitants of Louisiana as a million masters on conquered land. We shall encounter it again as a major element of the Alkalde's definitive ideological harangue in Colonel Morse's narration in *Das Cajütenbuch*; as I shall show, it, too, is a well-attested discourse of the antebellum South.

Another change is Sealsfield's evidently increased willingness to grapple with the issue of slavery. His views on and representations of slavery have been a quite contentious topic in modern scholarship. I shall return to them in detail later on; in this place I only wish to show that his treatment of the topic became more Jacksonian and American. In *The Indian Chief* slavery is barely visible. The few black characters receive, by Sealsfield's standards, neutral, even friendly treatment. The cultivated Creole complains that Copeland's men brutally beat a slave, to which Copeland, who "thought it his duty to take the part of his countryman against a negro," replies: "But them negroes are such beastly creturs" (5 [2]:228). In *Der Legitime*, however, Sealsfield begins to mount the defense of slavery common in the discourse of his environment. The narrator, not one of the characters, explains that, although the sight of slavery "dem menschenfreundlichen Auge wehe that," "die kleinen Wollköpfe" are in a cheerful and contented condition that many in the Old World might envy; the horrors claimed by abolitionists are rare, while the slaves' treatment in general redounds to the credit of the American character. Southerners do the best they can with their duties as slaveholders, which have been imposed on them; the thought of emancipation must cause one to shudder (7 [3]:7–9). In any case, slaves were property, with which, according to Jacksonian doctrine, government must not interfere: "For the government to legislate abolition would strike at the very foundation of American principles and institutions"; abolitionism was regarded as collusion between John C. Calhoun and John Quincy Adams.[16] It would be useful if Sealsfield scholars, especially European ones, would become more familiar with this contextual discourse, as it would help them comprehend his violations of our current horizon of expectations of where a "democratic" writer is supposed to stand. A recognition of his underlying and, indeed, intensifying racism would also contribute to clarity. In *Der Legitime*, for example, it is asserted not only that the white race is superior to the Indians, but also that even the proudest Indians must acknowledge this superiority (7 [3]:30, 38–39).

In addition to these adjustments and changes, *Der Legitime* exhibits two ingenious innovations. The first of these has not been much noticed by criticism, perhaps because it is a subplot that takes place largely offstage. Jackson, while preparing his defenses on his way to becoming the Hero of New Orleans, is at the same time being prosecuted for violating the rights of the state of Louisiana by arbitrarily imposing martial law and, ignoring a writ of habeas corpus, imprisoning a judge who defied him (7 [2]:226–38).[17] Copeland's militiamen spend a good deal of valuable time in democratic session debating this issue and deciding whether to obey the order to join the defense forces, going on record as censuring the commander while continuing to serve loyally under him. A regular army officer, who, significantly, spent his youth in aristocratic, hierarchical England, is shocked and offended by this insubordination, but he, in turn, is told that he is offending the democratic spirit of his countrymen, thereby putting his standing in the community and his career in jeopardy. It is difficult to imagine any other moment in the historical record better suited to Sealsfield's purposes. The people, constantly alert to the threat of despotism and encroachment upon their liberties, govern their rulers, even their military commanders, in a time of crisis. The local colonel is confident that Jackson himself will decide the matter justly (7 [2]:289–90), and it turns out that he is more democratic in spirit than the officers who defend his authority; he yields to the censure and the stiff fine imposed on him, if not enthusiastically, then with reasonably good grace (7 [3]:63, 251–22, 291). Needless to say, his authority is not damaged but enhanced by the episode. Here, if anywhere, is a message from America to Europe; such an event is, as Sealsfield supposes, unimaginable in any European country, unless one were to dredge up the memory of Frederick the Great's public-relations stunt in the matter of the miller of Sanssouci. The narrator sends the message quite explicitly:

> Es ist schwierig dieses republikanische Leben, das schwierigste das es gibt; denn zart ist die Grenzlinie des Rechtes, und leicht ist sie überschritten, wenn nicht die Millionen mißtrauisch wachen. Darum ist es nur bei einem Volke möglich, wo die Verstandeskräfte die höchste Stufe erreicht, wo selbst positiver Widerstand gegen den Machthaber noch die Grenzlinie seiner Pflicht erkennt, und so, ohne in Verwirrung und Anarchie auszuarten, seine Rechte behauptet oder die verlorenen wieder erobert.
> 
> (7 [2]:237–38)

Sealsfield's other innovative device, by contrast, cannot be missed by any reader, as it becomes a kind of leitmotif: the designation of the Indian chief as "der Legitime," thus paralleling him to the despots of Europe who claimed to rule legitimately by divine right. This metonomy is a correlative of the intensification in two directions of the Indian theme in *Der Legitime*: on the one hand the heightened pathos of oppression, suffering, and defeat; on the other a tightened insistence upon the inevitability and ultimate rightness of removal. Sealsfield establishes the first of these tones by setting to each of the three volumes a motto in which Thomas Jefferson is made to say that he trembles for his people when he considers the injustices that have been perpetrated against the original inhabitants. As we know, this remark of Jefferson's concerned not the Indians, but slavery, a sentiment for which Sealsfield had no use.[18] The bitterness of lost lands, of having been continually lied to and exploited, subverted by firewater, despoiled by relentless white greed, is passionately articulated by the Indians. Rosa, from her experience as Tokeah's forcibly adopted daughter, repeatedly defends him against the charge of savagery (e.g., 7 [3]:166). But Rosa is no longer a definitive voice in the novel, in which the images of savagery have been amplified. In the Indian camp James likens a dance to the sort of portrayal of Hell with which the church has tried to terrify believers; the Indian girls burn a Yankee in effigy, a scene not in *The Indian Chief* (6 [1]:172, 177).

Tokeah is made considerably more savage and is also diminished in stature. It appears more explicitly than in the earlier work that his poor judgment in allying himself with the thieving pirate Lafitte and his humiliating incompetence in battle are causes of the loss of his daughter (6 [2]:110, 118). At one point Tokeah charges the Great Spirit with injustice and, to El Sol's shock and outrage, wishes a curse on his own people (7 [3]:39–40). In a lengthy scene entirely new to *Der Legitime*, Tokeah, after having recovered his father's bones in Georgia, makes a detour through Alabama, encountering the rest of his tribe, which has repudiated him because of his persistence in making futile war against the whites; these Alabama Indians, here put in the right, were historically turncoats who had negotiated a land giveaway with Jackson.[19] Increasingly Tokeah is presented as blinded by paranoia. Instead of generously renouncing Rosa, as in *The Indian Chief*, Tokeah refuses to accept her return to white society, seizes her, and threatens her with a knife; she must be rescued by the wiser and cooler El Sol, to whom Tokeah has absurdly promised her, but who does know how to renounce (and to remove himself). Tokeah answers Rosa's plea for forgiveness with silence (7 [3]:297–308). Jackson's lecture to the chiefs is now augmented with material drawn from his "Second Annual Message" of December 1830 and his "Message on Indian Affairs" of February 1831:[20] the progress of civilization cannot tolerate a nomadic people wandering about the land; the Indians are welcome to settle as civilized farmers but otherwise must be removed. The Indians are silenced by the truth of what he says (7 [3]:278–82).

Historians believe that Jackson's apparent acceptance of Indian agricultural settlement was a hypocritical sop to liberal opinion;[21] he had been hostile to Indians all his life, he had made his first national reputation fighting the Seminoles in Florida, and he probably was consistently determined to remove all Indians from the southern states. But Sealsfield may have taken his statements at face value. It has been persuasively shown that *Der Legitime*, written at the time of the debate over removal, at first acknowledges but then suppresses the alternative of agricultural settlement.[22] Copeland, identifiable as a stand-in for Jackson in the novel, asserts that the Indians are disappearing by their own fault (7 [3]:296). In a probably fictive letter of dedication to "A. J. Smith, Esq." prefacing the novel, Sealsfield states that even though the sight of Indian removal is painful, they must for their own welfare be separated from the squatters and merchants (6 [1]:2–3). Sealsfield's later writing shows little interest in Indians. In the plantation novels they are minor characters. After a struggle over a buck in the Mississippi River, the Kentuckian Doughby defends a courageous Indian against prejudice (12:200–1), but elsewhere they are portrayed condescendingly, although as allies against evil blacks (13:78–79, 136).

No model for Sealsfield's identification of Indian chiefdom with legitimacy has been found, which does not mean that there was none. The notorious eighteenth-century purveyor of misinformation about America, Cornelius de Pauw, associated the degenerate and effeminate beardlessness of Indians with the clean-shaven fashion of European aristocrats.[23] Tocqueville hinted at the connection when he commented that the Indian "has his imagination inflated with the pretended nobility of his origin," and in his pride and disdain for labor "cherishes the same ideas, the same opinions, as the noble of the Middle Ages; and he only needs to become a conqueror to complete the resemblance."[24] But Sealsfield's ingenious device is to literalize the cliché of the noble savage. Eloquence, the stoic style, and the solemnity of hierarchical authority are noble *and* savage, dignified *and* obsolete, like the European aristocracy. The chief's "medicine" is revered by the Indians as a symbol of power just as scepters, tiaras, and crowns *used to be* by the European peoples (6 [1]:98). It is, on the other hand, the *legitimate* principle of Spanish and French satraps to look upon populations as herds of sheep (7 [2]:133–34). Jackson tells the chiefs they are bloodsuckers like the tyrants of the Old World (7 [3]:279–80). One of the colonel's daughters, while giving Rosa a geography lesson, explains that kings are like Tokeah, only greater; childish peoples require such rulers to govern them, make wars, sell their territories (as Tokeah has done), and fool the people into thinking they have been appointed by God (7 [3]:124–25). Later Rosa is taught that she will find living with American whites better than with Indians or with kings (7 [3]:295).

Might this concept of legitimacy not be a link to the European relevance commentators seek in Sealsfield? The novel takes place shortly before the convening of the Congress of Vienna, where legitimacy was one of the basic principles; the legitimacy of Louis-Philippe's accession in 1830 was a disputatious matter at the time the novel was written. Public discussion of such matters was tabu under the Metternichian censorship; might not Sealsfield have smuggled it in from an exotic perspective?[25] If that had been the case, however, one would think that the censors would have been the first to notice. In fact, there is no reason to think that Sealsfield ever had any measurable political effect, and it has been argued that his republicanism was hardly registered in the *Vormärz*.[26] Generally speaking, there is little republicanism to be found among the writers of the *Vormärz* at all, at least after the death of Ludwig Börne in 1837. It is by no means clear that Sealsfield ever intended to have a political effect; rather his posture is one of holding up the American example for contemplation and understanding, to Europe's more or less eternal shame. Wynfrid Kriegleder has shown that Sealsfield saw as threats *both* European poesy, implicated with degenerate sensuality, *and* European capitalism, regarded as an import rather than, as with most other observers, an expression of the American obsession with money.[27] He does not propose the exportation of American liberty to Europe; even in Latin America he sees no potential for republican government because of its Spanish character, as he asserts in *The United States* (2:44–55); and in *Der Virey* he endeavors to show that there is no hope of American democracy in Mexico (9 [2]:242–43; 9 [3]:306–7).

On the whole, he seems to turn his back on Europe as irrelevant to the progress of mankind, at least until his late novel *Die Deutsch-amerikanischen Wahlverwandtschaften*, but there he was unable to complete his intercultural chiasmus. Furthermore, in that novel his hope for an elective affinity is placed in a Prussian, not an Austrian. But, even there, he does not deviate from the posture of condescension toward Europe; it is merely that some Americans, urbanized and class-conscious, have deviated from true Americanism. The fashionables in the novel, who find Jackson and patriotism obsolete, regard the Louis-Philippes, the Metternichs, and the Wellingtons as among their friends (23 [3]:65–67, 71); such sentiments are infallibly a sign of assimilation to aristocratic degeneracy. Sealsfield seems to have directed his attention toward Germany in general rather than Austria in particular and to have lost interest in Austria after his polemic of 1828, *Austria as It Is*. A chubby scoffer with thick Austrian lips appears briefly in *Das Cajütenbuch* (17:148). The editors of the volume propose that the thick lips are an allusion to the Hapsburg physiognomy (17:398\*). This could well be the case, a little private, passing joke of Sealsfield's. But scholars grasp at straws when they highlight such matters, as though the text were a cryptogram whose secret message is to be extracted by exposing invisible writing between the lines, rather than comprehending the logic of the discourse as a whole.²⁸ Of course, Sealsfield's Central European origin must be a large presence in his consciousness and thought, but he does not direct much attention to it in his fiction. From within his American perspective, the first European object of concern and contrast is, of course, Britain, then France, then Spain. In Rosa's geography lesson, the rest of Europe is an undifferentiated collection of petty kingdoms (7 [3]:123–24). It is well to bear in mind also that in Sealsfield's account American liberty, as his insistence on the development of landed property and "Norman" conquests shows, is logically dependent on the taking and cultivation of vast tracts of land empty except for disposable aboriginal inhabitants. Such circumstances cannot, of course, be replicated in Central Europe.

The inward turn of *Der Legitime* appears also in many American allusions that must have been difficult for Central European readers. For example, Copeland grumbles: "Das alte Weib in der Bundesstadt schreibt und schwatzt Staatsrecht trotz Einem . . . ; wenn es aber darauf und daran kommt, so ist er Hamiltonianer über den alten John, und verliert den Kopf, wie er ihn hinter Baltimore verloren hat" (7 [2]:231). One wonders whether many readers will have recognized the allusion to President James Madison, whose brilliance as a constitutional theoretician was not equally matched by competence as an administrator and commander in chief, or have understood that he is being charged with susceptibility to the Federalist doctrines of the Adams faction and with confusion at an engagement at Baltimore after the burning of Washington (which the Americans won, incidentally, and which was the occasion for the writing of "The Star-Spangled Banner"). There are two allusions to the Hartford Convention, an episode right at the time of the Battle of New Orleans, when a number of New England Federalists opposed to the war and the hegemony of the South discussed secession (7 [2]:232; 7 [3]:144–45). It has been pointed out that the characters in the novel cannot have known of the event at that time; the allusion, therefore, derives from the author's political purpose.²⁹ The matter is undoubtedly relevant to the states'-rights issues raised by Jackson's high-handedness in New Orleans but of no detectable relevance to European politics. James, faced with the prospect of hanging, thinks of Major André, the British officer who was hanged as the contact with the traitor Benedict Arnold (7 [3]:190). American readers would probably have recognized the name, and perhaps many British ones also, even though the event was a good half century in the past, but what about Germans, Austrians, and Swiss?

Since the editors of the modern edition did not find it convenient to annotate *Der Legitime* with any thoroughness (even though many of the materials were prepared for the Riederer edition of 1937), interested non-American readers of today may still find the text intermittently inaccessible. It is hard to see how any political inspiration could have emanated from it in its time. The political dimension of Sealsfield's writings came to be disguised by their categorization as "ethnographic novels." This may not be entirely owing to the depoliticization of the German bourgeoisie after 1848, as Steinecke argues,[30] but also to an original incongruity with any conceivable readership in their time. Thus Ritter is right to conclude that Sealsfield's image of America is "weniger das Amerikabild eines europäischen Schriftstellers denn eines amerikanisierten Autors der Neuen Welt."[31]

Many, if not almost all of the German (as opposed to German American) writers about America have been regarded as never having quite left home and have often been criticized for a parochial inability to penetrate the variety and nuances of American life; this is true even, perhaps especially, of the exiles of the 1930s. Sealsfield's case is the opposite; he became so deeply involved in an important but circumscribed area of American society and politics that, while he was able to represent it with unusual ideological fidelity, he could not find, and perhaps did not even seek, efficacious political and ideological resonance in his readership. In the last analysis, an Austrian Jacksonian is an eccentric, and eccentrics maintain themselves in literary history only with difficulty, no matter how original and powerful their writing may be.

# 3. Slavery, Race, and Nation: The Antebellum Southern Context

Sealsfield's fiction strives to give a detailed and, in most of his writing, affirmative picture of American freedom. His stories act out a demonstration that people not only can live without rigid class distinctions, without their places and pursuits defined from above by the alliance of throne and altar, without the seamless discipline of the police state, but also that they can prosper and grow under these conditions, form functioning and mutually supportive communities, thrash out differences in contention and competition with one another, and maintain lawfulness and civil society without anarchy—propositions that were by no means universally acknowledged by European observers. Whatever he may have thought about the relevance of the model to the prospective politics of Europe, he certainly meant to hold it up as a new, epochal dispensation in human history, *Annuit cœptis novus ordo seclorum*, as we read on the Great Seal of the United States. In these respects he is one of the most systematically and programmatically democratic German-language writers in the entire nineteenth century.

In other respects, however, he is not, and his contradictions and ambiguities exactly reflect those of America in the time and place of his experience of it. For the center of that experience was the antebellum South, especially its western segment, from Louisiana roughly northward to Kentucky. Here in Sealsfield's time there was a great surge of local communal autonomy and egalitarian democracy—the movement we, like Sealsfield, associate with the iconic figure of Andrew Jackson—but it was a democracy for Americans only, and Americans are white men primarily of English and Scottish heritage. No one else is comprehended by the democracy—one more reason, incidentally, to suppose that Sealsfield did not even imagine it relevant to Central Europe. The crucial feature of this democracy, as it appears to us in historical retrospect and as it did also to many observers of the time, is that it is grounded on slavery.

Nearly all German writers about America were opposed to slavery, though with varying degrees of intensity, and some writers of the 1830s and 1840s acknowledged that there were German American slaveholders.[1] A German-born slaveholder appears as a shockingly evil character in Berthold Auerbach's pro-Union *Das Landhaus am Rhein* (1869). Still, a great many German Americans, mindful of the tyrannies and the serfdom they had fled, were abolitionists. It is true that ethnic propaganda has rather exaggerated the solidarity of the German Americans in this matter; like other Americans, many were indifferent or even hostile to abolition.[2] One contemporary historian has observed of the period after Sealsfield's novels:

> Contrary to the assertions of many writers, not all Germans were natural supporters of the new [Republican] party. Like immigrants everywhere, they had faithfully followed the Democrats, and while they were generally opposed to slavery, they, like other Americans, were intensely racist. Thus when the Republican party was being organized, only the so-called Greens, particularly the forty-eighters, joined the new grouping. The majority, including many of the Lutherans and especially those Catholics afraid of liberal freethinkers, remained Democratic.[3]

But a great many others supported Lincoln and the Republican Party, formed German units in the Union Army, and were instrumental in holding Missouri in the Union. For German like other foreign observers, slavery was the single greatest hindrance to acceptance of America's claims for itself. To those sympathetic to the cause of liberty, it was a source of grief; to the enemies of democracy, a welcome proof of hypocrisy. In the anti-American discourse from the beginnings to the present day, slavery and racism have been fairly consistently exhibit number one. The Jacksonian movement in the region in which Sealsfield experienced it was uniformly proslavery. Thus, virtually by necessity, his ideological discourse was also defensive of slavery.

In Sealsfield scholarship there has been some contentiousness on this point, owing largely to the unwillingness of some of his admirers to accept the evidence in the record. Some see "contradictions" or "ambiguities" in his position;[4] I see no ambiguities particular to him, except as they faithfully reflect irrationality and illogic in the slaveholding position.[5] Understanding has been particularly ill-served by his modern editors, especially Karl Arndt, whose commentary is recurrently obfuscating in this matter and who seems, if anything, sympathetic to racist and segregationist positions. There are two peculiarities in the contextual discourse that observers need to grasp if they are to comprehend Sealsfield's faithful replication of it. The first of these is that it was possible to believe that slavery was an evident evil, yet to hold that nothing could be done about it without creating a worse situation, so that slavery must remain undisturbed while society makes the best of it. This seems to have been largely Thomas Jefferson's view, and it came to be widely held: "there was little difficulty at the time in gaining theoretical assent from many slaveholders to the abstract proposition that slavery was an undesirable institution which posed a threat to republican government, national unity, and economic progress."[6] In John Pendleton Kennedy's *Swallow Barn*, the plantation novel that is numbered among Sealsfield's probable literary sources, it is agreed that slavery "is theoretically and morally wrong," with the unfortunate result that "it may be made to appear wrong in all its modifications."[7] But what was to be done? The childish, animal-like blacks, who could not or would not work except under duress and did not have the capacity to become autonomous adults, would, if set free, simply fall into helpless lassitude or, possibly, should their trammeled vengefulness be released, turn to crime and brutality. Sealsfield and his fictional spokesmen faithfully reproduce these positions. We have already seen this pattern in *Der Legitime und die Republikaner*, as was noted in the previous chapter.

In *The Americans as They Are*, he had seemed at first to deplore slavery; he praises the state of Ohio for having abolished it and Illinois for having repelled an initiative to introduce it (2 [2]:10, 86). From time to time he makes observations on the brutal treatment of slaves and their laborious existence, and he is able to see that slavery is a major threat to the survival of the Union. But even as early as *The United States of North America as They Are* he was persuaded that nothing could be done about it for the present: "Happily for the Union four of the Presidents were citizens of Slave States, and therefore, treated the point in question with corresponding delicacy, leaving it to time to remedy the evil" (2 [1]:55). Among the reasons for his pessimism about the future of the South American republics is that they "are about to place all races and colours upon the same footing" (2 [1]:56). While some blacks are honest and faithful, most "will exhibit the vicious nature of a debased and slavish character. There is no doubt that a malignant and cruel disposition characterizes, more or less this black race. Whether it be inborn, or the result of slavery, I leave to others to decide" (2 [2]:176–77). He goes on to say, in a passage that has no counterpart in the German version, that "emancipation is impossible," since the released blacks would slaughter the whites (he is thinking of Haiti) and, while it was unjust "to traffic in fellow-creatures, as though they were so many heads of cattle, it is equally unjust now to infringe upon a property which has been transmitted from generation to generation, without adopting some method of public compensation" (2 [2]:178), thus introducing his reiterated theme of the inviolateness of private property, however obtained; who, one of his characters wants to know, is going to compensate the owners if the slaves are freed (14:47)? The toss-up between environmental and innate explanations of the Negro character and the argument about the impossibility of emancipation are familiar features of the contemporaneous discourse; Jefferson concluded that the question of the Negro character needed to be left to future scientific investigation.[8] In *Der Legitime*, Sealsfield introduced the corollary that slavery was an inherited burden under which the slaveholders, "diese Zwingherren, schuldlos an diesem fluchwürdigen Dienstzwang" (7 [3]:9), suffered as much as the slaves, a point taken up by Tocqueville, who concluded that "the progenitors of Negro slavery had entailed upon their descendants a race problem for which emancipation provided no answer."[9]

These positions are consistently reiterated in the discourse of the plantation novels. It is regarded as common knowledge that slavery is "ein Uebel, ja ein Mackel unserer freien Verfassungen" (14:156). At the sight of young slaves the narrator George Howard muses how fortunate they are not yet to have felt "das Schreckliche des Fluchs ewiger Sklaverei" and to await "in harmloser Unwissenheit" the day of freedom that must come: "Ja, er wird kommen dieser Tag, der uns gestatten wird, das zu versöhnen, was unserer Väter Machthaber an euch verbrochen haben" (11:144). Southerners are not responsible for slavery, which was imposed on them by the evil British and French, leaving them with a burden of responsibility for the "uns ohne Schuld zugekommene Raçe" (13:88) with which they must deal as honorably as they can. Howard's friend Richards gives a detailed historical account of the culpability of the British in this matter, forcing the slave trade on the Americans, who protested and resisted it, but to no avail (14:134–40). Much stress is put on this burden; slaveholding is not "ein Liegen auf Rosenbetten" (13:84). Yet the responsibility and sacrifice can bring gratification also, as Howard explains to his bride:

> Nicht wahr, Liebe! sie machen uns vielen Verdruß, diese Geschöpfe, aber auch wieder Freude.—Mit unserem Vermögen könnten wir im Norden ohne Sorgen leben, ein glänzendes Haus machen, aber die Vorsehung hat uns diese schwarzen Creaturen—die Kinder thierischer Väter, durch geldgierige Ungeheuer aus den Sandwüsten Afrika's in unser Land herüber geschleppt—, in die Hände gelegt, sie uns zur Erziehung überlassen. Louise! wir wollen Vater-, Mutterstelle an ihnen vertreten. Es ist ein schöner Beruf, Vater, Mutter von fünf und zwanzig Familien seyn.
>
> (13:164–65)

The slaves themselves are treated with the greatest possible mildness and kindness, except by the occasional mean person of whom one hears, or the Creoles, who are more for whipping and unrelenting discipline and who, unlike Howard, support the policy of denying them schooling (11:151, 166–67; 13:82, 98). Their treatment would improve even more rapidly if it were not for the interference of the abolitionists (13:75–76). Howard's slaves celebrate his return to his plantation so enthusiastically that they nearly set fire to the house and bang their heads against one another (11:241–42). They are said always to be good-humored at their work if their master is also, indeed, more so than whites; sometimes the slave scenes are almost Arcadian in their innocence and love for the masters (13:69, 70–73, 162). Their work is light; they can easily save enough money to purchase their freedom, thus acquiring ethics through a sense of property (13:75); one old slave woman has several thousand dollars of her own (14:19–20). In any case, they are better treated than wage laborers under capitalism or Jews and serfs in Europe (14:66–67, 157–58).[10] But freeing them is not possible; if it were, why were they not freed by wise men such as "Washington, und Jefferson, und Henry Patrik [sic]"; it would take centuries to raise them from their animal condition (13:88). Sealsfield held consistently to these positions from the beginning to the end of his career. The conclusion of *Das Cajütenbuch* presents a Mississippi plantation quite literally as a paradise, exhibiting Old Testament conditions, in which the slave quarter is "ein anderer reizender Zug in diesem südlichen Gemälde"; in the North one has no idea how lovingly the slaves regard their masters (17:376, 378).

The second point is that Sealsfield's contemporaries did not necessarily see a contradiction between liberty and democracy on the one hand and slavery on the other; indeed, arguments developed that slavery was not only advantageous to the slaves but a foundation of a democratic civilization. The great scholar of the American South, C. Vann Woodward, observes: "When all who were white were invited to join the brotherhood of the free and equal and look down upon all who were black, unfree, and unequal, then American slavery did take on an ironic reconciliation with American equality as its underpinning, the underpinning of a strictly white egalitarianism."[11] This has been called the *Herrenvolk* ideology; its advantage was that it permitted claims of the true, antiaristocratic equality of all whites, diminishing class differences in proportion to the huge gap from Negro inferiority: "the planter class, whatever its own inner feelings, endeavored to maintain its *de facto* hegemony by making a 'democratic' appeal, one which took into account the beliefs, desires, and phobias of an enfranchised nonslaveholding majority.... *Herrenvolk* egalitarianism was the dominant public ideology of the South, because it was the only one likely to ensure a consensus."[12]

In Sealsfield's *Nathan*, reconciliation to slavery is put into a context of internalizing true Americanism and republicanism. The narrator, the French count Vignerolles, and his companions had come to Louisiana at the end of the eighteenth century with a deep antipathy to slavery, but, as they learn American ways: "Auch in Bezug auf die Schwarzen erlitten unsere Ansichten eine starke Revolution" (15:377). In the first place it is a matter of practicality; they realize the plantation they have acquired cannot be worked without slave labor. Some evils, Vignerolles remarks, cannot be evaded but must be confronted; he must overcome his inhibitions against buying and holding slaves, and he is warned against "sentimentale Antipathien" (15:382). The scene of the slave sale is constructed to be as charitable to Vignerolles's ethical sensibilities as possible. The slaves he buys are twenty-five half-dead rejects in steerage; the slave ship's captain tells him that, if they had not been taken, they would all be dead, as they were prisoners of war condemned to death. Several of them die before they can be brought to the plantation, but in time the remainder are nurtured to health and a semblance of civilization; again the burden assumed by the slaveowner is stressed. On the other hand, abolitionism has been earlier connected with the inability of a radical Frenchman to understand freedom and democracy (14:46–47). In the end, Vignerolles's assimilation is certified by the fact that he owns more than three hundred slaves (15:433), and it is this prosperity, evidently, that permits the fifty-nine-year-old count to marry the eighteen-year-old Yankee belle who, in the course of the series, had jilted both Howard and Doughby. In a private letter of 1837, Sealsfield praised slavery as a "safety valve warding off the deleterious influence of a too great influx of foreign populations, & keeping up that staunch republican sense, which distinguished the state of the Washingtons, Patrick Henrys, Jeffersons etc."[13] Thus Sealsfield is not ambiguous or contradictory in his own right; he merely replicates some of the convolutions of the proslavery apologists, with whom he "defended slavery as a natural part of a patriarchal-agrarian society."[14]

It is not possible to hold such views as these while believing that blacks fully share the humanity of whites, that they are included in the equality of all men asserted by the Declaration of Independence. Thus those who hold such views must *necessarily* proceed from racist presuppositions, Sealsfield among them. From one point of view, it seems futile to make much of this point; as one examines the record, it begins to appear that, with a few eccentric exceptions, virtually all whites were racist, though generally in an instinctive, unarticulated, prescientific way; biological racism came later. Racism was intensifying in the North, as people began to contemplate the prospect of a mass migration of emancipated slaves. Abraham Lincoln when debating with Stephen A. Douglas agreed that physical differences between the races made their dwelling together in equality impossible, and in 1862 he said the same thing to a delegation of blacks.[15] Nor is this an idiosyncrasy of Americans. Many if not most Europeans felt the same way; Tocqueville, for example, was persuaded of black inferiority. The two points peculiar about Sealsfield's case are the ferocity of his racist expression and the fact that it is not modeled in the American antebellum fiction upon which he is said to have drawn.[16]

Sealsfield consistently presents blacks as ridiculous, disgusting, and animalistic. They all speak the same barely intelligible, ungrammatical, and inarticulate jargon, "ob man sie in den Sklavenstaaten antrifft oder in der mexikanischen Provinz Texas, in Pennsylvania oder in New York";[17] in fact, their lips are too thick to allow them the use of human language (13:18). Not only blacks but even those of mixed blood are never able fully to master European language: "Ihre Sprache ist in der That mehr abgebrochenes Kindergeplauder, und klingt unangenehm in den Ohren" (14:272). The oddest of the anatomical claims is that their calves are in front of their legs rather than in back (13:14). Constantly they are compared to animals: they are like monkeys and odious orangutans because they imitate white dress (13:8, 13–14); Indian children, incidentally, also resemble monkeys (6[1]:85); blacks are demons, kobolds, a subterranean force; their children resemble piglets (13:67, 70–71). Vignerolles says of the debilitated slaves he has acquired that it is impossible to believe that these incredibly ugly beings, with the heads of orangutans and breasts hanging below their hips, devoid of memory, understanding, or instinct, can really be human; they are so much like animals that it is difficult to raise them even to the level of slaves (15:386–87). In fact, as the burdens of slave ownership are rendered in greater detail, the milieu appears substantially less Arcadian and idyllic. Slaves are liars and thieves, so stupid that a male exhorted to love Jesus believes Christ is a woman and is astounded to hear otherwise, while an inattentive mother causes her baby to die (13:61–62, 79–81). In *Die Prärie am Jacinto*, a Negro sent to get cigars and round up a jury gets his orders mixed up and must be given written instructions to show to others (16:176–77). They are violent: one bites off another's nose and a drunken, orgiastic group plots a genuine revolt, a scene that may well have been influenced by the rebellion of Nat Turner in 1831 (13:86–87, 95, 135–46).[18]

The fear of black rebellion becomes increasingly thematic in the plantation novels. It seems logical enough to Howard: people who are excluded from rights become malicious and vengeful, a condition that could only be cured by putting blacks on an equal footing with whites, which is, of course, not possible (13:104). But when the wayward group of his slaves does become rebellious, he professes not to be able to understand it, as they were always treated well; he wishes the best for his blacks, but the situation makes him tyrannical against his will (13:137, 146); his wife, for her part, has already sensed the potential of rebellion in the situation (13:97–98). In attempting to convert Creoles to Jacksonianism, Doughby argues that at the Battle of New Orleans Jackson saved them from a black revolt, as the British commander had brought uniformed blacks from the West Indies to instigate it (13:230). Howard fears that slaves listening to the harangues of the abolitionist Vergennes could get rebellious ideas: "Wir sitzen auf einem Vulkan—auf einem Pulvermagazin"; the frivolities of the French and Creoles could bring a repetition of the slave revolt in Haiti—"Zum Glück haben wir Uncle Sam im Norden" (14:62–63). Since blacks would not be able to function without masters, as they have no work ethic, if freed they would revolt under the leadership of a Spartacus (14:49).

Throughout there is an undercurrent of fear of black sexuality and a horror of miscegenation. One of the terrifying features of the rebellion of the bad slave is his intention of raping Howard's wife (13:137). The scene in "La Chartreuse" in chapter 2 of *Die Farbigen*, with its disturbingly sensual girls, is the most salacious in Sealsfield's generally prudish fiction (14:223–80). *Farbig* in his usage means mixed blood, and he leaves no doubt, here or elsewhere, that racial mixture leads to degeneration, a prominent concern of the contemporary discourse about slavery and race.[19] When the abolitionist Vergennes suggests intermarriage as a gradual solution to the race problem, the others, Americans, Creoles, and French, are horrified, especially as there are ladies present (14:150–54). As a result of his "Negerphilosophie," none of the ladies will have anything to do with him; the girls will not dance with him (14:362–63). Mixed-race people are vicious, asserts another of the Frenchmen, the children of unbridled passion who have stolen their way into the white race; to tolerate them would be to undermine the principle of marriage (14:153). Vignerolles asserts that one could not respect the American people if interracial marriage were allowed (14:158).

This opinion appears to be a consequence of Vignerolles's retrospectively narrated experience with "La Chartreuse" nearly thirty years before. The Frenchmen, in pursuit of a cow that had run off owing to the malfeasance of a slave, stumble upon this odd, bordello-like establishment with its atmosphere of a degenerate Arcadia or *Venusberg* of the Christian imagination, and find themselves erotically captivated by the sensuous colored girls and barebreasted slaves before making their escape upon hearing the warning of the Almighty in a clap of thunder (14:274). At this early stage of their American experience they are not properly sensitive to race distinctions; they still hold foolish views of racial equality like those of Vergennes (14:289). Schuchalter observes: "The ability to recognize that these near-irresistible creatures are not of the right race is an important step forward in becoming an American."[20] Subsequently they find themselves ostracized by their neighbors because of a rumor that they intend to install one of the girls on their newly purchased property. The French are at first offended at this puritanical challenge to their honor, grounded as it is in gossip, but they must free themselves from the imputation, whereupon the neighbors become cordial. An American supposes that a French cavalier and officer must "in diesen Punkten anders, oder, wie Sie sagen, liberaler denken; aber das ist eine böse Liberalität, die zum Glücke bei uns noch nicht Eingang gefunden hat" (15:329). A civil society that governs itself must make sure that the moral principles on which it rests not be injured (15:322). Thus racism and the fear of uncontrolled sexuality are closely connected, as was long the case in American society. Schuchalter points out the absences also: Sealsfield's narrator Howard "never mentions the beauty of the spiritual, the power of the slave service, the remarkable creativity of the slave dance. He never sees the expressiveness of the slave's verbal art, its wealth of stories, proverbs, and verbal games."[21] On the one occasion when a black dance is described, the portrayal is broadly satirical: the slaves are scorned for aping white manners and dress; two "ladies" even sport lorgnons; with their ducks' feet, cannonball thighs, blood-sausage lips, the "Wechselbälge" look like "ein Trupp bekleideter Orang-Outangs" (13:7–14). In fact, Sealsfield's portrayals of blacks are so abstract and cartoonish that one might wonder whether he had had much to do with them directly or could have been a slaveowner himself.

In any case, his representations of black-white relations are very different from those in the antebellum American novels he is believed to have consulted. There we see the most imaginably cordial, affectionate, and loyal relations between masters and slaves; it appears that the uprising of Nat Turner, rather than depositing in fiction an awareness of a revolutionary undercurrent among the slaves, led instead to elaborate denial. Abolitionist pressure and their own insecurity about the justice of slavery also motivated southerners to develop a benign scenario: "the strongest weapon which they possessed for justifying their peculiar institution to themselves and to others was the argument of plantation paternalism. The image of sunshine and happiness around the old plantation home would, it was felt, win the sympathies of many, especially women, whom the abstract justifiers—Biblical, Constitutional and historical—were unable to reach."[22]

It is true that Kennedy's *Swallow Barn*, in a mode of what the author doubtless supposed to be humor, has physiological representations of blacks that in places resemble Sealsfield's: a black child is "a little ape-faced negro ... flat-nosed pigmy"; the poverty of the clothing is also humorous—"the strange baboon in trowsers"; they have "wonderfully flat noses, and the most oddly disproportioned mouths ... a strange pack of antic and careless animals, and furnish the liveliest picture that is to be found in nature, of that race of swart fairies which, in the old time, were supposed to play their pranks in the forest at moonlight." They are somewhere between nature and civilization, and show gradations: "the veteran waitingman being well contrasted with the rude half-monkey, half-boy, that seemed to have been for the first time admitted to the parlour; whilst, between these two, were exhibited the successive degrees that mark the advance from the young savage to the sedate and sophisticated image of the old-fashioned negro nobility. It was equal to a gallery of caricatures, a sort of scenic satire upon mankind in his various stages, with his odd imitativeness illustrated in the broadest lines."[23] Yet all this, incredibly enough, is meant kindly. In *Swallow Barn*, all is mildness and domesticity (*this* is Biedermeier in an American setting); the blacks are usually called not slaves, but Negroes or servants. The whole of chapter 46, titled "The Quarter," is a depiction of the slave quarters suffused with good humor and loyalty; the blacks are well taken care of, for they are helpless in their present condition, which makes emancipation impossible. Slavery is wrong, but it is the southerner's responsibility and cannot be changed.[24] In the following chapter there is the story of Abe, a bad slave, corrupt and criminal, who is sent away to sea instead of to prison, whereupon his character improves. He becomes a good seaman and displays courage on a rescue mission in a storm, eventually losing his life. It is, a character comments, "a gallant sight to see such heroism shining out in an humble and unlettered slave of the Old Dominion!"[25]

One might also consider James Kirke Paulding, a northerner of old Dutch heritage who became a partisan of the South out of repugnance toward the industrializing North, and thus perhaps particularly attractive to Sealsfield, who praised his Indian elegies in a note (12:93). In 1836 he published a book in defense of slavery, and in the year before an admiring memorial of John Randolph, part of the lunatic fringe of American politics at that time, a virtually hysterical defender of states' rights, which he thought more important than the Constitution itself; Sealsfield had singled him out for special commendation in *The United States* (2 [1]:64–67).[26] The states'-rights principle was, of course, a pillar of the defense of slavery. In Paulding's *The Dutchman's Fireside* (1831), a faithful slave of the past is praised, though it is said that there are no more such since the "meddlers" have come;[27] in the preface to *Westward Ho!* (1832), the author asserts that he "yields to none in respect for the motives of those who are sincerely anxious to rid this country of the embarrassments of slavery; and none more heartily wishes the thing were possible, at a less risk to the happiness of both master and slave."[28] In the novel itself the slaves are grotesque and happy; one of them refuses freedom, and, when exhorted by an abolitionist in Philadelphia, he sees that the freed blacks are beggars, depraved women, and criminals, and realizes that he is better off in his enslaved condition.[29]

As I have indicated, William Gilmore Simms would be a pertinent figure for stylistic comparison if it were not for the chronological difficulties. However, in *The Yemassee* (1835), blacks volunteer to fight with their masters (the protagonist has no hesitation in arming them), and they refuse emancipation.[30] It might be noted here parenthetically that Sealsfield's hero Jackson, though he supported slavery on economic and political grounds, had no compunctions about arming *free* blacks and insisting on equal pay for them in the defense of New Orleans;[31] thus, even Jackson may have been less racist than his disciple. Simms's probably best-known novel, *Woodcraft* (1854), while too late to be relevant to Sealsfield's career, sheds a pertinent light on the literary context. Simms came to be a vigorous defender of slavery and the Confederate cause; *Woodcraft* is a rejoinder to *Uncle Tom's Cabin*.[32] Yet no other writer in this group portrays blacks so humanly. In *Woodcraft* he repeats the motif of a slave refusing emancipation, in this case on the grounds that he and his master are bound to one another: "*You* b'longs to *me* Tom, jes' as much as me Tom b'long to *you*; and you nebber guine git *you* free paper from me long as you lib."[33] The blacks are faithful, competent, brave, and loyal: "The negro guides did their duty with the exactness and promptitude of persons who knew exactly what was required of them, and what was the object of the arrangement"; on one occasion, they form an impromptu jury, and the master promises to be buried together with his beloved cook, Tom.[34] This is a writer who from the outset was explicitly racist in the modern sense; one character, very likely speaking for the author, argues that whites and Indians can never be reconciled, for "the very difference between the two, that of colour ... must always constitute them an inferior caste in our minds. Apart from this, an obvious superiority in arts and education must soon force upon them the consciousness of their inferiority."[35] Thus it appears that a similar ideology of racism can lead to very different fictional portrayals.

One might argue that the difference is one of representational purpose and interest: the Americans have a propagandistic need for euphemism and humanization while Sealsfield can reflect more realistically the true tone of southern white attitudes. This appears to have been the original view of Grünzweig, who argued that Sealsfield reflects the ambiguities of the southern intellectual climate and that he was freer, with his European audience, to depict them.[36] There is, furthermore, the question of voice, of what we are to make of his habit of splintering his narration among so many differentiated first-person narrators. While it has been argued that George Howard, one of Sealsfield's most persistently racist figures, is an imagined alternative identity of the author, Grünzweig interprets him as an unreliable narrator.[37] Recently the argument has become more deconstructionist: the racist discourse means the opposite of what it appears to mean. The grotesque, sometimes goofy behavior of blacks, such as the claim of astonishment that Jesus is a woman in *Pflanzerleben I*, is clever, imaginative pretense, signifying intelligent, potentially subversive resistance by the oppressed.[38] In fact, the thought occurs to Howard more than once that the displays of loyalty and enthusiasm on the part of his bondsmen might well have an element of pretense—for example, the hurrahs of the slaves upon his return to his plantation: "In dem Allem ist viel blauer Dunst, ohne Zweifel, wie es bei Sklaven nicht anders der Fall seyn kann; aber der Dunst, er riecht doch angenehm in unsere Nasen, er kitzelt unsere Nerven; das Souverainspielen hat doch auch seine angenehme Seite"—and he goes on to observe that what appears to be willful self-delusion makes him feel a few inches taller (12:245). The same thought recurs at a scene of parting: "'God bless Massa! our beloved Massa! Him Bless!' schreien Alle mit einer Stimme, die wenn sie nicht von Herzen kommt, ein Meisterstück schwarzer Ton-Modulation und Verstellung genannt werden kann" (13:162).

The gross stupidities of blacks, as in losing the Frenchmen's cow, or in a scene in which a slave cannot get fodder out of the barn because he is literally following orders to close the door and the window (13:17), may look to the modern reader as performances of ironic sabotage. Furthermore, Howard's insistence upon the contentment and good order of the slave community is repeatedly deconstructed, as it were, by the virtually concomitant complaints that the slaves thieve and lie whenever they can—that is, that their allegiance is to their own interest, not that of their masters. To be sure, Howard does not appear to get it, but interprets their behavior as simple perversity: "Der Neger giebt nie Wahrheit von sich, so lange noch eine Lüge möglich ist" (13:55). Are we to see through Sealsfield's narrator to the author's understanding? But we should be careful about ascribing modernist techniques to a writer of the past. There can be no doubt that Sealsfield complicates his perspective with his multiplicity of narrators, but it is not certain that he does so to undermine the narrators' authority. Another scholar argues that Sealsfield's texts do not sharply distinguish between author and narrator and that the narrator can speak in the author's voice; he refers to Sengle, who sees the unclear juncture between author and narrator as a Biedermeier characteristic.[39] The difficulty would be to find the countervoice. The abolitionist in *Pflanzerleben*, Vergennes, is portrayed as a shallow hothead and a potential terrorist in his association with the French Revolution. Schuchalter points out that "all of Sealsfield's narrators are profoundly unsympathetic to the plight of the slave."[40] Nor do matters change when he writes in a third-person mode, as we have seen in the examples from *Der Legitime* and can discover again in *Die Deutsch-amerikanischen Wahlverwandtschaften*, where the old black servant Priam is barely human in form, with the face of an orangutan and parts that do not fit, a nose that resembles a pickle, nostrils that open outward, the mouth of a frog, lips like snails, feet like fly swatters; he is stupid, pompous, and evidently deranged besides (23:4, 19–21). We must furthermore integrate the evidence from the nonfictional, expository essays on the United States, which indicate no contrast with the positions of the fictional narrators.

There are in addition other areas of consonance with the antebellum southern context that are not directly connected with slavery and race. One of these, briefly mentioned earlier, is Sealsfield's stated admiration for Scott, who was very popular in the antebellum South as a neofeudal model; he was the genuine predecessor of Simms.[41] In contrast, the more populist and egalitarian Dickens was less well received in the South.[42] Sealsfield, too, came to have little regard for Dickens. In his Brockhaus article, he rejected as frivolous any claim that he was a disciple of Dickens, and, in a letter of 1860, he denounces Dickens's writing as "ein miserables Geschreibsel, absolut ekelhaft, ohne Geist," and asserts that he should have quit with *Nicholas Nickleby*, that is, with his third published novel near the beginning of his career (*Briefe*, 292, 316). Bulwer-Lytton, from whom, as we shall see in chapter 5, Sealsfield drew an inspiration, was also popular in the South.[43] Occasionally there are traces of anti-Semitism (e.g., 2 [1]:182; 3:14, 132; 8 [2]:44; 9 [2]:291–92, 306–7); however, it is not very pronounced, and might be as much a Central European as an American element; doubtless American, but probably equally harmless, is the characterization of Yankees as "wahre doppelt destillirte Juden" or "doppelt destillirten Hebräer" (11:181; 12:18). Much more striking and specific to the environment is the treatment of Catholicism.

Sealsfield's intense hostility to Catholicism is a prominent feature of his texts and may at first look like the zealotry of the lapsed monk.[44] But here again he is drawing on an element from his American social and political environment, for there was a vast amount of anti-Catholic agitation in his time, to which he may be primarily reacting, for the antipathy grows stronger in the later works. In the plantation novels, a priest effectively speaks calming words during a hurricane (13:118–19). The two marriages of Americans to Creole women require Catholic ceremonies and in both cases the priests are amiably portrayed (11:277; 12:335), though Doughby is determined to remove his wife "so schnell wie möglich aus der creolischen Umgebung fort, weg von den katholischen Priestern und Mama's" (12:340–41). Later, however, Sealsfield twice refers with gratification to one of the most spectacular events of this epoch, the burning by a mob of the Ursuline convent in Charlestown, Massachusetts, on August 11, 1834: once in *Die Deutsch-amerikanischen Wahlverwandtschaften* (22 [2]:315), and again in *Das Cajütenbuch*, where the narrator, Colonel Morse, remarks that "das amerikanische Volk" burned such places down "mit dem sichern Takte, der es stets leitet" (16:36). However, despite the noisiness and vigor of the anti-Catholic agitation, it never became a successful political force; when it became organized in the Know-Nothing party, it foundered in ridicule after a few electoral successes.[45] Furthermore, so many of those in the forefront of the movement were such evident crackpots that it is troubling to see Sealsfield in their company.

Overall, one sees him absorbing the elements of American nativism with its hostility to difference. In this connection it is unclear to me whether he made any significant distinction among race, ethnicity, and national identity, whether "racism" is not too specific a term, and whether he does not show a tendency to treat all group identities and characteristics in a unitary way. Nativism was directed against the new waves of immigrants, prominent among whom were the Irish. In chapters 31 and 32 of *Der Legitime*, a stupidly and drunkenly comic Irishman, not found in the earlier English version, is dragged in to no benefit to the novel or its plot. In the story of the kidnapped child in *George Howard's Esq. Brautfahrt*, which Sealsfield took over from Timothy Flint,[46] the brutal kidnapper is easily identifiable as an Irishman: "das abstoßendste Gesicht, das mir je vorgekommen; eine hündisch verstockte, stumpfsinnig heimtückische Physiognomie, mit einem finstern, teuflisch-hohnlachenden Ausdrucke.... Beim ersten Anblick sah man, daß es ein Irländer war ... eine Gesichtsfarbe schmutzig grau, seine Wangen hohl, seine Lippen ungewöhnlich groß; der ganze Mensch ekelhaft, wild aussehend" (11:130). There are jabs at the Irish here and there in the later writing as well, and the central section of *Das Cajütenbuch, Der Fluch Kishogues*, is an extended ethnic joke in which Irish alcoholism is again thematic. In a private letter of 1854, Sealsfield complains that the three million Irish immigrants are "ein schrecklicher Dünger für dieses Land," bringing murder, drunkenness, and dirty vices (*Briefe*, 287).

A good deal more telling is Sealsfield's treatment of German immigrants, quite unique in my experience of reading German-language fiction about America. Many of these writers, from the nineteenth century down to the exiles of the 1930s, were strongly if not, in some cases, exclusively concerned with the Germans in America. Some of this portrayal is characterized by lament, self-pity, and resentment: the honest, frank, cultured German cannot compete with the crass, grasping Yankees and is harassed and scorned as a "damned Dutchman." In 1829, Sealsfield found it appropriate to present himself to the publisher Brockhaus as an American admirer of Germans: "that the German has more correct sense [than the Englishman] to value things & objects, is manifest from the circumstance, that they among all the nations of Europe, if properly guided, thrive best in America" (*Briefe*, 150). But in his writing he shows no trace of the conventional German or German American perspective. In general, he tends to ignore the German population, which, though it was not quite as vastly growing in the South as elsewhere at this time, had become established in the Louisiana Territory under French auspices long before Sealsfield got there, in a settlement on the Mississippi north of New Orleans well known as the "Côte des Allemands."[47] He makes a passing, historical reference to it, remarking only that the settlers had survived their early sufferings and were now enjoying the benefits of freedom (12:42 and n., 46–47). Elsewhere he restricts himself to remarkably unfriendly side glances at German immigrants, ranking them even below the Irish. His early story, *Christophorus Bärenhäuter*, 24:333–432), is, as is well known, largely copied from a tale of Timothy Flint; it tells of a slow-witted German whose spirited Irish wife is kidnapped by Indians; she winds up running the Indian tribe, and when she escapes and returns, only to find that Christophorus has taken a new German wife, she resolutely returns to the Indians to live out her life with them. Flint's story is conventionally anti-Irish; Jemima is a shrewish harridan. It is revealing that Sealsfield in his adaptation tells the story more in her favor, stressing her courage, competence, and dispassionate resignation, and making the German more of an oaf.[48]

In *Der Legitime*, German immigrants are comic in their un-American servility; idly drinking and nattering in a tavern, they are scornful of freedom and expect the British to defeat the American rabble in the Battle of New Orleans; they long for a king to create order as in the Fatherland; they spring to their feet and salute when a militiaman enters, and, though they sit down as soon as they realize he is only a sergeant, they nevertheless cease talking of politics in his presence (7 [2]:251–58). In *Morton*, the young man is rescued by a wise, dignified, and patriarchal German American farmer named Isling. However, he is not an immigrant but a former Hessian officer who belongs to the generation of settlers from the time of the American Revolution. A miserly German peasant who appears in the novel is less an immigrant than a redemptioner. German immigrants make a downright grotesque appearance: "Beim ersten Anblicke gewahrte man, daß es Kinder des unglücklichen Landes waren, die seit so vielen Jahren die Erde mit ihrem Blute zu düngen, die Welt mit ihrer Nacktheit und ihrem Elende anzuekeln bestimmt zu sein scheinen; eines jener Bilder servile Unterwürfigkeit, wie wir sie auf den Werften unserer Seestädte häufig als Exemplare dieser Nation zu schauen bekommen, und die uns bereits wider Willen gezwungen haben, der unbegränzten Hospitalität unsers Landes zu setzen" (10:48). Despite his own German lineage, Isling remarks icily: "Kein Engländer oder Franzose, und selbst der elende Irländer würde nicht so schamlos seyn, sein Elend da aufzudringen, wo er nichts zu suchen hat—in einem ganz fremden Lande" (10:55). In *Ralph Doughby's Esq. Brautfahrt*, Doughby disparages fruitful bottomland in Ohio because it is "deutsch wie Sauerkraut"; he does not want land in the half-German state (12:161). Perhaps this affect subsided as Sealsfield became more alienated from the American environment. The satirical portrayal of the impractical, unworldly Bohne in *Süden und Norden* is milder, friendlier, and more conventional. In *Die Deutschamerikanischen Wahlverwandtschaften* there is a certain amount of sympathy for German immigrants; however, some ambiguity remains even there, as we shall see in chapter 5.

Superior to the Germans are the Normans, as the Alkalde asserts in his harangue in *Die Prärie am Jacinto*; the Germans lacked the ruthless drive to conquest and freedom characteristic of the Normans and became slaves (16:217). The Alkalde's obsession with the pirate heritage of the Normans as the model for American conquerors, with which he justifies his decision to pardon the murderer Bob because the struggle requires such conscienceless and violent people, is skeptically regarded by Morse as slightly absurd monomania, and is likely to be particularly puzzling to today's readers.[49] However, young Morse, as appears from his own story, is a dangerously incompetent greenhorn and, moreover, an easterner from Maryland, thus of limited judgment, and the identification with the Norman heritage is a well-attested element of the antebellum southern ideology. It is initially connected with a notion that traces the dissimilarity of the North and the South to the parties of the English Civil War, Roundheads and Cavaliers: the northern Yankees have inherited the blood of the plebeian Roundheads, the aristocratic South that of the Norman Cavaliers.[50] This neofeudal concept was widely disseminated in the discourse of the antebellum South.[51] Once again it is *Der Legitime* that already shows Sealsfield's assimilation of the contextual discourse. The motif of the energetic, conquering Normans, barely adumbrated in *The Indian Chief* (4 [1]:180), appears more explicitly in *Der Legitime* (7 [3]:249), where Copeland describes the inhabitants of Louisiana as a million masters on conquered land. In *George Howard's Esq. Brautfahrt* the great Mississippi River is "das leibhafte Bild eines nordischen Eroberers, der mit seinen stinkenden Horden hervorbricht aus seinen öden Steppen, um eine halbe Welt zu verwüsten" (11:209)—an early image of the "Huns" who were to become so notorious at the time of World War I.

Mentioning *Die Prärie am Jacinto* brings us to the most extensive area of discourse about national character, the contrast of Americans and Hispanics. It reflects, of course, the American pressure westward, the infiltration of the Mexican province of Texas, the Texan struggle for independence, and, prophetically, the Mexican War and Texan statehood after the conclusion of Sealsfield's writing career. Here especially are signs that race and nation are not distinguished from one another, for Mexicans are described in much the pejorative way that blacks are: the Indians in Mexico look like orangutans (8 [1]:78); Mexicans are the products of miscegenation between Indians and whites and, therefore, have the worst qualities of both races (8 [1]:298–99); Mexican soldiers are skinny, dwarfish, and weak (16:28). In *Der Virey und die Aristokraten oder Mexiko im Jahre 1812*, a novel of chaotic political struggles, the often opaque narration reproduces the confusion of civil war in a wild, bizarre land, the complexities of class and race, and the intrigues of the British. The point is to demonstrate that Mexicans, unlike Americans, are not mature enough for liberty, and the story ends in compromises by the privileged designed to control the masses. *Die Prärie am Jacinto* depicts the heavily outnumbered American settlers as naturally superior to the treacherous, brutal, and incapable Mexicans, thus ultimately invincible; much of the mythmaking concerning the Texas episode in

American history has already been codified in Sealsfield's work. Although the late novel *Süden und Norden* has a more complex, not to say, puzzling fabric, it, too, as I have mentioned, vividly portrays Mexico as a morass of superstition, corruption, and oppression. Prominent in this perspective is Sealsfield's pervasive anti-Catholicism; the superiority of American culture over the Mexican that justifies Texan independence is, in part, a confrontation with the obscurantist, repressive, superstitious hold that the Catholic Church maintains over the Mexican people. The narrator of *Süden und Norden* remarks that the Catholic religion is good for uncivilized, childish peoples (18:70), while the love-struck Cockley is willing to be anything for the girl he loves: Tunker (*sic*), Baptist, Quaker, Shaker—but never Catholic; he would sooner become a Negro (18:194).

Even in this matter, however, the American writers from whom Sealsfield is presumed to have drawn exhibit a more nuanced perspective. Flint, who was himself a Protestant clergyman, takes a sufficiently condescending view of the Spanish culture in Mexico, and one of his main characters is an evilly intriguing priest. Yet he is able to see the situation also through Spanish eyes: "They had been accustomed to consider us as a nation of pedlars and sharpers, immoderately addicted to gain, and sordid in the last degree; that we were a kind of atheistic *canaille*, on an entire level, without models of noble and chivalrous feelings; in short, a kind of fierce and polished savages, whose laws and institutions were graduated soly with a view to gain."[52] To this it is replied, not altogether fairly, that only lower-class Americans have an analogous prejudice against the Spanish.[53] But at least there is a comparative view of intolerance. Flint's novel ends with a Protestant-Catholic marriage in a Catholic ceremony; the boys are to be raised as Protestants, the girls as Catholics, and the narrator remarks, quite in contrast to Sealsfield's views of miscegenation, that "crossing the breed," as in agriculture, "is considered a great improvement."[54] An 1838 novel of the Texas conflict by Anthony Ganilh, no less insistent on Mexican backwardness in the grip of Catholic bigotry, nevertheless begins and ends with mixed marriages; the consequence of the first liaison is a protagonist who is raised as a Mexican aristocrat, thus providing through much of the novel a contrasting point of view to that of the Texans, one internal to the Mexican cause. In one place, the author introduces a refugee from anti-Catholic persecution in the United States who makes a direct reference to the notorious convent burning and predicts that all Catholics will emigrate to Texas when Mexico has completed its conquest;[55] thus we see how bigotry cuts both ways. We also see once more that Sealsfield drew his perspectives more from the general, popular discourse of the time, which gives "a picture of Mexicans in general as an ignorant and indolent people demonstrably incapable of self-government,"[56] than from literary sources.

These views of society and politics that Sealsfield absorbed from the American context raise questions about the influence on him of the teachings of the theologian Bernard Bolzano (1781–1848), who, initially a kind of intellectual prodigy, received an appointment in 1805 at the age of twenty-four at the University of Prague, where he became a prominent figure and where the young Postl certainly must have attended his lectures. In a fine display of Metternichian despotism, he was removed from his teaching position in 1819 and placed under investigation for six years in what was essentially a heresy trial, though, as in all such matters under the Holy Alliance, one with political aspects. Sealsfield commented briefly but pungently on the persecution of this "very liberal and eminent thinker" in *Austria as It Is* (3 [1]:75–77; the English typesetter has turned Bolzano into "Bolpano" and his enemy Jakob Frint into "Friut"). Since, as it is important to remember, practically nothing is known about Sealsfield's youth and education apart from its main outlines, the impressive dissenter Bolzano has been found to be a key to the development of the young man's thinking.[57] One rather isolated but nevertheless weighty voice of skepticism about this is that of Franz Schüppen, who finds the treatment of the Bolzano affair in *Austria as It Is* ironic and dismissive, not indicative of a strong allegiance, and argues that Bolzano's collectivist theories of property and his utopian view that trade and commerce should be managed by the state wholly incompatible with Sealsfield's convictions in these matters.[58]

The question has never been exhaustively treated and it would be a formidable task, as Bolzano was extremely prolific. I have naturally not undertaken it myself; what follows are comments based on some probes into the material.[59] Bolzano was an anti-Kantian rationalist who tried to reconcile Christian ethics with a set of notably progressive views on society and politics. They might strike one as those of an early Christian socialist, resembling those arrived at somewhat later by his almost exact contemporary in France, Félicité de Lamennais, though more disciplined philosophically and without Lamennais's exalted *Schwärmerei*. In religious matters, the remarkable thing is not that Bolzano was charged with heresy and sedition, but that, apart from losing his academic position, he was left at liberty and not defrocked as Lamennais was. He owed this result partly to exceptional dexterity in walking a tightrope of assertions of belief and partly to what is known in Austria as *Protektion* in high places. (A less well-connected disciple was not only removed from his position as seminar director but spent four years in ecclesiastical custody.) For Bolzano's religious views were exceptionally liberal: he spoke against the literal interpretation of doctrine, treating it as metaphor; against the enforcement of orthodoxy; for the right of believers to choose or remove their own clergy; for the right of conversion to any religion. He joined Christianity to Jeremy Bentham's utilitarianism, holding that the central meaning of religion lies in intelligible, objective ethical truths and that its purpose is activity in the interest of the greatest possible social welfare. He seems to have contemplated the separation of church and state. One can well imagine that such views might meet with a thoughtful response in a young man questioning his clerical vocation and even his allegiance to the Catholic Church.

Bolzano's political views, conceived, to be sure, not as a revolutionary program but as utopian projections, were in many respects radically democratic. He regarded the republic as the best form of government; he was opposed to inherited privilege and advocated individual freedom and equality of all men before the law. Citizens should elect their judges and representatives, and defend themselves with a people's militia. They have a right to rise up against tyranny. All activity should be directed toward nourishing in the commonwealth the greatest possible happiness of others. He was for the pursuit of prosperity but against the accumulation of wealth and proposed that its inheritance be abolished. Thus far, except for the last point, Sealsfield might well have heard echoes of Bolzano in American doctrine. Schüppen is right to indicate, however, that in economic matters they must have diverged. Bolzano quite explicitly advocated "einen oder den anderen Zug von jener sozialistischen Verfassung auf Erden . . . , die meiner Meinung nach die allerzweckmäßigste ist."[60] Socialism, as we know, tends to bring with it authoritarian structures. He proposed that land, industry, tools, machines, books, and works of art should be social property; the state should set prices and wages, provide free education and health care, publish all books, and in general guide people to freedom.[61] Compared with one who holds these propositions, Sealsfield is a limited anarchist of the American type, holding to the once emancipatory, today right-wing and reactionary doctrine that the best government is the one that governs least. Bolzano's ideas in this area belong to long-lived European traditions; it is important to see that Sealsfield is not rooted in them, but in American practices. One can imagine what Sealsfield, the apostle of Andrew Jackson, relentless opponent of the Bank of the United States, would have thought of Bolzano's proposal that the state should manage all credit, if he thought about it all.

But in another area Sealsfield deviates even more, and it is precisely one that is at the center of the revived interest in Bolzano in our time. For he propagated not only the equality of men and communities with one another, but also of nations and languages. Needless to say, the issue was crucial in the Hapsburg lands, and Bolzano particularly appealed for mutual respect and understanding among Germans and Czechs; he also opposed anti-Semitism. The majority of both the Bohemian Germans and the Czechs took a dim view of Bolzano's arguments against linguistic-nationalist exclusivity, then and later, because they considered it much more just and right to hate one another and the Jews.[62] Today, of course, his position seems eminently pertinent. I cannot see that this important facet of Bolzano's teachings made any impact on Sealsfield at all. He never shows any signs of a belief that nations and races are equal to one another, even potentially, or deserving of mutual respect. Therefore, when the relationship of Sealsfield to Bolzano comes to be exhaustively researched, it will be found to have had limitations.

With this kind of attention, Sealsfield's reputation as a radically democratic writer must undergo considerable revision. For it emerges that he celebrated just those features of America that have come to be least loved in the world at large: a virtually fanatical commitment to the acquisition and defense of private property, and a conviction of the unquestionable superiority of the American way of life, with its imperialistic contempt for other peoples, justifying the historical mandate to shove them aside. In fact, he does not appear at his best as a writer of politics in the specific sense. He was not only intolerant but an impatient and sometimes gullible observer. He repeatedly veers from observation into satire and caricature; although he read and admired Tocqueville, as he indicates in a note to *Die Farbigen*, where he praises *La démocratie de l'Amérique* (*sic*) as the finest work from a French pen since the days of Montesquieu (14:221), he had nothing of Tocqueville's liberality, spirit of inquiry, or sense of the limitations of his own perceptions.[63] He seems to have taken many exaggerated anecdotes and bits of campaign propaganda at face value; he even hoaxes us with a well-known canard when he claims that a Yankee tried to sell him a wooden nutmeg (2 [1]:187). Schuchalter remarks on "a curious inability to distinguish between ideological bombast and party conflict."[64] Long misunderstood as a "realist," he was in fact an ideologue, a utopian prophet of Manifest Destiny.

But it is just this excess, this satirical indifference to pedestrian reality, the colorful language with its often impossible diction, the vigor and violence of an excited and prejudiced imagination that give his texts their great originality, their unique place in nineteenth-century

German prose. Some of the best modern work on him has taken him seriously as a literary artist, indeed more seriously than he appears to have taken himself. Even among German writers, his nature descriptions stand out by reason of their dynamic vividness and plasticity. He delineates personality types with confident and spare strokes, and he had a good ear for dialogue, achieving impressive results in his effort to reproduce the levels and cadences of American speech patterns in German.[65] His tone differs dramatically from that of the majority of German observers, who tended in varying degrees to be shocked and dismayed by what they perceived as the rudeness, disorder, and lawlessness of American life, which only the cultivated, spiritual, honest, and frank German might mitigate if he were not overwhelmed and trod underfoot. Sealsfield wanted nothing to do with cultivated Germans and did not give a hoot about the alleged absence of culture in America; as a matter of fact, he thought it a good thing. Whereas most German commentators shrank from violence, Sealsfield revels in it, imaging by the exuberance, the hyperbole, and the structural insouciance of his narrations the burgeoning of American freedom as an explosion of historical energy, an inchoate but energetic and comic newness, a mighty force shoving aside the lugubrious detritus of centuries, and a victory, as he always believed, over tyranny and superstition, an upheaval that consigns all the proprieties of European civilization, which are in the service of bondage, to the dustbin. He was an aggressive writer, not least toward his reader. He grasped the nettle, so to speak, of American frontier society with an exuberance that most German writers were too timid to match. We shall turn in the next chapter to some details of his portrayal of the phenomena of freedom.

# 4. The Shape of Freedom in the Plantation Novels

The main thematic thrust of the great centerpiece of Sealsfield's oeuvre, the plantation novels, collectively titled *Lebensbilder aus der westlichen Hemisphäre*, is the exposition of American freedom. This endeavor has two main axes. One is the replication of American self-understanding, always, of course, in its southern and southwestern variant. I do not believe that any other German-language writer at any time has placed himself so insistently, indeed repetitiously, within the discourse of American democracy and patriotic rhetoric. It is this obsessive assumption of citizenship that accounts for Sealsfield's self-identification as an American writer or, simply, as an American, down to the inscription on his gravestone. Whenever he speaks of Americans, even in third-person or expository writing, his pronoun is not "they" but "we." Thus the narrator's posture, whether in first-person mimicry or third-person omniscience, is in intimate contact with his setting and located over against his presumably European reader. The other axis is the distinction of American concepts and practices from the European mentality. In this matter Sealsfield's focus is stronger than that of any American-born writer is likely to have been; thus it may be said to constitute the European dimension of his writing that some commentators have so avidly sought. However, his projections of European mentalities are more stereotyped and cliché-ridden than the representation of American values and habits; while this perspective may have something to do with the device of first-person narration, it is of no little significance that the narrator of *Die Farbigen* and *Nathan* is by origin a French aristocrat. Another question is whether the two axes are entirely on the same plane and graph a coherent image of America.

American freedom in Sealsfield's representation is grounded in individual independence. The independent individual is a monad, so to speak, of society. In American civil society, where "jedes Individuum sich als absolutes Seyn betrachtet," French and Germans, conditioned for centuries to see themselves as parts of a machine operated by government, are incapable of competing successfully either as individuals or communities (14:218–20). Out of the multiplication of individuals the community and the society grow. The state does not form the person but is an instrumentality of individuals in combination. One impor-

59

tant though less explicit corollary to this is that the state is not identical with the nation but merely its administrative device. An absolutely necessary precondition of this independence is the availability of unowned land on which to settle. This is the reason why the claims of the Indians cannot be acknowledged, however uneasily the execution of the policy of removal may rest upon the moral conscience. In the particular case of the Louisiana Territory, the consequence is that the sovereignty of Spain and France, though in some sort acknowledged as a legal fact, lacks the reality, the solidity, and the potential for the future of the community created by the squatters on the ground. Subsequently the same view will be taken of Mexican authority in Texas. While the term "Manifest Destiny" was not articulated until the 1840s, the concept is intact and in place in the discourse of Sealsfield's fiction. Prior to the Louisiana Purchase, it was known as "geographical predestination," and a Jacksonian paper spoke in 1825 of "a country *manifestly called by the Almighty to a destiny.*"[1]

Illustrations of these points abound in the texts. Americans spontaneously organize themselves into collective action, for example, on board a steamboat, where they form a committee to investigate a quack salesman and his Negro shill (12:40). In the primitive backwoods society of *Nathan*, the squatters solemnly debate the important question of the relationship of assumed squatters' rights to Spanish sovereignty in the territory, and, not without sharp disagreement, come to acknowledge limits to their challenge to Spanish authority and, grudgingly, to allow Acadians to settle with them. The newly arrived French aristocrats at first observe this display with disdain and find it absurd that the crude barbarian Nathan speaks of "principle" (15:227), but they are soon obliged to a more respectful view. Justice under the system of locally appointed "regulators" is raw but not arbitrary. The Frenchmen are horrified to witness the tar-and-feathering, whipping, and expulsion of a man, but they afterward discover that he is the odious crook Balot, who, in the guise of a river guide, robbed and stranded them; the backwoodsmen, meanwhile, recover and restore the stolen possessions intact. Justice is possible, explains Nathan, "ohne Courthaus, Perrücken oder Richterstuhl . . . , ohne Sheriffs, Constables und Galgen," and, in fact, can be more humane than in the lawyerly North, where Balot would have been hanged (15:270–71). The Frenchmen are amazed that backwoodsmen, in order to bring their produce more easily to market, have on their own initiative built a road through a swamp without the help of the government (15:336). *Nathan* also has a scene of a communal house-raising "frolic" for the newly arrived Frenchmen, one of the archetypal American scenes of free individuals combining spontaneously to communal action, a point caught also by Gerstäcker, as we shall see, but missed by many European critics of isolated, egotistical individualism in ungoverned America. The Frenchmen discover that work without frivolity generates republican consciousness and realism (15:376–77).

In chapter 4 of *Pflanzerleben I*, entitled "Der Stumpf-Redner," we get an enactment of grass-roots democratic activism, where Ralph Doughby, on board a boat on the Red River, gathers the passengers in a meeting to plan election tactics in support of Jackson and, not incidentally, to grab the share of the spoils promised by Jackson's principle of administration (13:182), to appoint campaign workers for each locale, and even to win over a Federalist as a poll watcher, for, as the less democratically inclined Howard observes, morality is different in politics: "Unsere Mitbürger in der Politik zu betrügen, ist eine unserer Bürger-Seligkeiten" (13:204). However that may be, those who work at it win in democratic politics; the Federalists are too lazy to bestir themselves in this detailed, local way.

It is in fact the consciousness of freedom and civil rights that permits the individual to submit himself to society; it is on such public occasions "daß man fühlen lernt, was es ist, ein geachtetes Glied eines freien, sich selbst beherrschenden Volkes zu seyn" (12:85). Thus the country needs no police, for every citizen takes on the responsibility of policeman (15:10). The resulting society has a solidity and strength that antidemocratic observers had often doubted; Americans can never be rebels, it is remarked, on this point overoptimistically, for they are born free (15:27). This is the ground of the constant self-praise of the Americans as the greatest, indeed the only important nation on earth, for which the narrator Howard occasionally apologizes but nevertheless repeatedly articulates; foreigners cannot understand this pride, for the United States is our bride with whom we are in love. The patriotism is not like any other nation's, for we have made the nation ourselves; nothing is owed to authority, no debts, no forced labor, no aristocratic masters; anyone who wishes can call the president a fool (12:88–90).

The very primeval nature of America is more natural than the "verkünstelte[ ] Natur der alten Welt" (15:7), and thus its product, American freedom, is natural; American settlers will make Louisiana "zu dem..., wozu es Gott der Allmächtige bestimmt," and it will grow like a natural plant (15:291, 295). This point is interesting, although I doubt that it derives from Herder, as the editor Karl Arndt has argued (15:XI*–XII*, XXXIX*–XL*); it seems rather to flow directly from the Jacksonian discourse about nature.[2] Sealsfield undoubtedly reacted intensely to nature, and his vivid nature descriptions, whether of the colorful, almost subtropical Louisiana landscape or, in *Die Prärie am Jacinto*, of the infinite Texas prairie and its great live oak, the "Patriarch," with its cathedral-like interior and vast religious associations, have been justly admired by critics, but sometimes also overinterpreted. We must be careful not to reromanticize him or see him in the light of Cooper's lament at the shrinkage of the natural realm. His ideology is one of land clearing and the spread of settlement.[3] Howard associates the primeval forest, sublime as it may be, with a place where crimes can be hidden: "Ja, die Wirklichkeit ist oft grausamer, als die glühendste Dichtung—schauderhafter als die schreckenvollste Phantasie—sie malen kann" (11:98–99). In *Nathan*, the Creole and Spanish inhabitants of Louisiana complain that the encroaching American squatters are depleting the wildlife, but the squatters reply that there can never be too many hunters; the sooner the game disappears, the better, for then the land can be turned to its appropriate use, raising cotton, sugar, and corn (15:61). The implication is that hunting for its own sake is a useless, aristocratic pastime and should not be encouraged beyond practical necessity. On this matter, Gerstäcker, as we shall see, took a quite different view.

All the millions of elements yield a divine power; a society formed through the "Geheimnis der Individualisirung" is one of responsibility and self-respect, with the power of multiplying "die Zahl der *free agencies* . . . , im Gegensatze von Euch, die Ihr blos durch Massen handelt" (13:266–67). The patriotism is most strongly oriented locally, where one has settled; it grows weaker with distance from the county, the state, and finally the Union, "über die sich die Wärme unserer patriotischen Gluth oft recht matt hinbreitet" (13:177–78).[4] It is in such details that one sees a perspicacity about politics that is rarely found in any other German fiction about America. Sealsfield presents the Jacksonian movement as one of resistance to centralizing tendencies in the federal government (see his note explaining this, 12:156); thus the Federalists, in the demagogic jargon of the time, are disparaged as "Tories" and "monarchists." In this regionalism lie seeds of the doctrine of states' rights, of which the defense of slavery, at least at this time, was a subtext, and of the stresses that will lead to the Civil War. Sealsfield sees this quite clearly and represents it with unusual accuracy. The vision of Manifest Destiny is as explicit as it well can be at this early date; Americans are bursting out of the original states to the West and the South. It was, of course, easy for Sealsfield, with authorial hindsight, to have Nathan predict in 1799 that Louisiana would be American within ten years (15:291), but he was more prophetic in his prediction that in seven decades there would be a hundred million free citizens from sea to sea, "einen Coloß . . . , der mit dem rechten Fuße am Gestade des atlantischen Oceans, mit dem linken am stillen Meere . . ., unter dem Gesetze Christi leben, die Sprache Shakespeares, Miltons reden" (13:291)—a calculation, to be sure, quite similar to one made by Tocqueville.[5] Seventy years from the time the novel was published brings us approximately to the census of 1910, when there were ninety-two million people living from the Atlantic to the Pacific, though, of course, not all Christian and not all speaking Shakespeare's and Milton's English.

Manifest Destiny is a vision that implies conquest, for all the pretense that America is an empty, unpopulated, unowned land. Conquest requires violence by men of action and ruthlessness. Sealsfield not only recognized this requirement but embraced it; he acknowledges with remarkable enthusiasm the utility of men of violence for the cause of triumphant freedom. In this he is unique in all my experience of the German image of America, fictional and nonfictional, at any time. German observers have been and remain pained and repelled by the violence of American society and its apparent integral place in our habits and imagination. The representation of America as an incurably violent nation is a staple of the tradition of anti-American discourse,[6] but the concern that violence belongs to America's original sins is not restricted to explicitly anti-American observers. In the Jacksonian era there was real and endemic violence in American society; new emigrants were warned about it, though some modern historians see it "as a means of participation and expression that was based on a perception of moral right and political expediency" and "a valid means of expressing concerns over perceived social and political injustice."[7] But among European writers of the time, Sealsfield alone saw violence, dialectically, so to speak, as a force with positive consequences made necessary by the energy of freedom's explosion, ultimately to be sublated in a new, higher civilization. It is a temptation to speculate that this acceptance correlated with some element in his psychological disposition; evidently an impatient, intolerant, bearish man, he may well have entertained fantasies of the ruthless *conquistador*.[8]

The best-known exemplar of the utility of criminal violence is, of course, the hallucinating murderer Bob Rock in *Die Prärie am Jacinto*, spared from hanging by the Alkalde because he can die a useful death while applying his violent nature to the cause of Texan independence. His conditional pardon becomes a practical illustration of the Alkalde's obsessive theory of the conquering Norsemen. But there are other examples, such as Lafitte and his pirates in *Der Legitime und die Republikaner*, whose savage skills are turned to account by Andrew Jackson in the defense of New Orleans. The theme recurs in several places in the

*Lebensbilder*. The drunken, rowdy sailors from the *Constitution* may give a poor impression of public order in America, but that does not matter; these uneducated men are burning patriots and brave fighters: "Solche Männer verdienen, daß man ihnen ihre Lust nach ihrer eigenen Weise gönne. Sie werden schon wieder nüchtern werden ohne Polizei, Gendarmes und Wachhaus. Ihr rohes Treiben ist nicht den zehnten Theil so verderblich für des Volkes Sitten, als euer raffinirter *bon ton*" (11:32–33). Note the *euer* that Sealsfield employs throughout Howard's discourse, one of the many gestures of dissociation from the presumed European readership. Howard goes on to remark that these sailors are evolving into free men who can rightly look down on other peoples; British sailors, by contrast, become ever more stupid, "weil Knechtschaft immer zurück, Freiheit immer vorwärts führt" (11:35). Trappers are the uncouth, irreligious refuse of civilization, fugitives from justice, but they, too, toughened by nature, serve the cause by destroying the wild animals and developing valuable skills; they, too, will find their way to understanding. This new race of helots with its piglike children is nevertheless healthy; only they could prepare the way for civilization (11:197–201, 212–14).

The absentee landlord Howard discovers on his return that the justice of the peace has a higher regard for Howard's thieving, slave-driving overseer than for Howard himself, because the overseer is on the ground and works there; for that reason the judge did not interfere with his thefts, a view that he considers "echt patriotisch"; also in the community Howard finds that the overseer has more prestige than he has himself until he returns to take charge of his property (11:239–40; 273). In a passage that prefigures *Die Prärie am Jacinto*, it is remarked that Austin's settlement in Texas is flourishing despite the desperate characters it has attracted (12:221). The addlepated abolitionist Vergennes is astounded at the sight of the rough backwoodsmen, who look like murderers—"Aber könnt ihr lauter Washingtons, Jays und Franklins haben?" It is natural that the refuse of the world collects in the West. The reign of gamblers, murderers, thieves will be brief; they are unconsciously laying the base for civilization, and better men will come after. They move on, leaving the "Grundlage . . . des Glückes von Millionen freier, aufgeklärter und religiöser Bürger, die den Gott ihrer Väter in tausend und abermals tausend Tempeln, an Stätten preisen, wo zuvor der wilde Indianer gehaust." In any case, our women will know how to deal with them: "Es haben unfehlbar unsere Weiber zur Gesittung des Westens mehr beigetragen als alles andere" (12:233–37).

The main figure in this regard is the wild Kentuckian Ralph Doughby, who, to be sure, is anything but a criminal; he is just a good old boy, "kein übler Junge" with his heart in the right place (12:202). But he appears as a large, loud, impetuous, hard-drinking primitive, whose crudity permanently alienates him from his Yankee fiancée and distresses the prissy Creoles. He instigates a steamboat race that runs the risk of disaster but must be carried out against all counsels of caution as a matter of honor; after all, the Americans *invented* the steamboat (12:144–53). This scene may appear particularly infantile, even an anti-American canard, but social history reports that such races were not unknown, and the estimate in Sealsfield's novel that they cost five hundred lives a year (12:155) may not be excessive.[9] Sealsfield, employing a tale he had read in a book on Ohio River navigation and reported in *Die Vereinigten Staaten von Nordamerika* (1:2, 50–51, not in the English version),[10] has Doughby terrify his companions and nearly lose his life in a superhuman leap over a chasm; he appears, in fact, as a rather comical hero, as his disgusted fiancée must rescue him by hauling him up with her shawl wrapped around a sapling (12:160–70). Not long afterward, Howard's friend Richards describes Doughby as a true American and democrat (12:178–80).

He emerges, in fact, as the political hero of the *Lebensbilder*. The narrator Howard becomes persuaded that he is not a bad fellow after all, and his ability to apply his wildness to democratic political skills wins the grudging admiration of Howard and his Federalist companions (12:202; 13:192). For Howard he calls to mind the way other great American politicians have evolved: "ich sehe die Art und Weise, wie sich unsere großen Autodidakten, die Clay's, die Henry Patrick's [sic], und so viele Andere zu Rednern, zu Staatsmännern gebildet, gewissermaßen in Doughby personifizirt" (13:231). Like the rough-hewn backwoodsmen, Squire Copeland in *Der Legitime* and the squatter Nathan Strong in the later, retrospective segments of the *Lebensbilder*, he is a stand-in for Andrew Jackson himself. In fact, Doughby says of himself that he is not really wild compared with Jackson (12:329–30). As we know, Jackson was regarded, especially by his enemies, as a man of violence. He had killed men; he had fought fiercely against Indians; he had had alleged friends of the Indians and deserters executed; and, perhaps worst of all, he was charged with bigamy because he had married his wife, apparently unwittingly, before her divorce from her first husband had become valid. Doughby, in a performance of political, not to say, demagogic skill that impresses his skeptical companions, defends Jackson in an impromptu speech to anti-Jacksonian Creoles. He confronts them with the charges from a broadside and refutes them with lawyerly eloquence; chastity is a problem, however, being of greater importance than life, so he makes a show of admitting Jackson's error in the matter of his marriage, but, hoping to appeal to the Creole character, he extols young Jackson's passion and asks them to defend Mrs. Jackson chivalrously (13:232-45). Unfortunately, this fine speech falls flat with the Creoles who, as we shall see, are preoccupied with other concerns.

I have mentioned before that Sealsfield appears to have been an anarchist of the American sort, persuaded that the less government, the better, though with low tolerance for disorder in the immediate environment. Anarchism is an ideological emotion, however, irrelevant to practical politics. The surging energies of freedom, enacted by the wildness of backwoodsmen and settlers and the crudities of a man like Doughby, must somehow be contained if people are to live together in a community. In fact, as Walter Weiss noted at an early point in the modern reconsideration of Sealsfield, his democracy is authoritarian; the republic "ist für ihn ein Absolutum, das an die Stelle des absoluten Monarchen und der absoluten Katholischen Kirche in Europa tritt."[11] Since government is not really available in Sealsfield's landscape, there are three forces in his representation of the realization of freedom that support order. They are religion, respect for property, and American pride in distinction from the habits and characteristics of foreigners.

Sealsfield supported the separation of church and state, as he rightly observed that it strengthened religion rather than weakening it (2 [1]: 136-39). There is not actually a great deal of religion to be seen in the *Lebensbilder* or in Sealsfield's writing generally. There are moments of awe before phenomena of natural sublimity, such as the great live oak in *Die Prärie am Jacinto* or the imagined Southern Cross in *Süden und Norden*. But, on the whole, the religious aspect is a matter of rhetorical insistence, and its function is control of waywardness and anarchy. Only religion can replace the inner discipline that the still unfinished, unstable social order cannot provide.[12] The Conde in *Der Virey* worries that, if one deprives people of their "Aberglauben" in religion and monarchism, the result will be "nicht Freiheit sondern Zügellosigkeit" (8:267); here, to be sure, as so often, one must be careful about the interpretation of the various voices in Sealsfield's texts and not necessarily identify him with the viewpoint of a character.[13] Still, in *Nathan*, an American major defends puritanism to libertine Creoles: "Wehe uns, wenn diese letzten und einzigen Schranken bei uns niedergerissen werden, wir müßten in eine Anarchie, ja in eine Zügellosigkeit verfallen, größer als selbst die, deren Ihre Sansculotten beschuldigt waren, und unheilbarer" (15:330). In *Die Deutsch-amerikanischen Wahlverwandtschaften*, true peace comes to the plain American folk in the storm at sea from the Protestant prayer book, whereas one of the negative characteristics of the emancipated, loud, aggressive, allegedly wealthy but in fact fraudulent "Big Lady" is a religious skepticism that is spurned by all the other passengers (21:2, 28, 54–56). Sealsfield—and in this he resembles a great many German observers of the American scene—is altogether unsympathetic to popular sectarianism, especially as it is likely to stir up slaves and Indians rather than discipline them. Thus Howard complains:

> Heilig, wie mir Religion ist, und wie sie jedem reflektirenden Wesen seyn muß, und Achtung, wie ich vor der vollen Gewissensfreiheit jedes vernünftigen Geschöpfes habe, so ist mir diese Religionskrämerei, dieses Oppositionswesen unserer Methodisten, Tunker, Presbyterianer, Quäcker, und wie sie heißen, ein wahrer Gräuel, denn alles wird Euch so kaufmännisch betrieben, sie ziehen Euch umher, werden ausgesandt wie Musterreiter, diese ehrwürdigen Herren; die vielleicht vier Wochen zuvor die Nadel oder den Riemen verlassen haben, um die Köpfe unserer Indianer und Neger mit ihren krüden Ideen zu füllen, und sie aus halb blödsinnigen Tröpfen zu totalen Narren zu machen. Ich habe noch nie einen Neger oder Indianer durch diese Missionäre gebessert oder bekehrt gefunden, wohl aber Hunderte, die eine noch weit empörendere Sprache führten, als die ich so eben gehört. Alle Achtung vor dem wahren geistlichen Berufe und den Männern, die sich in die Wildniß begeben, um unsere Indianer durch sittigende Beschäftigung zur religiösen Erziehungen vorzubereiten;—mit diesen Camp-Meeting-Predigern aber verschont mich.
>
> (13:63–64)

Sealsfield is clearly resisting the extreme evangelism of the Second Great Awakening, the religious revival that swept the United States at this time. One might see this as a European posture, for German writers about America consistently opposed a rational Protestantism to the bewildering variety of religious expression found here, but, of course, there were many Americans who opposed "fanaticism." In his expository writing, Sealsfield gives an irritable account of a Methodist camp meeting, and though he makes a gesture of tolerance toward the "sects," he hopes Unitarians and deists will become extinct and denies that Catholics are Americans at all. Religion is needed for public discipline; Unitarianism in particular leads to "demoralization," for how could a Unitarian uphold morality and law (2 [1]:148–66)? He does not associate himself with any particular church or refer to mainline denominations very often. The scene of children singing Presbyterian hymns toward the end of *Nathan* is unusual, and, as we have just seen, elsewhere the Presbyterians are accounted among the sectarians. In *Süden und*

*Norden*, it is observed that Gourney's strict Presbyterian upbringing is not proof against the seductions and importunities of the fantastic Mexican ambience (18:193). The religion Sealsfield propagates is a generalized Protestant piety. Vignerolles, the narrator of *Nathan*, ranks the children's hymn-singing as an inspiring experience above "die Zauberflöte und Iphigenie..., die Entführung aus dem Serail und das Miserere der sixtinischen Kapelle" and asserts that religion binds the classes together: "sie ist doch das Band, das Wesen und Wesen an einander knüpft, und dem Hinterwäldler und dem Pair in dem, der droben über den Sternen thront, den Vater zu erkennen gibt!" (15:347–48). Nathan, for his part, disapproves of his guests reading secular newspapers on the Sabbath and gives them the Bible instead: "Ist die Zeitung, die uns lehrt, ein ruhig achtbares Haus, und uns selbst und unsere Leute in Zucht und Ordnung zu halten. Gibt Euch und ihnen den Halt..." (15:352). Thus the use of religion as a discipline against moral and social anarchy is explicit enough and is a feature of Sealsfield's outlook that is not very much out of the ordinary.

The matter of property as an important bulwark against anarchy is sufficiently pronounced to have attracted the attention of Sealsfield scholars.[14] It is doubtless also drawn from contemporary discourse, in which private property was an axiom. Jefferson's view has been summarized this way: "All persons had a natural right to enough land to produce their subsistence, as well as a right to the property produced by mixing their labor with the land."[15] The maintenance and defense of property—by which Sealsfield always means landed property—is a central concern of the order of liberty, to which his narrators constantly recur. Thus in *Der Virey*: "Eigenthum und vorzüglich Grundeigenthum ist, was auch Ultraliberalismus dagegen sagen mag, eine Basis, deren Solidität auch dem schwächsten Verstande einen Halt gibt, den der geistreichere Eigenthumslose vergeblich anspricht. Es liegt etwas Zähes, aber zugleich auch etwas Positives im Grundeigenthum, das seinen Besitzer gewissermaßen zwingt, unabhängig von seiner persönlichen Vorliebe und seinen Vorurtheilen, das Wohl des Landes zu berücksichtigen, in dem sein Eigenthum liegt" (8:318). Around property is formed the basic agrarian, patriarchal order that has come to be regarded as Sealsfield's central ideological value and, as Claudio Magris has observed, displays "einen paradox anarchisch-patriarchalischen Charakter."[16] Whoever is propertyless must be at least temporarily subjugated to the patriarchal extended family, or, like the blacks, who are incapable of property ownership by reason of race, kept in permanent dependence. For Sealsfield, the only alternatives to this patriarchal extended family, now threatened by the historical development, are a neoaristocracy or an anarchic, because propertyless, proletariat. He seems to have had no concept of a bourgeois democracy. In his picture of society the normal workers, artisans, and mechanics, the servants, employees, and small businessmen, the physicians, scientists, and engineers are largely absent, not to speak of intellectuals and artists. In this regard, as we shall see, Gerstäcker is able to throw a much wider net.

How is property, that is, landed property, secured? In the West, it seems, mainly by settlement and land clearing, "what historians of the frontier have called 'state-making.'"[17] Those who have improved the wilderness land are now its owners. Property can be purchased, as occurs now and again, but Sealsfield is never comfortable with money transactions, a point to which we must recur. Property can also be granted by sovereign government. However, in the plantation novels there is a good deal of ambiguity about the validity of Spanish and French land grants. Sealsfield did not wish to concede any validity at all to Spanish or French sovereignty in the Louisiana Territory—also a point to which we shall return shortly—but, despite his divagations about ruthless Norsemen, did not wish his exemplary Americans to appear as lawless and rapacious conquerors. Thus Nathan, after he leaves Louisiana because the rule of government is approaching too closely to him and who makes a new and ultimately very prosperous beginning in Texas, we are told, almost as an afterthought, initially acquired his property, through connections, to be sure, as a grant from the Mexican government (15:434–35; by *Die Prärie am Jacinto* such consideration for Mexican authority is no longer in evidence). One of Nathan's claims of his right to settlement, apparently cited from contemporary public discourse, appears at first to be something of a fiasco: he asserts that Louisiana is American because it is formed by alluvial soil deposited by the Mississippi, which has washed it from American land (15:72–75). Even his brother-in-law Asa has trouble accepting this argument, and the Frenchmen listening to Vignerolles's account of it find it hilarious. At the time Vignerolles thought this was a parody; a European who mounted such arguments would be thought crazy (15:81). But in all probability it is an indication of an epochal consciousness that is more powerful than reason. The Frenchmen also find it amusing that Nathan refers to the Spanish and French as foreigners in what is still their own country (15:242–43); here, too, however, they fail to hear the voice of destiny.

The most spectacular assertion of property rights is constituted by the defense of the blockhouse in *Nathan*, a scene that appears to reflect the ideological import of the siege of the Alamo, which occurred during the genesis of the novel, if it was written in 1836 as we suppose; the

Alamo siege is described in some detail in *Das Cajütenbuch*, although one critic has complained that Sealsfield did not make as much of the event as he ought to have.[18] The blockhouse battle, in fact a conflict over property rights between Americans and non-Americans, in which six American rifles are victorious against eighty-five French and Spanish muskets but Asa is killed, consecrates the property in blood, and a virtual cult is made of the blockhouse. Because the ground is consecrated, the battle becomes a magnet that attracts more Kentuckians to settle there, and this kind of settlement secures the American claim to the land permanently; because of the blood they shed, they have the right to keep out the French, Canadians, and Acadians who want to settle there (15:124–25, 146–47). It would seem that the mystique of property is born in Manifest Destiny.

In the plantation novels, property is an element both of freedom and of social cohesion. Near the beginning of the sequence, Sealsfield supplies a preposterous note explaining why the social critique of Fanny Wright has no impact in the country at large: violent revolution is impossible in the United States because nine-tenths of the citizens are owners of landed property (11:19 n.). The property issue is, of course, associated with that of slavery, property in slaves being as inviolable as any other. But, beyond that, the inviolability of property is crucial to the order of liberty. Thus Nathan articulates the basic principle of his community: "Ist aber unser Prinzip immer gewesen, und wird immer, calculire ich, seyn, das Prinzip freier Männer, *Unabhängigkeit der Person und des Eigenthumes*" (15:229). Anyone who transgresses the rights of property is appropriately treated as a man without principles, like a Negro, for a Negro acts not from principle but from animal instinct (15:237–28). An example emerges promptly. The Acadians who have come from Canada are animal-like, ignorant people, who "nicht so viele Notion von der Heiligkeit des Eigenthums haben, als Ebony-Neger" (15:247). That is, they steal pigs and cannot understand what difference it makes until they are instructed by whipping.

As we can see, both religion and the sanctity of property are employed to define the difference between Americans and foreigners. Americans, though their freedom is born in revolution and they are now engaged in the second, Jacksonian "Staatsumwälzung" (11:273) against the centralizing Federalist aristocracy, are not *French* revolutionaries, that is, leveling sans-culottes running mindlessly amok. It is amusing to note, by the way, that the distinction of the American Revolution from the bloody French chaos and anarchy was a point of importance to the Federalists. In an essay of 1800, Friedrich Gentz, who was to become Metternich's ideological factotum, played off the American against the

French Revolution as "only a conservative defense of established rights against British encroachment." None other than Sealsfield's bête noire John Quincy Adams published a translation of Gentz's essay as campaign literature, making the point that it "rescues that revolution [the American] from the disgraceful imputation of having proceeded from the same principles as the French."[19] In general, the discourse of the *Lebensbilder* regards revolutionary thought in Europe as futile, an intellectual concoction without a base in the people. Freedom is possible only when the spark is struck among millions; where it is an isolated flame, it sputters (11:248). Vergennes, the enthusiast for the French Revolution, is told scornfully that the French are children, whose unbounded vanity makes them manipulable; economic inequality makes a strong ruler necessary, where, unlike in America, three to four million have nothing, three million have little more, only a slim majority has subsistence, and a few hundred thousand live in excess. Thus Old World republicans are playing an unnatural role and always look foolish or repellent; the role only fits Americans (12:95–100). A revolutionary of Vergennes's type lacks the least notion of the sacredness of property, the basis of our commonwealth, and would slaughter the noblest citizens, on whom culture depends, in order to achieve equality (12:100). Nathan, who is, after all, a contemporary of the French Revolution, explains that French republicans "statt sich selbst zu regieren, sich vom ersten besten Gassentyrannen am Gängelbande herumführen lassen;— Tollköpfe, die, wenn ihnen ein solcher Ohnehosen ein Wort sagt, den Feuerbrand in das Haus des Nachbars schleudern, und dann wie böse Buben sich über das Unheil freuen, und rauben und plündern." It is madness to make a land free against its will (15:290). American society, without priesthood, police, officials, or king, requires the maintenance of the strictest principles—by which is meant, principles of sexual morality and the separation of the races—otherwise it will fall into the anarchy of the sans-culottes (15:330).

In an odd passage, the narrator muses that Europe is wrestling for the birth of a new freedom, but forgets the threat from the north (12:50–51). In the usage of Young Germany and the *Vormärz*, the "threat from the north" always meant Russia, feared for the alliance of its barbarous despotism with the dominant Central European powers, Austria and Prussia. Thus this is one of the very few places where Sealsfield drops out of his American role and speaks from a European perspective. In general, however, few hopes for Europe of any kind are expressed. Schuchalter associates Sealsfield's position with Frederick Jackson Turner's thesis of the frontier, for which "Europe is the antithesis of everything American. Where Europe is corrupt, America embodies virtue, where Europe is rife with superstition, America is an embodiment of reason, where Europe is despotic, America is democratic and free."[20]

The scorn for the French Revolution as inauthentic and immature is a component of a more general condescension toward the French, and they, in turn, stand in here for Europeans generally.[21] In *The Americans as They Are*, Sealsfield observed:

> The French are of all men the least valuable acquisition for a new state. Of a lavish and wanton temper, they spend their time in trifles, which are of no importance to any but themselves. Dancing, fighting, riding, and love-making, are the daily occupation of these people. Their influence on a new and unsettled state, whose inhabitants have no correct opinion of true politeness and manners, is far from being advantageous. Without either religion, morality, or even education, they pretend to be the leaders of the *bon ton*, because they came from Paris, and they in general succeed. As for religion and principles, except a sort of *point d'honneur*, they are certainly a most contemptible set, and greatly contribute to promote immorality.
>
> (2 [2]:174–75)

Once again, in the fiction, this discourse dwells within the narrative voices projected by the ventriloquist author. But the effect is in no way mitigated by the fact that the most important of the first-person narrators after George Howard is the Frenchman Vignerolles. On the contrary, though he gives a detailed account of the resistance mounted to the challenges of American experience by his socially and nationally constructed consciousness, his story is one of Americanization, that is, assimilation and capitulation. When Vignerolles relates the tribulations he and his friends suffered upon first arriving in Louisiana, the Americans can hardly keep from laughing at the pettiness of their troubles. They are just children, according to Howard, who treat frivolities seriously and serious matters frivolously: "Kaum waren die ersten Baracken der elenden Stadt zusamengestoppelt, als auch ein Theater da seyn mußte, und Spielhäuser und Ballhäuser, und noch schlechtere Häuser.— Das nennen sie ein Land civilisiren" (14:126–27). Nathan, for his part, can hardly bear to discuss questions of property rights with French people, "da sie keine Amerikaner, sondern bloß Franzosen waren, mit denen zu disputiren wir unter unserer Würde hielten" (15:148). To be sure, their inferiority is not their fault; their character has been debased by despotic government and, consequently, "sie brachten eine debauchirte Civilisation in ihrem Gefolge mit" (15:341).

Bearing the brunt of the discourse of American self-definition are the

Creoles, the Louisiana-born French and Spanish. A striking feature of the *Lebensbilder* is the diminishment of the stature of the Creoles in the course of the novels. This may be a parallel to the excision of the Creole planter Gentillon as an explicator of American doctrine in the transformation of *The Indian Chief* into *Der Legitime* (see chapter 2); it is perhaps also a parallel to the intensification of the anti-Catholic affect after the relatively benign treatment of priests in the earlier plantation novels. This development is difficult to explain; one must suppose that Sealsfield came increasingly under the influence of the environmental discourse, its biases and obsessions, as summarized by a modern historian:

> Lousianians . . . were a people speaking a foreign tongue and steeped in foreign ways, exhibiting unusual and even questionable values and behavior (festivals and frolics on Sundays!), used to authoritarian government, unlettered in representative institutions, following strange legal customs and laws. . . . Common perception and reference viewed it [Louisiana] as being divided between two peoples, the "Americans" and the "French," or "Creoles." . . . [Creoles developed] a strong sense of distinction from the Americans, who regarded them all with disdain. . . . In Anglo-American eyes, the French were tainted by their tendency to mix and socialize too freely with other races.[22]

But the novels, after all, were written in Switzerland, where one might suppose that Sealsfield had some perspectival distance from the American environment. The progressive hardening of the nationalistic discourse through not only the plantation novels but also *Das Cajütenbuch* and to some extent *Süden und Norden* therefore provides something of a puzzle, as does what appears to be a weakening of the discourse in *Die Deutsch-amerikanischen Wahlverwandtschaften*.

For at the outset of *George Howard's Esq. Brautfahrt*, Creoles are portrayed quite positively. When the absentee landowner Howard returns to his plantation, his crooked overseer gives him a totally false accounting. But his neighbor Menou has kept a close watch on Howard's affairs and is able to give an exact accounting and to impeach the overseer, an eminently significant service to Howard, who, quickly concluding that he prefers the ingenuous Creoles to the clever Yankees, employs Menou's son as a more competent overseer, who transforms the somewhat negligently managed operation (11:220, 236, 268). Menou also turns out to be a competent surgeon, and he takes over the task of buying Howard's slaves for him, as Howard is still somewhat skittish on this point (11:263, 270). Madame Menou's naturalness and the tone of the Creole family are praised (11:245–46, 249–50, 256–57). Once it is established that there is no black or Indian blood in the family (11:256–57), the path is clear to Howard's marriage with Menou's daughter Louise. In the second volume, where Howard criticizes his friend Richards's prejudice against the Creoles as a mental habit inherited from the English (12:12–13), Doughby will marry Louise's sister Juliane. Howard actually praises the French for their strength and endurance as settlers, who are more than conquerors, but Promethean creators who transcended the frivolity of their rulers; mindful of their support of the American cause in the Revolution, he again sets his face against English prejudices: "Nein, der Franzose ist nicht der tanzend leichtfertige Johnny Crapaud, als welchen ihn der grobkörnige John Bull der Welt gern zum Besten geben möchte" (12:48–50). All of this looks very much like integration.

Nevertheless, there is from the beginning a competing discourse of condescension toward the Creoles. Howard observes that Menou's household effects and decorations are not American and republican, but French and royalist; only Americans and the English know true domestic comfort; all others have luxury and dirt (11:242). We call a Creole, like any foreigner, "Monsieur," "ein Mittelding zwischen Herrn und Sklaven, während der Mister oder Master—der Meister—den freien selbständigen Mann bezeichnet, und deshalb für uns vorbehalten wird" (11:252). Richards warns Howard to keep his distance from Creole company, remarking that not all Creoles are Menous (12:83). In later parts of *Ralph Doughby's Esq. Brautfahrt*, even Menou comes into a more critical light by objecting to Doughby as a son-in-law because he is a barbarian and a Jacksonian. Now Howard judges him as "wirklich einen Franzosen und keinen Amerikaner"; his view that he has a right to dispose of his daughter shows that he may be civilized but will never understand true freedom (12:264, 316–18). When Menou insists he is French—"Je suis Français, né en Louisiana quand Louisiana était française. Je suis Français"—Howard thinks him a fool; being French weighs like a feather against American citizenship: "Ein geborner, freier amerikanischer Bürger ist das schönste Attribut, das es für den Mann geben kann, und dieses Attribut, wie der dumme Esau sein Geburtsrecht für ein Linsengericht des Franzosenthums hingeben!—ich kann solche Narrheiten nicht ausstehen" (12:267). The bluff, buoyant Doughby wins Menou over by sheer force of personality, but a disparaging discourse about the Creoles has now established itself permanently in the text. During a hurricane in *Pflanzerleben I*, they are cowardly, but pretend to be heroes afterward (13:124–25).

Creoles hover on the edge of frivolous sensuality and an ambiguous racial character. A central motif of this discourse of suspicion is dancing. The obsessive employment of the leitmotif of the dance comes to suggest to the reader a puritanical malady in Sealsfield's psychic disposition.[23] As we have just seen, Howard in one mood defends the French against the imputation that they are a frivolously dancing people. But increasingly, dancing becomes a sign of unseriousness and incompatibility with the American character. There is, to be sure, a certain attraction to the sensuousness of the dancing even of blacks and mixed-race people: "diese Natursprünge und die *con amore* Tänze unserer Creolen-Negerinnen.... Wollust und Sinnlichkeit leuchten aus jeder ihrer Bewegungen" (13:47). But, as appears in *Die Farbigen*, the combination of racial impurity and sensuality implies depravity and libertinage. The alluring temptresses in "La Chartreuse" dance bewitchingly before their visitors (14:273–74). While Doughby works to organize the passengers on the riverboat for political action, the Creoles are dancing; they talk of a forthcoming ballet and do not even know the following Monday is election day (13:216–17, 224–25). This contrast escalates gradually into a major conflict between Doughby and the Creoles over democratic participation and responsibility. A Creole complains that there is no firm government; it is always changing, and there is constantly change around them, hurly-burly, busyness, more and more building of roads, dams, canals, improvements, bother with meetings and juries (13:254–55, 258). In their complaints they become increasingly agitated about the instability of everything. Presidents are at first extolled as great men, then disparaged, first "Shefferson," then "Maderson," then Monroe, now "Shekson"; can't we keep one if he is a good man?—"*Au diable* mit ihrem Selfgovernement!" (13:271–72). They continue to grumble about improvements and the nuisance of the public good (13:296). The Americans, unsurprisingly, are offended by this display, and Howard concludes that freedom and democracy cannot suit "zarten, parfümirten und überpolirten Personalitäten" (13:278).

From this point the representation of Creoles and, in *Nathan*, Acadians becomes increasingly derogatory. In an odd but well-received simile, Creole huts are compared to a huddled group of Swabian peasants seen by one of the Americans in the Rotunda of the Capitol in Washington (13:297). The Americans hoot at the Creoles' houses; they are ridiculous like those of the Shakers, but the people themselves are lazy and provincial; eighteen out of twenty are illiterate; the women are vulgarly seductive; a meal is tastelessly served (13:298, 300–1, 303, 307, 310–11). An old man tells of the French settlements of the past: the settlers did not work, lived off royal funds, put on plays and gambled, and they *danced*. The first building they erected was a casino; the American carpenters were disgusted by "das wüste leichtfertige Leben" (13:326–

28). Nathan's community initially excludes the Acadians because they dance on Sunday and passes a law against dance music; after six months in wistful banishment, they are admitted upon renouncing "die Abomination des Tanzes," and gradually became partly assimilated: "wurden nach und nach ordentliche Leute und wohlhabend dazu, und sind jetzt brave tüchtige Bürger, freilich keine Amerikaner" (15:147–48).

Sealsfield makes even his French narrator, Vignerolles, continue this discourse; he reminisces that, at his first encounter, the admittedly crude and sometimes absurd backwoodsmen seemed to have a nature "himmelweit verschieden von der der Creolen und unserer importirten Landsleute, die mir in dem Augenblicke, wenn ich es frei gestehen soll, wie zweimal aufgewärmtes Ragout vorkamen" (15:9). They are shabby people who keep their word as little as Negroes; drunken, dishonorable, semihysterical, and cowardly louts (15:63). Vignerolles becomes totally persuaded of the superiority of Americans; though they leave their environment rough and uncivilized, they invest what they achieve year by year in their property, building a base for the future; a Creole would have used his first harvest to decorate himself and his house, to impress others with *Schein* (15:310–11). When contemplating the road the backwoodsmen have built through the swamp, he observes that the French would have built a dance hall and a theater instead; the Creoles are pretty enough "mit ihren ewigen Bällen und kindischen *Plaisirs menus*, ihrem Faulleben," but they have vegetated for fifty years without improving their situation (15:339).

The increasing xenophobia of the discourse in the *Lebensbilder*, for all that it is placed on the account of Sealsfield's primary and secondary narrators, is a symptom of a narrowing of vision that constitutes his misfortune—one might almost say, tragedy—as a writer. His burrowing into the discourse of the antebellum South is the source of his strength as a writer, because he reproduced vital dimensions of American reality with a fidelity matched by few German-language writers, before or since, but it also came to be a weakness, because it locked him into an ideological space that, as he himself sensed in one part of mind, was not wholly suited to a plausible depiction of the range and possibilities of freedom and democracy. Schuchalter has remarked: "he saw too literally into the nature of Jacksonianism and was fascinated by the least viable of the myths surrounding Old Hickory."[24] Jacksonianism itself is said to have been "oriented toward a period in American social development that was slipping away at the very moment of its formulation" and to have failed owing to its rigidity.[25] The ambiguities and subliminal insecurities in regard to the matter of slavery, which have exercised the academic critics, are in my view segments of the larger problem, namely, that Sealsfield did not wholly believe in the democracy so colorfully detailed and eloquently praised in the texts. For example, an analysis of the occurrences of his repeated leitmotif, "Wir sind in einem freien Land," would show that it is regularly called upon by characters seeking license for a mean or selfish act.

Sealsfield achieves, if not narrative irony, then a certain distance from the thematic preoccupations of the *Lebensbilder* through his narrator Howard, who is more of a Federalist than a Jacksonian and rather skeptical of democracy. Early on he makes fun of the ignorance and crudities of a backwoods orator who, while fulminating against John Quincy Adams, confuses the Creek Indians with the ancient Greeks (11:90–95). He seems to moderate his views as his narration goes on; he remarks at one point that he is not as rigorously anti-Jacksonian as some of his friends (13:213), and the elaborate Creole display of refusal of progress and the responsibilities of democratic citizenship on the riverboat is so repellent as to propel him to greater respect for democracy's contribution to the public good (13:266). Yet, upon reflection, he thinks the Creoles, who are, after all, men of property, may actually have a point; the busyness of democracy is like a noisy tavern in which one would like to get some rest (13:277–81). For all his admiration for Doughby's performance on this occasion, he sees in it a form of demagoguery that is beginning to affect the whole of civil life (13:205). Doughby, he thinks, has the makings of an intriguer, "einen zweiten Van B——n" (13:208).

At the time when Sealsfield was writing his novels, it had become evident that Martin Van Buren was to be the Jacksonian crown prince. But he was never admired and loved as Jackson was. There are several reasons for this, but an important one is that he became a master of partisan political cunning. Thus he did not appear to have the simplicity, the transparency, the alleged naturalness of Jackson, a sort of *Kerl* out of the *Sturm und Drang*. Doughby's view that elections are won by grass-roots political work and his efforts to organize his region as advantageously to his party as possible seem quite normal to us, but such partisan activity was not only relatively new at the time but something that the revered Founding Fathers had done their best to inhibit. Sealsfield, with his characteristic preference for prejudice over inquiry, yielding, as Grünzweig has remarked, not sociological analysis but a "Kette von konventionsmäßig determinierten Bildern,"[26] appropriates an image from the public discourse instead of looking more closely to discover what Van Buren, dismissed in *Die Deutsch-amerikanischen Wahlverwandtschaften* as "der kleine fliegende Holländer-Kneipensprößling" (22 [2]: 278–79), might have been able to contribute to the evolution of democracy.[27] In fact, it is not clear that Sealsfield gave American politics the same close attention after the middle of the 1830s as he had done earlier. Some of the resulting confusion is evident in *Die Deutsch-amerikanischen Wahlverwandtschaften*, as we shall see in the next chapter.

Howard worries about the spread of a moneyed aristocracy (12: 84–95). The wise Vignerolles makes an ominous prediction: "je republikanischer eine Regierung wird, desto selbstsüchtiger, egoistischer, geldsüchtiger das Volk" (14:54). At the end, Nathan is apotheosized as "[e]in wahrer Sterling-Charakter, noch aus der alten Zeit, nicht durch das Geldmäckeln, Wuchern der heutigen Tage verdorben. Es ist etwas Patriarchalisches in seinem ganzen Wesen. So müssen die alten Patriarchen gedacht, gesprochen, gehandelt haben, mit dieser Kraft, Natürlichkeit und Gott vertrauendem Sinne" (15:419–20). However, Nathan himself is to some degree an incoherent figure. The whole story of his settlement is one of bringing American civilization to Louisiana. But when the civilization reaches the point that land titles need to be clarified, he betakes himself to Texas, "wo kein Sheriff, kein Gesetz ihn ein Haus weiter weisen kann"; he would rather fight Spanish muskets than the law (15:399). The contradiction has been noted in Turner's frontier thesis also.[28]

The preference for a "patriarchal" society based on landed property as the true form of American democracy, increasingly threatened by the cash nexus and the more materialistic and egotistical greed it brings with it has, of course, been noted by many Sealsfield scholars. But, perhaps in some cases animated by an anticapitalist affect, they have not always seen how dubious this position is and how it trapped Sealsfield, with the potential to be one of the most progressive German-language writers of his age, in stasis. For the position that wealth based on agricultural estates and the production of export goods such as cotton, and counted by the number of slaves owned, is more moral and democratic than wealth based on cash and credit, trade and industry, surely will not bear any kind of scrutiny. In fact, Sealsfield's antipathy to the money economy seems to me to have been grounded in superstition, if not in states'-rights opportunism, as, indeed, Jackson's campaign against the Bank of the United States, paper money, and a system of credit generally may have been.[29] He was unable to see that the Jacksonian position itself was contradictory and self-delusory: "Despite contradictions of patriarchy, racism, and fee-simple property, they rallied around enduring human values of family, trust, cooperation, love, and equality." The kind of expansion that Nathan represented threatened "patriarchy, conformity, and circumscribed horizons."[30] How this self-imposed myopia came to sabotage one of his most ambitious literary endeavors will appear in the next chapter.

# 5. *Die Deutsch-amerikanischen Wahlverwandtschaften*: An Attempt at a Social Novel

Over the years, especially in recent times, a considerable body of criticism has grown up around most of Sealsfield's works. There are valuable major studies especially of *Der Legitime*, the *Lebensbilder*, *Das Cajütenbuch*, and *Süden und Norden*. By contrast, the uncompleted novel, *Die Deutsch-amerikanischen Wahlverwandtschaften*, which appeared in 1839–40 with what looked like a new series title, *Neue Land- und Seebilder*, has remained rather a stepchild of criticism. One reason for this relative neglect may be that the text did not become available in the modern reprint edition until 1982. But it never established itself very firmly. Although a number of more or less appreciative reviews appeared,[1] and although it was one of the first of Sealsfield's novels to be translated into English in 1844, the year of the to-do about the identity and origin of the "Great Unknown,"[2] the novel faded from view. The publishing house retained remainders of the carelessly and unattractively printed first edition until after World War II (21:XIII). The publisher reported to the author in 1857 that fifteen copies had been sold since 1850 (*Briefe*, 305). The reason may not necessarily be that the novel is a fragment, for it is a quite large fragment, perhaps, as Grünzweig has suggested, Sealsfield's most ambitious undertaking;[3] furthermore, his other fragmentary novel, *Morton*, has attracted considerably more attention. One explanation may be that, since the novel takes place in New York State and Switzerland, it lies outside the expectations brought to Sealsfield as a writer of the American Southwest. Moreover, it is not all that easy to read. It is not only, even by Sealsfield's standards, prolix and diffuse, but also somewhat confusing when looked at closely. The last two points form the basis of my effort to approach a degree of understanding of this work: its distinctiveness as a commentary on Sealsfield's oeuvre from the periphery, and the significant confusions in content and theme that any reasonably attentive reader must sense.

The novel consists of five large segments that are not congruent with its external divisions. In the first segment we meet a young American, identified in the course of the narration as Harry Rambleton, taking his leisure at the Lake of Zurich sometime in the mid-1830s. At first sight

Rambleton appears to be a fashionable, cold man who looks down upon the Germans with contempt. The acquaintance of a Prussian baronial family named Schochstein is imposed upon him, more or less against his will. However, the affable urbanity of the German nobleman causes the aristocratic American to thaw; a friendship develops with the baron's liberal son Wilhelm, while Rambleton appears to fall in love at first sight with the daughter Luitgarde. But pressing business soon calls Rambleton back to America. The second segment consists of the forty-two-day sea voyage from Le Havre to New York. This journey provides the opportunity for a broadly based social satire, the points of which are highlighted by the effects of a storm lasting for days and the following calm, also lasting for days. For long stretches of this segment, the figure of Rambleton disappears completely; not until the arrival in New York does he emerge again, as he is pleased to see that the Schochstein family has also sailed across on a different ship. The third segment shifts the perspective to the fashionable society of New York and especially to Dougaldine Ramble, a stunningly beautiful, fabulously rich, and extravagant society belle, a coquette notorious for devouring men, who is being courted by a jovially cynical financier named Erwin Dish. In this segment the first traces of the political content of the novel appear: the looming financial crisis and the evil conspiracy to introduce paper money and a credit bank. The young Baron Wilhelm von Schochstein, who as a nobleman is already on his way to becoming a social lion and who has made a strong impression on Dougaldine, is drawn by curiosity into the political dispute; toward the end of the segment he rides in an omnibus with a number of uncouth activists to a political meeting. At the same time the somewhat consternated Dougaldine goes to Acreshouse, the seat of the Rambleton family on the Hudson north of New York City. For the experienced reader of Sealsfield, this move from the city to the country is a sign that good qualities are slumbering in Dougaldine and that she is on the way to moral reflection and regeneration.

The fourth segment contains the prehistory of the foregoing. It begins a year earlier and bears the title, in Sealsfield's inimitable German American idiolect, of "eine fashionable Liebe." Rambleton and Dougaldine, who have not seen one another since childhood, meet, at first without recognizing one another, on an outing to an island in the Hudson, where he falls head over heels in love with her. After their return, his search for her takes him to the resort of Saratoga Springs in the company of the still unsuspecting Dish, who plays the role of Rambleton's mentor in matters of fashion and dandyism. Among the dandies, American patriotism is now passé, "der alte Metternich jetzt *en vogue*"

(22 [3]:66). But, in Saratoga Springs, Rambleton suddenly rebels against Dish's tutelage and appears, to the latter's annoyance, in his traveling dress, sunburned and unkempt, in the dining room, where Dougaldine, still not recognizing him, regards him with shock and disgust. Thus Rambleton has no other alternative than to change his identity—the elements of traditional comedy in this segment are manifest. He transforms himself into a properly groomed, affluent young man named Digby, under which name he successfully woos Dougaldine. But when she learns of his deception, she is deeply insulted in her American pride and cancels the wedding. This causes her to become almost a pariah in the Rambleton family, which misunderstands her as a coquette, while her blustering, avaricious, domestic tyrant of a papa tries to force her into a marriage with Erwin Dish. Harry Rambleton flees in his desolate frame of mind to Europe, where we have made his acquaintance on the shores of the Lake of Zurich. The narrative strand is continued into the present, in which Dougaldine pines for Baron Wilhelm Schochstein and the firm of Ramble and Rambleton fails in the financial crisis. But this segment also has a subsection, the elaborately described prehistory of the Ramble and Rambleton families, which descend from an originally Dutch family named Rambel and whose contrasting fates in the economically developing New York State have shaped their present character. That the "Americans" of the German American elective affinities are originally Dutch and still exhibit a Dutch stamp points to the literary context of the novel, to which we shall return farther along.

The fifth segment rejoins the third: Wilhelm, bewildered by what he takes to be Dougaldine's avarice, finds himself in the omnibus among drunken rowdies extolling their invincible political power. They ride to a phantasmagorical political meeting, which degenerates into a huge riot in which Wilhelm is beaten up. But immediately thereafter he is invited to a political dinner; the Prussian consul shows Wilhelm the lies about the meeting that have already appeared in the newspaper, and Wilhelm and Erwin Dish realize that they are rivals for Dougaldine's favor. At that point the fragment breaks off.

At first this unusual organization may remind us of the unconventional structural characteristics of Sealsfield's better known texts. But this impression would be mistaken. Perhaps apart from the family history in the subsection of the fourth segment, there is little trace of his otherwise characteristically tangled and encapsulated narrative habit. The related technique of first-person narrations succeeding one another also disappears here. Within the segments the narration is more novelistic than in the *Lebensbilder*; in this respect *Die Deutsch-amerikanischen Wahlverwandtschaften* looks forward to *Die Prärie am Jacinto*. Still, Sealsfield's narrative experimentalism has not totally vanished, for the narration of the storm at sea and the following calm in the second segment is maintained throughout in the second person plural, so that you, the readers, shall feel the anxiety and misery of this experience as directly as possible. But, in general, with this work Sealsfield approaches the structural conventions of the realistic novel in the nineteenth century. The placement of the first segment at the beginning out of chronological order has the purpose of thematically stressing the German American cultural antithesis that is to be overcome.

This brings us to another significant difference, the appearance of a German American concern. This is new in Sealsfield, who had previously avoided the topic to a degree that is striking when one compares his practice to the subsequent development of the theme of America in nineteenth-century German literature. To be sure, it is possible that his works were conceived before the emigration had become such a widespread topic of public discourse in Germany. But in his personal experiences in the United States he must have come into contact with German Americans and the persistent debates about immigration. In his other novels there are only two, at best ancillary, German American characters, Isling in Morton and Bohne in Süden und Norden, on whom I have remarked earlier. In Die Deutsch-amerikanischen Wahlverwandtschaften the theme is approached from two directions: on the one hand, by way of the German American elective affinities alluded to in the title, which appear to point toward paired bonds of love at the end, the one between Baron Wilhelm and Dougaldine Ramble, the other between Baroness Luitgarde and Harry Rambleton; on the other hand, in the depiction of the miserable condition of the German emigrants on the ship in the second segment.

As I have mentioned, Sealsfield in his other works treated German immigrants with rather extraordinary disdain. But in Die Deutsch-amerikanischen Wahlverwandtschaften the emigrants on the ship are more sympathetically portrayed; they are distinguished by moral conduct, humane fellow feeling, and simple religious faith. However, when they are robbed by French passengers, it is impossible for them, in contrast to the French, to defend themselves collectively (21 [2]:71). This is an evident commentary on the political conditions of Germany and the German character shaped by them, perhaps also a dramatization of the Germans' chronic sense of vulnerability before the aggressions of the "hereditary enemy," thus indicating that Sealsfield, at least for the moment, had become a national liberal. At the same time there is a faint but unmistakable foreshadowing of the uncertain future that awaits the Germans in America; at home Rambleton has often seen German immigrants with "dieselben getäuschten Hoffnungen, Leiden, Trübsalen auf den verkümmerten Gesichtern" (21 [1]:179). Upon arrival in New York, the Germans are intimidated by the military fortifications in the harbor; they are beset by "Ahnungen der düsteren Zukunft," grow conscious of their poverty, and begin to weep as they realize that they will not be "Kinder des Hauses" (21 [2]:109–11).

There is nothing unusual about this kind of commentary; it fits easily into the German discourse about America and the emigration at the time. One might recall Heine's image a few years earlier of Swabian emigrants, on their way not to America but to Algiers, who must leave their homes in a sad and dejected frame of mind, for "was sollten wir thun? Sollten wir eine Revoluzion anfangen?"[4] Less familiar is the role that Sealsfield ascribes to the German noblemen in the novel. When we meet Wilhelm von Schochstein for the first time, he is much more liberal than the haughty American dandy Rambleton. For example, Wilhelm defends the politically engaged literature of the Young Germans (21 [1]:52). To be sure, the elder Schochstein is occasionally somewhat shocked by Wilhelm's avant-garde attitudes, but no harm is done to family relations; instead, the relationship between the generations is cordial, in contrast to the strained American family relations depicted in the novel. It looks as though Sealsfield at this juncture, in the midst of the Metternichian restoration, placed a certain amount of hope in an enlightened Prussian liberalism, just as his politics in later years, as far as they can be defined at all, seem to envision a *großdeutsch* solution to German unity—not, however, under Austria, as one might have expected from a writer of his provenance, but under Prussian leadership, a probably objectively impossible solution, but one shared, as we shall see, by another Austrian of the next generation, Ferdinand Kürnberger. Thus, at first glance, the German American elective affinities seem to imply a fusion of Prussian German enlightenment and cultured liberalism with American republicanism and practical business sense (cf. 23 [3]:361). On the other hand, however, Sealsfield's typical ambiguity emerges on the satirical level of the novel, where the young American ladies despair disgustedly when they learn that Wilhelm is "Deutsch wie Sauerkraut," but then instantly change their opinion when they realize that he is of noble rank (22 [2]:227–33). For his part, Wilhelm feels insulted in his republicanism by this snobbery (22 [2]:249).

We must resist the temptation to seek an interpretative connection of the word "Wahlverwandtschaften," which recurs as a leitmotif in the text from time to time, with Goethe's novel. It is hardly more than a weightless reminiscence, although a parodistic intention is imaginable. Goethe belongs to the few German writers to whom Sealsfield owed any allegiance, but his admiration was not unconditional. In his most extensive statement of his sense of literary tradition, the preface to *Morton*, the praise of Goethe is qualified with reservations, especially moral ones strongly recalling those expressed at the time by the anti-Goethean literary historian Wolfgang Menzel,[5] and in the work at hand there is an allusion to the reprehensible theme of adultery in the German novel doubtless aimed at Goethe's *Wahlverwandtschaften* (21 [1]:49). In matters of morality and sexuality, Sealsfield was quite clearly located on the threshold of the Victorian age; in this regard he differs notably from his Young German contemporaries and, indeed, seems to have absorbed not a little of the American puritanism that other European observers were inclined to find quite strange.

In any case, the literary genealogy of the novel is to be sought elsewhere: in Edward Bulwer-Lytton's then renowned novel *Pelham* (1828) and in the writers of Dutch New York, in the first instance James Kirke Paulding. Bulwer-Lytton's first novel was an instant success not only in England but also in Germany.[6] This witty, in places even cynical work has little of the cumbersome style, the display of learning (apart from a tendency to Latin quotations and wordplays), and the philistine morality normally associated with Bulwer-Lytton's name. He was a great admirer of German culture and was particularly inspired by Goethe's *Wilhelm Meister*,[7] although Goethe would not have found *Pelham* very edifying. It is a kind of *Bildungsroman*, narrated by an upper-class young man who has consciously taken on the role of a dandy and fashionable fop. Sometimes it appears, however, that he uses his pretended egotism to mask his real egotism; in any case he ultimately develops into a reasonably enlightened and morally responsible member of society. As with Sealsfield, the political world is portrayed as shallow and corrupt. The novel had a great reputation as a critically realistic picture of English society of the time. Sealsfield entirely shared the general estimate of it, as, indeed, he admired Bulwer generally. That, in the *Lebensbilder*, one of the fashionable belles in New York finds Bulwer in *Paul Clifford* (the novel with the notorious "dark and stormy night" opening) "ein unausstehlicher Fantast" and Scott "alt und abgedroschen" while longing for a new Cooper (11:10, 13) is doubtless a sign of her impaired sensibility. Sealsfield mentions *Pelham* in several places, and in *Das Cajütenbuch* he has his hero Morse assert that it has remained Bulwer's best book (17:333).

Sealsfield seems to have been primarily fascinated by the phenomenon of an elitist, aesthetically immoralistic, fashion-mad dandyism that had been imported from aristocratic England by a neoaristocratic stratum of extremely rich Americans, a clear sign of defection from republican virtue and a regression to the European class society. But, like Bulwer in *Pelham*, Sealsfield stresses the sound human core that has been concealed by these fashionable distortions. Just as a healthy, natural girl is hidden in the often absurdly fashionable figure of Dougaldine, so a proper man is slumbering behind the dandy in Rambleton (22 [3]:160). When Dougaldine and Rambleton (in his role as Digby) get into a genuine conversation with one another in the country, both have difficulty keeping the coquetry intact: "die amerikanische Natürlichkeit schlug sie so derb ins Genick, guckte hinter der angelernten fashionablen Verschrobenheit so naiv hervor" (22 [3]:196). Although it would be idle to speculate too far on the further course of the fragment, it is at least imaginable that this purification process was to have taken place under the influence of the urbane but still virtuous, morally disciplined German nobles.

So far as the American scene is concerned, Sealsfield, as I have indicated, was less taken by Washington Irving than by Irving's contemporary, friend, and occasional collaborator Paulding.[8] Largely forgotten today except by specialists in American studies and antebellum history, Paulding in his own time was a highly prominent and successful writer. He was himself of Dutch descent and wrote with intimate attachment of the region in which Sealsfield's novel takes place. It is not unlikely that Paulding's satirical treatment of the fashion circus in Saratoga Springs in his travel book, *The New Mirror for Travellers; and Guide to the Springs* (1828), influenced the portrayal in the third segment of Sealsfield's novel; to be sure, the resort of Cheltenham is presented in exactly the same spirit in Bulwer's *Pelham*. Paulding's extraordinarily successful novel *The Dutchman's Fireside* (1831), which was translated into five languages, is also relevant, even though it takes place before the Revolution. It draws a picture of the Dutch settler community that exhibits some similarity to the historical account in the fourth segment of Sealsfield's novel, and Paulding introduces a female figure, Catalina, who shares certain characteristics with Sealsfield's Dougaldine.[9] Here, too, the course of true love is made difficult by misunderstandings deriving from vain social role playing.

But more important than these thematic similarities is Paulding's ideological tone. It is elegiac, grieving for the past, refusing accommodation with an industrializing, urbanizing America growing socially and economically more complex; thus it tends to a conservative if not reactionary spirit. This is the reason why Paulding developed from an opponent to a defender of slavery. He displays the paradox of a passionate patriotism, sometimes bordering on xenophobia, oriented, however, not on the present but on a past America. The parallels to Sealsfield are obvious, especially in the novel under discussion. As I have indicated, it has often been supposed that the increasing incongruence of the agrarian ideal with which the *Lebensbilder* are permeated led to the abandonment not only of this novel but of Sealsfield's whole literary career.

When one asks why a novel has remained a fragment, it would seem useful to look more closely at the place where it breaks off. This place is at the end of the long, perhaps overlong, political phantasmagoria through which Wilhelm, at least temporarily, as far as we can judge, is cured of his republicanism. We recall that Wilhelm rides in an omnibus with a gang of drunken, violent political storm troopers who have been recruited from the *Lumpenproletariat*. At first he is insulted as a German and mistreated, then praised and respected as a Prussian, allegedly out of gratitude to Frederick the Great (Prussia was one of the first foreign nations to recognize the United States diplomatically). The political meeting in the hall is broken up by feuding gangs and deteriorates into an epic battle into which Wilhelm is drawn; bloody and battered, he is immediately afterward invited to a dinner. The political background of this scene can be fairly exactly identified.[10] It has to do with the financial crisis of the time, the tendency of Jacksonian populism to degenerate into unbridled lawlessness, the resistance to Jackson's successor Martin Van Buren, the disputes over the Bank of the United States and the credit system, and so forth. A modern historian gives an account of the volatile political scene not so different from Sealsfield's depiction:

> In New York and Philadelphia each election after 1834 was the occasion for violent street fighting between rival Irish factions or between natives and foreigners. Bloodshed was common and deaths were not infrequent. In 1834 in New York Irishmen armed with stones and cudgels put the mayor, sheriff, and a posse to flight and terrorized the city. A year later police who tried to quell Irish fighting in the Five Points area were driven back and the turmoil was not ended until a man had been killed. The spring election of 1842 brought a pitched street battle in New York between Irish and Orangemen aided by native Americans.[11]

Tomy, the boss in the omnibus, is very likely modeled on the "Irish rabble-rouser" Mike Walsh, a left-wing supporter of Calhoun, who led working-class gangs employed to coerce political meetings. He subsequently became a member of Congress and a New York drunk, dying in a St. Patrick's Day mugging in 1859.[12]

These are all matters that were probably not unknown in Europe at that time, at least in general. But Sealsfield's portrayal of the political conditions cannot have been wholly comprehensible even to the reasonably well informed German reader of the time. The political storm troopers belong to the dreaded "Workies," that is, the militant working class. As early as *Pflanzerleben I*, Howard, offended at the sight of a carpenter with egalitarian airs, lectures his wife on the destructive political power of the working class and its determination to level society down into mediocrity (13:30–34). But in *Die Deutsch-amerikanischen Wahlverwandtschaften*, the working men are in fact fighting for the finance aristocracy and the supporters of the Bank, that is, against Jackson. That the Locofocos, who storm the hall and spread a Satanic stench with their symbolic matches (23 [4]:272), belong to the radical wing of Jackson's Democratic Party is by no means made clear. Sealsfield blurs and muddles these political details intentionally in order to present republican activism itself as degenerate nonsense. Years later, in 1854, he lamented that in America "das Übermaß von Freiheit ist in eine Mobocratie ausgeartet, das alle sozialen legalen und finanziell[en] Verhältnisse zu zersetzen droht" (*Briefe*, 298).

Through long stretches of his work, Sealsfield is a comic writer, to a degree that has not been sufficiently recognized. His often quite drastic, even violent comic quality differs from the comedy of the Austrian theater and Biedermeier humor; it has to do with his view of America, since it is derived from the "comic triumph" of American "western humor," thereby acquiring a democratic and democratizing character.[13] It is the comic newness of this country, the raw, vital, historically potent explosion of freedom, simply ignoring the manners of the Old World, that drive the energy, the hyperbole, the structural insouciance, and the relentless chattering of the texts. In *Die Deutsch-amerikanischen Wahlverwandtschaften* the comedy can still be employed for political commentary, for example, in a chapter of the third segment titled "Eine Belle's Sitzung," where young ladies in earnest democratic assembly recite feminist parodies of the Declaration of Independence and the Constitution, and debate a motion never to marry a man who drinks alcohol. Sealsfield simultaneously lampoons the women's emancipation movement, the democratic endeavors of the disfranchised, and the temperance movement, hated by almost all Germans and German Americans.[14] But in the last segment the comedy has turned sour, has been transformed into a satire lit with hellish colors. What has happened? The problem is the threat of anarchy. The energetic, in its way revolutionary reshaping of life and culture, enacted in Sealsfield's novels, constantly touches the boundary of anarchy; Sealsfield himself, as I have mentioned, shows no little affinity for the anarchy that lurks within the militant frontier society. For just that reason, the repudiation of anarchy through religion and property is of the greatest urgency, as we have seen.

When Wilhelm von Schochstein is confronted in New York City with the corrupted, morally and religiously rootless, propertyless and anarchistic radical democrats, he is in that moment cured of his liberal republicanism, thus of his faith in America; the effect makes "sein liebes Deutschland theurer denn je" (23 [4]:204). In the face of the corrupt politics of the public meeting Wilhelm even senses "die ächt deutsche, sich durch fremdes über eigenes politisches *Misere* tröstende, Schadenfreude" (23 [4]:253). But this change had begun to take place in him earlier. For in a rather implausible but doubtless significant scene we have learned that Wilhelm's republicanism fell away immediately at the sight of the blindingly beautiful society belle, Dougaldine (22 [2]:251). Were the German American elective affinities to lead to neoaristocratic alliances that repudiate democracy? Or were there to be still further alterations in the characters, not yet indicated in the text? Given the mutability of the characters in this novel, that is not improbable. There is no way we can know; it would probably be safer to assume that Sealsfield himself saw no way out, no resolution of his own impasse and therefore abandoned the novel. Bernd Fischer has made a convincing argument that Sealsfield's *Weltanschauung* was burdened with irreconcilable contradictions from the outset, and just those contradictions are responsible for his structural peculiarities and his unruly narrative drive.[15]

But the contradiction that makes this novel so bewildering lies at a deeper level. His artistic gift was stronger than his intelligence, but he wanted to be not an artist in the first instance—the word *Dichter* hardly ever occurs in his writings—but an evangelist of revolutionary truths. When he could no longer maintain these truths on account of their inner contradictions and discrepancies with reality, his art failed him. As I have shown earlier, he took little interest in literature as such; in fact, his indifference to artistic considerations was even more radical than that claimed by the Young Germans or even Heine. From the partisan debates of the Age of Jackson he borrowed a by no means original ideology, to which he held with remarkably stubborn tunnel vision until it was no longer viable for him and had abandoned him to conservative despair. "Er erscheint," observes Alexander Ritter, "restlos eingesponnen in seine konsequent vertretene Vorstellung, obgleich er sehr wohl den gesellschaftlichen Wandel aufmerksam und äußerst kritisch wahrnimmt."[16] Bernd Fischer adds, "daß sein Geschichtskonzept von dem komplexen Phänomen der Neuen Welt weit überfordert wird."[17]

The consequence of such insights has been that Sealsfield's artistic standing has become insecure among scholars. For my part, I consider him a gifted, almost great writer. The reverse of his literary insouciance is a fearless experimental instinct uninhibited by normative or generic scruples. If it is true that his structural complexity mirrors his ideological confusion, this does not mean that it is artistically ineffective; rather the contrary. Despite some misunderstandings and hearing mistakes, he had a sharp ear for the American idiom and undertook heroic efforts in the thankless task of reproducing it in German. His language is of a forcefulness without compare in the German literature, his narrative talent brilliant. For example, in his description of the storm at sea in the second segment of the novel, he reaches a mastery that one without hesitation might set beside the great achievements of this kind, such as Joseph Conrad's *Typhoon*.[18] The figures in *Die Deutsch-amerikanischen Wahlverwandtschaften* have become more complex, insofar as they display antithetical, even contradictory characteristics. The characterization is deepened further psychologically in *Die Prärie am Jacinto* and still more in *Süden und Norden*. These achievements apparently did not satisfy him, but they might continue to challenge us.

# Excursus I. The Emergence of the German Western: Balduin Möllhausen and Friedrich Armand Strubberg

Some years ago there came into my hands for review a book that surprised me a good deal: a study of the German detective story in the nineteenth century.[1] For it was a received opinion that the Germans had been unable to develop the detective genre before the epigonal, imported imitations in modern times. Like many other received opinions about German literary history, this one turned out to be quite wrong. Stories of criminal detection began to emerge in Germany nearly two decades before Edgar Allan Poe is alleged to have invented the genre with the publication in 1841 of "The Murders in the Rue Morgue" in *Graham's Magazine*. The author of the study argued that the genre was quantitatively even more widespread in nineteenth-century Germany than in England, France, or America, and that it obtained its modern shape in the years between 1860 and 1880, well before the impact of Sherlock Holmes in the 1890s. The point here, of course, is not to argue some sort of German priority, but merely to show once again that German literature of the nineteenth century, taken as a whole, belongs to the literary history of the Western world generally.

Speaking of the Western world, another example is the relatively early emergence in Germany of the genre of the Western. By this I do not mean fanciful accounts of adventure and noble savages in a utopian New World, well known from the eighteenth century, but fictional reflections of the opening up and settlement of the American Far West based upon experience and knowledge. These also came to be a substantial type of fiction available to the German public. It has been pointed out that Sealsfield's own narrations move westward.[2] If it is true that Sealsfield's *Cajütenbuch* was misunderstood as a Wild West adventure story, this, too, indicates the kind of reader expectations that had been generated.[3] The exceptionally well informed Ray Billington wrote of the succession to Cooper: "Westerns became the standard literary fare of Britishers, Germans, Scandinavians, Frenchmen, Spaniards, even Hungarians and Poles, for a century to come."[4] I cite this to show how Billington, unencumbered by the presuppositions of German *Literaturwissenschaft*, easily and naturally locates the Germans into a shared international context. There was, in fact, a substantial amount of German writing, both reportorial and fictional, about the West,[5] but for our purposes two authors in particular stand out: Balduin Möllhausen (1825–1905) and Friedrich Armand Strubberg (1806–89).

Möllhausen was born in Bonn into an initially prosperous but increasingly dysfunctional family, the effect of which on him seems to have been to make him in later life an exceptionally loyal and affectionate family man. His mother was a baroness, his father a commoner; whether this mésalliance was a source of stress is difficult to make out, as are many of the details of Möllhausen's childhood and youth, but there is no doubt that his father, an architect, construction engineer, and, increasingly, speculator and adventurer, abandoned the family in 1835 to knock about Texas and Louisiana for fourteen years. In 1840 he attempted to persuade the government of the Republic of Texas that he was a confidant of the king of Prussia and was in a position to mediate commercial relations with Prussia and Russia as well as to encourage emigration to Texas.[6] He turned up in Berlin in 1850, where he published a set of descriptions of Texas translated from English,[7] but it is not known whether he had communication with his son at this time. We do not have a record of any contact until 1867, when the seventy-year-old father offered to help his now prominent son write his novels, undertake translations, and found a newspaper; Balduin replied with dutiful circumspection, and the father died later that same year.[8] His mother having died at the end of 1837, he and his siblings were raised by various stern upper-class relatives in Pomerania, where he seems to have acquired the hunting skills that stood him in good stead later. He wished to study art but was not permitted to do so; instead, like Gerstäcker in comparable circumstances, he was trained in agriculture. In 1849 or 1850—we are not sure just when or why—he took off for America; he may have regarded himself at the time as an emigrant. He went out into the wilderness as a hunter, then, in order to improve his English, got a job through various German American connections as a court clerk in Belleville, Illinois. There, in nearby Mascoutah, he was to make a providential acquaintance: Duke Paul Wilhelm (1797–1860), the adventurous nephew of the king of Württemberg.[9] Married to a wealthy princess of Thurn and Taxis, he lived a life about as far away from his class and social milieu as possible. An accomplished outdoorsman and explorer, he was a genuine contributor to geographical and anthropological knowledge; although only one of his book-length works was published in his lifetime, he was acknowledged in his own day, receiving an honorary doctorate from the University of Tübingen. He adopted and brought back to Germany Baptiste Charbonneau, the son of the Shoshone heroine of the Lewis and Clark expedition, Sacajawea. He was also a tough and hardy man who owed his survival not only to skill and endurance but also to a considerable amount of luck. In 1851 he took Möllhausen with him as an assistant and maid of all work on a journey in the direction of the Rocky Mountains, reaching Fort Laramie in October.

On the way back things began to go wrong. The weather turned hostile. Another assistant became separated from Paul Wilhelm and Möllhausen, never to be seen again. They were harassed by Indians; one wagon broke, and another got stuck in the middle of a river with Paul Wilhelm in it. On November 19, in a place on the Platte River Möllhausen calls Sandy Hill Creek,[10] the weather closed in and the travelers, freezing and threatened by wolves, could go no farther. On November 25, a mail coach from Fort Laramie came by; it was full, but Paul Wilhelm paid $100 for a place. He and Möllhausen drew lots for it and, perhaps unsurprisingly, the duke won. Promising to send help, he left Möllhausen, ill with fever, on the wintry plain. The help never came. For six weeks Möllhausen struggled with cold, weakness in his limbs, short rations, wolves, and a pair of marauding Indians whom he was obliged to ambush and kill. Finally, in January 1852, he was rescued by friendly Indians, with whom he spent several weeks, evading the offer of one or even two Indian wives. He returned to Belleville, where he wooed a half-breed woman, who did not, however, relish the prospect of Möllhausen's plan to live like Robinson Crusoe on an island in the Missouri River. In the spring of 1852, Paul Wilhelm, who had given up Möllhausen for lost, wrote to him to say how nice it was that he had survived. The duke has been much criticized, as he was at the time, for aristocratic insouciance toward his companion's welfare. However, his attitude may just have been the stoicism of the frontiersman, taking the hard times and the high costs as they come. Möllhausen appears never to have held anything against him. They met in New Orleans and traveled together again for a while, as Möllhausen had obtained a commission to conduct an animal transport for the Berlin zoo. He accomplished this task, sailing to Bremen by way of Havana and arriving in Berlin in early 1853.

The adventure in the Nebraska Territory was clearly the crucial, shaping experience of Möllhausen's being; it radiated through the rest of his life; more than fifty years later he was buried in his trapper outfit.[11] A protracted near-death experience, it proved him strong, competent, and fortunate. The combination of anxiety and exhilaration fueled his remaining Western adventures and a long writing career. Though it looked for a time that he might settle down in Berlin, it is not surprising that his thirst for adventure was not yet slaked. In the meantime he had become something of a minor celebrity, obtaining the patronage of the elderly Hinrich Martin Lichtenstein, founder of the Berlin zoo and a prominent naturalist, and of the most famous man of science in Germany at the time, Alexander von Humboldt. He arranged an audience with Friedrich Wilhelm IV, who in turn took steps to find Möllhausen a post. He fell in love with and eventually married Caroline Seifert, a member of Humboldt's household who figured as the daughter of his private secretary. Today it seems all but certain that Caroline was, in fact, Humboldt's natural daughter.[12] This would in part account for his unwavering public support of Möllhausen and affection for Caroline and the children. Möllhausen, for his part, faithfully loved Caroline to the end of his life.

For the time being, however, he found another opportunity to go to the West; Lichtenstein arranged for a grant to send him to America to collect specimens and fossils. But no sooner had he presented his letters of recommendation to the Prussian minister in Washington than he found himself appointed to assist Lieutenant Amiel Weeks Whipple of the Army Corps of Topographical Engineers on the southernmost of three expeditions initiated by Secretary of War Jefferson Davis to determine the best route for a transcontinental railroad. Möllhausen's main task was to make illustrations; his drawings and watercolors of landscapes and Indians are in several museums today, including the Smithsonian Institution, with whose assistant secretary, the acclaimed zoologist Spencer F. Baird, he was on terms of friendship, and they constituted a valuable supplement to Whipple's highly regarded report on the Indian tribes. Some of the drawings were widely and repeatedly reproduced in Europe and the United States.[13] The journey proper lasted for nine months, from Fort Smith in Arkansas in July 1853 over the prairies and deserts of the Southwest via Albuquerque and across the Rocky Mountains to Los Angeles in March 1854, a trek, needless to say, full of adventures, hardships, and dangers. The task completed, Möllhausen went on to San Francisco, sailed to the Isthmus of Panama, which he crossed by rail, and continued to New York, Washington, and Berlin, where he arrived in August. The product of this experience was a splendid, luxurious travel work, *Tagebuch einer Reise vom Mississippi nach den Küsten der Südsee*, elegantly printed in Roman type, bearing a rare introduction by Humboldt, and published in Leipzig in 1858.

While this book was in the press, Möllhausen was off on his third American journey, as an associate of Lieutenant Joseph Christmas Ives, a Yale and West Point graduate with a literary flair whom Möllhausen had met on the Whipple expedition and who had been charged with determining the navigability of the Colorado River. After having been introduced to President Buchanan and other dignitaries in Washington, Möllhausen traveled from New York to San Francisco, again crossing the Isthmus, and reaching Fort Yuma in December 1857. This journey lasted until July 1858. The Colorado did not prove to be very navigable and some of the mishaps that plagued the expedition have a rather comic aspect. But the frequent occasions when the boat they employed got stuck gave Möllhausen an opportunity to roam about, hunting, observing, and collecting. Ultimately there was recompense in the sublimity of the Grand Canyon. Ives and his companions were probably the first white men to reach its floor, and Möllhausen's illustrations were the first representations of it published in Europe.[14] When the expedition had been completed, he traveled to Cleveland, where he visited the home of the expedition's geologist, and departed for Europe from New York in September. Except for a trip to Norway in 1879, that was the end of his career as a traveler. The result was a second major work, also introduced by Humboldt: *Reisen in die Felsengebirge Nord-Amerikas bis zum Hoch-Plateau von Neu-Mexiko*, published in Leipzig in 1861. He settled into a bourgeois existence in Potsdam, opening his literary career with his first novel, *Der Halbindianer*, also in 1861.

I have gone into these experiences in some detail—although there is a great deal more detail known about them—because they constitute Möllhausen's genuinely significant achievements. As an author of works of travel and exploration he deserves all honor and credit. He was undoubtedly a fine outdoorsman and a useful member of these strenuous expeditions. In a number of his comments there is an element of self-realization in the crucible of danger, and he was well aware of the literary sources of his yearnings: in his first travel work he observed, in the midst of freezing and suffering in the Nebraska Territory: "Ich war glücklich, überschwenglich froh, weil die Träume meiner Jugendzeit, hervorgerufen durch Cooper und Washington Irving, verwirklicht worden waren" (*TR*, 1:133). In a letter from Washington of July 12, 1858, after the Colorado expedition had been safely completed, he cheerfully tells his wife of having written a farewell message to her from a perch in a tree while being besieged by Mohave Indians.[15] He airily reports that his journey to Cleveland was without any particular incident except for a train wreck in which the locomotive and tenders went into a river just as they uncoupled themselves from the passenger cars (*RF*, 2:391). Duke Paul Wilhelm, though occasionally grumbling in his highborn way about the young man's minor insubordinations and tendency to illness, nevertheless once wrote that Möllhausen was the most courageous companion he had ever had.[16] He was not as skilled an artist as the abler depicters of the West, George Catlin and Karl Bodmer,[17] nor was he, of course, a scientist of the stature of Humboldt. But his illustrations were widely regarded and unquestionably of utilitarian value in his prephotographic age (Ives took a camera on his expedition but did not regret its loss when it was blown into a river).[18]

Möllhausen's travel works were not without scientific ambition. From time to time he gives latitude and longitude of his location. He provides the Latin names of plants, animals, and birds when he knows them, as he often does. He was among those who discovered the Petrified Forest, and he recognized what it was. He convincingly communicates the wonder of the first sight of the great saguaro cacti of the desert, and he must have been one of the first Europeans to describe and sketch the giant redwood trees. Some of what he reports is interesting even today, such as the account in the third chapter of his second travel book of the U.S. Army's experimental camel troop. At the same time he relieves the sometimes plodding report with anecdotes and stories, some from his own experiences—through the two volumes he serializes his adventure in the Nebraska Territory and its aftermath—some related by companions, some taken from other published accounts, such as the hair-raising exploits of John C. Frémont, who had been the Republican candidate for president in the year before the Colorado expedition. The books were well received at home and abroad. Charles Dickens published a translation of the peril at Sandy Hill Creek in his periodical.[19]

However, as a writer of fiction, Möllhausen is not to be taken seriously; recent attempts to upgrade him strike me as evaluative muddle. Many in his time found him entertaining, though the majority of these were probably youthful readers. One might doubt, to be sure, the importance of Gerstäcker's harsh dismissal of Möllhausen, since, as it was expressed to their common publisher, it is likely to have been motivated by competitiveness:

> Apropos die Möllhausischen Bücher, über die Sie von mir ein Urtheil wollten. Mein guter Herr Costenoble, ich gebe Ihnen das nicht gern, da Hr. M. gleichen Stoff mit mir behandelt, wenigstens ein gleiches Terrain hat. So viel kann und muß ich Ihnen aber sagen daß es meiner Meinung nach der reine Schund ist, & ich meinen Namen nicht um vieles Geld unter einem dieser Bücher, haben möchte. Ich will mich verbündlich machen einen solchen Roman einer Anzahl Stenographen in drei Tagen zu dicktiren.
>
> Das aber natürlich nur unter uns. Die Leihbibliotheken werden sie kaufen, denn es ist deren Futter: Spieß & Cramer ins Amerikanische übersetzt, mit lauter unmöglichen Charakteren.[20]

*Schund* is too harsh a word, but the rest of the judgment seems to me fair enough. Someday it ought to be possible to program a computer to write novels like Möllhausen's; perhaps it is already possible. Plots are generated by secret and often distressed family relationships; it may well be, as Andreas Graf has argued, that this preoccupation is a psychological reflex of Möllhausen's childhood experiences, but in my view that does not elevate them literarily. As in Karl May's stories, information is obtained by eavesdropping from hiding places. The moral status of characters is immediately legible in their physiognomy, and there are only two possibilities, good and evil. The good are virtuous, generous, and kindly; the evil are greedy, selfish, calculating, and malicious, especially toward one another, a logical source of their inevitable failure. Plots turn on the exposure of criminals and are driven by patterns of flight and pursuit, but lack suspense, as the narrator tells all. Möllhausen's succession to Cooper has probably been overemphasized in the past, but, like numerous others in his time, he takes over one of Cooper's main devices to make plot possible, the contrast of Indians between those who are good, cooperative, and well intentioned and those who are evil and hostile; in Möllhausen the latter tend to be degenerate and criminal also.

All these characteristics are the marks of a kind of automatic writing, fundamentally commercially driven, though it is probably also true that Möllhausen for many years lived emotionally from the adventurous epoch in his life. His novel type has been defined by one of his admirers as an amalgam of subliterary types: "eine Verbindung des transatlantisch-exotischen Abenteuerromans mit dem Schema des Liebes- und Intrigen-, aber auch des Schauer- und Kriminalromans, verwoben mit zeit- und sozialhistorischen Elementen."[21] He is not without certain technical skills; his best moments, to my mind, are scenes of raucous comedy, such as the episode in the second volume of *Der Halbindianer* when a St. Louis fire brigade literally cleanses a bordello by pumping streams of water into it. It is sometimes pointed out that Möllhausen had some association with Theodor Fontane and may have influenced his novel *Quitt*, which has the structure that became characteristic of Möllhausen—a two-part novel, split between Germany and America. But *Quitt* is not one of Fontane's finest achievements, and although in 1882 he wrote a subdued preface to a volume of Möllhausen's stories, trying to make a virtue out of the sameness of his writings, in a letter to his wife Fontane called Möllhausen's kind of writing "Mittelgutsblech."[22] In general his works show the signs of mechanical production. He wrote "twenty-five large works in one hundred and fifty-seven volumes, eighty novelettes in twenty-one volumes"; between 1871 and 1879 alone he wrote seven novels totaling twenty-five volumes.[23] Few writers in world literature have been able to maintain standards of quality at such a pace. As a result he was very prolix, lacking in density; even friendly reviewers sometimes suggested that his novels might have had fewer volumes. The productivity was necessary to maintain his success. His books sold modestly and few went beyond the first edition; his continued prominence over several decades was owing, therefore, to a steady stream of new works.

While acknowledging that he is unimpressive in plot and characterization, Möllhausen's admirers give him credit for one of his main motivating themes, the critique of American racial prejudice. In his second travel book he presents himself as insisting that there is good in all men regardless of color, but he is told that few Americans would share his view (*RF*, 1:165). He characterized his first novel as "eine Geschichte, in welcher namentlich die Vorurtheile der Amerikaner gegen jede dunkler gefärbte Haut, und die daraus entspringenden Folgen dargelegt werden" (*Hi*, 1:ii–iii). The armature of the novel is the quest of the half-breed Joseph to overcome his father's rejection of him because of his dark skin. The topic of prejudice is frequently raised in Möllhausen's texts. He was a firm abolitionist who, like Gerstäcker, attacked Germans who supported slavery;[24] his ten later novels dealing with the Civil War exhibit unequivocal Union sympathies, though by that time he was long out of contact with the American scene. However, a closer look indicates that he did not think very systematically or reflectively about race matters. His attraction to half-breeds and mixed-race characters is, to be sure, an improvement on Sealsfield's hard-line views on miscegenation, but is not without a race-conscious motive, because it is the white component that gives the character access to civilized, bourgeois norms and brings him or her closer to the reader's sympathies. Joseph's mixed blood confuses him; sometimes he acts red when he should be white and vice versa; when Indians attack, his "indianisches Blut war bei dem verrätherischen Angriff in Wallung geraten" (*Hi*, 1:57; 3:197). This is a pattern often met with; we shall see it in a different form when we come to Strubberg, and it is probably useful to remember that the admirable Eliza and George in *Uncle Tom's Cabin* are of mixed race and nearly white in appearance.

I mentioned earlier that Möllhausen took over Cooper's plotting device of dividing Indians into good and evil tribes; Indians with whom Möllhausen is not in sympathy are depicted most disparagingly. Once again the not quite explicit touchstone is assimilation to the values of white civilization. He admired the Choctaws and Cherokees because they had adapted to agricultural settlements and improved the status of women, observing that Indians are capable of civilization with proper guidance, and he praised Lieutenant Ives's policy of treating the Indians with kindness, denying them handouts, persuading them of the power of the U.S. government, and encouraging them to aspire to work habits and greater effort (*TR*, 1:16–18; *RF*, 1:287). In one of his stories, a white trapper adroitly kidnaps an Indian princess, who much prefers him to the chief to whom she is betrothed.[25] On the whole, he is quite dismissive of the Plains Indians as primitive savages, absorbed in such a struggle for subsistence that they cannot possibly develop civilized qualities of gratitude and rectitude (e.g., *Hi*, 3:29–31; *Md*, 1:12), and much is made in various places of their uncontrollable mania for alcohol. A trapper observes that vengeance is a characteristic of the Indian, but not of the white man (*Md*, 4:154). Among the Indians of the Far West, Möllhausen appears to have most admired the Zuñis and Pueblos because their way of life appeared civic. He regarded the Indians of California as degenerates who had been unable to profit from the ministration of the missionaries (*TR*, 2:445; *Md*, 1:229); as we shall see, Gerstäcker took a quite different view of that matter.

Although Möllhausen certainly was an abolitionist and repeatedly expressed sympathy for the plight of the black, the blacks he depicts are almost without exception grotesque, comical, and simple-minded. In his second travel book he ascribes the comically simple ideas and gauche conduct of a black to the suppression of his abilities, but then, in a quite Sealsfieldean vein, pretends to praise him by making fun of his big feet and heels, large mouth, fat lips, protruding ears, and hard skull (*RF*, 1:68–69). Much is made of the superhuman hardness of Negroes' heads; in *Der Halbindianer* Joseph flees because he believes he has killed a belligerent slave of his father's, but it turns out long afterward that his hard head saved him.[26] Slave or free, they sing at their work on idyllic plantations. As slaves: "Das geräuschvolle lustige Volk der Negersklaven arbeitete weit abwärts in den Baumwollfeldern"; "zeigten sie nichts von einer thierischen Unterwürfigkeit, sondern [schauten] mit einer Miene und Freimüthigkeit, die darlegten, daß sie sich, trotz ihrer niedrigen Stellung, als Mitglieder der Familie des Pflanzers betrachteten, und auch gewohnt waren, wie solche betrachtet zu werden" (*Hi*, 1:123; 4:27). Once freed, the blacks work just as happily on the master's Missouri farm (*Hi*, 4:276). Thus it is quite unexpected that in one place Möllhausen mounts a prophecy of an apocalyptic slave rebellion: "*Die meisten aber der nordamerikanischen Sklavenzüchter und Sklavenhändler werden erst zur Erkenntniß ihrer schmachvollen Stellung gelangen, wenn diejenigen, die ihrem Herzen am nächsten stehen, unter der heraufbeschworenen Rache der entfesselten Race verbluten, das heißt, wenn es 'zu spät' ist*" (*Hi*, 4:265; emphasis in the original). There can be little doubt that he found the congenial sorts of Indians more agreeable than blacks.[27]

His pronounced hostility to the Mormons seems to be largely a prejudice that he absorbed from his American environment, but also little more than a special case of the common hostility of liberal German observers to American religious sectarianism.[28] The account of the Colorado expedition is full of anxiety about threats from hostile Mormons, and a visibly malignant Mormon spy with a wolfish expression attempts to infiltrate the camp (RF, 1:397–98); in fact, the "Mormon War" of 1857–58 was largely a fizzle that came to be known as "Buchanan's blunder." Möllhausen treats the Mormons as a cult bent upon luring into it unsuspecting victims, especially innocent maidens to be condemned to polygamy. This is the theme of one of his most popular novels, *Das Mormonenmädchen* (1864). He does, to be sure, point out the hypocrisy of abhorring polygamy while tolerating slavery: *"Die Vereinigten Staaten, voller edler Entrüstung darüber, daß auf ihrem gesitteten Continent eine Religionssecte lebte, die der ihrem Glaubensbekenntniß vorgeschriebenen Polygamie huldigte, anstatt das, nach den unumstößlichen Ansichten, damals noch der meisten Amerikaner, von Gott eingesetzte System der Sclaverei* weiter zu verbreiten, hatten den Mormonen den Krieg erklärt" (*Md*, 3:41; emphasis in the original). While nowhere nearly as condescending to Hispanics as Sealsfield, he does not seem to be a very intimate observer of their culture.[29] In California he found solace from Mexican chaos with a German vintner near Los Angeles (*RF*, 1:27). He depicted Jews in a quite anti-Semitic manner, especially in his social novel, *Die Hyänen des Capitals* (1876); but, like other writers of the time—one thinks particularly of Gustav Freytag and Wilhelm Raabe—he endeavored to counter, if not to balance, these portrayals with positive Jewish characterizations.[30] In Santa Fe he was happy to see Americans and German Jews living comfortably together despite religious and national differences (*RF*, 2:288–89). He is simply not thoughtful about any of these things, and his critique of American prejudice based on skin color is as conventional and mediocre as all other aspects of his fiction. In some places the ordinary folk, such as the fire brigade in St. Louis, seem to have no racial prejudice; only the rich and bourgeois do. In another place, however, it is the brutalized lower class that mistreats the Chinese (*Md*, 3:116). Möllhausen does, to be sure, notice that racial prejudice is not restricted to Americans; in one place he observes that degenerate Indians and Chinese look down on one another, while the whites regard both with contempt (*Hi*, 4:86–87). His own view of the Chinese was that they all look alike and have "denselben Ausdruck in den nichtssagenden häßlichen Zügen"; they deserve the contempt in which they are held (*TR*, 2:462–63).[31]

Möllhausen was not actually much interested in the United States beyond the issues of race and slavery, and, to the extent he was, he might be numbered among the anti-American writers if he had cared enough to become one. His West is, in a sense, anterior to the United States, a wilderness and desert inhabited by prehistoric peoples; he remarked that, with the passing of trappers and buffalo, the North American continent would lose its poesy (*Hi*, 4:273). Americans as such are often depicted, equally conventionally, as greedy and soulless. Exceptions tend to be woodsmen and trappers, who are, however, often French, nearly as sensitive as Germans. While Gerstäcker, as we shall see, encouraged and praised the adaptability of the immigrant in the new land, Möllhausen is sarcastic about it; at a trial in the gold-mining territory of California, one Baron Kreuzer turns up as a juror: "Früher deutscher Student, dann Officier, dann badischer Freischärler, dann Literat, dann Schenkwirth in Neu-York, dann Zeitungs-Kolporteur in Cincinnati, dann Farmer in Minesota, dann Methodisten-Prediger in Illinois und zuletzt Viehtreiber in Missouri!" (*Hi*, 4:183).

Peter Brenner has observed that Möllhausen's America is generally a land of criminals and swindlers: "Obwohl er durchaus nicht prinzipiell amerikafeindlich eingestellt ist, kann ihn nicht einmal der trivialliterarische Zwang zum guten Ende dazu bewegen, dieses Ende Amerika gutzuschreiben."[32] Right at the beginning of his first travel book he observes that an American on the Mississippi sees nothing of the glorious nature around him because he concentrates exclusively on obtaining riches, adding: "Dieser bei einem grossen Theile der Nation fast gänzliche Mangel an Sinn für die Schönheiten der Natur ist dem Europäer ebenso unbegreiflich, wie dem Amerikaner die laute Begeisterung der Europäer bei einem derartigen erhabenen Anblicke spasshaft dünkt" (*TR*, 1:2–3; the thought is repeated in *RF*, 1:168). One might object here that those he is observing are not tourists but working people. But soon after he contrasts competent but wild and immoral American workers with a German who sings "In einem kühlen Grunde" and "Ich weiß nicht, was soll es bedeuten" as he works (*TR*, 1:9–10; the names of Eichendorff and Heine are not mentioned, possibly because any reader of the time would know, possibly to avoid mentioning the latter). Of an apparently untypically positive American character, the narrator observes that if all Americans had "halb so viel Gemüth" (a familiar German shibboleth), the United States would be a happy land "anstatt mit schnellen Schritten seinem innern Verfall entgegen zu eilen" (*Md*, 4:144). Apart from the matter of slavery and secession, he was not much of a democrat. He regularly spoke ill of the revolutionaries of 1848 and established himself comfortably on the boundary between the prosperous bourgeoisie and the aristocracy. One of his characters, addressing the narrator, trivializes political oppression in Germany while scorning refugees from it: "mehrmals verächtlich ist Derjenige, welcher sein Heimathland vergessen, ja schmähen und sich desselben schämen kann, wie so viele Eurer deutschen Landsleute thun und zwar, weil ihnen die eine oder die andere Regierungsform nicht zusagt, als ob der Boden die Schuld von wirklichen oder eingebildeten Bedrückungen und Ungerechtigkeiten trüge."[33] His first travel book was dedicated humbly and gratefully to the despotic Friedrich Wilhelm IV (the list of subscribers consists largely, apart from dealers in New York, of kings and princes); the second to Prince Friedrich Wilhelm, subsequently Kaiser Friedrich III. For twenty years Möllhausen spent leisure hours in a largely aristocratic circle around another Prussian prince, Friedrich Karl, who took Möllhausen on his yacht to Norway.[34] As a writer he was forgotten soon after his time; at the end of his career, he himself doubted that he had achieved much or would be long remembered. This verdict seems just.

Möllhausen was a man of a moral purity bordering on stupidity. His contemporary Friedrich Armand Strubberg, by contrast, was a shadier character or at any rate a more opaque one. For one thing, he was involved in a manner still not entirely clear to us in the greatest scandal of the German emigration, the project of the so-called *Adelsverein* to organize a large German settlement in the Republic of Texas.[35] For another, the account he gave of his life seems to be as seriously misleading as his self-representations in his fiction are rather obviously self-aggrandizing.

Strubberg's account of his life was summarized with occasional mild skepticism by Preston Barba years ago.[36] According to it, Strubberg was born in Kassel in 1806 as the son of a prosperous tobacco merchant descended from the landgrave of Hesse, later king of Sweden. He grew up in a cultured home visited by prominent literary figures, among them the young Heine, whom Strubberg thrashed for his impiety. In 1822 he was sent to Bremen to be apprenticed as a business clerk. There, having become enamored of a young woman, he seriously wounded her disapproving cousin in a duel, whereupon he fled to America. What he did there we do not know, except that in October 1828 he visited Niagara Falls. Meanwhile his father's business began to become a victim of the tariff boundaries of the petty German states, and the son was called home to rescue it. This he was, at length, unable to do, so he returned to America, where he set himself up as a commission agent for European export houses in New York. He achieved some success and social standing, but again became involved in a duel with a disapproving cousin of an heiress he had courted, and this time killed his opponent. He was obliged to flee westwards; the steamboat on which he was traveling sank, stranding him in Louisville. There a German academic encouraged him to study medicine for two years, after which he styled himself a doctor and evidently took great pride in his medical abilities. He then determined to settle, against all advice, as far west as he could get, in the company of three other men, only one of whom, Königstein, is ever named in any of his accounts. Together they built a fort on the Rio Bravo, where they lived from hunting and planting. At first the only white men in that part of the country, they began to be joined by others. Strubberg gave up homesteading and, under the name of Dr. Schubbert or Shubbert, was employed by the *Adelsverein* in March 1846 as director of the town of Friedrichsburg, north of the main settlement of Neu-Braunfels, a position in which he served until July 1847.

In this post he strove conscientiously and selflessly to serve the colonists, cure disease, establish a mill and a church, combat the incompetence of the *Adelsverein* bureaucrats, defend the settlement against hostile Indians, and make peace among those Indians willing to enter into a treaty. However, he quarreled with malign associates and was cheated out of a farm he had been promised. He then joined General Winfield Scott's troops in the Mexican War, during which he encountered Sealsfield in Vera Cruz. Subsequently he became a celebrated physician in Camden, Arkansas, where he was engaged to a wealthy lady, but an insect sting in his eye obtained on a bear hunt obliged him to return to Europe for treatment in 1854. On this journey he was warmly received by the dying Heine on his "mattress-grave" in Paris. He returned to Kassel to visit his sister, a translator and teacher of foreign languages, and after some wandering from town to town, settled permanently in Kassel in 1860. At the age of fifty-two he had begun his literary career with *Amerikanische Jagd- und Reiseabenteuer aus meinem Leben in den westlichen Indianergebieten* (1858), published under what was to become his literary pen name of "Armand." Thenceforward he endeavored to live from literature; within ten years he had published forty volumes; altogether he wrote twenty novels in fifty-four volumes. He met and married his former beloved, only to discover that she was a madwoman who had been released from an asylum and had to be confined again, and, supposing himself a lawyer as well as a physician, became involved in a tedious lawsuit of the deposed ruling house of Hesse against the Prussian government. In 1885 he moved to Gelnhausen, his literary abilities steadily declining; like many German writers of the century, he was mesmerized by the prestige of the drama, with results that even those best disposed toward him have been unable to admire. He died in Gelnhausen on April 3, 1889.

How much of this story might be true is uncertain, but, although this is not the place to enter into a thorough evaluation of it, there can be little doubt that substantial parts of it are fabricated.[37] It has been commented that his life was like a "Kolportageroman," but that may well be so because the account of it is a kind of "Kolportageroman."[38] To begin with, there is no independent evidence of either of Strubberg's duels. Kassel and New York were not places in which a prominent man of society might be critically injured or killed in a duel without leaving any public record, especially as the latter event, in Strubberg's account, led to an extensive interstate manhunt. It is certain that he did not make Heine's acquaintance either in Kassel or in Paris; we are well informed about such matters, and the account of the visit to the mattress-grave follows the conventions of the celebrity journalism that battened upon Heine's illness. Whether or not Sealsfield was ever in Mexico, Strubberg cannot have met him in Vera Cruz in 1847, when he was living in Schaffhausen, Switzerland.[39] In any case, General Scott's forces had left Vera Cruz well before Strubberg's appointment in Friedrichsburg was terminated, and it seems probable that he never served in the Mexican War at all.

His role in Friedrichsburg is mired in controversy. In accounts published in 1896, his conduct is represented as dictatorial, egotistical, and violent, as well as incompetent both as a physician and a frontiersman.[40] Strubberg, an excellent shot, is said to have intimidated opponents with threats of duels, whereupon one man committed suicide. While other reports speak well of him, modern historians do not:

> Besides disease, another evil of early Fredericksburg was an imposter known as Dr. Schubert who managed to have himself appointed as director of the settlement. Both his quackery as a doctor and his acts as an administrator worked mischief for the settlers until he was fired by Meusebach [the second commissioner of the *Adelsverein*] in 1847. Late in 1846 Schubert appointed himself to head a group of men who went into the grant. His cowardice toward Indians on this occasion helped necessitate Meusebach's treaty with the Indians in March, 1847.[41] This man seemed to heap favors on his circle of friends; the people whom he disliked he dealt with summarily, even to the point of sending them out of the community, making it indelibly clear that they were never to return.[42]

From these and other accounts it appears that it was Meusebach, not Strubberg, who achieved a rapprochement with the Indians. In any case, it is evident that the *Adelsverein* colony, lurching from one catastrophe to another, beset by fevers, hostile Comanches, the inability to arrange transport because all wagons in the area had been commandeered for the Mexican War, and a horrifying mortality rate, was a morass of intrigue, with officers, agents, and speculators at each other's throats. Strubberg's effort to maintain the farm he thought had been promised to him culminated in a genuine Western shoot-out in which one of his men was killed, leading to a charge of murder against the head of the *Verein* in Texas.[43]

The impeachment of the transmitted account of Strubberg's life leaves us with no very clear picture of it. It is certain that he was at Niagara Falls in 1828, that he was director of the Friedrichsburg colony for sixteen months in 1846–47, and that, past the age of fifty, he launched upon a literary career in Kassel and Gelnhausen; beyond that, we are in a realm of fiction that he wove around himself, undoubtedly based on real experience, but to what extent heightened and adjusted to a heroized self-portrait is difficult to estimate. At the outset of his fictionalized account of his directorship, *Friedrichsburg, die Colonie des deutschen Fürsten-Vereins in Texas* (1867), he determinedly elides the boundary between memoir and fiction: "Wenn ich nun in diese, treu und wahr dem Leben entnommene Erzählung als Würze den Faden eines Romanes eingeflochten habe, dessen einzelne Momente jedoch gleichfalls auf wirklichen Begebenheiten beruhen, so greift derselbe in keiner Weise störend, oder entstellend in das Geschichtliche des Werkes ein, sondern dient vielmehr dazu, dem entworfenen Bilde noch lebendigere Farbe und hellere Beleuchtung zu verleihen" (*F*, 1: unpaged preface). Any reader who believes that will believe anything. One rather gets the impression of a person who was frustrated in his failure to reconcile his real self with his imagined self. Strubberg was intelligent, if not very well educated, lively, and not without abilities, one of which was in handling weapons. He was a tall, handsome man of exceptional physical strength. One imagines that he might have been attractive to women, but this seems not to have been the case. The sequence of frustrations and calamities in relations with women in his fiction and, apparently, in his life becomes a peculiar leitmotif; it has been pointed out that his narrative persona always manages to avoid marriage;[44] other characters, however, succeed in getting married all the time. For all his airs as a frontiersman, he seems to have had aspirations to elegance. He tells us that, in his Western blockhouse, when tired of hunting, he put on bourgeois clothes "mit Spitzen und Manschetten, mit Frack, seidenen Strümpfen und glanzledernen Schuhen."[45] He dedicated *Friedrichsburg* to Duke Ernst II of Saxe-Coburg-Gotha, one of the sponsors of the *Adelsverein* and brother of Queen Victoria's Prince Albert; an earlier novel, *Sklaverei in Amerika oder Schwarzes Blut* (1860), was dedicated to Wilhelm I, king of Prussia and future emperor.[46] There is reason to think that the life he masked was marked by disappointments and failures, and that finally he came to writing as compensation and a reconstitution of his imagined self.

Although not generally recognized as such, Strubberg is in some ways a better writer than Möllhausen. He is crisper and gets on with it; his narration, one might say, is action-packed. His characters are more complexly motivated. There is a harder substratum in his writing. Like any nineteenth-century popular writer, Strubberg is moralistic, makes unequivocal distinctions between good and evil, and guides his plots to poetic justice most of the time. Yet the thoughtful reader may sense a kind of amoral indifference lurking under the surface. His stories are strikingly careless of life; characters die quickly, in substantial numbers, and often violently. There is a good deal of meanness and selfishness, not just among his villains, but in his world generally. Sometimes a rather freakish sense of humor breaks through. In the third volume of *Bis in die Wildniss*, a corpse is transported by boat in a cask of rum from which the deckhands have been tippling; they become distinctly queasy when they are made aware of what they have done. It is true that he is inclined to sensationalism and melodrama, suggesting an influence from Eugène Sue. He is rather good at Sue-like scenes of horror, such as New Orleans under a plague of yellow fever in *Bis in die Wildniss*. He also has a tendency to moments of rather soppy sentimentality that contrast oddly with the moral chill one often feels. Possibly this is an attempt to reach the female readers who were believed to be the majority consumers of fiction in his time, since his mode of adventure writing was presumed to be primarily attractive to a male readership. Some of his self-dramatizations read as pretty tall stories, and it is odd that until recently critics were not more skeptical of retranslating fiction into biography. Mustangs leap a forty-foot chasm; Strubberg, though debilitated with fever, rescues his dog from the jaws of an alligator.[47] Such scenes as those in which he pursues and kills an Indian despite having taken an arrow in the breast, or fights off thirty Indians at a time, or, armed only with a knife, defeats three grizzly bears by getting two of them to fight with one another,[48] as well as the practice of projecting an invincible, all-knowing persona who, appearing under various near anagrams of "Friedrich Armand"—Farnwald, Farland, Franval—both is and is not identical with the author, remind us forcibly of Karl May, who undoubtedly drew extensively on Strubberg; readers of May will remember that one of Old Shatterhand's first feats in establishing his superiority is the killing of a grizzly with only a knife. Strubberg is a kind of proto–Karl May, the predecessor who resembles the later writer most, though less extravagantly and pathologically.[49]

This effect is evident in a number of places where the narrative persona exceeds all others in competence and skill. Examples abound in all the writings in which he foregrounds his persona. Almost everything that goes wrong in Friedrichsburg, including fatalities, is a consequence of not taking Dr. Schubert's advice. A traveling German botanist dies at the hands of Indians for the same reason (*AJR*, 56). During the harrowing sea voyage to America in *Bis in die Wildniss*, the narrator repeatedly saves the ship and particularly the Creole family with whose daughter he has fallen in love, finding means to make both stagnant water and sea water potable. He can tell character by reading faces. In New York he is recognized as musical and artistic, a graceful dancer and fine rider, and all-around good fellow; on the prairie, another man, lacking his skill in butchering a buffalo, would starve to death; in Friedrichsburg he cures an epidemic with his medical skill. He is especially competent with rattlesnakes; in *Bis in die Wildniss* he shoots one about to bite his Creole beloved; in Friedrichsburg, Dr. Schubert, against the skepticism of others, saves a young woman from death by applying an onion to the snakebite, an Indian cure he had already displayed in his memoir (*BW*, 2:101; *F*, 1:99–101; *AJR*, 84). An Indian acknowledges that Armand is an even better Indian than they are themselves, a passage that gives a clear premonition of Old Shatterhand (*BW*, 4:229).

Like Möllhausen, Strubberg was critical of American attitudes toward race and opposed to slavery; nearly half of his novels are concerned with slavery and the Civil War, though, like Möllhausen's, written long after the author had departed the country, and some of his scenes of abuse look as though they might have been taken from *Uncle Tom's Cabin* more directly than from experience. A black named Daniel in *Carl Scharnhorst. Abenteuer eines deutschen Knaben in Amerika* (1872), actually a juvenile novel, is said to have been "the most interesting Negro in Germany's Western fiction";[50] he is a skilled frontiersman who has been raised as an Indian warrior, and he prefers Germans to Americans because they are less prejudiced, another note that prefigures Karl May, as does the boy Carl himself, a "youthful Leatherstocking" who develops into a mighty hunter.[51] In other places, however, blacks are grinning, obsequious, comic figures or "garstige schwarze Niggers" (examples in *BW*, 1:47–48; 2:280). A house slave named, of all things, Tom, "war ein freundlicher alter Mann und ganz das Bild des Glücks, welches diese abhängige Menschenklasse unter einem guten Herrn in so vollem Maße genießt"; like most German fictional blacks, he speaks ungrammatically with his thick lips (*BW*, 2:10). The Armand of *Bis in die Wildniss* abandons a prospective marriage partner because she is alleged to have had intercourse with a slave. Having grown lonely for civilization in the wilderness, Strubberg tells us that he was glad when neighbors with slaves moved near him (*AJR*, 219).

His primary focus, however, was on beautiful, mixed-race women, such as Melina in *Bis in die Wildniss*, who "has beauty, intellect, poise, virtue, and typical feminine fragility"; she is "too well educated and gifted to associate with the people of her mother's blood."[52] Melina, whose father had attempted to settle her in society, comes within a hair's breadth of being reenslaved; the model here may well be Cassy in *Uncle Tom's Cabin*. However, it is also possible that he has the motif from Gerstäcker's novella "Jazede," originally published in the *Novellen-zeitung* in 1845 and then in the third volume of *Mississippibilder* in 1848; we shall return to it in chapter 8. One of the narrator's acquaintances overcomes his aversion to black blood to marry Melina, but must move to Europe to do so. The fourth volume contains a quite vivid description of a quadroon ball in New Orleans. Strubberg puts great stress on the role of beautiful quadroons as career mistresses of young men who cannot marry them: "Wie viele junge Männer der ersten, angesehensten Familien von Louisiana beugen sich unter dem süßen Joche einer bezaubernden Quadrone, entsagen den matten Reizen der weißen Schönheiten und stürzen trotz aller Bitten, aller Wünsche ihrer Familie, ihrer Freunde, trotz der ihnen Rache drohenden öffentlichen Meinung, wie der Abendschmetterling in die verzehrende Gluth der Flamme, trunken von Seligkeit in die geöffnete Arme eines solchen heißliebenden Engels des Südens" (*BW*, 4:10–11). The heated sensuality of the language here is striking; it reminds one somewhat of Sealsfield's depictions of alluring mixed-race women, but with much less of his neurotic censure. The whole scene maintains this atmosphere and lacks the studied innocence of Möllhausen's descriptions of Mexican fandangos in the Southwest. Armand does not, naturally, cross the boundary of decency; the narrator stresses the decorum of an evening he spends with one of the ladies and her mother (*BW*, 4:55). Still, there is an edging toward sexual arousal in his scenes of romance that is different in quality from the other writers of my acquaintance.

His Indians, like those of all writers in the Cooper tradition, are divided into good and evil, depending upon their degree of accommodation to white society. In his memoir of his Far West adventure, the Plains Indians are several times referred to as subcivilized cannibals; of an Indian girl he says she would have been beautiful had she had white skin (*AJR*, 8, 11, and passim; 374). At the end of *Bis in die Wildniss*, Armand's former Creole beloved is punished for having been more faithful to Methodist superstition than to him by making her the contented wife of an Indian who kidnapped her: she could not be his for reasons of religion, now she is the "Weib eines Anbeters der Sonne!" (*BW*, 4:251). In *Friedrichsburg* he stresses that the moral superiority of the whites intimidates the attacking Indians; like virtually all German observers, Dr. Schubbert sympathizes with the plight of Indians, but agrees that the land was not made for aborigines to hunt and wander in (*F*, 1:14–15, 158). Interestingly, however, the fictional protagonist, the kindly young colonist Rudolph von Wildhorst, several times expresses his empathy with the most hostile and treacherous of the Indians, recognizing that his land has been occupied and his way of life destroyed. Still, Rudolph fights him all the same.

Strubberg was a more explicitly anti-American writer than Möllhausen. *Ralph Norwood* (1860) is said to have been, of all the German novels of the time, "the only one that has an American scoundrel as its main character."[53] The American steamboats and railroads that fascinated others leave him cold: steamboats "rauben der Schiffahrt die Poesie, wie auf dem Festlande die Eisenbahnen das Dasein in Prosa kleiden" (*BW*, 1:52–53). There are the usual clichés about Americans gobbling their food to run off to business, or calling tricksters "smart," "wofür man im Deutschen kein Wort hat" (*BW*, 1:259; 2:117–18; 1:268–69). Like Möllhausen, he presents the Americans, in an ironic tone, as too busy to take note of the natural surroundings: "Einem solchen Volke taugen nicht die weinerliche Gutmüthigkeit, die bange, ängstliche Zärtlichkeit, womit man in dem alten Lande an der Scholle, an Verwandten und Freunde hängt, es kann solche Gefühle nicht in seinem Kampf mit der Natur, mit der Roheit gebrauchen, sonst bliebe es weit hinter seiner Bestimmung zurück."[54] A murder trial in the second volume of *Bis in die Wildniss* is a contest of corrupt factions in which justice occurs all but accidentally before a fickle public that engages in an orgy of drinking, fighting, and killing. The familiar scene of a passenger steamboat race ending with the explosion and sinking of one is there also.

In his emigration novel, *Alte und neue Heimath* (1859), he takes, in contrast to Gerstäcker, a downright contemptuous view of the emigrants and their motivation. He certainly gives a vivid picture of the sufferings, mistreatment, greed, and meanness of the *Adelsverein* colonists. But it is their own fault for being there in the first place. The father of the Werner family has been deluded by utopian literature and emigration propaganda. He wishes to flee "dem übervölkerten und ausgesogenen Deutschland" for "dem gesegneten reichen Texas, wo die Natur dem Menschen Alles, was er bedarf, umsonst giebt," but the narrator insists that he and everyone else had it good in Germany: "bis jetzt noch keine Noth zur Auswanderung getrieben hatte" (*AH*, 1:10, 13). As the horrors mount, the emigrants think sadly of their nice home in Germany. All but two members of the Werner family die miserably. The daughter Mathilde is rescued by a salt-of-the-earth German Catholic family. At the end of the novel, her brother, even though he has become a U.S. Army officer occupying defeated Mexico, is able to marry a beautiful and wealthy Mexican woman because he is Catholic and German, not American (Strubberg's occasional pro-Catholic gestures are another feature that reminds one of Karl May). The other family, of a totally incompetent schoolmaster named Kunze, suffers from terminal stupidity; the fatuous wife allows her daughter to be taken in and ruined by a suave debauchee, after which she commits suicide. The peasants, fops, officials, businessmen, soldiers, artisans, actors, tenant farmers, bourgeois, and noblemen stranded on the Galveston coast, one more helpless than the other, reveal the occupation of their consciousness by literary images in their fantastic dress (*AH*, 1:21–22).

In the second volume of *Bis in die Wildniss*, witless peasants, who refuse to take advice from the omniscient Armand, are duped into buying nonexistent land as soon as they are off the boat; the narrative tone does not show them much sympathy. If the *Adelsverein* emigrants are foolish, Americans, like the Johnson brothers, who charge $500 for a wagon, strand the Werners, take their last food money, and allow them to starve, are cruel primitives. The Americans in the semifictional Friedrichsburg novel are Mormons. Their polygamy strikes Dr. Schubbert as somewhat wanton, but they form a solid community of good neighbors outside the town while building the sawmill the town needs. However, one day the whole community just vanishes, leaving unpaid several thousand dollars in debts to the German colonists (*F*, 1:124–25, 2:225–27). Perhaps we are supposed to think of the Hebrews despoiling the Egyptians, but my guess is that it is just another case of American crassness and greed. In the historical sources, the Mormons' helpfulness is stressed; nothing is said about them despoiling the community when they moved on.[55] The German way of life in Friedrichsburg is much praised; we see "die richtige deutsche Bürgerfrau mit Haube und Schürze beim Rechen eines Beetes" and a true German Sunday, the colonists in German dress contrasting with the American dress worn on workdays; Germany is toasted; still, the colonists do not seem to want to live there (*F*, 1:41, 187, 193). While critical of some of the incompetent agents of the *Adelsverein*, Strubberg tends to defend its good intentions, a view not wholly borne out by the historical record. Chapter 6 of *Alte und neue Heimath* contains debates on the responsibility of the *Adelsverein*, which the narrator cants in its favor.

In the allegedly autobiographical *Bis in die Wildniss* (which does not get him to the wilderness until halfway through the fourth and last volume), a substantial part depicts commercial life in New York, where the always innocent protagonist is set back by having guaranteed a note for a man who dies and whose father and in-laws hoot at the idea of making it good, and is nearly bankrupted by an exporter who changes his mind about which supplier to use. These are more examples of Yankee crassness and greed; Gerstäcker might have observed, however, that Armand was evidently one of those naive, starry-eyed Germans attempting to do major business by handshake rather than by contract and legal agreement. *In Mexiko* (1865) attacks the Mexican War as unjust and imperialist, as, of course, many Americans did also at the time. Still, in one of his shorter stories, although Americans in Mexico are shown as rude and greedy imperialists, Mexican women turn to them because they despise their weak men for having lost the war, and in another, energetic, restless, progressive Americans are contrasted, quite in Sealsfield's spirit, to lazy, weak, and superstitious Mexicans.[56] While he wrote against slavery and the Confederacy, he was not a partisan of the Union, ascribing to the northern abolitionists motives of economic aggression against the South. His German hero of the Civil War leaves America disillusioned with republicanism, placing his hopes in the new order in Germany.[57] Like Möllhausen, Strubberg was not much of a democrat. He scorned the refugees from the Revolution of 1848; one of them, an exiled lawyer, is portrayed as a ruffian, criminal, and detested troublemaker, and Strubberg appears to have disapproved of political partisanship, "da der unglückliche Geist der Eifersucht zwischen dieser [Whig newspaper] und der der Demokraten schon für die Republik eine Gefahr drohende Höhe erreicht hatte" (*AH*, 1:76–77; *BW*, 2:180). There is also, to be sure, a quite exhilarating scene of a political rally in Baltimore for Henry Clay that concludes with a prediction of American world power (*BW*, 3:170–74); perhaps a future researcher will find that Clay was Strubberg's man.

For the present, however, we must be content to say that Möllhausen and Strubberg are writers of historical, anthropological, and perhaps sociological interest who should not be elevated into a literary standing that they cannot sustain, lest we come to be unable to recognize relative excellence when we encounter it. Where such relative excellence might be identified I should like to suggest in the next section.

# Part II. Mimesis: Friedrich Gerstäcker

# 6. The Revealed Vocation

In some ways, Friedrich Gerstäcker's career resembled that of Möllhausen and Strubberg. He, too, came from a defective family, though one less emotionally stressed than theirs. He, too, never had a complete bourgeois education; like Möllhausen, he was shunted into agricultural training. Like them, as a young man he took off for America, more as an adventurer than an emigrant, without any clear goals or prospects, and there he accumulated a vast amount of exhilarating and sometimes terrifying experience far beyond the boundaries and perhaps in many cases the imaginations of the average German of his generation. Like them he did not set out to be a writer and came to a literary career by an indirect route, but one somewhat less accidental than theirs. He did not fall into fiction writing by chance like Möllhausen or in lieu of something else to do like Strubberg; there was in him a subliminal creative vocation that was revealed rather than imposed on him.

Friedrich Gerstäcker was born on May 10, 1816, in Hamburg; the place was something of an accident, for his parents were transient artists: his mother a singer and actress, his father a successful opera tenor, indeed, apparently something of a star. For a time the family lived in Dresden, then in Kassel. But the father died in 1825, grieving the boy and leaving the family in straitened circumstances; his mother settled in Leipzig but he was sent to live with an uncle in Braunschweig. The uncle, Eduard Schütz (1799–1868), was an actor and theater director who obtained a place in literary history in the role of Faust at the premiere of Goethe's drama in Braunschweig in 1829. He may have been an eccentric, self-aggrandizing, and manipulative personality; in any case, he is portrayed with merciless satire in Gerstäcker's late novel, *Im Eckfenster* (1872).[1] The youth began to train for a commercial career in Leipzig, but it did not suit him, so he was sent as an apprentice to an estate near Grimma in Saxony to learn agriculture. Thus he had no real hometown and was consequently, by the standards of his time, unusually uprooted. Although today he is associated with Braunschweig, the center of researches on him, in his adult life he was settled there only during his last three years. When he was homesick, as he often was during his travels, it was not so much for any particular place as for Germany in general.

It is clear that he long entertained the idea of taking off for America, though initially he may have thought of South America, particularly

Brazil. In 1837, at the age of twenty-one, he finally sailed to New York, his first extended journey in an exceptionally restless life; by the end of it he "had lived in Hamburg, Kassel, Braunschweig, Gotha, Dresden, and Leipzig, not to mention New York, Cincinnati, New Orleans, San Francisco, Pittsburgh, Valparaiso, Sydney, Adelaide, Bolivar, and Rio de Janeiro. He had traversed the deserts of Egypt, the jungles of Latin America, the shores of the Mississippi, the Pacific coast of the United States, the pampas of Argentina, the islands of the South Seas, and sections of Australia."[2] In America he had a wide variety of occupations, a series of which he ticked off in a letter of February 22, 1840, to the friend of his youth, Hermann Schultz, as his "Stände" (*Br. 1*, 209–12). It was a list in which he invested considerable pride for adaptability and competence, which he presented as defining American requirements of the ability to change course as circumstances require, in contrast to the lifetime assignment of a trade characteristic of German society. He stressed the point in his emigration manual (*Wie?*, 9) and on many other occasions. In New York a partner cheated him out of an investment in a tobacco shop on Broadway—an experience he always valued as an archetypal lesson in American commerce. He often repeated a German American saying: "Es kann kein Deutscher einen Cent in Amerika verdienen oder vielmehr sparen, bis er nicht den letzten europäischen Pfennig losgeworden ist" (*DAFS*, 59; cf. 115, 260); to Schultz he gave the wording as: "So lange noch einer einen Pfennig deutsches Geld hat kommt er auf keinen grünen Zweig" (*Br. 1*, 197). The saying seems to have been in wide circulation; the redoubtable Amalie Schoppe reported it in an account of her crossing in 1848 as "Der Einwanderer kommt zu nichts, solange er noch einen Cent europäisches Geld im Säckel hat."[3]

After having absorbed this lesson, Gerstäcker traveled through New York State, Ontario, the upper Midwest, Illinois, Arkansas, Louisiana, and Texas. He lived off and on in Cincinnati, where he passed a schoolteacher's examination without ever practicing, worked for a chocolate maker, assisted a silversmith, constructed pillboxes for an apothecary, and sold cane for pipe stems that he had cut on the banks of the Mississippi. He worked briefly as a fireman on a Mississippi riverboat and as a woodcutter in Memphis, and at the end of his first stay in the United States he was manager of a hotel in Louisiana. It is true that a memoir in a German monthly in Cincinnati portrays him as fantastically incompetent in these occupations.[4] But, if so, he did not allow himself to be inhibited by lack of qualifications. When he took on his job as hotel manager, he realized he had no idea how to do it—he had rarely been even a guest in a hotel—but he agreed to try, "denn man muß eben alles in der Welt versuchen, und weiß vorher nie, was man wirklich kann" ("Mein Eintritt in das Ferry-Hotel zu Pointe-Coupée," Z5, 355). As he observed in a truly programmatic statement, "Dem Amerikaner ist übrigens Alles möglich, und was nicht *gut* geht, das geht *schlecht*, aber es *geht* doch auf jeden Fall" (*Wie?*, 97).

The largest block of his time was spent as a backwoodsman in Arkansas, living primarily from hunting, which was the great passion of his life and to which we shall return in somewhat more detail in the next chapter. In consequence he has become a figure of some interest to Arkansas historians, one of whom has published a volume of his backwoods stories in English translation with the observation that Gerstäcker "probably wrote more about the state than any other writer who was not an Arkansas native"; in 1957 another historian induced Governor Orval Faubus to grant him posthumous honorary citizenship, the only good report of Faubus I can recall ever having heard.[5] Some of Gerstäcker's papers are archived at the University of Arkansas at Little Rock, which is generous of them in view of his response to a settler's claim that there is only one Little Rock: "und darin hat er vollkommen recht, denn es wäre fürchterlich, wenn auf der Welt noch solch ein zweiter Platz existirte" (*AWS*, 2:18). But that was just Gerstäcker's feeling about cities; later in the same story a character comments that Arkansas is the best state in the Union (*AWS*, 2:68). Toward the end of his life he was to say that Arkansas was the first place where he had felt free and independent: "Ein wahrer Zauber lag auch schon allein in dem Wort für mich" (*NR*, 1:277).

In an autobiographical memoir in the *Gartenlaube* in 1870, he wrote that when he returned to Germany in 1843 he found to his surprise that he was a published writer: he had been sending his diary to his mother, who had had excerpts published in the journal *Rosen* (*KENS*, 1:3; cf. *SJ*, 1:ix). Modern scholars have not been able to verify this account, as there are no extant copies of those issues of *Rosen*. He did not make the claim in the letters to his friend Schultz, to whom he chronicled his difficulties in establishing himself after his return, though five years later he said something similar to the publisher Cotta (*Br.* 2, 14). In any case, there is no good reason to doubt the tale. This unexpected success encouraged him to submit for publication his first book, *Streif- und Jagdzüge durch die vereinigten Staaten Nord-Amerikas* (1844), which appeared with a preface by Traugott Bromme (1802–66), a well-known travel and geographical writer, who praised the author as "ein deutscher 'David Crockett'" (*SJ*, 1:vii). To earn a living after his return to Germany, he put the English-language skills he had acquired to use by translating English and American books; one of the most important was

Herman Melville's *Omoo*, which he translated within months of its appearance in 1847.

By then he had begun to wonder if he might have a talent for creative writing himself and soon launched himself on a busy literary career as a writer for magazines, drawing initially on his American experience; from time to time he collected the stories in book form, beginning with *Mississippi-Bilder* (1847-48) and *Amerikanische Wald- und Strombilder* (1849). He also achieved early success with two wild and woolly novels of crime and adventure, *Die Regulatoren in Arkansas* (1846) and *Die Flußpiraten des Mississippi* (1848). A Texas scholar has credited *Die Regulatoren* with being not only the first German Western, but the first Western ever.[6] Abridged segments of these books, as of others, appeared as pirated translations in the form of dime novels. The books are lively and reasonably entertaining for those who like that sort of thing, but, as is sometimes the consequence of early writing successes, they came to be harmful to Gerstäcker's long-term reputation. For one thing, since they are probably best appreciated by young readers, they contributed to his reputation as a writer of children's literature; in fact, the oldest German children's book prize is named for him. He did, indeed, write books specifically for young readers, among them *Fritz Waldau's Abenteuer zu Wasser und zu Lande* (1854), which combines South Sea adventure with nautical and anthropological information, and which had a long life in English translation as *Frank Wildman's Adventures on Land and Water*, first published in 1855. But his success as a writer of adventure tales came to obscure the more important theme that began to preoccupy his sense of obligation and civic duty: the emigration.

The emigration was a major social concern in Germany for the greater part of the nineteenth century; it generated a huge public discourse and is today an extensive subspeciality among historians. While large segments of the educated middle class chafed and burned in a perpetually reactionary, repressive, caste-ridden environment, the common people were buffeted by episodes of famine, inflation, depression, and the dislocations of an accelerating capitalist order. The statistics alone indicate the weight of the problem. Some 20,000 emigrants left for America during the horrible Rhenish famine of 1816-17. The number dropped below 7,000 in the 1820s, but jumped to more than 150,000 in the 1830s, to 434,000 in the "Hungry Forties," and to nearly a million in the 1850s. From then on the figures wax and wane, peaking in 1882 with a quarter of a million emigrants in that year alone. For the eighty years prior to 1900 the official total surpasses 5 million. However, this figure may well be too low if one considers the totality of German speakers. By 1910 more than 9 million Americans spoke German as their mother tongue, some 11 percent of the population and more than a quarter of all foreign-language-speaking Americans.[7] In 1864 the population of the German states was estimated at 46 million and that of German Austria at 8.8 million.

One can see from these proportions that the emigration question must have touched the consciousness of a large fraction of the people; there must have been few who did not think about it or know someone who did. As Gerstäcker wrote in the introduction to *Nach Amerika!*: "keiner ist unter uns, dem nicht ein lieber Freund, ein naher Verwandter den *salto mortale* gethan, und Alles hinter sich gelassen, was ihm einst lieb und theuer war—aus dem, aus jenem Grund—und täglich, stündlich noch hören wir von anderen, von denen wir im Leben nie geglaubt daß *sie* je an Amerika gedacht, wie sie mit Weib und Kind und Hab und Gut hinüberziehen" (*NA*, 1:viii). It was thus first of all a personal concern: individuals had to make up their minds about it. Should one go? What was America really like? Could one hope to survive and thrive? What would be the cost in terms of security, uprootedness, the loss of a familiar, sustaining, and venerable culture? But there was a public dimension as well. For thoughtful and patriotic people, the waves of emigration raised troubling questions about Germany itself. What was wrong that so many thousands of people were willing to accept grave risks, dangers, and losses in order to leave? Was it a failure of character or intelligence, or was it a reproach that demanded change? On the other hand, was America really so advantageous, or was it not a chimera, a trap for the unwary?

In regard to these matters, Gerstäcker was in an unusual position. On the one hand, he was not really an emigrant himself, so he had no particular commitment to defend or rancor to avenge. On the other, he had unusually extensive and profound experience of America, which, as we shall see, was to expand over the years. He was not in principle opposed to the emigration, though he often looked upon it sorrowfully, as a reflex of lamentable conditions in Germany. It has been observed that his warnings were the more plausible and persuasive because he was not one of those implacably opposed.[8] He wrote that the emigration would create a united Germany in America, and should be encouraged, for it was the only way to relieve class suffering (*AzW*, 1:18, 20–21). At the time of the revolution of 1848, he gave a heartrending account of the profound structural poverty of the lacemakers of the Erzgebirge in Saxony (a milieu similar to that into which Karl May was born), demanding that the government sponsor the emigration of the whole community to America—doubtless an impractical proposal, but one that indicates the intensity of his concern (*AzW*, 2:363–400).[9]

Conversely, he became equally concerned that large numbers of people were heading into serious trouble owing to ignorance and misinformation, romantic imaginings derived largely from literature and from the sheer utopian self-hypnosis of the deprived and frustrated, letters home from immigrants inflating their attainments while suppressing out of shame their failures and disappointments, and the blandishments of agents of every kind of scam, especially of transatlantic transport. He did not, by the way, think much of claims that the emigration was impelled by the hatred of tyranny and the love of freedom. In a speech he made to the German community of Rio de Janeiro in 1861, he dismissed such claims as "Redensarten"; the two essential factors, he said, were "die *Noth*" and "die *Phantasie*."[10] Gerstäcker could not do much about *Noth*, but he made of *Phantasie* a cause of conscience. It must be said that he tried everything he could think of, employed every medium at his disposal, to affect the discourse.

One obvious approach was to offer advice directly. As early as 1849, he published an emigration manual, *Wie ist es denn nun eigentlich in Amerika?* In mid-nineteenth-century Germany, the emigration manual became a genre in its own right. I have seen a number of examples, which were well meant and doubtless useful, packed as they are with information about transportation, land acquisition, agricultural produce prices, and the like. But none of my acquaintance is as entertaining or, for that matter, compact, as Gerstäcker's. He begins on a somewhat ironic note, remarking that he had written it not only for the reader's welfare, but because he had been plagued with inquiries "und bin dabei mit den peinlichsten Kreuz- und Quererkundigungen in einer solchen Fluth von tausend und tausend Mal wiederholten Antworten gehalten worden," so that he determined to answer these questions once and for all (*Wie?*, iv). Actually, he was only beginning to experience the nuisances that fame would bring with it. In 1868 he published an amusing vignette, "Ein Besuch," of an especially importunate visitor who besieges the author with questions but rejects the answers because he knows everything already (*KENS*, 1:643–49; the original magazine piece is reproduced in *Haz*, 41–44).

One of his main concerns was to counter romanticized, fictional images by warning emigrants against the wilderness and the frontier as too demanding of labor and stamina for most people, advising them instead to seek cleared land. My favorite passage in his manual is his advice to the prospective settler in the wilderness to take an ax, go to the nearest woodyard, obtain doubtless readily given permission to practice chopping and splitting logs three feet in circumference, and see how he would like this work all day long every day (*Wie?*, 76–78). Gerstäcker commented several times on the ax as the symbol of the skill of the American woodsman. He once observed that logs hewn by the ax were so straight and true that one would think they had been sawed (*MB*, 3:125). Strubberg also has a scene where more experienced Germans in Texas comment on a recently arrived "Federfuchser" that he will find out how things are when he tries to use an ax (*AH*, 72). Gerstäcker constantly insisted that emigrants gird themselves for hard labor: "Amerika ist ein Land der *Arbeit* und des *Fleißes*"; one need not be ashamed of any kind of work and the lowest laborer is respected (*Wie?*, 6, 8). The 127-page manual was wisely conceived; while, as has been pointed out, its informational content is vague and the specific advice not very concrete, its aim was "mentale Voraussetzungen beim Auswanderer zu schaffen. . . . Die konkrete Detailinformation tritt gegenüber der affektiven Komponente zurück, die die Stelle des persönlichen Kontaktes mit dem potentiellen Auswanderer einnehmen soll."[11] There was no shortage of information; indeed, there was a plethora of it. Gerstäcker realized that the consciousness of Germans needed to be prepared to process it. He also intermittently published warnings, some of them no more than a page or two, in periodicals, especially the widely read *Gartenlaube*, persistently attempting to counter the inexhaustible ingenuity of swindlers and confidence men (examples in *Z*3, 44, 54–55, 64–67). In San Francisco he wanted to found a German newspaper, but German type could not be located, the costs were too high and the subscriptions too few, and his partner was itching to go off to the gold mines (*R*, 2:244–45).

Another obvious approach was to cast his admonitions in fictional form. His initial efforts hyperbolized the problems with a degree of melodrama. His first emigration novel, *Der deutschen Auswanderer Fahrten und Schicksale* of 1847, reflects its didactic purpose by including a foldout map of the United States, but is otherwise a chamber of horrors. It concerns an effort to organize and establish what Gerstäcker always called a "colony," that is, a collective, cooperative community. The endeavor fails for a number of characteristic reasons: Germans, conditioned to submissiveness, do not easily develop initiative, nor are they really interested in cooperating with one another, but are concerned with their own advantage; their heads are full of irrelevant German ideas of things, especially as regards farming and household implements; class stresses break out as the poorer members run out of funds and become a burden on the others; the group is naively vulnerable to swindles, especially in land sales. The whole undertaking collapses in quarreling. Gerstäcker has some difficulty wrenching a conventional happy ending out of this mess, which looks as though it is meant to reflect the catastrophic project of the *Adelsverein*, contemporaneous with the genesis of the novel.[12]

In a similar way, Gerstäcker directed his attention to a particular situation that developed in northern Brazil.[13] This concerned what was known as a "parceria" contract, an arrangement similar to indentured servitude, in which emigrants would contract to work off their passage and land costs while sharing in the profits of the community. It ought to have been easy to see that such a contract is highly vulnerable to abuse. Apparently, as in today's multimillion-dollar movie industry, somehow there never were any profits to share; loss was built into the accounting. The settlers were reduced to permanent servitude in an arid, unfruitful land. Gerstäcker knew and acknowledged that there were successful, indeed thriving, German settlements farther south in Brazil, on which he wrote a novel,[14] but he was very concerned to warn emigrants off the projects in the north, and to this end published a story in book form (*Ein Parcerie-Vertrag*). In it the victims of the contract are reduced to a condition of white slavery. Another of Gerstäcker's persistent concerns comes up in it: the unreliability of diplomatic protection of Germans abroad owing to the absence of a unified German state (see also "Unsere Vertretung im Ausland," Z3, 49–50); he argued also that Germany's petty states were easier for emigrants to renounce than a unified nation would be (*R*, 2:232). Later, in Australia, though he spoke well of German prospects there on the whole, he worried that emigration manuals had told gigantic fables about Adelaide (*R*, 5:265). In the mid-1850s he published "Das Auswanderer Schiff. Skizze" (Z5), a grueling story of an awful storm at sea and a wreck in which most of the emigrants, turning violently on one another in mortal fear, perish.

In contrast to these grim admonitions, he also called upon his considerable resources of humor and satire. The most amusing example of my acquaintance is a story originally published in 1848 entitled "Ein Versuch zur Ansiedlung, oder wie's dem Herrn von Sechingen im Urwald gefiel." It describes the concentrated misery that a German nobleman, whose head had been turned by reading Cooper, experiences in Arkansas. He finds himself instructed by a German farmer:

> "Der Urwald verliert aber doch sehr in der Nähe," erwiederte Sechingen, als er durch eine Spalte der Wohnung hinaus auf die, von grauen, nassen Regenwolken überhangenen Baummassen blickte, während der Wind, unheimlich pfeifend, durch ihre Wipfel brauste und ihnen die großen, klaren Tropfen aus den schwankenden Häuptern schüttelte, "ich hatte mir in mancher Hinsicht ein anderes Bild davon entworfen."

"Sie hatten nicht daran gedacht," fiel ihm sein freundlicher Wirth lachend in's Wort, "daß die gewaltigen, stattlichen Bäume auch im Sumpfe stehen, oder gar quer über den Weg hin liegen könnten, und dann die Passage eher versperren, als verschönern, daß nicht allein das romantische Geheul der wilden Thiere, sondern auch das sehr prosaische Gesumme der Mosquitos den Wald erfüllt, und daß sich eine Landschaft, wo der Sturm auf den Flügeln der Windsbraut die Fläche durchsaust, wo tolle Regengüsse aus den Wolken niederfluthen und trockene Wege zu Bächen und Bäche zu Strömen werden, sehr hübsch und interessant auf der Leinwand, keineswegs angenehm aber im wirklichen Leben, in der nüchternen hausbackenen Wirklichkeit ausnehmen. Ja, das geht Manchem so, das giebt sich aber, und zuletzt lernen wir selbst die Unannehmlichkeiten eines wilden Lebens lieb gewinnen."

(*AWS*, 2:65–66)

It takes Herr von Sechingen twenty-four hours to become persuaded that he is not going to learn to like it.

In 1852, Gerstäcker called upon the evenhandedness that was one of his basic instincts to assemble a variety of voices in an anonymously published story, "Aus dem Briefsacke des Pacquetschiffes 'Seeschlange'" (original text in Z1, 47–65). In the first set of letters from New York in March 1848, a young *Bildungsbürger* breaks out in enthusiasm at American freedom; a steerage passenger, complaining of his terrible journey, the difficulty of farming, and other irritations of American society, already wants to give up; an unorthographic peasant finds that everything is great, as cattle is for the taking, and, having become a thief for the Mormons, that this is the place for "Kommunismus"; a debt-burdened count complains that the republic is ruled by merchants but gets invited and celebrated as an aristocrat; a tradesman has failed as a carpenter and has been cheated out of his tools, cannot farm because he does not know how to use an ax, and now works for $4 a month because he is unadaptable; a hunter buys a farm in Indiana for $250 and gushes about the game; and a Jew, traveling as a peddler in the frightening countryside, gripes that there are no profits to be made because there are too many Jews. In the second batch of letters a few months later, the youth, ill in Cincinnati, is wholly disillusioned, the republic is a fraud, the Germans are despised, he has been cheated by a land agent and a lawyer, no one pays for his journalism, he is reduced to working as a steamboat fireman and must share sleeping quarters with dirty Negroes; the poor man is doing better and is cautiously optimistic, having begun to work some cheap land and to appreciate the qualities of his fellows; the peasant, having discovered there are police in America, is nearly hanged in Texas for horse theft, but, having heard that everything is being divided up in Germany, wants his share and, in the meantime, some money from his wife; the count, having been robbed and ostracized, is now also a steamboat fireman together with the disillusioned young man, whose opinions he dislikes, and thinks he will go into Mexican military service; the tradesman has learned that most descriptions of America are lies written out of shame, that one should avoid Germans and learn English, that a poor man can change his trade and learn to farm; the hunter finds he has been swindled and the only game around is disgusting possum, so he decides to go West; the Jew, now ecstatic, invites his whole family, having made 700 percent profit selling German silver to the rubes as the real thing (*AzW*, 2:299–362). All this encapsulates the points Gerstäcker was constantly trying to stress and that are more patiently elaborated in the ambitious emigration novels to be discussed in detail in chapter 9.

It is difficult to estimate how effective his campaigns were. The historian James Miller thinks that he failed to reach the audience of emigrants, who were mostly peasants and artisans, too poor to buy books and in many cases functionally illiterate.[15] There were, to be sure, literate bourgeois emigrants, especially among the legendary forty-eighters, who were also, in Gerstäcker's view, sadly in need of reliable advice and information. We know that at least one emigrant of the 1870s paid some attention to him, the subsequently well-known *armer Teufel* Robert Reitzel, who wrote: "When I came to America I had a small arsenal of weapons, for anyone who has read Gerstäcker's novels of travel would think he couldn't manage without weapons." He also had the typical Gerstäcker experience that things did not work out as planned: "The beautifully carved sword cane had already been stolen at the Freiburger Hof [in New York], and one of my revolvers had been sold."[16] But Gerstäcker himself had to complain that his warnings against an ill-conceived settlement project in Peru had been ignored, blaming "der faule Fleck in unserem deutschen Vaterlande, daß die unteren, oder vielmehr die arbeitenden Klassen fast gewaltsam davon fern gehalten werden, sich selber zu belehren" (*Cost. Corr.*, col. 1156, n. 74). After having married in 1845 and skirmished for a time in the revolution of 1848, it occurred to him that he ought to look at the situation for himself.

In the aftermath of the revolution, he persuaded the short-lived Frankfurt Parliament to grant him 500 talers to report on German settlements abroad.[17] Paltry as the sum was, this was quite an achievement, on which he remarked: "die Leute sagen, ich sei der Einzige, der damals etwas vom deutschen Reich gehabt" (*KENS*, 1:5). He then turned to Baron Cotta for an advance of 1,500 talers and after some haggling got 400 (*Br.* 2, 16, 21–24)—pocket money, one would think, for the most prestigious publisher in Germany. Thus Gerstäcker set off on a three-year journey around the world with 900 talers in his purse, an indication of his resourcefulness, indifference to hardship, and, perhaps, conscious and intentional foolhardiness. He may also have been fleeing the disappointments of the revolution; in Batavia he remarked that he avoided German newspapers in order to spare himself pain (*R*, 5:10). He traveled to Brazil, then to Argentina, crossed the Cordilleras to Chile in winter, and sailed to San Francisco in time for the gold rush. He mined gold to scrape a little money together, then sailed to Honolulu; from there he voyaged on a whaleboat to the island of Moorea (which, following Melville, he called Imeo) and in a fragile native vessel to Tahiti, thrilled to find himself in Melville territory. He went on to Australia, where he determined to paddle the Murray River in a handmade canoe; it and most of his belongings were lost, and he continued on foot to Adelaide across 700 miles of hardscrabble outback through tribes of hostile aborigines.[18] After returning to Sydney, he sailed to Java, and returned home around the tip of Africa. For his investment Cotta got five volumes of *Reisen* (1853–54), surely one of the most engaging travel works in the German language.

In the period after his return he published two of his three major emigration novels, to be discussed in chapter 9: *Nach Amerika!* (1855) and *Gold!* (1858; the sequel, *In Amerika*, was a very late work, published in 1872). But in 1860 he was off again, on a year-and-a-half journey to South America, spending his time primarily in Peru and Ecuador; this experience generated years of reportage, stories, and novels. On his return in the fall of 1861, he found that his wife had died a few weeks earlier. Partly as a distraction from his sorrow, he accompanied Ernst II, duke of Saxe-Coburg-Gotha, to Africa, traveling up the Nile from Cairo to Luxor and Karnak.[19] One member of the expedition was the naturalist Alfred Brehm (1829–84), later to become famous for his *Illustriertes Tierleben*, found in nearly every German middle-class home and translated into many languages. The account of the journey, *Reise des Herzogs Ernst von Sachsen-Coburg-Gotha nach Aegypten und den Ländern der Habab, Mensa und Bogos* (Leipzig: Arnold, 1864), was apparently written largely if not wholly by Gerstäcker, but the duke and duchess took credit for it (see *Cost. Corr.*, cols. 1107–8 and n.). Gerstäcker was doubtless disappointed, but made no complaint; he was rising in the social scale and the last thing he needed was an altercation with a ruling duke, whose grateful hunting companion he had been (*AmT*, 1:196). After his return he married in 1863 a Dutch woman he had met as a girl in Java.

In 1867 he set out on another journey, landing in New York thirty years after his first visit. He traveled by train to the oil fields of Pennsylvania, where he made pungent observations on air and water pollution around Titusville; later he visited Cincinnati, Louisville, and St. Louis. There he heard of a meeting that General Sherman was to hold with Indian chiefs in the Nebraska Territory to persuade them that their hostility to the ruin of their hunting grounds by the railroad was futile, a view in which Gerstäcker fully concurred. He set off via Chicago, Council Bluffs, and Omaha to observe the conference, traveling in the capacity of a reporter on Sherman's train to the construction point of the Union Pacific at Julesburg in the northeast corner of the Colorado Territory, then back to the conference in the vicinity of North Platte. After the conference he rode on the Smoky Hill branch of the railroad through Kansas, encountering the genuine Wild West, then returned to Arkansas, where the impoverished and depressed condition of the South made him very melancholy. He went on by steamboat to New Orleans and sailed to Vera Cruz, where he commenced a leisurely journey through Mexico, today's Panama, Ecuador, and Venezuela, returning home via Trinidad. This journey generated another of his elaborate travel memoirs, the three-volume *Neue Reisen* (1868), and another series of works of fiction and nonfiction about Central and South America.

By the time of the Franco-Prussian War, Gerstäcker was one of the most beloved and admired of German writers, and this high repute gained him easy access as a war correspondent to the royal and noble commanders at the siege of Paris. He most enthusiastically took the Prussian line on the conflict, portraying France as an unprovoked aggressor that had received its just deserts and exulting at the unification of the German nation. In one of his dispatches, he observed that, despite his tendency to softheartedness, he was gratified by the artillery explosions destroying the war-mongering French, and he celebrated the fall of "das Sodom der 'Civilisation'"; he insisted that Alsace and Lorraine must be retained despite the hatred of their populations for the Germans (*KENS*, 2:60, 62, 93). In his zeal he got into a most uncharacteristic verse polemic with Georg Herwegh, the last and most faithful of the radical political poets of the *Vormärz*. In 1869, before the war, Herwegh had published a poem in Vienna, in which he prophetically deplored its cost and, by implication, national unification under the aegis of undemocratic Prussia.[20] Gerstäcker struck back in the same Vienna newspaper denouncing Herwegh as un-German and lacking in feeling for the fatherland, hooting that poets do not found great nations, and returning to his old theme that Germans abroad are endangered as long as Germany was held in contempt among the nations.[21] Elsewhere he violently attacked the "Phrasenmacher" Victor Hugo's proclamation to the German people as hypocritical, for it was the French who were megalomaniacs (*KENS*, 2:185).

This may look like a not untypical case of the evolution of a national liberal from democratic to imperial and chauvinistic commitments. However, he had always been a middle-of-the-road liberal. In his first social novel about Germany, *Pfarre und Schule*, he portrays radicals in the revolution of 1848 as opportunistic simpletons; in fact, his view seems to have been that the radical democrats were responsible for the failure of the revolution and to have concluded that Germany was not then ready for it (*PuS*, 2:135–37). To be sure, he hoped for an enduring peace after the Franco-Prussian War: "Nur das kann uns auch für das viele Theuere Blut in etwas trösten. Die Schlachten werden dießmal nicht umsonst gekämpft werden" (to Costenoble, August 29, 1870, *Cost. Corr.*, col. 1190). He stressed that the victory was achieved not under Prussian colors but under the black, red, and gold of a federated Germany, and predicted: "Das Wort *Deutschland* ist eine *Wahrheit* geworden, und wir dürfen jetzt getrost einer frohen und glücklichen Zeit entgegen sehen" (*KENS*, 2:75). This was the realization of a hope that he had expressed throughout his career. While sailing from Australia through the Torres Strait twenty years before, he was pleased to see a ship flying the Prussian colors, but wished they were the national black, red, and gold (*R*, 4:501). Upon hearing the British national anthem played to a German melody by Haydn, he was sad that the Germans needed no anthem, because they had no nation (*R*, 4:441). He held fast to a long-lived self-image of the Germans as innocent, idealistic, and humane in contrast to other peoples. The Germans could never, he wrote during the siege of Paris, begin a war of conquest or permit themselves to be sent against other peoples (*KENS*, 2:176). Doubtless he hoped that principles of freedom and democracy would develop in Germany; even at the height of his elation he commented that the press was not respected by the authorities, in contrast to America (*KENS*, 2:88). One can only speculate as to whether he would have been disappointed by developments in the Reich, as others who held similar views came to be, but it is not improbable. However, he was spared this distress, for the apparently indestructible adventurer died unexpectedly of a stroke on May 31, 1872, in the midst of plans for a journey to the Far East.

Whatever else one may think of him, Gerstäcker is one of the most amiable and attractive personalities encountered in the history of German letters. Three-quarters of a century ago, a young scholar at Yale, who made an attempt at the still unwritten biography of Gerstäcker but later abandoned the effort (and the profession), wrote of "the probity, the benevolence, the lovableness of his . . . character."[22] Fifteen years later another observer wrote of "the simplicity of his tastes and habits, his matter-of-factness, his love for the outdoors, his joy in an unrestrained life, his admiration for personal and national freedom, and, above all, his realistic outlook," and the historian Miller speaks of his "basic honesty."[23] To be sure, not all was sweetness and light. Probably he could not have managed as he did on the frontier without a certain amount of roughhousing. On one occasion, a rebuke from a riverboat captain for having given food to a poor old woman led to a quarrel in which Gerstäcker attempted to throw the captain overboard, and the captain marooned him in the middle of the night on a swampy riverbank (*SJ*, 1:141–43; a more personal account in *Br. 1*, 194). He tells of having to beat up a drunk, of problems with his boss on a plantation because he is not inclined to take orders, of a donnybrook in a tavern (*SJ*, 1:104; 2:18, 240). On the whole, however, he seems not to have been excessively combative, considering the circumstances.

He does appear recurrently irritable in correspondence with publishers. He even managed, to Cotta's astonishment, to get into an irreconcilable quarrel with the editor of the Augsburg *Allgemeine Zeitung*, Gustav Kolb (1798–1865), of whose fidelity and integrity we know from Heine's biography (*Br. 2*, 55–56). However, the cause of the stress lay in the conditions under which nineteenth-century German writers labored, in a poor, not fully literate, disunited, economically inefficient, and censorship-ridden land. Gerstäcker's great public success has deceived some observers about his prosperity; I doubt that he ever surpassed by much a level of modest subsistence. At the beginning of his career, he had difficulty getting paid for his writing at all (*Br. 1*, 248–49). Cotta professed to think well of the *Reisen*, which he predicted the public would take up "mit Begierde"—but 2,000 copies of a five-volume work? Such sales were hardly to be expected (*Br. 2*, 39). By comparison it might be noted that, not long afterward in America, free of censorship, internal tariffs, and, to be sure, royalties, a multivolume German-language edition of Heine's works sold 18,000 copies.[24] Like Heine and many others, Gerstäcker complained bitterly of book prices. In a literary satire he has the Devil remark that he is not stupid enough to lend money to a German writer (*KENS*, 1:25–26). The only recourse of the mid-nineteenth-century German professional writer was to write as unremittingly as possible in every possible genre and medium. The consequence is that their life works tend to be very large, and Gerstäcker's is no exception. Once he complained that one could not shake works out of one's sleeve and always be in a productive mood (*Br. 1*, 264), but, in fact, this is just what was required. Despite the admirable labors of the devoted amateurs of the Friedrich-Gerstäcker-Gesellschaft, we still do not have complete bibliographical control over his hundreds of publications in periodicals or the pirated editions and translations. Gerstäcker himself kept records, which are helpful, but they are not completely precise or exhaustive.[25] Like other writers of his time he composed, along with fiction, essays, and memoirs, also verse and dramas. The unsurprising result is a great qualitative range. Gerstäcker could be a skillful writer, but he could also turn out routine stuff that is as dull as any of the magazine fodder of his time. He produced not only books formed by his most conscientious intentions, but also outright potboilers. Once he perpetrated by plagiaristic synthesis of English-language sources a book on China without ever having been there.[26]

Some parts of this oeuvre will be left out of consideration here, such as the substantial amount of his writing about Latin America. It has received little attention, because most people in the German field, like myself, are not equipped to address it knowledgeably.[27] But it is also a less attractive part of his writing, because he could never bring to Latin America the level of sympathy and understanding that he felt for the United States. He found the countries chaotic, with their tiresome successions of revolutions and military dictatorships, their landscapes for the most part (excepting Mexico, *KENS*, 2:22) bleak and uninspiring, and the people undisciplined. They leave things unrepaired that "Americans" would fix (*Haz*, 18) and are inclined to procrastination (*KENS*, 1:242); they just cannot work like "Americans" (*R*, 1:244–45). They have, it is remarked in an account of an anarchic carnival in Lima, "Laune," but no true "Humor und Witz" (*AmT*, 1:149). The class differences in Ecuador he thought greater than those in London (*KENS*, 1:229), and the dirtiness of Quito he found beyond belief ("Bilder aus Quito," *Z6*, 3). Chile he thought the only country free of civil war and despotic generals (*KENS*, 1:207–8). One scholar has claimed that his 1871 novel *In Mexico* was influenced by the writing of "Sir John Retcliffe" (Herrmann Goedsche, 1815–78), the revolting yellow-journalist author of sensational current-events novels, one of which came to be a source of the *Protocols of the Elders of Zion*;[28] if true, this link would certainly put it into degrading company. While some of the stories are characteristically exciting, the settings, on the whole, are dispiriting. However, these works are not as integral to Gerstäcker's writings on the United States as Sealsfield's Mexican novels are to his, so they can be left aside for my purposes.

Another body of his work that has not been much addressed is his social fiction set in Germany. The first novel, *Pfarre und Schule,* is a polemical tract demanding the emancipation of schools from the oversight of the clergy. While this is an admirable purpose and some of the scenes of the torment of the virtuous by the malignant have a Dickensian flavor, the novel is not very good. It does give a picture of the widespread poverty of Germany at the time of the revolution of 1848, and there is a portrayal of a schoolmaster's hopeless poverty that anticipates a similar description in Raabe's *Der Hungerpastor* a number of years later. His last social novel, the witty and satirical *Im Eckfenster,* published in the year of his death, is a considerable improvement. It is, like many of Raabe's novels, a story of a returnee to his homeland who has become somewhat alienated by his foreign experience, and it is thought to be in some degree autobiographical, reflecting Gerstäcker's own experiences after his return from America. It has been given a little attention,[29] but Gerstäcker's writing of this kind, while not uninteresting, is probably not strong enough to invite study on its own merits and would have to be dealt with in a comprehensive account of his life.

A third area is rather surprising, given his generally rational and commonsensical nature: he liked to write stories of the supernatural. He wrote a book-length ghost story, *Das alte Haus,* and collected the short stories in a two-volume work, *Heimliche und unheimliche Geschichten* (Leipzig: Arnold, 1862). The former, with its interpenetration of a realistically depicted contemporary world and a fantastic realm, suggests an influence from E. T. A. Hoffmann, but it is rather good of its kind and is intriguing because the mystery is never fully clarified. This is true also of what became the most famous of the collected stories, "Germelshausen," a tale of a town that appears only once every hundred years. It was widely reprinted and translated, and it has had a long life as a German-language textbook, beginning in 1893;[30] it was still in use in my high school. I have been told that it was dramatized on the radio in the 1930s,[31] and it was said to have been the source of Alan Jay Lerner's and Frederick Loewe's musical *Brigadoon* in 1947.[32]

Until the relatively recent revival of interest in Gerstäcker, almost all of his career had disappeared entirely from view, except for the ghosts of Germelshausen in the elementary German classroom. An early student of our subject evidently could not get past the *Regulatoren* and the *Flußpiraten*: "it cannot be denied that the cultural and literary value of Gerstäcker's novels is far inferior to that of Sealsfield's works. . . . Gerstäcker is hardly more than an ordinary story-teller . . . his novels appear crude, superficial and without ideas."[33] A more recent scholar exhibits the same limitation: "Compared with Sealsfield's works, Gerstäcker's novels appear exceedingly superficial and somewhat crude. His plots are little more than a chain of exciting, suspensive adventures."[34] Neither critic seems to have penetrated to *Nach Amerika!* or *In Amerika*. It is possible that such judgments were abetted by a certain unliterary posture on Gerstäcker's part. At the outset of his writing career, he denied that he was a *Dichter* (in the sense of a poet, *Br.* 2, 233), and he never pretended to be anything other than a popular storyteller, though, as has already been pointed out, he was able to distinguish himself qualitatively from another of that sort, Möllhausen, and like any right-thinking writer he despised Eugène Sue (*R*, 5:49, 284; see also the reference to "die überspannte Phantasie eines Victor Hugo oder Eugen Sue" in *IA*, 3: 177). To Costenoble he had sufficient critical acumen to recommend another writer, unfortunately completely forgotten, on the strength of "ein besonderes Geschick psychologische Conflicte zu schildern" (*Cost. Corr.*, col. 1149). He made a point of being unlearned, merely a direct, unencumbered observer of people and nations (*KENS*, 1:6).

While he made no display of *Bildung*, he was rather better read than he let on. In 1844 he wrote and had performed a verse drama, *Kunibert von Eulenhorst der geschundene Raubritter*, the title of which clearly signals parody of a subliterary genre, only to be astonished that the audience took it "für baare Münze" (*Br.* 1, 240), so that, whatever his level of literary sophistication, it seems to have been somewhat more advanced than that of the general public. His allusions to Goethe, Schiller, and Eichendorff show that he had a command of the tag lines familiar to the normal middle-class German. He begins one of his letters to Schultz with a quotation that concludes: "wenn ich Euch auch einen goldenen Engel male, so wird er doch wie ein rother Löwe aussehen!" (*Br.* 1, 64; left unexplained by the editor). The passage is taken verbatim, almost down to the orthography, from the preface to the first volume of Heine's *Der Salon*, published a couple of years earlier;[35] the allusion suggests a discriminating alertness to contemporary literature. In a letter to Schultz he included a poem clearly under Heine's influence (*Br.* 1, 242–43), but that was not unusual at that time. There are some signs, especially in the *Regulatoren*, indicating that he knew of Sealsfield. As a young man Gerstäcker read, among numerous American and English writers, Washington Irving and Bulwer-Lytton, and, in his earliest youth, *Robinson Crusoe*, which, he tells us, set him dreaming of faraway places (*Br.* 1, 16, 29; *KENS*, 1:1–2). While drifting in a boat in the Pacific, he read Thomas Moore's still famous *Lalla Rookh*, he says, for the tenth time (*R*, 3:254). Like everyone else he read Dickens (allusion to *The Pickwick Papers*, *SJ*, 1:291). He recommended to Schultz the complete works of Captain Marryat, whom he later met in person in Cincinnati (*Br. 1*, 160, 202). He was quite conscious of the debt he shared with a large fraction of his generation to Cooper; in one place he trades for a long rifle "wie sie Cooper bei dem alten Hawkeye schildert" (*SJ*, 1: 272). This acknowledgment was important, because he came to regard Cooper as one of those consciousness-occupying writers who misled prospective emigrants about what they would find in America.

Although he seems to have looked upon his translation labors as hack work, one of the texts clearly left a strong imprint on him: Herman Melville's *Omoo*. He recalled it in the South Seas, where he had, according to his account, an experience of the interfusion of reality and imagination. Drifting in a whaleboat between Maiao and Moorea, he wonders if he is living in his imagination: "Und schrieb ich in diesem Augenblick nicht etwa einen Roman?" He remarks with a touch of self-irony: "vor allen Dingen bin ich als Köngl. Sächs. Schriftsteller vollkommen berechtigt irgend etwas Unmögliches zu träumen oder zu empfinden." Although he is drifting and running out of fruit to combat thirst, and must row the whaleboat with canoe paddles, he feels it is a miracle of God that he is able to be there (*R*, 3:262–64). Somewhat later he has a vision of an undersea town, and thinks it is perhaps the dream of his childhood, now realized (*R*, 3:276–79). When he gets to the island of Moorea, however, fiction and reality clash. He has a breakfast like that described by Melville, only messier, a contrast that leads to one of his most thoughtful passages:

> Das Alles ist die Prosa, das Ganze nimmt sich doch weit besser in einem Roman, als in der Wirklichkeit aus.—Und mit wie vielen vielen Sachen geht es so, vorzüglich mit Verhältnissen, an die wir nicht den Maßstab unseres gewöhnlichen Lebens legen können, weil er nicht dorthin paßt, und wir nun unserer Phantasie überlassen sich den Gegenstand nach Gefallen auszumalen. Thut man das nun allein zu seiner Unterhaltung, so ist die Phantasie gerade die beste Aushülfe, die man auf der weiten Welt dazu finden könnte—will man einen ernsten und wichtigen Zweck damit verbinden, handelt es sich, wie zum Beispiel bei alle den Schilderungen und Beschreibungen, die mit der Auswanderung in Verbindung stehen, um eine *Lebensfrage*, dann wird die eigene Phantasie unser gefährlichster Gegner, und hat uns da schon manchen entsetzlichen Streich gespielt, hat schon manchen armen Teufel auf das schauerlichste in die Dinte geritten, und die Leute haben dann *Recht* und *Unrecht*, wenn sie eben nur den Beschreibungen die Schuld geben, denn die Beschreibungen mögen ganz wahr seyn,

aber—sie hielten sich eben nur an die freundlichen Punkte des Beschriebenen, und schwiegen über das Andere.

(R, 3:308–09)

For a number of reasons it seems that his vocation as a writer was not accidental but was revealed to him. Perhaps the diaries sent to his mother were not written with publication in mind, but the descriptiveness of the letters to Schultz even before leaving Germany often looks like practice writing, and Schultz seems to have perceived this, for, reminded of "Cooper, Scott u. Irving" (Br. 1, 87, 88), he replied: "höre Fritz, quittire die Oeconomie sammt Stallfütterung und Mistfuhren und werde ein Schriftsteller!" (Br. 1, 88, 87). By 1845, Gerstäcker is able to give Schultz advice about writing (Br. 1, 256). In the preface to his first book, while he claims no other ambition than "eine schlichte Erzählung und Schilderung meines dortigen Lebens und Treibens," he apologizes that his six years away from the German language may have harmed his style, suggesting that he was not indifferent to craft (SJ, 1:x). Although this is a travel work, in the first sentence he begins to novelize it in the form of dialogue (SJ, 1:1). For his second journey he had obtained an English copybook that enabled him to make duplicates while writing and to send the originals directly to one of his publishers.

In the course of time he found his fame emotionally gratifying; he called having been recognized as a known writer on board ship to California "ein Liebeszins, den mir die Schriftstellerei abwirft" (R, 1:445). When he arrived there he remarked upon the richness of storytelling inspiration: "ich selber hätte kein günstigeres Land, keine günstigere Zeit abpassen können, Stoff für ein Lebensalter zu sammeln. Die Hauptsache war dabei, daß ich Alles fix und fertig—vollkommen reif und ausgebildet fand; ich brauchte nur einzuschneiden und zu trocknen" (R, 2:219). Later he remarked that the gold mines did not yield him much gold, but for the writer they were an "Eldorado" (R, 2:357). It did not go unnoticed that he was seeking adventure for the sake of writing. In 1852 the prominent caricaturist Carl Reinhardt, who was to be one of the illustrators of *Nach Amerika!*, published a cartoon entitled "Friedrich Gerstäcker auf der Reise," showing him in the forest primeval: an alligator has him by the coattail as he endeavors to subdue a fierce snake with his rifle butt; from the front he is being attacked by a rampaging buffalo and a most barbarous-looking Indian. The caption reads: "Hurrah! das gibt wieder einen prächtigen Artikel für die Allgemeine Zeitung!"[36] In the middle of his career he wrote movingly of what his fate had brought him: "Ueberhaupt gehöre ich zu jenen glücklichen Menschen, denen Gott seine wunderbare schöne Welt nach allen Richtungen hin ausgebreitet und gezeigt hat. Ich durfte dem Rauschen der Palmen, wie dem der Gletscherwasser, dem donnernden Sturz des Niagara, wie der Brandung der Südsee über den Corallenriffen lauschen, durfte dem Hirsch und Bär im amerikanischen, dem Rhinoceros im indischen Urwald, dem Kängeruh im australischen Busch, dem Guanako in den Cordilleren folgen" (*Amt*, 1:195–96). Yet it would be consonant with his character if he had not always been so comfortable in his vocation as he sounds here.

Everyone who has observed Gerstäcker closely, almost without exception, has commented on the oscillation in his temperament. For example: "Nowhere was he ever *really* comfortable; nowhere . . . did he ever settle, either physically or psychically"; "no matter where he was, he wanted to be somewhere else"; "Die Spannung zwischen Fernweh und Heimweh wird, sobald die Ferne nahe genug gerückt ist, zur Spannung zwischen Erwartung und Enttäuschung, die die Erfüllung des Wunsches nach Abenteuern verzögert."[37] When he was at home in Germany, the most acute wanderlust would beset him, for he could not live, as he repeatedly said, as a philistine (*Br. 1*, 185); when he was on his travels, driven through the world, as he once put it, like a masterless dog (*Br. 1*, 247), he was beset by homesickness. No sooner had he got on board ship on his first journey to America than he began to wonder if he would be homesick (*Br. 1*, 167). As a traveler he was more dogged than heroic; his accounts and stories are full of the miseries of heat, cold, hunger, mosquitoes, swamp fevers, apparently hopeless situations, and dangers real and imagined; with wry self-irony he sometimes implies that only a moron would have gotten into such scrapes. The loneliness could be fierce; at his first Christmas alone on the frontier he felt himself on the edge of insanity and must choke down his homesickness; a man is a fool to long to get away from his home and family (*Br. 1*, 191, 193–94, 197). But soon afterward, as he is about to give up his job with the silversmith in Cincinnati: "Lange hat nun das wilde mit dem ehrbaren Leben gestritten, aber Gott sei Dank das wilde hat den Sieg davongetragen" (*Br. 1*, 200). Upon reaching New Orleans after a stressful journey: "die große gewaltige Stadt machte, nach dem langen einsamen Leben in der Wildniß einen merkwürdigen, fast beengenden Eindruck auf mich" ("Canoefahrt auf dem Red-River in Nordamerika," *Z5*, 48). In winter, eating bear meat three times a day, he longs for a warm house in Europe, and he could be attacked by homesickness in the midst of duck hunting; he has another acute attack on New Year's Eve in the wilderness of the Ozarks, feeling lost to the world with no attractive future and imagining himself as an old, white-haired, friendless hunter, like Cooper's Hawkeye (*SJ*, 1:270; 2:86, 142). No sooner is he back in the fatherland than he reports his unhappiness, thinks it is improbable he will ever have a "Heimath," and longs to depart "vielleicht wieder nach America, Afrika, Australien oder Ostindien es ist Alles so ziemlich egal"; now he is homesick for Arkansas; the Germans all seem too political and hypocritical, and he feels like a wallflower; just before getting married, he is homesick for the forest (*Br. 1*, 230, 231, 240, 254).

The pattern is permanent. "Ich habe das Reisen herzlich satt," he wrote Cotta from Java, "& sehne mich nach der Heimath" (*Br. 2*, 32); in his travel book, however, he reported that he wanted to go home, but not just then; he longs for his fatherland, but does not have one (*R*, 5:309, 451). No more traveling, he says after arriving at Bremen, perhaps intentionally arousing a smile in the reader (*R*, 5:472). Amid the ecstasies of reaching the ridge of the Cordilleras in the face of great dangers, he is touched by homesickness (*R*, 1:312). He longed to leave the mines of California, and when he does so, he has the pain of parting, for he has come to love the "cedars," that is, the redwoods (*R*, 2:432–33, 437). He was quite aware of this tendency in himself. To his friend he wrote, after praising the peaceful life of an American farmer in the green forest with his dear wife, "Hermann das ist der Wurm der mir am Herzen frißt, diese ununterdrückbare Sehnsucht nach stiller Häuslichkeit und dabei wieder der wilde Hang ins Weite," applying to himself Faust's lines about having two souls in his breast (*Br. 1*, 188). One observer has remarked that his *Heimweh* and his *Fernweh* were actually the same feeling.[38]

This permanent unease and feeling of homelessness may, of course, derive from the circumstances of his childhood, when he had no real permanent home. It is also clear from his letters to Schultz that the death of his father when he was nine years old left him feeling bereft. In one despairing night he attempted to summon his father's spirit (*Br. 1*, 24). He also intermittently ascribed his unstable emotions to lost love, but his disappointments in courtship seem, as he recounted them, to be commonplace adolescent experiences; they cannot be more than symptomatic of a deeper disposition. One constant is the combination of his perpetual loneliness with his tendency to seek solitude. During the Red River trip cited earlier, he fell out of his canoe, causing him to consider the dangers of solitude—"Der Mensch ist nun einmal ein geselliges Geschöpf"—but for his part he prefers to be alone than be bored by a companion; he is then immediately delighted to find a sign of *people* at a farmstead, but there is no one there but a dog; he helps himself to a piece of cake, leaves a quarter, and departs (*Z5*, 41).

If one surveys his life, one finds that, in comparison to most people, he spent a large proportion of his days alone. Even when he is in company or groups, his associations are rarely intimate. In fact, I think he did not like many people very much, and that he had a relatively low opinion of the general run of mankind. Even in his children's book he observes: "Der Mensch ist ja einmal ein blutdürstiges grausames Thier—wie der Panther" (FW, 202). He generally avoided heroic depiction and tended to inject his oscillating temperament into the heart of his characterizations. A compact example occurs in an otherwise slight Californian story, in which an alcoholic Irish vagabond, having been expelled by the proprietor of a liquor tent, besieges it by building a smoky campfire right outside it. Here occurs the following sentence: "Sein Wirth war ein Franzose und hatte den fidelen Burschen eigentlich gern, auch aus ihm schon herausgeschraubt, was nur herauszubekommen war und dafür vielleicht mehr Geduld mit ihm später gehabt, als mancher Andere in Californien, dem Land des Augenblicks, gehabt haben würde" (Z1, 96). Here, in the very rhythm of the sentence, Gerstäcker asserts but then relativizes cordiality, then makes opportunistic materialism a motive for forbearance. The Australian harbor police, whose task it is to return escaped sailors to their tyrannical captains, are very active and competent, but somehow are unable to catch any of the sailors, who are wandering the streets and dives of Sydney, as long as the bounty is only one pound sterling per head (Z7, 98); when it increases, they do much better. There are many examples of this kind of checkered characterization, through which realism takes the form of a moderate cynicism about the human condition.[39]

Gerstäcker had a highly developed witty and humorous side, and at times he could exude high spirits and self-confidence. To Schultz he would from time to time gaily describe his exotic appearance; in Cincinnati he looks so wild that "in Deutschland wäre ich sicher nicht der Policey entgangen!" (Br. 1, 195). He finds his transformation into a gentleman when taking up the management of the Louisiana hotel just as amusing: "anstatt des ledernen Jagdhemds, leggins und Moccasins habe ich einen kattunen Frack couleurte Sommerhosen mit Gamaschen nach der Mode gemacht & geputzte Stiefeln an, statt des Messers & der büchse an der Seite ein seidenes Schnupftuch in der Tasche, von dem der Zipfel eine Kleinigkeit heraussieht..." (Br. 1, 226). To Cotta, as self-advertising for his advance but also truthfully, he ascribes to himself "ein gesunder Körper, ein guter durch Nichts zu störender Muth und eiserne Ausdauer" (Br. 2, 19). Though occasionally felled by injury or illness, Gerstäcker must certainly have been an exceptionally strong and tough man. Yet he was highly susceptible to an almost existential pessimism. In the first and gloomiest of the emigration novels, the narrator muses that the emigrants arriving in New York will be deceived by the beauty of the coast and fail to foresee "all die Noth, all den Gram, der auch unter den Bewohnern dieses, *wie jedes andern Landes* herrscht" (*DAFS*, 38; my emphasis). In Java, where he experienced one of the most interesting and stimulating episodes of his traveling career, a meditation on the grievous hatred that must obtain between the natives and the foreign colonialists generates a sorrowful commentary:

> es ist ja auf der ganzen Welt nicht anders, und wohin wir auch kommen, wohin wir blicken, schauen wir, unter oft güldener Oberfläche, Jammer und Verzweiflung, Elend und Tod—wir gehen auch zuletzt gar nicht selten gleichgültig, und tausendmal unbewußt daran vorüber; richtet man dann aber Blick und Geist einmal fest auf einen solchen Punkt, dann kann man's auch nicht gut verhindern, daß es Einem mit Schmerz und Galle durch die Seele schneidet.—O wer all das Elend auf der Welt zu lindern vermöchte.
>
> (*R*, 5:388)

Thus the oscillations of his temperament are not just a matter of shuttling between wanderlust and homesickness, as they have often been described, but constitute a labile dynamic fundamental to his personality that caused him to be more self-reflective than he might otherwise have been and may be one source of his creative energy as a writer. So fundamental were they that, as we shall see in the next chapter, they even occasionally penetrated the most enduring passion of his life.

# 7. The Multicultural Bear Hunt: An Introduction to Gerstäcker's Narrative Devices

My contention is that, while Gerstäcker's *most important* works are his major novels of America, his *best* writing is in his stories. Not, to be sure, in all of them. Generally he seems artistically unambitious, that is, he relied upon certain native storytelling gifts without endeavoring to stretch or refine them very much. But these gifts were considerable, with an instinct for shape, pace, and suspense, and sometimes an unexpected turn that may remind us of O. Henry. When reading a large number of his stories, it is easy to see, even taking their considerable qualitative span into account, how he became a star of the domestic periodical in mid-nineteenth-century Germany. One can readily imagine that many readers turned to the page on which they found his name. He puts no intellectual demands on the reader, but he can be ingenious and dexterous, and he often does have something of substance to say. What I should like to do here is to see him for a bit inside out, so to speak, that is, to look at a fairly simple story and expand some observations on it. It is a very early story, written before he came to his great theme of the emigration, and for that reason might serve as an introduction to some of his narrative procedures and ways of representing an American experience.

The story was originally published in 1844 in the Leipzig *Novellenzeitung*, then as "Höhlenjagd in den westlichen Gebirgen" in the first volume of *Mississippibilder* in 1847 (*MB*, 1:65–109). It tells of three backwoods hunters on a chilly winter day: a German named Werner, an Indian named Tessakeh, and an Englishman named Redham. It almost sounds like the beginning of a joke—a German, an Indian, and an Englishman go into a bar—but although Gerstäcker could be a witty and sometimes quite comic writer, he is not so here, as the story maintains the even, neutral, middle style that is his most characteristic tone. The hunters come across a vertical entrance to a cave in which they suppose a bear to be hibernating. The German and the Indian climb down into the cave, while the Englishman remains above, maintaining a campfire. As the hunters crawl through the cave, they come to a deep chasm. The German leads the way across by squeezing himself against the walls of the cave. A tense encounter with a rattlesnake causes the bear to wake up. The German shoots the bear, but not fatally; the wounded animal rushes past them back into the passage, as the Indian attacks it with a knife. The bear dies just on the other side of the chasm, its carcass blocking the passage. The German, weakened by hunger and exertion, makes a desperate effort to cross the chasm and push the bear back, but fails and winds up hanging by his hands from the edge. The Indian works his way across backward, with great effort squeezes by the bear, and manages to pull it a little way from the edge, from where he is able to rescue the German, who has been hanging on with his last strength. Now the exhausted men must move the bear through the passage and figure out how to get it up to the top. When they have succeeded in dragging the carcass to the exit, they find that the Englishman, who has been waiting patiently, has been joined by a number of other backwoodsmen; together they haul the bear up with a rope, and the story ends with a feast of bear ribs. Altogether, the German and the Indian have been in the cave for eighteen hours.

I picked this story because it exhibits good qualities of its kind. It is economical and well formed, composed in a rhythm of suspense and relaxation. It effectively exploits the claustrophobia to which many of us are subject to a greater or lesser degree. It occurred to me that it might be suitable for a movie treatment, though it would have to be a film noir in the literal sense, since much of the action takes place in the dark. In considering it, we might begin with the aspect that may be the most recalcitrant for many modern readers: that it is a hunting story. In fact, even those who are not opposed to or disgusted by hunting in principle might ask what sort of a sport this is, shooting a hibernating bear. The story makes the reason explicit: it ought to be easier and safer to kill a sleeping bear than an alert one—though this turned out not to be exactly the case here.

Stories and reminiscences of hunting make up a substantial part of Gerstäcker's oeuvre. Hunting was his passion. He even produced a kind of coffee-table book, containing verses on the hunting possibilities of each month of the year, hunting stories, and, for children, an illustrated alphabet of game animals with verse captions, entitled "Moralisches Jäger-A-B-C."[1] There is good reason to think that hunting was his major motive for going to America in the first place, where, if there were any laws about hunting, in contrast to Germany they were not obeyed (*AWS*, 1:7–8), and where he undoubtedly became very skilled. At an early stage of his first journey he went to Canada because he heard there were wolves and bears there, and killed a bear with the help of an Indian (*Br. 1*, 187; *SJ*, 1:83–85); in the Arkansas backwoods he had hand-to-hand combat with a bear, and later he told of a hunt for a male bear in a cave (*SJ*, 1:152–54; 2:146–47; for the direct source anecdote of our story, see 2:189–204). When he first got to California, he tells us, he initially went hunting for bear instead of gold (*R*, 2:22). Now it is true that the hunting in the story at hand is for sustenance. The men are hungry and out of provisions before the bear hunt begins; they are weak from hunger at the end and in need of the meat. As a backwoodsman, Gerstäcker sustained himself almost exclusively from game. In one place he commented that to make money from hunting, as in fur trapping, turns it into murder (*AWS*, 1:75). However, that is not all there is to it. For he also became a sporting hunter, a companion eventually of the duke of Gotha and the archduke Johann of Austria, an experience that doubtless inclined him to his opinion that in Germany hunting tended to break down class barriers somewhat (*R*, 5:162). He actively sought opportunities to hunt, for example in Java, where he gives an entertaining account of his futile efforts to oppose his solitary backwoods habits to the Indonesian custom of hunting in groups, with beaters and servants (*R*, 5:170–74, 258–82). It is interesting to note in this connection that while Gerstäcker consistently advised emigrants to defer in their ideas of things to Americans and experienced settlers, he does not feel obliged to do so in colonial Java (but see the footnote, 281–82, somewhat justifying the Javanese customs).

The hunting impulse seems psychologically significant and also connected in a complex way with his writing, since, although originally his writing was a by-product of his adventures, it seems clear that subsequently his adventures were undertaken for the sake of writing. He knew that the passion for hunting was not shared by all his potential readers and that it might be incommunicable to those who did not share it (*R*, 5:157). In one place he wrote rather irritatingly that those who do not share a love of hunting—I am one of them—are unmanly, but then, in a more forthcoming mood, he tried to help the nonhunting reader share his feelings about it (*AmT*, 1:197, 216). Of course, hunting plays a large role in the German Western, and bear hunts are not uncommon. Strubberg has a scene in which an Indian goes after a bear in a cave and drives it out, whereupon the narrator shoots it; afterward the Indian and the white cooperate in pursuing the wounded animal and killing it (*AJR*, 193–94). It is not inconceivable that this scene was influenced by one of Gerstäcker's tales. Even in Reinhold Solger's *Anton in Amerika*, of which there will be more to say in excursus II, the citified protagonist fights a bear in an exciting scene: his lady friend has shot the bear, which chases her; Antonio jumps on top of it, so that she can shoot it in the ear and kill it (*AA*, 2:49). A study of German adventure literature has pointed out: "das Motiv des 'Bärenkampfes' wird in der Abenteuerliteratur häufig und mit zahlreichen Änderungen wiederholt; es erhält seine Bedeutung aus dem archetypischen Bild des Drachenkampfes."[2] But such comparisons only highlight the realistic ground of Gerstäcker's narrations. Putting them into a mythic context is a literary-critical extrapolation; Gerstäcker really did hunt bear for long periods, accompanied for a time with a dog named Beargrease, as Karl May and his disciples noted.[3] There is every reason to think that Gerstäcker's accounts are reflections of experience and his fictions shapelier formations of them.

Naturally, Gerstäcker's story might be put into the context of the hunting literature of the American South. In a sense, he did so himself by translating, to considerable acclaim, Charles Fenno Hoffman's *Wild Scenes in the Forest and Prairie* (1839, translation 1845).[4] Hoffman (1806–84), despite losing a leg in a boyhood accident, became a fairly adventurous westerner. Gerstäcker published a number of chapters of the translation separately in the Leipzig *Pfennig-Magazin der Gesellschaft zur Verbreitung gemeinnütziger Kenntnisse* (Z4) and in the Stuttgart periodical *Das Buch der Welt* (Z6), including one in 1846 on a confrontation with a bear. However, Hoffman's tone is whimsical and faux-naïf: "folks that ain't used to the woods, sometimes get mighty flurried when they meet these wild animals."[5] The story is a slight anecdote about a man in a boat who shoots a she-bear, which then climbs into the boat and indicates a demand to be rowed to the other side of the lake. The editor of the periodical appended a superfluous note: "für die Wahrheit der Geschichte mögen wir nicht bürgen" ("Eine Bärengeschichte," Z6, 351). This is clearly not on Gerstäcker's own level. To adumbrate comparisons with American images, we shall have to go beyond his own purview.

An essay entitled "In Defense of Blood Sports," by Walter Sullivan, evidently an epigone of the so-called Southern Agrarians, does not help us very much. Sullivan reminds us that "the authorization of blood sports is in Genesis" while asserting that the hunter is "the Nietzschean tragic figure, the synthesis of the Apollinian and Dionysian impulses," and in general seeing hunting as the recovery of a lost sense of the sacred and unity with nature.[6] A more pertinent starting point might be the hunting essays of William Elliott of South Carolina, which were printed in periodicals before appearing in book form in 1846 and are thus contemporaneous with Gerstäcker's story. Among these is a yarn about having killed two bears with one shot, a feat that Elliott's fellow hunters at first, understandably, find hard to believe. There is a facetious intimacy with the reader in Elliott's mode of narration that is lighter in weight than Gerstäcker's tone. It has been pointed out that Elliott was a minor writer whose imagination, like that of other antebellum writers, was limited by the need not to release it to the point where it would challenge the ideological structure of his public, and that his story did not have literary dignity for the author but was no more than a hunting sketch.[7] Still, Elliott is able to imply the connection between hunting and writing, for his fundamental posture is one not so much of the hunter as of the storyteller: "The sportsman, who gives a true description of his sports, *must be an egotist*. It is his *necessity*. The things, which *he* has seen or done, are precisely those which make the liveliest impression; and with none other but such as are thus brightly enshrined in his memory, should he attempt the difficult task of interesting the careless or preoccupied."[8] Elliott's defense of hunting has two dimensions. One is of male bonding: hunting generates social skills and virtues of foresight, punctuality, observation, sagacity, and promptitude, and "promotes social intercourse and the interchange of friendly offices between neighbors"; the other is that it is a form of pleasure and amusement to be defended against puritanical repressiveness.[9] Male and social bonding is not a very prominent issue for Gerstäcker, despite the valued cooperativeness in our exemplary story, because of the tendency for his hunter, both in memoirs and fictions, to be largely solitary; and, as we shall see, amusement is not exactly the affect that he associated with such adventures.

To go forward almost exactly one hundred years to William Faulkner's elaborate novella *The Bear* of 1942 would be not quite fair to either of these writers.[10] The story's virtually medieval atmosphere of quest and entitlement and the anthropomorphization of the great bear Old Ben as a worthy adversary and, in his own way, mentor in a young man's process of *Bildung* would have been foreign to Gerstäcker, as Faulkner's highly colored, surgically subjective style would have been foreign to Gerstäcker's sense of limits, of the ordinary. The most basic difference, however, lies in the attitude toward the wilderness. Gerstäcker, like Elliott, saw the diminution of the wilderness in the face of cultivation, but regarded the process as inevitable. Elliott pointed out that bears were hardly ever found by hunters any more in South Carolina,[11] at the same time as Gerstäcker, farther west in Arkansas, was aware of the depletion of game by hunting, which would soon be found only in the Indian Territory and the Rockies, owing, as the relentless hunter rather captiously put it, to the American "Vertilgungskrieg gegen die armen Hirsche und Bären" (*SJ*, 1:xii; see also his advice to emigrants on this matter, *Wie?*, 120–25). Faulkner, the more modern writer, is also the more nostalgic. The sacral unity with nature, the command over and at the same time subordination to the instincts that are the goal of *Bildung* as a skilled hunter and woodsman are incompatible with civilization. Thus Ike McCaslin, on reaching his majority, renounces his inherited property, not only because its acquisition has been associated with injustice but also because property and nature are incongruent with one another—that is, what he has acquired in his quest cannot be owned. This is one of the myriad ways in which literature of the twentieth century retreats from the frontiers of nineteenth-century literature into regressive utopias.

In any case, one element in Gerstäcker's motivation was the courting of danger. He preferred hunting bear because it was the most dangerous game. The cave story is by no means the only depiction of hunting as a risky contest. In one of his autobiographical accounts he tells of a hunting companion being killed by a bear, while he himself was seriously injured (*SJ*, 2:226–27). On another occasion some hunters are nearly killed by a mother bear protecting her cubs, but the men kill and eat her instead; as one of them remarks: "Die Bestie hatte so große Lust mich zu verzehren, daß ich auf jeden Fall wissen will, wie *ihr* Fleisch schmeckt" (*MB*, 3:111). Despite this flippancy, the bear is no joke. If Gerstäcker could have lived long enough to encounter the scene in the first volume of Karl May's *Winnetou*, in which the recently dubbed Old Shatterhand blinds a grizzly by shooting out its eyes and then kills it with his knife, he might have died laughing. In the short novel *Der Flatbootmann* of 1858 there is an amusing scene in which a boatman goes off to hunt alligators and gets himself into a situation in which the alligators are hunting him. Since the hunting that involves danger and physical effort is best, the most preferable game in Germany, we are told, is the mountain goat (*AmT*, 1:194).

He conspicuously sought out difficulty and danger. This urge seems to have been a matter of proving himself primarily to himself; Brenner has claimed that he was the only one of the travel writers realistic about danger and difficulty,[12] and, while this may be an exaggeration, he does not make many of his experiences sound like fun. It may be a somewhat self-aggrandizing gesture when he occasionally minimizes perceived dangers: the grizzlies in California, he tells us, are not as frightening as people say (*R*, 2:304), a matter on which he may have been mistaken and for once failed in his endeavor to provide prudent information; lions, he found, just run away and there is no danger from any animals in Africa except, perhaps, elephants ("Die Jagd in Ober-Abyssinien," *Z5*, 60–61); the dangers of rhinoceros hunting have been exaggerated

(*R*, 5:255). Another gesture of minimization is his list of the dangers of civilized life:

> Eisenbahnunglücke fallen alle Augenblicke vor, Häuser und Brücken stürzen ein, Feuer bricht aus, der Blitz erschlägt Leute am Kaffeetisch oder im Bureau, Pferde gehen durch, tolle Hunde laufen herum, Trichinen bringen ganze Familien um, Petroleumlampen explodiren, so daß einem armen Wilden da draußen im Urwald ganz angst und bange werden müßte, wenn er von solchen schrecklichen Geschichten hört, und er gewiß Gott danken würde, daß er dort, wo er sich gerade befindet, zwischen seinen sehr ungefährlichen Tigern und Schlangen sitzt, und nicht jenen zahllosen Gefahren eines civilisirten Lebens ausgesetzt zu sein braucht.
>
> (NR, 1:viii–ix)

Much of the time, however, he seems avid for situations that will test him. During his adolescence he expressed the hope that the Brazilian wilderness might confront him with unspeakable dangers (*Br. 1*, 13). In one of his less lucid comments, it is asserted that danger belongs to travel, unless one is compensated with scenery: "Ueberhaupt gehört, meiner Meinung nach, etwas Gefahr mit zu den und zwar nothwendigen Annehmlichkeiten einer Reise, die Scenerie müßte denn so wundervoll seyn daß sie für alles Andere, also auch für diesen Mangel, genügende Entschädigung böte" (*R*, 4:489).

It becomes almost a leitmotif that he will insist on doing something against which others have warned him. On his first Atlantic crossing he went swimming in the sea against the captain's orders and hoped for a storm (*SJ*, 1:49; private account *Br. 1*, 170–71, where he tells of climbing the ship's rigging and being chased by the sailors). He is told by others that it is impossible to travel on foot through Indiana and Illinois in the winter, "so will ich es denn mit Gottes Hülfe frisch versuchen," and finds that the others were not so wrong (*Br. 1*, 187, 190). On the Red River he is told that he cannot maneuver a canoe through the "raft," that is, a mass of cut timber blocking the river, so he decides to try it ("Canoefahrt auf dem Red-River in Amerika," *Z5*, 43).[13] In Argentina he is told that it is impossible to cross the pampas in winter, so he does it anyway (*R*, 1:80–81). Everyone said that it was not possible to travel to Chile across the Cordilleras in winter; he feels greatness in himself at the challenge (*R*, 1:190, 234). Everyone was nearly right; his account of the crossing is rather harrowing, but there is an exhilarating description of the hot springs he found in the midst of the ice and snow (*R*, 1:301–2). In Australia he was warned against traveling into the interior, so he determined to go (*R*, 4:11–13). Everyone said that it was not possible to paddle the length of the Murray River in a hand-made dugout canoe, and this time everyone was right; the canoe with most of his belongings was lost, and he was obliged to cover the 700 miles of outback to Adelaide on foot. He called it the wildest, most adventurous march of his life (*R*, 4:120). The consequence of it was a certain amount of notoriety; in an isolated police station he discovered that his plan to canoe down the Murray had already been reported in a Sydney newspaper (*R*, 4:176). When he reached Adelaide, he found that the governor of South Australia had heard of him; he was pleased to be presented to Colonial Secretary Charles Sturt (1795–1869), who had been an intrepid explorer of the Murray River system around 1830; and he was invited to write an article in the local newspaper on the navigability of the Murray—a matter on which he had doubtless acquired a pessimistic opinion (*R*, 4:280–81). This is a compact example of how his intrepidity related to a public image and a modicum of fame as a writer. Having resumed his journey, he also ignored the advice not to travel into the interior of Java (*R*, 5:9). This pattern is too repetitious to be accidental. There is a degree of self-dramatization in it, of foregrounding the persona as uncommonly independent, skeptical of the anxieties of ordinary people, and confident of managing adversity. He was also capable of observing himself acting out this role; he was, he says of himself, "jung und gesund und hielt mich für einen Mitbesitzer der ganzen Welt" ("Canoefahrt auf dem Red-River in Nordamerika," *Z5*, 37).

Yet his characteristic oscillation emerges in his attitude toward danger, also. He observed reasonably that when traveling he wanted a strange place, strange people, and some danger—but not too much, as in the Australian wilderness (*AmT*, 2:211), where he found an armed band of aborigines too exciting to be pleasant (*R*, 4:168). On more than one perilous occasion, he commented that things were becoming, as he put it in connection with his crossing of the Cordilleras, "ein *klein* wenig zu interessant" (*R*, 1:319); still, he recurrently undertook such things. In this respect he differs somewhat from the German in his story of the bear hunt in the cave, which, nevertheless, like much of his fiction, repeats or varies motifs found in his autobiographical writing. The fictional version, despite its almost superhuman triumph over adversity, ends on a curiously wry, antiheroic note. The German and the Indian are both of the opinion, "daß sie, und wenn zwanzig Bären darin steckten, in *die* Höhle nicht mehr hineingingen, denn es wäre, wie der Indianer gar nicht unrichtig bemerkte: Zu viel Mühe und zu wenig Fleisch" (*MB*, 1:109).

Like Werner and Tessakeh in our story, he, too, could occasionally get too much of adversity. In one such mood he declines an invitation to hunt bear, as he has had enough of slogging through swamps and hunting for a while ("Canoefahrt auf dem Red-River in Nordamerika," Z5, 40). It also occurred to him that his repetitious tales of hunting might become monotonous for the reader (*Br. 1*, 225). But more interesting are his occasional reflections on the barbarity of hunting and his addictive complicity in it. In a reminiscence of 1858 over his whole hunting career thus far, he recalled the enormous gratification he felt at the age of eighteen when he had shot his first rabbit and his tremendous desire to become a hunter. Attracted by the forbidden, he became a violator of hunting regulations, remarking of this that every passionate hunter is an instinctive poacher (*AmT*, 1:154–59). This anarchistic affect is a basic symptom of the resistance to philistinism and civilization that impels the adventurer, as the awareness of it is a symptom of belonging to civilization nevertheless. In a curious and telling juxtaposition, he remarks of alligators that, despite their terrible reputation, he has always found them "liebe, harmlose Thiere," which he nevertheless zealously hunts (*SJ*, 2:285). In the Cordilleras he comes to ruminate on the cruelty of hunters, as he realizes that he wants to kill a fox for no reason: "Jäger sind eigentlich recht grausame Geschöpfe. Obgleich mir die arme Bestie in ihrem ganzen Leben noch nichts zu leide gethan, ja trotzdem, daß ich nicht einmal den geringsten Nutzen aus ihr ziehen konnte, wenn ich sie wirklich erlegte, war doch mein erster Gedanke *Mord*, und ich erwartete mit wahrhafter Schadenfreude den Augenblick wo der Fuchs in Schußnähe kommen würde" (*R*, 1:305).

As is commonly the case, his level of empathy with animals was anthropocentric. He speculated some on the behavior of bears but concluded, Who knows what bears think? (*SJ*, 1:286).[14] Monkeys, however, are too anthropoid to shoot (*R*, 5:244–45). From his account of his life in the backwoods, it appears that there were many days in which his diet consisted exclusively of meat from the game he had shot. But his description of a slaughterhouse in Buenos Aires sounds like a modern vegetarian tract; he was so disgusted that he almost lost his taste for meat and ate none for two days (*R*, 1:125–34). Thus the habit of oscillation reaches into the most elemental components of his personality. Strubberg, too, incidentally also a passionate hunter who described himself as shooting everything that moved, including magnificent condors, expressed ambiguity about the sport and the fragility of its motivation: "Die Jagd ist das grausamste Spiel, welchem der Mensch sich hingeben kann.... Der Reiz liegt lediglich in der Frage: 'triffst du oder triffst du nicht?' nimmt man diesen Zweifel hinweg, so ist es aus mit der Leidenschaft, und niemand wird mehr zum Vergnügen auf die Jagd gehen" (*AJR*, 197–98, 61–62).

There is a misguided tendency in some work on Gerstäcker to see him as a Romantic writer of Cooperian, perhaps Thoreauvian, even Rousseauistic outlook, impelled by longing for Edenic nature and primitive relationships. It is true that he loved nature and there are many passages of eloquent nature description in his writing. But, after all, much of North America *is*, in actual fact, beautiful or sublime to this day; why should it not be accounted as realism so to describe it? Gerstäcker does not notably spiritualize nature, which has also its insalubrious, destructive, and even life-threatening side. The wilderness in his writing can be a bleak and intimidating place, and there is plenty of strife and meanness to be encountered in it. There may seem to be Edenic elements in our story, despite the danger and discomfort it depicts, in the instinctive sense of community that obtains among the characters, but Gerstäcker merely wishes to show something about the way human relations can develop in America. The German and the Indian accomplish together what neither could have done alone. When one falters, the other takes the initiative. It is the Indian who fashions a ladder from a sapling that allows them to descend into the cave, who suggests that the German drop a bullet into the chasm to test its depth, who kills the rattlesnake with his tomahawk, and who effects the rescue from the major crisis. At other times the Indian is cautious and must be urged on by the German; it is he with his strength who finds the way across the chasm; the Indian is just as glad to see the German assume the greater danger by leading. To be sure, the German, to whose inner thoughts the narration is closer, is more self-conscious and therefore insecure about proving himself: "verdammt will ich sein," he says to himself at one point, "wenn Du Furcht an mir bemerken sollst" (*MB*, 1:81)—a fear he certainly does feel. But at the end he graciously praises the Indian for saving his life twice, to which the latter replies: "Tessakeh und sein weißer Bruder sind eins!" (*MB*, 1:106).

Nor is the Englishman devalued for his prudence in not entering the cave. He performs a service by maintaining the campfire and waiting patiently through the night for the others to return, and also by attracting the wandering backwoodsmen, without whose help it probably would have been impossible to hoist the bear from the cave. All in all, it is an encouraging picture of the way free men spontaneously and generously cooperate in adversity. Gerstäcker's characterizations, although they have typological limits, are varied and flexible. His German Werner is not *the* German, or *the* German American. Nevertheless, he is a German for a reason: he shows how a German can conduct himself in a free society. The cave story is an example of how human beings, despite their differences, can work together in rational solidarity, free of sentiment or pathos.

Tessakeh is not exactly a typical Indian either; the narrator describes him as more muscular and handsomer than the norm. Nor does he much resemble an Indian of Cooper, a model about which Gerstäcker was to become increasingly skeptical. This is another area in which those who have not got past *Die Regulatoren* and *Die Flußpiraten* have misperceived him, taking the heroic, abstemious Assowaum in *Die Regulatoren* to be one more reincarnation of Chingachgook, as he may well be.[15] In some matters the relationship of transmitted image to direct observation is not clear, at least to me. For example, it would be interesting to know whether Gerstäcker's assertion in an 1846 article on the Indians that the men were much less strong than whites because they made their women do all the work is a retained reminiscence from Cooper or an empirical observation (*MB*, 3:334; elsewhere, *R*, 2:334, he commented that the men make their women do all their work and lie around waiting to be called to eat, "gerade wie in Deutschland"). His claim that whites could acquire tracking skills equal to or superior to those of Indians may have made an impression on Karl May (*MB*, 3:335). Several times he purports to reproduce Indian songs (*Reg*, 236, 490; *AzW*, 1:128–29; 2:70). These might have been drawn from the contemporary published discourse on Indian rhetoric, as a quoted example of Indian declamation must certainly have been (*MB*, 3:368–71). On the whole, however, Gerstäcker probably had more direct experience of native Americans than any other German literary personality at any time, and he had a larger perspective on them than many commentators have seen.[16]

In the wilderness they simply belong to the inhabitants, sometimes to be avoided, sometimes to be joined or cooperated with. I have mentioned that, on his third journey to America, he made a special point of traveling to the Nebraska Territory to witness an Indian council conducted by General Sherman, with whom Gerstäcker became personally acquainted.[17] By and large, his savages are not very noble; figures like Tessakeh do not recur much in his mature writing. He "blame[s] the white American for Indian hostilities,"[18] and consistently deplores the aggression of the new Americans against the natives, the destruction of their culture, their forced removal, their consequent despair and degeneracy (see, e.g., *MB*, 3:332–33). In *Nach Amerika!* a German traveler, having encountered a bigoted fellow passenger who wants to exterminate all the Indians, observes that they are emigrants like himself, having been expelled to the reservation, and that "das Banner der Staaten fügte einen blutigen Stern zu seinen weißen" (*NA*, 4:23–25). In one early story—perhaps a historical vignette—a man with a demonic hatred of Indians captures one while repelling an attack, has him infected with smallpcx, and returns him to infect the whole tribe, an expedient that is successful ("Die Rache des weißen Mannes," originally 1845, *MB*, 3:165–208).

At the same time Gerstäcker sees in this development a historical necessity. In his major travel book he observed that the Americans were responsible for all conflicts with the Indians. "Doch," he went on, "das sind traurige und—nutzlose Betrachtungen—Jene gehen den Weg aller wilden Völker, einige langsam, andere schneller, aber alle unaufhaltsam ihrem gewissen Untergang entgegen" (*R*, 2:317). Wild life must yield to culture, he comments in one place, and the bones of Indians fertilize the ground of progress (*AWS*, 1:187). By the time he arrived, the policy of Indian removal was a settled fact; he waxed somewhat sentimental about the traces of the "Trail of Tears" and pronounced them "traurige Folgen der Civilisation" (*SJ*, 2:124–25), but he did not seem to have any alternative to suggest. Sometimes his expression of historical necessity sounds virtually Darwinian. The North American Indians and the South Sea islanders are equally doomed by the spread of civilization: the Indians will become as extinct as the dinosaurs; steamers will puff and locomotives wheeze where today the palm trees wave (*Z*3, 4).

> Aber wie bald wird die Zeit kommen, wo man von diesen Helden der Prairien nur noch wie jetzt von den alten Spartanern und Römern spricht; die östlichen Stämme sind schon fast vernichtet, die Mohikaner und Delawaren, die Oneidas, Senecas, Yamasees und Algonquins leben nur noch in der Erinnerung der Staaten, die sie früher beherrschten, und selbst die Sioux und Sauks, die Huronen, Pawnees, Cumanches und Blackfeet haben Tausende und Tausende ihrer Krieger verloren, schmelzen mehr und mehr zusammen, sehen sich weiter und weiter in ihre Wildnisse zurückgedrängt, wo sich selbst die Anzahl der Büffel, ihr einziges Subsistenzmittel, verringert, und bald wird Tomahawk und Friedenspfeife neben einander ruhen und rasten, und dort, wo jetzt der Büffel mit trotzigem Huf und Horn die Erde aufgewühlt und brüllend und schnaubend über die Fläche stürmt, werden an seiner Staat feuersprühende Maschinen einherbrausen und schwarze Fabrikschlünde stampfend und zermalmend die Eingeweide jener herrlichen Gebirge verdauen.
> 
> (*MB*, 3:364–65)

As he indicates in this passage, one reason for this inevitability is the exterminatory slaughter of the buffalo, without which the Plains Indians cannot carry on their traditional way of life, and into complicity with which, in fact, the Indians, lacking a sense of deferred gratification, have been lured in order to trade hides for firewater (*MB*, 3:367): "Mit dem letzten Büffel stirbt auch der letzte Indianer" (R, 2:341). He repeats these views after having witnessed Sherman's conference: "was vermögen alle wilde Horden gegen den fortschrittlichen Geist"; "so ist auch der Untergang der Indianer unvermeidlich" (NR, 1:1530, 200–1). Di Maio sees Gerstäcker as "ultimately implicated" in the decimation of the Indians.[19] But, if so, he had a lot of accomplices, for his views were widely shared by European observers. Billington has observed: "The Indian was the most tragic victim of the spirit of progress and utilitarianism that shaped social thought in Europe and America during the nineteenth century. His fall from grace was an inevitable by-product of changing attitudes toward nature"; most observers agreed that the case was hopeless and the Indians must perish.[20] Gerstäcker took much the same deterministic view of colonialist imperialism. He was regularly critical of colonialism, for example, of the French in Tahiti and especially the Dutch in Java, but there was no way to resist it: "die Macht und der Einfluß der Holländer wachsen dort von Tag zu Tag, ihre Flagge weht schon am Strand, und nicht lange wird es dauern, so flattert sie auch von den Bergen des einst freien Volkes" (Z2, 85). The oppression of native peoples, he observed in Java, is the same all over the world (R, 5:53).

The process is not a pretty one. Many of his Indians are pathetic and wretched, insatiably alcoholic. The Plains Indians at the conference are dirty, treacherous, and manipulative (NR, 1:156–57). The first Indians he encounters in Arkansas are drunk; of course, it is the fault of the palefaces (SJ, 1:134–35). On the other hand, he remarks not long afterward that the Indians spoke better English than he did at that time, and he joined them in a hunting party (SJ, 1:156–57). On one occasion Indians reset his shoulder, which had been dislocated in an encounter with a bear (SJ, 2:232–33). A recurrent observation that may in fact be a romantic hangover because of its apparent concern with primordial authenticity is a deprecating depiction of the adaptation of western dress. His first sight of Indians in St. Louis he found repellent because of their mixture of native and western dress (Br. 1, 192; cf. MB, 3:364). Di Maio, in discussing this point, mentions also that Gerstäcker sometimes described his *own* dress as converging to Indian garb.[21] The Indians have been infected by the palefaces with the mercantile spirit, for which he eventually blames the Indians, who have become so grasping that they sell their pipes and tomahawks as souvenirs ("Eine Stunde in einem Lager der Sioux," KENS, 1:657–63). Unlike some other writers, he claims never to have seen a pretty Indian girl; here, too, he finds that literature has been misleading, for the active, Amazon-like Indian girl lacks the feminine character "der ihr so gern in Gedichten beigelegt wird" (KENS, 1:680). The Californian Indians, the most harmless and peaceful of all (*R*, 3:317), are simply pushed to the periphery by the gold rush. Gerstäcker observes that the missionaries do not even bother to Christianize them, since they are not needed for exploitation (*R*, 2:58, 171). In a scene in *Gold!*, to which we shall return in chapter 9, an Indian chief can get no justice for a murdered tribesman (*G*, 2: chap. 2).

A story of 1853 entitled "Civilisation und Wildniß" works a twist on the familiar trope of the child kidnapped and raised by Indians. In this case nurture gains the upper hand over nature, for the young man, after having been reunited with his family and the white community, chooses to return to his life as an Indian brave (*AzW*, 2:229–98). Of course, Indians could be hostile, also. In a story originally published in 1868, "In der Prairie," there is an Indian attack on a railroad train (*KENS*, 1:535–79); it is one of Gerstäcker's contributions to Karl May's plagiaristic synthesis.[22] Nor does Gerstäcker otherwise consistently depict Indians as passive victims.[23] Sometimes they are ironic and sly in their contentions with whites. In one story, an Osage, who wants whiskey, asserts with a straight face that he is a good Indian because he likes whites and goes to church; when told that only bad Indians drink, he replies with equanimity: "Ich ein verdammter Schurke!" whereupon his drink is poured (*MB*, 1:177). Later in this story the same Indian outwits a white who attempts to cheat him by doctoring his gun in a turkey shoot.

Gerstäcker copes with the Indian theme by placing himself empathically inside an American perspective without becoming totally absorbed by it like Sealsfield's narrators. He pointed out that Europeans admire the Indians on account of "Coopers reizende Erzählungen" and from sympathy with their lot, while the situation of American pioneers and settlers does not permit them to share this sensitivity; their situation instead determines a relationship of hostility and contempt, especially as the Indians they know have become degenerate through contact with those very pioneers and settlers (*MB*, 3:331–33). In one place he bitterly charges federal Indian agents with corruption (*NR*, 1:200–1), though elsewhere he tells of one who was attacked by the settlers for attempting to help the Indians and provides a verbatim translation of the agent's published protest (*R*, 2:342–43). Then, after pointing out that Indians cannot get justice because the law will not accept their testimony against a white, he delivers a philippic against American hypocrisy:

Wie oft, wie entsetzlich oft sind die Indianer dort wirklich auf das Nichtswürdigste von Menschen behandelt worden, die überhaupt nichts Heiliges auf der Welt kannten, und offen aussprachen, daß es ihnen eben so viel Vergnügen mache einen Indianer zu schießen wie einen Wolf—und nie hat das Gesetz der Weißen, trotz all seinen wehenden Freiheitsflaggen, prahlerischen Reden und hochtönenden Gerichtsnamen ihnen auch nur den mindesten Schutz gewährt. Und dann nennen sie diese armen Teufel "mörderische Schufte," wenn sie zur Verzweiflung getrieben, und aus ihren Jagdgründen verjagt, jedes Subsistenzmittels beraubt die blutenden Leichen der Ihrigen vor sich, einmal das Wiedervergeltungsrecht übten, und nach ihren Gesetzen und vor Gott im besten Recht, Einzelne derer zu tödten suchten, die Tod und Verderben über ihre Stämme gebracht.

(R, 2:344–45)

Still, he knows no remedy but to trust in the mysterious compensatory ways of fate. He thinks little of projects to turn the Indians into agriculturists, remarking that it was as though one of us were given a bow and arrow and told to make a living with it (NR, 1:200).

One sees, perhaps, in this extrapolation of Gerstäcker's quasi multiculturalism with particular clarity the limits of unmediated, unanalytic mimesis, the reproduction of the self-evident, what Lukács would have called "naturalism." But perhaps one might also conclude that the spirit of realistic inquiry can be relatively flexible. As Di Maio observes: "In Gerstäcker's North American narratives specific issues concerning the encounter of the Native American with the European-American remain consistent, yet the narrator's representation of the Native American changes in perspective according to Gerstäcker's experience, the passage of time, and the nature of the literary genre."[24] We may keep this in mind as we turn to a review of his social and political observations in America.

# 8. Gerstäcker's America: Social and Political Observations

To claim for Gerstäcker relatively unmediated mimesis is not to make a claim for "objectivity," whatever that might be. It means, rather, that his perceptions were not organized by a predetermined agenda. He had prejudices and unarticulated determinants of consciousness like anyone else, but he was not fanatically attached to them, so that they were subject to modification by experience while maintaining a certain recognizable continuity, with the result that his perceptions are not chaotic or aleatory. It may seem odd and obvious to say that he did not know what he would find in America. But in the large and growing body of study of the German or, more comprehensively, European image of America, it is constantly discovered that observers bring their image with them, that in many cases it is surprisingly impervious to modification, and that therefore "America" is, as the French have it, not only an *image* but a *mirage*. However that may be—the point is often overemphasized—this is not Gerstäcker's failing, one reason being that he was, or came soon to be, aware of the occupation of consciousness by prefabricated images, particularly from a romanticizing literature, so that he arrived sooner at the point that his response to experiences was not: "Aha, I knew it all along," but to measure them against expectations and try to read them in their own right.

The other side of this receptivity, however, was that he lacked analytic mental discipline. For better or worse, he brought less of a philosophical and ideological armature with him than many other observers. Consequently, he would have been baffled, I expect, by a concept like "political correctness," that is, a reflective mental and moral exercise applied to acknowledge and defuse one's own prejudices and stock responses toward the end of fairer understanding and acceptance of the other. For a mind like his, a thing was what it was and not some other thing, and this applied to people also. Combined with his relatively unencumbered flexibility of response, this perceptual habit yields a differentiated and dynamic representation of the surface of American life. For deeper organizing principles, one must go to a writer like Sealsfield. Given Sealsfield's results, however, I am not sure that Gerstäcker's mode of perception was inferior in principle.

## Slavery and Blacks

As I have indicated in the introduction, my foregrounding of the topic of race is not merely a matter of current concern. Slavery and the discourses about race may have been the most prominent aspect of America in the eyes of most mid-nineteenth-century foreign visitors, overrunning and, indeed, to some considerable extent displacing both the more abstract issues of freedom and the more concrete details of politics. For those well disposed toward America and to democracy in general, slavery was a source of grief, for it was the one eminent defect that made wholehearted pro-American partisanship difficult to sustain. Most German writers about America were intensely opposed to slavery. Perhaps a majority of German Americans were also. This does not mean, however, that their attitudes on race corresponded to ours today. Those of the immigrants of the 1830s and the forty-eighters have been characterized as "a mixture of idealism, racism, and politically expedient ambiguity."[1] I have come to think that it is all but futile to charge any white person of any nationality in this era with racism. In the sense in which we currently understand it, racism was virtually universal, a consideration that shows both the distance we have come and how difficult racism is to combat because it so profoundly natural. Karl August von Varnhagen's niece Ottilie Assing reported to the Augsburg *Allgemeine Zeitung* in the midst of the Civil War that racial hatred was universal among Americans, North and South.[2] What would require comment and explanation would be a distinctly nonracist or antiracist phenomenon. We will not find it in our amiable author.

Gerstäcker might be called a racist abolitionist, a category that at that time must have been very large. As a modern historian has put it, abolition was complicated by

> the White dilemma over what to do with free Blacks—that is, how to keep such a potentially large body of people from participating fully in American society and polity, and how to contain the explosive pressures inevitably generated by such denial.... Visions of great waves of free Blacks moving to the North and West were an effective polemic... because of the widespread and deep-rooted antipathy of American Whites to *any* Blacks in their communities.... Throughout the nineteenth century, White Americans were in such basic agreement about Black inferiority that no model of an American society accommodating the two peoples on anything like equal terms was seriously considered.[3]

For the most part Gerstäcker was grieved and horrified by what he saw of slavery. It is true that one of the American writers he translated was William Gilmore Simms, vociferous defender of the slaveholding South, though it is curious that Gerstäcker left that translation out of his personal bibliography.[4] At first he seems to have fallen victim to that part of the southern discourse arguing that slaves were no worse off than the industrial proletariat (*SJ*, 2:279–82); he thought they were better treated in the West and in Arkansas and Missouri than on the plantations of the Old South, that they were happy if they had good masters, and that they were in any case better off than farmhands in Germany (*Wie?*, 69).[5] Brenner charges the discovery of many visitors that slavery was not as bad as they expected to their latent racism.[6] Landa observed in Gerstäcker another reflex of southern evasiveness: "Every slave dealer encountered in his works is a Yankee"; Landa also points out how irritating Gerstäcker finds blacks when they imitate white dress and manners, a pattern we have seen in his view of Indians.[7] Even after the Civil War, when his views had become more differentiated, he describes freed slaves as incompetent, unwilling to work without direction, and so insouciant of the future that they tear down huts for firewood (*KENS*, 1:585–86). When, in *Der Flatbootmann*, an overseer is shot, the slaves are unable to do anything without whites' orders (*Fl*, 161); it is unclear whether Gerstäcker senses this obstinacy as a form of resistance.

Nevertheless, he was implacably opposed to slavery itself. He was particularly incensed by that particular evil at the core of *Uncle Tom's Cabin*, the breakup of slave families, which caused him to comment that slavery was "der Schandfleck der nordamerikanischen Freistaaten" and to predict that the Union would break up over it; the sight of a slave auction oppressed him (*SJ*, 1:252–53; 2:279; also touched upon in his children's book, *FW*, 55). He hinted at treatment of slaves so horrible that he did not even want to describe it ("Canoefahrt auf dem Red-River in Nordamerika," *Z5*, 45). In Java, after observing that the Dutch were less cruel to slaves, he burst out in a prayer that American slavery might be abolished (*R*, 5:58). A story entitled "Schwarz und Weiß. Aus dem Farmerleben Missouris" is a kind of underground railroad tale. An escaped slave, pursued by a posse, seeks refuge with a farm family, which, though split on the slavery issue, succeeds with great ingenuity and presence of mind to shield him until he rides off to Canada on the posse leader's horse. Some weeks later the horse is returned, a gesture certifying the black's character and even motivating the posse leader to treat blacks better (*AzW*, 1:137–226). Once in a while Gerstäcker touched upon the neuralgic point of the slavery discourse: the possibility of rebellion. In *Der Flatbootmann*, a northern sailor in Louisiana thinks the slaves will rebel (*Fl*, 50). One curious story, *Der Pflanzer*, originally published in 1845 and said to have occurred five years earlier, tells of a mass escape. The slaves appear to die of cholera and the bankrupt master by suicide, but it turns out to be a plan for all of them to escape to Texas. They are caught by a cruel slaver, but one of the blacks obtains revenge by tying him up and throwing him into the river. In this tale the blacks are both loyal to their good master and clever (*MB*, 1:305–26). In the same year appeared an ambitious story of suspense, "Jazede," which also touches on black resistance. It tells of a plot of Spanish Creole smugglers to abduct and free a fair-skinned slave whose father has died without manumitting her and who is to be sold at auction by the heir to the property, an evil Yankee, naturally (the reader will perhaps recall Strubberg's appropriation of the motif in *Bis in die Wildniss*, discussed in excursus I). One of the accomplices in the endeavor is an Indian whose humorous, facetious manner masks a rage against the oppressive whites. Jazede is guarded by slaves, but the conspirator manages to turn them by offering them freedom, so they join in what is de facto a mini-uprising against the slaveholding community (*MB*, 3:1–74).

"Jazede" is one of Gerstäcker's most accomplished stories, recommendable to an anthology of his best work.[8] But one will note, as in Strubberg's version, the heroine's fair complexion, her lily-white fingers and light brown complexion, of which much is made; the blacks call her "der weiße Nigger" (*MB*, 3:33). Though she has only one black great-grandmother, even her lover has to get over his hesitation when he hears that she is "äthiopischer Abkunft" (*MB*, 3:48). The motif repeats in "Die Sklavin," where there is, in addition, a pale-skinned male of Negro blood who is viciously treated (*MB*, 1:1–64), and in *Der Flatbootmann*, where the girl rescued (by purchase, incidentally) is an octoroon, completely white in appearance, identifiable racially only by her fingernails (an old wives' tale Gerstäcker evidently absorbed); even so, the protagonist hesitates: "Es war *nur* ein Nigger, und das Vorurtheil konnte er nicht so leicht besiegen, das selbst in den Herzen der nördlichen Amerikaner wurzelt" (*Fl*, 144). The matter of color seems confused in Gerstäcker's mind. In his first, less accomplished emigration novel, an evil slave has "das hellgelbe, teuflische Antlitz eines Mulatten, mit gierig glühenden Augen und fletschenden Zähnen" (*DAFS*, 248). A Javanese girl is said to be pretty despite the color of her skin (*KENS*, 1:425). However, a young Dutch painter of native girls is free of any such considerations: "Er war Künstler und gerade *durch* seine Kunst stand er frei und unbeschränkt allen lästigen und ungesunden Vorurtheilen gegenüber" (*KENS*, 1:442); what about the *Künstler* Gerstäcker? Different skin colors, we are told, contribute to the exoticism and beauty of New Orleans (*MB*, 3:323). Of an Australian black woman who attempts to rescue her white, criminal husband, it is said that the loyalty of the "Frauenherz" knows no color; when he proves faithless, she conscientiously guides the police despite their distrust of her and at one point "glich einer aus schwarzen Marmor gehauenen Statue, einer dunklen Najade" ("Gentleman John," *Z5*, 301, 344). The cliché that all people of another race look alike is ironized in the other direction: the fleeing protagonist of *Der Flatbootmann* is told that Negroes won't recognize him: "*Ein* Buckra sieht aus wie der andere" (*Fl*, 194). In the late, retrospective novel *Im Eckfenster* there is an implicitly antiracist dialogue in which evidence is developed that there is no relationship between hair color and character (*Eck*, 3:14–16).

The Australian woman is also an example of black competence, of which there are scattered examples. In a whimsical story, "Der Leichenräuber," about an Irish doctor determined to steal a skeleton out of an Indian burial mound to sell in New York, a scared but alert black boy rescues the band of miscreants from enraged Indians by successfully imitating an Indian cry (*AWS*, 1:95–96, 100; original version in *Z1*).[9] In an anecdotal memoir, we are told of a slave boy able to identify a steamboat by name before Gerstäcker can even hear it, much less see it ("Eine Mississippifahrt," *Z5*, 37). However, such cases are rare. In his first book, he deplored the segregation in New York, despite the civil-rights improvements achieved by "General Jakson's Güte," and he comments on the contradiction between slavery and the assertion of the Declaration of Independence that all men are created equal (*SJ*, 1:62–63). Yet in that same work he mentions that he was obliged to share a bed with a black because he was a greenhorn; had he known then how shamefully that was regarded, he would have broken every bone of the innkeeper (*SJ*, 1:94).

At one time I thought that it might be possible to detect a gradual improvement and mellowing in Gerstäcker's feelings about race as he became more experienced and wiser. Even between the two early adventure novels there seemed to be some movement. *Die Regulatoren in Arkansas* exhibits a virtually Sealsfieldian representation of blacks as rascals and "Canaillen" (*Reg*, 341–42), whereas in *Die Flußpiraten des Mississippi* there is more awareness of the mistreatment of blacks. Here it is the criminals who make race distinctions: a black is forced to dance Jim Crow and to break open a cheese with his head—Gerstäcker was another who believed in the incredibly hard skulls of Negroes—and the pirates lynch a black for laying hands on a white (*Fp*, 199, 206–7,

378). But there is no sustained development, one reason for this being that, whatever his principles, Gerstäcker certainly did not care for the company or presence of blacks. In his earliest correspondence he spoke of working side by side with blacks as demeaning (*Br. 1*, 262). There is a lot of stress on black criminality. In the first emigration novel, a new arrival is mugged immediately upon landing in New York by two blacks, on which a companion observes: "er habe einen 'schlagenden' Beweis von der Bösartigkeit der Neger erhalten"; immediately thereafter a shoemaker's equipment is stolen by a Negro (*DAFS*, 43, 49). In *Der Flatbootmann* it is said that they steal whatever they can (*Fl*, 23). There is another lynching, more positively seen as a democratic proceeding, of a black who has raped a white deaf-mute girl on a riverboat; the vigilantes are tried but freed by popular demand (*MB*, 2:152–79).

Gerstäcker's most racist piece of writing of my acquaintance is an essay of 1860 entitled "Die Neger in St. Thomas: Skizze." Here again he complains that the loafing blacks dress like actual gentlemen and act the part: "nur das verwünschte, schwarze, äthiopische Gesicht stört die Illusion und wirft sie über den Haufen." The facial configuration is an apelike characteristic: "Die echten Negerhasser, von denen wir auch in Deutschland eine wenn auch nur sehr kleine Anzahl aufweisen können, haben der afrikanischen Rasse oft das Affenähnliche in ihrer ganzen Natur vorgeworfen—und zum Theil haben sie recht." Thus Gerstäcker pleads for emancipation and segregation simultaneously: "Ich gönne dem Neger seine Freiheit aus vollem Herzen, und bin der Meinung, daß sie ihm nie hätte genommen werden dürfen, aber—ich verlange nicht seine Gesellschaft und vermeide sie sogar wo ich nur irgend kann. Es mag das nicht christlich sein, aber es ist natürlich. Wir beiden Rassen passen nun einmal nicht zu einander, und je getrennter wir uns halten, desto besser" (*Haz*, 11–12). The best that can be said for this is that he did not include it in his collected works. After having observed the freed slaves in the postwar South, however, he stated flatly: "Es läßt sich nicht leugnen, daß die schwarze Race an geistigen Fähigkeiten der weißen untergeordnet ist" (*NR*, 1:345). The naturalness of racism is supported elsewhere by the claim that alligators fear whites, but hate and chase Negroes (*SJ*, 2:289), the reason being the blacks' peculiar odor (*AWS*, 2:4).

The St. Thomas essay is an indication that the racist affect became stronger outside of North America. The Negroes in Brazil are described as hideous; working under a mulatto is humiliating. It is remarked that the successful, more southern Brazilian colony of Blumenau freed its slaves, thus relieving itself of their company (*PV*, 60, 111, 146). When it came to the Australian aborigines, Gerstäcker could not arouse even much sense of common humanity.[10] Despite the honorable woman of classical demeanor in "Gentleman John," mentioned earlier, and the observation in that story that the blacks aided the highwaymen because they were also persecuted (Z5, 296), in his travel work they are described as nasty, cowardly, and sneaky, and as the race most neglected by the Creator (R, 4:86, 174, 333). It is true that they invented the boomerang, but only by accident; it is possible for them to learn, but it is hard to see this (R, 4:148, 282). In a story called "Booby Island," they are just thieves who need to be taught respect for whites by force (Z6). It will remain to be seen in the next chapter whether there is any improvement of vision in the major emigration novels.

## Religion

In his youth, Gerstäcker's religious feelings seem to have been quite conventional. There are occasional references to gratitude toward and hope in God in his letters to his friend Schultz. I imagine that he held without much reflection to the kind of domesticated Protestantism that, because it was integrated with the state, presented no challenge to society or morality, and that educated German Protestants had always regarded as the wellspring of liberty and compatible with reason because it derived from the Reformation. In the course of his travels, however, his views on religion became much more militant. His attitudes developed mainly two aspects. One, which will not be pursued at length here, because it would lead away from our topic, was a wrathful indignation directed toward missionaries, whom he regarded as self-seeking agents of colonialism imposing a regime on native peoples for which they had no need and which merely distorted their way of life, sometimes causing bloody conflict. His views on them were doubtless reinforced if not actually shaped by Melville, who in his South Sea narrations commented repeatedly on the intolerance of missionaries and lamented their destruction of native dress and custom. In New Zealand the missionaries are the vanguard of artillery, firearms, and enslavement (AzW, 1:283–86; for similar views on Hawaii, see R, 3:40). Christianity, Gerstäcker observed, would not make the Javanese better people (R, 5:224). His pungently expressed views on this matter created atypical frictions in his otherwise relatively uncontentious career. Cotta refused to publish the novel *Tahiti* because he did not wish to be associated with what he regarded as its anti-Catholic tendency, so it was brought out by Costenoble in Jena in 1853 (Gerstäcker sent Cotta a copy, Br. 2, 9, 47). Another novel in this vein, *Die Missionare*, published by Costenoble in

1868, drew a published protest from a Christian zealot named Gustav Jahn.[11] Gerstäcker mounted a diatribe against those who collect money to feed parasitical missionaries and send stockings for pagan children while German children go barefoot (R, 3:364). In the late novel *Im Eckfenster*, we see one of these people, a woman who is said to hate everybody but the Hottentots, and who is so reminiscent of Mrs. Jellyby in Dickens's *Bleak House* that she may be her literary descendant.

The other response was a kind of culture shock in the face of the variety of religious experience encountered in America, with its emotionalized communal expression and its plethora of uneducated, often self-ordained ministers. This feature of American life struck European observers almost universally and often disgusted them.[12] For Germans, so used to religion in its orderly place, American sectarianism was horrifying, especially when it interfered with beer drinking on Sunday,[13] a remarkably abrasive issue that led eventually to the entanglement of anti-German sentiment with Prohibition. Gerstäcker, who might enjoy a glass of beer or wine but otherwise does not seem to have been much of a friend of alcohol at all, did not care about that point, though he did complain like many others of the boring American Sabbath (*Br. 1*, 206). Otherwise he came to regard American clergymen as fools and/or knaves, when they were not outright criminals, as one turned out to be in *Die Regulatoren*. Miller points out that when Gerstäcker arrived in Arkansas, "evangelical Christianity ... was the predominant form of religion," Baptists and Methodists being the largest denominations, and he adds: "There is not a single frontier clergyman in Gerstäcker's writings who is not portrayed as either a buffoon or a hypocrite."[14] He reports gleefully on a riot in church caused by a sermon (*SJ*, 1:61; private account *Br. 1*, 180), of the "Religions-Unsinn" of Methodists howling, jumping, and rolling on the floor in grotesque prayer meetings (*SJ*, 1:173, 209; *DAFS*, 75–77), and with more outrage than humor on a Catholic exorcism in Cincinnati (*SJ*, 1:174). He tells of a preacher who sings a hymn for three hours but has to give up because he cannot remember any more verses (*SJ*, 1:292–93).

Nor did he think much of the religious communities founded by immigrants, on which he commented that they end badly "wenn sie nicht durch den strengsten fanatischen Despotismus und mit Hülfe des Aberglaubens und religiöser Schwärmerei auf das Volk einwirken." Then they may thrive, but "der liebe Gott bewahre uns vor einem Leben, wo Geist und Körper gleich fest in Banden liegt.... Nein, deshalb sind wir nicht nach Amerika gekommen, wir wollen die Freiheit, das schönste Gut dieses herrlichen Landes, genießen" (*DAFS*, 262). He exhibits the same hatred of the Mormons that we have seen in Möllhausen and that has very likely been absorbed from the American environment. In a report entitled "Die Vertreibung der Mormonen aus Missouri," written in 1845 for an illustrated newspaper but apparently not published in it, the Mormons are hateful, bloodthirsty, fanatical, deluded rebels against the government; Joseph Smith was criminally insane; and, anyway, what with Methodists, Quakers, and Baptists there are enough sects already (MB, 1:245–304).

Once in a while Gerstäcker gives an indication of his own ideals, of "natural," human-centered religion. He describes an idyllic outdoor Sunday service in Canada, without any clergyman talking unctuously about reward and punishment (Haz, 14). In his novel appealing for the separation of church and school, a young deacon wishes he could preach of love and of Christ as a man (PuS, 1:42–43). Gerstäcker was enough of a freethinker to venture a satirical fantasy about God: things are so bad in Germany that God cannot figure out how to help. He cannot alter the natural laws, and though he taught Moses all of religion in a quarter of an hour, no one would believe fiery inscriptions or voices in thunder any more, so he decides to write a book. But the publishers are balky, fear the censorship, and find the religious parts unthinkable. After having been arrested for traveling without a passport, God gives up and goes home (AzT, 2:93–108). Gerstäcker never became irreligious or unspiritual, but after some observation of the world he subsumed organized religion under fashion and concluded that, like fashion, it is simply imposed on people by happenstance (Z1, 77).

Parenthetically, it might be remarked that, if it is any consolation to the clergy, Gerstäcker was just as hard on the medical profession in America. There is scarcely an American physician in any of his writings who is not a quack; in fact, he flatly stated that they were all quacks (SJ, 1:127; Fl, 70). He thought the physicians downright dangerous; in one place he tells us that he survived a fever because no American doctor could be found to treat him (SJ, 1:246). The truth of the matter seems to have been that, while most medical men were not charlatans, "medical practice was only sporadically effective in curing disease and easing pain. Many of its treatments were not only uncomfortable but potentially dangerous to patients";[15] another historian concludes: "there must have been plenty of quacks, for the examinations for admission to the medical corps were a mere formality."[16] In fact, licensing came to be regarded as a "restraint on practice"; after 1830 most states *repealed* penalties on unlicensed practitioners, with a natural consequence of "rampant charlatanism."[17]

## Jews

There are no important Jewish characters in Gerstäcker's writing. I have the impression that he had no close acquaintance with any Jewish people. It is therefore surprising how many references he makes to Jews; while collecting materials on other matters, I found myself with pages of notes. The topic does not belong under "religion"; like many others, Gerstäcker did not perceive the Jews as a religious community, but as an alien presence living by a morality incompatible with normative society. The material is more closely related to considerations of race, and it does not shed the most agreeable light on him, though here, too, one occasionally encounters his characteristic oscillation.

In the letters to Schultz accompanying his first voyage, he comments several times on the unpleasantness of having to travel with a large number of Jews (*Br. 1*, 165, 168, 170). But it is not as bad as it might be, for the Jews are girls; if they had been nothing but "schmutzige Krämer," he would have jumped overboard. Still, they are unpleasant enough, for they throw up the bacon he claims the rabbi permitted them to eat on board (*SJ*, 1:15, 17). Gerstäcker seems to have regarded them as little better than prostitutes, who engage in a sexual orgy during a Fourth of July celebration of a sort that he could not report to his mother (*Br. 1*, 175); the considerably cleansed public version of this event observes only that one drunken woman is disgusting, but thirty are interesting (*SJ*, 1:41). Yet he appointed himself the brotherly defender of one of the Jewish girls, who was decent and mistreated by the others, because, as it turns out when she is dressed for arrival in New York, she resembles his lost love (*Br. 1*, 170, 177). In California, he tells us, he rescued Jews who could not swim (*R*, 2:131).

Gerstäcker's representations of Jews recurrently exhibit elements of the traditional anti-Semitic discourse. Jews are cowardly, avoid danger, and become hysterical when unable to do so (*SJ*, 1:44; 51, where they confuse "hip hip hurrah" with the pogrom cry "hep hep"; "Gentleman John," *Z5*, 290, where the shabby, fearful Jew claiming poverty turns out to have hidden money); they have flamboyant but inauthentic tastes (*SJ*, 1:48); they are preoccupied with obtaining wealth (*R*, 4:409); they cheat (*SJ*, 1:69; *DAFS*, 50–51); they speak (or write) "jargon" (*Fp*, 455; *AzW*, 2:324–27, 358–62); in Germany they tend to socialism and demagoguery out of greed (*PuS*, passim) and jack up prices after the Franco-Prussian War (*KENS*, 2:76). On board ship to Rio de Janeiro, the sailors use the pretext of a kind of blindman's buff game to whack a dirty, disgusting, universally disliked Jew for an hour, a punishment Gerstäcker seems to regard with equanimity (*AmT*, 2:203–9). In Louisiana, a German sheriff, too inhibited by European principles to carry out a death sentence, hires a Jewish peddler as hangman for fifty dollars; the locals are so incensed by this greed that they attempt to lynch the cowardly Jew, who drowns while hiding in a cistern and is buried with his fifty dollars ("Der erkaufte Henker," MB, 1:185–228). In the Australian gold mines, a Jewish merchant is said to have had a magnificent Sabbath, having taken in so much money, indicating that either he or Gerstäcker is indifferent to Jewish religious practice; when he is robbed, he howls and laments in despair (Z7, 76–77).

However, Gerstäcker's main point with respect to America is that the Jewish character is too ingrained to be liberated by freedom, or, alternatively, that mercantile America with its moneymaking obsession is the place for Jews to thrive (e.g., *DAFS*, 183).[18] The reader may recall from the story of the epistolary accounts of emigrant fates the case of the Jew who makes a large profit by selling German silver as the real thing. Gerstäcker came back to this point several times (e.g., *AWS*, 2:181–83, where the German silver is peddled to mulatto prostitutes), suggesting that he was generalizing a single example. After having been in the United States for a while, he proclaimed that the Jews on his ship had all become rich by such practices and with them had driven an honest German peddler in Cincinnati out of business (*SJ*, 1:310–11). There they are said to run the whole clothing trade (*AWS*, 2:199); in the first emigration novel, a pushy tailor in Cincinnati tries to force the new arrivals bodily into his shop, at first will not speak so as not to give away his dialect, but then pours scorn on their clothes (*DAFS*, 112; cf. their "liebenswürdige Dreistigkeit," *AWS*, 2:177). Later he was to claim that a fellow passenger had risen from impoverished peddler to millionaire and, having changed his name from "Süßengut" to "Seasongood," had become "einer der geachtetesten Bürger Cincinnatis" (*NR*, 1:94–98). In Louisiana, however, Gerstäcker finds that Jewish competition has made his clothing cheap, and that the merchants have become "ganz andere Wesen . . . als die Schacherjuden bei uns in Deutschland" (*SJ*, 2:274–75). But this was not his usual view, which was, that since Jews in free America might have become anything, but nevertheless revert to trade, it is proven that trade is their "Lebensprincip" (*AWS*, 2:176–77); elsewhere they are compared with the Chinese in this respect, though, unlike them, the Jews lack a work ethic, the odd proof of this being that they would rather carry a heavy bundle than do regular light work "und dabei dem unwiderstehlichen Reiz des 'Profitchens' entsagen" (*R*, 5:27–29). In San Francisco, too, "unsere deutschen Schacherer" have occupied the whole clothing trade up and down the coast "mit lauter Firmas wie 'Kaufmann, Levi und Comp.,' 'Rosenberger und Feigenlaub,'

'Herz, Löwenhaupt und Sohn,' 'Meyer, Schwerin und Gutmuth' 2c"; of course, no one associates with them socially (*R*, 2:452). The affect here is an association of the Jews with the American mercantile spirit, which, as we shall see, is one of the flickering remnants of anti-Americanism in Gerstäcker's views.

On this matter there seems to be a turn toward more wisdom in the late novel *Im Eckfenster*, where, as in Annette von Droste-Hülshoff's *Die Judenbuche*, an innocent Jew is a victim of a murder. Here it is the protagonist's hidebound aristocratic father who complains that all capital will fall to the Jews and old families will be dispersed and scorned like "der Stamm Israel's" (*Eck*, 4:235); his son tries to open him to more republican ideas, but without success. In an essay attacking pompous forms of address such as "Wohlgeboren" and "Hochwohlgeboren," Gerstäcker associates them with days when Jews were put in ghettos and knights were highway robbers, thus implicitly associating himself with the emancipation process (*Z3*, 56). On the whole, however, this part of the record does not redound very much to the credit of Gerstäcker, who took pride in scaring a couple of anxious, obnoxious Jewish travelers by making them believe he intended to rob them (*SJ*, 1:105–6). Yet, as we shall see in the next chapter, in the late novel *In Amerika* he performs an inversion on this kind of scene that vindicates an unjustly suspected Jew.

## Women

On the whole, women do not play a very large role in Gerstäcker's travel works, and many of those in his fiction seem to be present for plot requirements. While one cannot be certain about such things, the evidence suggests that he was quite chaste; it would not be incongruous to claim that, as wild as his life was, in this respect he was a Victorian. He once remarked that he did not know how to dance, suggesting that he was not much of a ladies' man (*R*, 4:497). In his youth he moaned about his rocky and ultimately unsuccessful love affairs, but no one will find anything in his letters out of keeping with commonplace adolescent experience, and he stressed the chastity of his lovemaking (*Br. 1*, 46). In Cincinnati he observes that he had no need to refine his wild appearance, since he had no contact with the female sex (*Br. 1*, 208); in the California gold mines he remarked that life without women was miserable (*R*, 2:475–76). At one point he seems to have fallen in love with the daughter of his host family in Louisiana, but, he says, he kept silent so as not to cut himself off from his homeland (*Br. 1*, 227–29), a telling episode, since it proves that he did not wish to be an emigrant. He married a second time after his first wife died and had children in both marriages. It is true that he was away from home a great deal, but, as he explained to Cotta, his wife was obliged to understand that he could make his reputation only through additional travel (*Br.* 2, 20). There is no trace of the lurking salaciousness found in Strubberg and even in Sealsfield; he was genuinely repelled by lewdness in women, for example, by coquettish bar girls and obscene pictures in California or by prostitutes in Australia, whose degradation he describes not without sympathy but with explicit disgust (*R*, 2:461, 463; 4:38; *Z*7, 104). Nor does he anywhere show a trace of approval of male aggression or impropriety toward women. I have mentioned his private account of the scandalous goings-on during the shipboard Fourth of July celebration, from which he claims to have hid in his bunk (*Br.* 1, 176). To be sure, when his friend Schultz's sister was, as it appears, left violated by a faithless lover, he counseled forgiveness and solace toward her, with reference to Goethe's Gretchen (*Br.* 1, 36, 41–42).

He was not insensible to female charms, but he tended to accompany his responses with gestures of timidity. He seems worried about the Hawaiian girls, who are said to be "feil" (*R*, 3:44), but he was nevertheless entranced by a dance on Moorea, which he describes as graceful, strong, natural, and indecent, like a cancan or a bacchanal (*R*, 3:319–20). He found Javanese girls pretty and their dancing beautiful (*R*, 5: 104, 126). Initially he felt the music of the gamelon to be nerve-wracking (*R*, 5:72), but it is good to discover that he became reconciled to that wonderful instrument and declared its effect beyond his powers of description (*R*, 5:132). He did not find the unclothed Australian aborigine girls good-looking in general (*R*, 4:205), but he did eventually discover one who was and put a shirt on her, remarking sheepishly that it was a strange situation for a married man (*R*, 4:497).

Some of his first impressions are the conventional ones, found repeatedly in European writing about America, of hyperemancipated American women tyrannizing their men; they are doubtless grotesquely exaggerated and symptomatic of nothing more than an unreconstructed allegiance to Old World social rigidities. He was shocked in New York at the sight of men shopping for groceries with baskets on their arms: "Es macht aber keinen angenehmen Eindruck daß die *freien* Amerikaner sich von ihren Frauen so tyrannisiren laßen!" and he insists that women have monstrous rights, their oath equaling that of four men (*Br.* 1, 178, repeated 197–98). He apparently made these observations after having been in New York for about an hour; perhaps someone had been bending his ear, but he repeats the point about the comic sight of men shopping (in *AWS*, 2:104). On his way home, Gerstäcker allegedly traveled with an American wife who beat and bit her patient German husband, until she is somewhat checked by being told that in Germany a man has a right to sell his wife to anyone he likes, although she might have considered "daß Niemand in Europa so dumm sein würde, für solchen Drachen Geld auszugeben" (*SJ*, 2:306–7).

He did, however, develop a great admiration for the resolute, even heroic endurance of American women in the backwoods. The historian Miller has said that he "is unusual among male writers of the period" in the extent of these observations.[19] The solitude of frontier women was noted by others,[20] but Gerstäcker was particularly struck by it. In the first emigration novel, a German woodcutter tells the new arrivals, concerned about whether their women will be able to stand the suffering, that in time they show that they can bear a lot (*DAFS*, 164). On the whole this is Gerstäcker's view, although in the fever country of the Mississippi he sometimes calls attention to their pale and wasted appearance (e.g., "Eine Mississippifahrt," *Z5*, 34). In 1845 he devoted a lengthy article to "Die Frauen in den 'Backwoods' oder Wäldern des Westens" (*MB*, 3:135–64), in which he stresses their courage and endurance of deprivation, along with their good manners as compared with those of cloddish German peasant women and their absence of class pride. He points out that they marry very early for practical considerations and not for love. In general, he describes frontier women as civil and competent, but rather low-keyed emotionally, although in one place he indicates that this reserve masks the true affection between man and wife (*SJ*, 2:58). In the essay on the backwoods women he adds an anecdote of the resoluteness of a widow with children whose husband has been killed by a snake. Gerstäcker also noted elsewhere that, because of the dangers of frontier life, widows were not uncommon, and he describes them as bearing up with dignity and competence. Like other visitors in this era, he is particularly struck by the courtesy and even gallantry men show to women (that is, to white women), even in the backwoods (*MB*, 3:144–45; *Wie?*, 59; *Fp*, 341). At the same time he is critical of the western custom of making the women eat after the men (*SJ*, 2:100).

Compared with many other writers, who could not stop complaining about the faults of American women, Gerstäcker on the whole seems to admire the result. In his story "Curtis Brautfahrt" (*ASW*, 1:131–84; the reprint of the original in *Z1* is missing several pages), a persnickety and vain widower, who goes courting around the neighborhood while ignoring the attractive girl who serves as his housekeeper, is fopped by the girls he woos, who, it turns out, have been cheerfully conspiring against him. One of these is described as "ein liebes, holdes Mädchen, schlicht und einfach, doch brav und häuslich erzogen, und eine amerikanische Jungfrau im reinsten und vollsten Sinne des Wortes" (*ASW*, 1:146). The diction here does not suggest that Gerstäcker was an early feminist, nor was he. In fact, in 1868, he published an attack on women's emancipation in the *Gartenlaube*, praising an American who refuses to give up his seat in a train to a woman traveling to a suffragette meeting, and worrying that women are losing the dignity for which Schiller praised them in his notorious poem (*Haz*, 40–41). This apparently aroused a protest from women, to which Gerstäcker replied that he was not against women turning to "passenden Wissenschaften und Erwerbszweigen" or to unmarried women having a place in society, only against American and English nonsense such as seeking the vote and mixing into politics, which would unfit women for domesticity (*Haz*, 41). This was the customary view of the German American press, which also opposed suffrage.[21] Deviant women get short shrift from Gerstäcker. A gold rush story cynically entitled "Eine gute Frau" tells of a woman who separates from her pioneer husband, takes up with a gambler, denies knowing her husband, pretends to a kind of reconciliation, and when the gambler is hanged for murder, steals all his gold and flees (*KENS*, 1:372–420). Mormon women are dismissed as immoral (*MB*, 1:296). Thus Gerstäcker, here as everywhere, had limits, but within those limits his respect for American women on the frontier and in the wilderness is manifest.

## Germans

No other German writer about America of my acquaintance, Sealsfield not excepted, writes as critically and satirically about Germans in America as Gerstäcker.[22] Of course, there are fine men and women among his German characters, but there is also a large population of crooks, swindlers, loafers, dimwits, fantasts, and snobs. Taken together, these characterizations have a multiple significance. In the first place they are part of the pattern of warning emigrants, of inculcating in them caution and distrust. It is particularly important that they should not presume that others will be their friends and benefactors just because they are also German. This is a special hazard on the alien American ground, where the immigrant is susceptible to real-estate swindlers and gouging innkeepers because they are one's countrymen (e.g., *DAFS*, 210). A German doctor in California will not treat a sick man without pay, even though it is another German (*R*, 2:157). Gerstäcker himself was cheated by a gold-mining partner named Böhm, who disappeared; since it is unusual for Gerstäcker to name his acquaintances except in his last travel book, *Neue Reisen*, he doubtless did so in this case out of particular wrath, predicting that justice would catch up with Böhm (*R*, 2:356–67). In his emigration manual he stressed that the *"Betrüger"* were "leider größtentheils Deutsche," adding, however, that this was not a peculiarity of Germans, merely that it was convenient for persons of all nations to prey upon their countrymen (*Wie?*, 33, 42–43); Americans, after all, do not know enough German to cheat them (*AzW*, 1:6). But this danger begins in Germany itself, where there is no end of land salesmen, indenture contractors, and transatlantic emigration agents. It is just as important that dangers also come from within their own consciousness, and this not only because it may have been beguiled by Cooper or Gottfried Duden.[23] Their minds are parochial, their ways are set, and they have an insufficient grasp of the foreignness of America. Germans can learn only in the hard school of experience because no one can tell them anything (*DAFS*, 299). It makes no difference whether they are clodhoppers expecting someone to take care of them, middle-class people insisting on hauling their heavy furniture and implements with them, or intellectual "Latin farmers" who have mastered agriculture from books—they are all in danger unless they can learn flexibility and adaptability, and acquire a new self quickly.

And here lies the other side of the significance. The Germans are in danger because they are Germans. This is not primarily owing to anti-German hostility in America, although Gerstäcker from time to time touches upon the topos of the "damned Dutchman," who, he once remarked, is, like the Irishman, no more respected than the Negro (*SJ*, 1:62; cf. also *Fp*, 27). Rather it is because they have been socialized by an authoritarian, oppressive, and infantilizing homeland that has not bred them for freedom and independence. After over a year in America Gerstäcker grumped that if the Germans were regarded with contempt by the "dummen eingebildeten Amerikaner," it was their own fault, "denn fast alle die Deutschen die hier herüberkommen sind wahre Horn & Rindviehextracte, meist plattdeutsche denen der Amerikaner darin natürlich in allem überlegen ist" (*Br. 1*, 201). German settlements have a tendency to fail because each has its own little despot (*SJ*, 2:32). Gerstäcker was not an American and did not, like Sealsfield, pretend to be one; he was a German who deplored conditions in his homeland and hoped for progress, for which aspects of America were a model of possibility. He did not like the German immigrants much at first, finding that they imposed their egalitarianism on educated people (*Br. 1*, 223). In Cincinnati he depicts Germans as poor, dirty, exploited, and unemployed (*SJ*, 1:170–71, 304); when he finds the taverns in Pittsburgh full of Germans, he thinks that not a good sign (*SJ*, 1:323).

It is important to keep in mind, however, that Gerstäcker arrived in the midst of a severe economic crisis, at the peak of the Panic of 1837, although it is not clear that he understood the situation; it may be that, at the beginning, his English was not good enough to read newspapers regularly, for, even as late as the fall of 1840, "mit meiner englischen Grammatik sah es noch trübselig aus" (*SJ*, 1:315). In a detailed essay on Cincinnati originally published in 1845 but doubtless going back to his first experiences, he tells of many Germans with no means of support and much misery among immigrant families (*AWS*, 2:89, 92). In his first emigration novel, he claims that Germans constituted half the yellow fever victims in New Orleans (*DAFS*, 193). He sometimes finds the immigrants, with their habits brought from the fatherland, uncouth: a German ball in gold-rush San Francisco ends "auf ächt deutsche Art mit einer tüchtigen Prügelei" (*R*, 2:242). Having mastered English, he finds the German American jargon amusing: "Er spricht dabei natürlich nur von 'guten Claims' suchen, oder noch besser, 'Platz clähmen' von 'ein Tuhl hinein stellen,'—ein Loch 'diggen,' von 'Grawell' und 'Cleh,' von 'Ledge und Rock streichen' von 'cayoten und crowbar' und Gott weiß was noch für entsetzlichen Dingen, und läßt den unglücklichen Ankömmling, der sich gar nicht einmal getraut eine Erklärung all dieser ihm völlig chinesichen Wörter zu verlangen, in einem wahren Chaos von Begriffen und noch viel verwirrter zurück als er ihn kurz vorher aufgefischt" (*R*, 2:396).[24] We hear this macaronic German also in *Nach Amerika!*: "wie gleicht ihr das Bild?" (*NA*, 3:216), and in *Gold!*: "Die *store keepers* werden reich, *yes* . . . , aber die *miners*, die in der Erde *worken* und mit ihren *cradeln* schukkeln, blasen Trübsal. Puh—Namen—*der* Art nennt solche Plätze on Purpes so, um recht viel *people* herzukriegen" (*G*, 2:4; cf. 3:328).

But at length, except for the crooks and predators, he did not normally apply his satire to Germans who were settled and had learned how to function. He comments that German farmers, once they have learned to start from scratch, were widely admired (*AWS*, 2:89; *AzW*, 1:13). It is those who are still carrying their homeland with them who flounder and founder, some comically, some tragically. Often he describes them as not only unworldly but ignorant from poor education. The reason he ventured to get himself certified as a schoolteacher in Cincinnati was that, after the German population had induced Ohio to institute bilingual schools, the German schoolteachers were fearful of submitting themselves to the examination (*SJ*, 1:315). The experienced reader in this topic will recognize at once how atypical his outlook is. Gerstäcker was as far from trying to turn America into a province of Germany with the agency of the racially superior German Americans, whose self-image he subverts by pointing out that there were not a few German slave-owners (*Wie?*, 64), as he was from defining it as the antithesis of everything good, decent, and German. Sometimes one must listen a little to catch his drift. It should be remembered that Gerstäcker began publishing under conditions of severe censorship, and, although the regulations became less onerous after 1848, there never was anything like full freedom of the press in the German Confederation.

It is therefore surprising how often he is able to get in a dig, sometimes in a subordinate clause. He could not, he remarks in one place, describe in decency the state of his underwear: "ich darf ihn nur, wie es die Redaktionen der politischen Zeitschriften mit Rußland, Oestreich und Preußen machen, ihren Zustand *ahnen* lassen" (*R*, 1:345). Speaking of his sound health, he remarked that he did not have a German constitution, but a good one (*R*, 5:85). This is one of his few direct references to his bitter feelings about the course taken by the Revolution of 1848. Another is his observation that there hangs in every German tavern in America the portrait of Robert Blum, the revolutionary democrat martyred in Vienna (*AmT*, 2:173).[25] The Civil War, he remarked in passing, was in the news in the whole world, "China und Preußen natürlich ausgenommen" ("Eine Musterung," *Z5*, 421). When remarking upon poisonous king snakes, he added a note: "An die Redaktion! In Preußen würden Sie eine Verwarnung bekommen, wenn Sie die Königschlange als *giftig* denuncirten" ("Eine Mississippifahrt," *Z5*, 35). This last remark, incidentally, was published in an Austrian journal; though he may appear to play Austria off against Prussia, it was not out of any love of Austria, which he described after a visit in 1844 as a reactionary horror a hundred years behind the times, which he hoped never to see again (*Br. 1*, 248). In a rather amusing dream story of 1865, a simpleton imagines he is working his passage to America on a whaler and, after being mistreated by the sailors, slips to the bottom of the sea, where he finds a community of shipwrecked emigrants, complete with gendarme demanding papers and forced military service, for, where there are six Germans, there must be "Obrigkeit" (*Z1*, 137–53).

Schools in the backwoods certainly have their deficiencies, "doch darf man sich darunter ja keine Schule denken, die mit denen unseres lieben Vaterlandes die geringste Aehnlichkeit hätte, wo der Bakel in gewaltiger Hand regiert, und die armen Schulkinder zitternd den donnernden Worten des Schulmonarchen lauschen" (*SJ*, 2:49–50). In the first emigration novel, the duped colonists cannot stand up to their despotic "Vorstand" because of their built-in "Untertanengeist" (*DAFS*, 34–35). They carry their authoritarianism abroad (*R*, 1:122–24), and because of their habits of servility, they are easily bought off by political parties and therefore scorned, like Negroes (*AzW*, 2:331). A German who has gone native on the Argentine pampas still is fearful of the police (*R*, 1:202). A couple in a recreated orderly and industrious German settlement in Australia wish they were back home: "Und gewiß ist's in Deutschland besser, wenn—wir nur einen Doktor fänden, der uns einmal so recht von Grund auf heilen könnten" (*R*, 4:247; doubtless the doctor turned out to be Bismarck). Gerstäcker tells anecdotes of Germans who bring their submissive habits to Australia, and sighs: "Armes Deutschland" (*R*, 4:329–31). A repeated theme is the inability of Germans to unify and cooperate among themselves, clearly intended as an analogue to the disunited condition of the homeland. A German farmer Gerstäcker meets in Buenos Aires complains, just like those in North America, primarily about other Germans; they do nothing for one another (*R*, 1:92, 115). The Germans in San Francisco are nice enough, but one cannot expect unity from them (*R*, 2:453). It is no different in Java (*R*, 5:349–50). The only place Gerstäcker found Germans not disunited was Tahiti, and that was because there was only one German there (*R*, 4:262). When he was outside the range of German censorship, he spoke distinctly: before an audience in Rio de Janeiro in 1861 he recited a satire on German disunity, asserted that it was maintained in the interest of the princes at home, and prophesied that a united Germany would be the mightiest land of Europe, perhaps of the world.[26] Thus the topic of Germans shades easily into that of politics.

## Politics

There is a received opinion that Gerstäcker was an unpolitical writer, especially in comparison to Sealsfield, whom he is said to have displaced *because* the post-1848 public had lost interest in politics.[27] Brenner's claim that Gerstäcker does not mount a critique of German conditions until *Im Eckfenster* at the end of his life must be modified by the observations made in the preceding section.[28] Durzak's assertion that the only national political event to which Gerstäcker referred was the election of William Henry Harrison in 1840 is also not strictly correct.[29] He did comment on that event, both privately, when he predicted that Van Buren would lose and added that it made no difference to the likes of him (*Br. 1*, 224), and in his first book, where he observed that almost all the Germans in Cincinnati were Democrats (*SJ*, 1:314–15). The election itself he experienced in Pittsburgh, where he commented on the campaign symbols, especially Harrison's log cabin (*SJ*, 1:321). But he also wrote a story about the presidential election of 1844 in an Ohio town, in which he asserts that all immigrants are Democrats, although one quixotically attempts to found a German-language Whig newspaper in the expectation that Clay will win and make him attorney general or a Supreme Court justice (*MB*, 3:255–302). Gerstäcker shows an awareness of the issues of Tyler's precedent-setting succession from the vice-presidency and veto of the bank bill, but, since he was not in the United States at the time of that election, the story must be a product of the imagination or something he read about. In the first emigration novel there is a comic scene of the 1844 election, where the speakers at a German political meeting, instead of praising Polk, tear down his opponents, giving Gerstäcker another opportunity for a jab at the deficiencies of the mentality of the Germans, who "wissen und verstehen so wenig von der amerikanischen Politik wie die meisten deutschen Recensenten gewöhnlich von den Büchern wissen, die sie recensieren—sie werfen einen Blick hinein und urtheilen nun das Blaue vom Himmel herunter" (*DAFS*, 125); again, this scene must be a product of the imagination. As we shall see, *In Amerika* contains substantial reference to post–Civil War politics. In the *Flußpiraten* farmers talk of the threat of monarchical principles from Clay, "Henry Unsinn" (*Fp*, 40). Even the backwoodsmen, Gerstäcker tells us, interest themselves in electoral politics: "die Majorität der westlichen Squatter ist stets demokratisch gewesen"—which at this time still means Jacksonian—because they expect the president to defend their interest in cheap land (*MB*, 3:121–22).

To be sure, from this and his other references, one sees that Gerstäcker perceives these matters locally, not in the national and historical perspective of Sealsfield. But politics are local also, and it is at the communal and even interpersonal level that his political observations were most astute. One of his deepest convictions was the importance to the commonweal of schools. We have seen how he elaborated the need to emancipate German schools in his novel *Pfarre und Schule* and how he compared the kind atmosphere of a backwoods school with the terror customary in Germany. In an essay for the *Gartenlaube* in 1859 entitled "Die freie Rede," by which he meant not the civil right of freedom of expression but the rhetorical ability of the citizen to express himself forthrightly and effectively, he argued that in an age of progress there is much to do in the schools, for the teacher is the most important person in the state, although the worst paid. He pointed to the training of effective speech in American schools by encouraging children to debate serious questions, and he describes a scene in Arkansas where he proposed humorous topics (Z3, 11–13). This lightness of treatment notwithstanding, debate is at the core of a democratic polity. The whole system of government in the German states before 1848 was designed to prevent debate, and it was still not clear after the revolution that governments saw the necessity of it. The scene is a recapitulation of one described in his first book (SJ, 2:206–9), but in the meantime he has come to take a more contextualized view of its significance.

In 1845 he came back to the debating scene in a more systematic essay on the backwoods school, in which he mentions also a spelling bee, necessitated by the peculiarities of English orthography. He gives some statistics about the growth of education, mentioning that there were 173 universities and colleges. While he points out that there is very little child life, since children must go to work at an early age, he stresses a teacher-pupil relationship of freedom and equality completely different from that in Europe; teachers play with the children and never hit them. In the more urbanized part of the country, in the East and in Cincinnati and St. Louis, education is improving every day. He tells of a practice in the wilderness of setting aside a tract of forest for the benefit of the schools, which the backwoodsmen vigorously defend against criminal timber poachers ("Unberufene Gäste," KENS, 1:664–75). Only when he comes to Indian education does he turn bitter: it is conducted by missionaries for their own welfare, pacifying the Indians in order to obtain large farms for themselves (AWS, 1:185–205).

Legal procedure also caught his attention. In *Die Regulatoren*, one character, defending vigilantism, mounts a complaint about courtroom technicalities that sounds like a grievance recited on one of today's talk shows: "Eben das hat uns gezwungen, selbständig aufzutreten, daß vor dem Gesetz des Staates Kniffe und Ränke der Advocaten stets die ärgsten Verbrecher der Strafe entzogen, weil vielleicht irgend eine Kleinigkeit in der Anklage versehen, oder ein Zeuge fehlte, oder sonst ein Haken gefunden werden konnte, mit dem man Den, der im Stande war zu bezahlen, herausriß aus Noth und Strafe" (*Reg*, 473). But later Gerstäcker gave a humorous but respectful account of a case in Arkansas about a stolen pig, stressing the orderliness of the procedure and the presumption of innocence (*MB*, 2:225–64).

Such a court is communally organized, an example of the way free people cooperate together, an American characteristic, as I indicated in connection with the story of the multicultural bear hunt. This aspect of American life regularly caught the attention of European observers.

Tocqueville stated: "In no country in the world has the principle of association been more successfully used or applied to a greater multitude of objects than in America."[30] One aspect of this cooperativeness is hospitality. Gerstäcker's wilderness was populated; he always seems to have been able to find a house and shelter when he really needed it. In one place he thanks the Americans for the way they care for foreigners (*SJ*, 1:257). He describes how a country road is built by calling all men from eighteen to forty-five to work on it (*SJ*, 2:48) and adverts to one of the classic scenes of American cooperativeness, the communal house-raising (*SJ*, 2:91). Perhaps also under this heading comes the humorously described "quilting frolick" (*SJ*, 2:20–26).[31] The importance of neighborliness and mutual aid is stressed also in *Die Regulatoren* (*Reg*, 356).

The readiness to cooperate is part of the egalitarian spirit, of exceptional importance to European observers. "Among the novel objects that attracted my attention during my stay in the United States," Tocqueville wrote at the beginning of his treatise, "nothing struck me more forcibly than the general equality of conditions among the people."[32] It struck Gerstäcker also. He describes the republican spirit of steamboat passengers helping to load wood (*DAFS*, 132), though in another place Germans try to get out of it (*MB*, 2:97). Aristocrats tend to be incompetent in this environment, as in a comical story, "Eine Hochzeitsreise," in which an oversupplied baron gets lost while hunting, fails to reboard his steamboat, and becomes separated from his baroness, who searches for him in the backwoods; that is all the America they will want (*KENS*, 1:307–71).[33] Emigrants, Gerstäcker stressed, had better understand the fluidity of class relations:

> Dort drüben stehen Grafen und Barone neben dem Neger vor den Kesseln der Dampfer, mit der Schürstange in der Hand, oder hinter dem Schenktisch, um irgend einem durstigen Gast ein Glas Cognac und Wasser zu mischen, oder *hinter* der Table d'hôte—an der *sie* sonst die Kellner springen ließen—mit der Serviette unter dem Arm; dort drüben klopfen Gelehrte und Ungelehrte Steine an den Chausseen oder hüten Schafe oder Kinder (fand ich doch in Australien selber einen österreichischen Lieutenant als Kindermädchen)—da kehren alle Schichten der Gesellschaft die Straßen, tragen Theaterzettel und Zeitungen aus, schleppen für Reisende Koffer von der Landung in's Haus, oder Mehl- und Kaffeesäcke, und rollen Fässer mit Schweinefleisch oder Spiritus vor sich her—um kargen Lohn.
>
> ("Eine Mississippifahrt," Z5, 34)

His eye is naturally always on his homeland in such matters. When he was received in his rough clothing by the daughter of the president of Argentina, he commented how different that was from Germany, though he otherwise took a dim view of the state of democracy in that country (R, 1:119–22).

To be sure, one might note in this anecdote a symptom of the characteristic desire of the post-1848 bourgeois to assimilate to the elite rather than to destroy it (he also dedicated *Neue Reisen* to the president of the state of Guyana, later Bolívar, in Venezuela). It has been asked whether it was appropriate for an alleged democrat to accept the patronage of the duke of Saxe-Coburg-Gotha.[34] One does find him quite often in such company; for example, he made the acquaintance of Duke Bernhard of Weimar in Java (R, 5:65–66). However, this must be seen in a context. Bernhard was the commander of the Dutch troops in Java, thus the agent of an imperialism with which Gerstäcker had no sympathy whatever. What, he asks, have the peoples of the earth done to be punished with European masters and missionaries? (R, 5:57). He was just as severe about the brutality of the French in Tahiti (R, 3:339). Although he lived before the age of American imperialism and colonialism, he did comment that the United States had no right to force an entry into Japan (R, 5:355–56). It may be that his original idea of freedom, which he extolled in his letters to Schultz, was not strictly political, but an anarchic freedom from governance: "ein freies unabhängiges Leben gründen" (Br. 1, 13). But there is a political dimension in his constant contrasts with the Old World. He wrote from New York: "Was seine Freiheit anbetrifft so ist Amerika wirklich ein herrliches Land und blüht und grünt, und daß das alte Europa unter seinen Despoten zu sehr einschrumpft" (Br. 1, 184). Even when he does not have many happy hours, he feels free; he never worked so hard in Germany, "aber frei, frei, frei!—Das ist das Zauberwort was Alles versüßt," and after a time he worries that he will not be able to adapt himself again to German unfreedom (Br. 1, 188, 196, 222). He never really abandoned republican instincts. On his journey to South America, he noted with approval that the steerage passengers elect a president and make rational laws; they even have term limits, as a new president is to be elected every fortnight (R, 1:15–18). In the late novel *Im Eckfenster*, the returnee, Hans von Solberg, eventually says of his aristocratic parents that they have good hearts despite their good manners, but, in fact, he is unable to persuade his father of the idea of republican government, which sounds to him like an oxymoron, while Hans with his American perspective sees little good in the aristocratic class (Eck, 4:253–54; 1:33; 4:199). Even here, at the end of his career, Gerstäcker depicts aristocrats as stiff and purblind, not with ironic sympathy, as his later-starting contemporary, Theodor Fontane, will do. None of this means, however, that he was a fanatic devotee of the United States.

## Anti-Americanism

At an earlier stage of my inquiry into this topic I was surprised to find Gerstäcker included in Hollyday's study of anti-American novelists,[35] because I had come to think of him as the writer with the most positive view of America. In fact, however, one can find many bitter comments about America in his writings, private and public, perhaps another example of his habit of oscillation. They tend, however, to cluster around only two themes. The most deep-rooted and persistent of these is the familiar topos of German and, no doubt, generally European anti-Americanism from the beginnings until today: the pervasive commercial atmosphere, the subordination of all values to moneymaking. This complaint emerges so promptly upon his arrival that one wonders if it was not a mind-set that he brought with him. He concluded promptly that there was no freedom, just commerce, "eine große Kaufmannsschule, die den Geist erstickt und von weiter nichts handelt als Geld"; because of the heartless pursuit of money, the people no longer live up to their own excellent Constitution and laws; the merchant spirit makes him want to flee the United States in disgust (*Br. 1*, 200, 222–23, 214).

These strictures recur intermittently. In the gold mines Gerstäcker suddenly dilates on a theme found frequently among others but rare for him: the temperamental superiority of the German to the American:

> Der Amerikaner mag sich auch in einem solchen ewigen Drängen und Treiben gefallen—sein Hauptsinn ist das Geld, der Gewinn, und so lange er eine Muskel am Körper regen kann, so lange ist ihm das Drängen danach ein unentbehrliches Bedürfniß. Der Deutsche aber hat einen ruhigeren, ja ich möchte sagen natürlicheren Charakter. Das Ziel nach dem er strebt ist nicht nur der Erwerb selber, dieser kann ihm nicht genug Ersatz bieten auch seine Belohnung darin zu finden, nein es ist auch der *Genuß* desselben, den er sich durch denselben erringen will, und meine Landsleute werden sich deßhalb auch nie, es mag blühen und gedeihen soviel es will, auf die Länge der Zeit wohl in Californien fühlen.
>
> (*R*, 2:253)

The Pennsylvania oil field Gerstäcker visited is, not surprisingly, a scene of cynical materialism, where things have value only insofar as they can be sold (*KENS*, 2:483–534). For an American, *anything* can be bought and sold, except perhaps his family ("Canoefahrt auf dem Red-River in Nordamerika," *Z5*, 48). A consequence is an unfriendly coldness in human relations (*Br. 1*, 202). It is typical that Gerstäcker never learns the names of his companions in a tavern (*SJ*, 2:242). Life itself is cheap, as is illustrated in a scene where the body of a man who has been squashed to death by a low bridge on the Erie Canal is unceremoniously left behind (*DAFS*, 102–3); the cheapness of life is the reason Gerstäcker gives for the appalling casualty rate in the Civil War ("Eine Musterung," *Z5*, 421). In another place, to be sure, he asserts that he prefers the indifference to life and safety to the "widerliche Polizeiaufsicht in unserem 'geordneten Deutschland'" (*NR*, 1:36).

The demonization of money and commerce is an antimodern affect, a superstitious anxiety from which even Karl Marx was not entirely free. It fails to see how the pursuit of prosperity is a consequence of the freedom from the authoritarian society that determined each person's place and treated poverty and deprivation as an inescapable, perhaps even divinely ordained fate, and Gerstäcker in particular usually failed to see how it related to the freedom and, indeed, necessity to choose and, when required, change one's course in life that he repeatedly and consistently praised. Like many cultists of the anticapitalist left and right, he seems to have believed that anything earned by trade or finance was stolen from someone else, not an increase in the wealth of the community. These misapprehensions are related to Gerstäcker's attitude toward the Jews and also to his dislike of cities, his flight from "all dem dumpfen Stadtleben" (*Br. 1*, 186). Cities seemed all the same to him, philistine, possibly beautiful like Philadelphia, but boring (*DAFS*, 181); there was not enough new in them to visit with interest and they were too expensive (*R*, 4:40); the cities of the urban East were not different enough from those of Europe to describe (*Wie?*, 44–45). He was disappointed that Honolulu turned out to be so civilized (*R*, 3:32), and, although when he got to Tahiti after being long at sea, he was astonished to see street lamps and embraced one, he was soon deflated by the signs of commercialism and the Californian motto, "Geld um jeden Preis" (*R*, 3:334–38). By the time he has encountered the French bureaucracy of Tahiti, which wants to see his papers, he has grown ironic: "Aufenthaltskarte, Straßenlaternen, Polizei—o süße, süße Erinnerungen!" (*R*, 3:341). He does seem to take a friendlier view of San Francisco, but that is described more as a camp than a city, which fascinates because it keeps burning down and rebuilding itself.[36] For all that cities lay on the periphery of his interests, critics sometimes dismiss his observations too curtly. When it is asserted that he was unable to grasp

Cincinnati because he saw it as a German "Kleinstadt" (which it may to some extent have been) or that he made Valparaiso less strange by describing it as a European town (which it may have tried to some extent to resemble),[37] once again his mimetic dimension is being sacrificed to critical clichés.

Related to the poverty of human relations in commercial society is the other theme, that of manners. Here one encounters observations that are so familiar from the body of writing about America that it is hard to tell whether they are images transmitted from book to book or reflections of American reality; social history tends to suggest the latter. There are, first of all, the racing and exploding steamboats familiar from Sealsfield and others (*SJ*, 1:177; *Fp*, 508–9; *DAFS*, 268; *MB*, 2:99; *R*, 2:465). In the face of all this havoc, it is rather disconcerting to read in the emigration manual that the steamboats are not as dangerous as believed (*Wie?*, 3; similarly in *NA*, 3:188–89, where the carnage is ascribed to the obsession with making money, but the danger is not as great as reported). There is the asocial, fast, silent eating (*Br. 1*, 206; *Fp*, 38–39; *AmT*, 2:175), a trait confirmed by social historians.[38] There is the eye gouging (*Fp*, 310–11; *MB*, 3:242–43), which appears to have been a canard, though certainly a widespread one.[39] There is the rudeness in public places, at first surprising to Gerstäcker (*Br. 1*, 179, 197), which shocked some but could be interpreted as a form of sincerity and cordiality, as it was by Tocqueville.[40]

The informed observer will be struck by how much of Gerstäcker's "anti-Americanism" is conventional, part of a larger, standardized discourse. His praise is more distinctive: his admiration of canal locks, an outstanding technical achievement for a young country (*SJ*, 1:75); his assurance that, although there are many bad people in Arkansas, there are many more decent ones (*SJ*, 1:254); and, above all, his constant stress on competence, hard work, efficiency, and flexibility. He wanted to warn, but not to crush hope: "Für den Armen, der arbeiten will, ist daher Amerika noch ein Land der Verheißung" (*AzW*, 1:12). In the conclusion to his emigration manual, after all the dire admonitions, he urges people to go if they have the spirit and resources of character, for: "Amerika ist ein so glückliches gesegnetes Land, wie nur je eins aus der Hand des Schöpfers hervorging, und bietet dem Europäer Alles, Alles, was er nur vernünftiger Weise hoffen und erwarten kann" (*Wie?*, 125–26). This, I believe, remained his overall judgment and message.

# 9. The Immigration Trilogy: *Nach Amerika!, Gold!, In Amerika*

The foregoing has been a detailed and, I am afraid, somewhat verbose introduction to Gerstäcker's major novels of the emigration. They require this context for their achievement in concentrating and refining the issues that he scattered across his vast oeuvre. Several circumstances have conspired to obscure the view into these works. One was, as I have mentioned, the popularity of the two early adventure novels. The constricted literary market for ambitious novels was probably another. Ironically, Gerstäcker's publisher Costenoble seems to have sabotaged *Nach Amerika!* with ambitions for excessive elegance. For its original publication in six volumes in 1855, volume one was illustrated by the prestigious painter Theodor Hosemann (1807–75) and volumes two to six by the prominent caricaturist Carl Reinhardt (1818–78). Perhaps for reasons of cost, Costenoble shared publication with the firm of Gaertner in Berlin, but the imposing price of 6.40 talers inhibited sales; Gerstäcker complained fifteen years later that, on account of the price, the edition of 2,000 copies had still not sold out (*Cost. Corr.*, col. 1189). In general, the novels have been stepchildren of literary scholarship; in a dissertation of 1930, applying normative principles of novel form, it was said of *Nach Amerika!* that it "klafft . . . an allen Ecken und Enden auseinander und zerfällt in eine Fülle einzelner Szenen."[1] Even Durzak, who is unusually well disposed toward Gerstäcker, connects *Nach Amerika!* to Gustav Freytag's degenerated form of the *Bildungsroman* and remarks on stock figures and the prefabricated parts of the subliterary novel before arguing its outstanding and even unique qualities.[2] The criticisms are not irrelevant, but Durzak is one of the few to have seen that they do not exhaust the import and strengths of the novel.

## *Nach Amerika! Ein Volksbuch*

One of the strengths of *Nach Amerika!* as a novel about emigration to America is that nearly a quarter of the more than twelve-hundred-page book takes place in Germany. Anterior to the process of emigration is the process of decision. Gerstäcker thus anticipated the position of modern scholarship:

S[ocio]-H[istorical] M[igration] R[esearch] does not view migration as an event, but rather as a very complex social process: with the exception of abrupt compulsions such as flight or expulsion, this process spans the genesis of the latent intention to migrate, and the thereby fostered, mostly gradual mental segregation from the social context of the emigration area, whereby a last, external cause may transform the latent intention into the actual decision to migrate. In addition, the carrying out of this decision, and the integration into the social context of the immigration area, form the topics related to viewing migration as a complex social process.[3]

No other writer, to my knowledge, has concentrated so intensively on this part of the issue, because most others thought, depending upon their political and social standpoint, either that the motives for emigration were obvious, or, conversely, that emigrants were simply deluded when not ungrateful and unpatriotic. For Gerstäcker the matter is much more complex. Motivation differs by class, economic condition, and level of education as well as by gradations of character. He strives to provide a panoramic depiction of the emigrant population, fleshing out their motivations, of which he gives an ambivalent summary in his introduction (NA, 1:vii–viii). To do this he must deal with a substantial number of differentiated characters, and it is by just this requirement that the features objectionable to normative critics are generated. In the first place, the multiplicity of figures invites stock, or, as we might more charitably say, typological characterization; Gerstäcker is interested not in individual fates but in representative ones. Second, the multiplicity of figures and fates, once they begin to spread through the American continent, virtually requires episodic narration. As the novel goes on, we are bounced from group to group in a mosaic of contrasting experiences.

Neither of these devices ought to bother readers accustomed to the modern novel. However, Gerstäcker was not a modern novelist; he was as constrained by the conventions of the well-made novel as the normative critics, but his efforts to conform to the generic type weaken rather than strengthen the work by those standards. In the first place, he felt obliged to impose a plot; it takes the form of a detective story, employing elements resembling those of subliterature. The daughter of a wealthy family, Clara Dollinger, is the fiancée of a rather flashy and boastful German from New Orleans, Joseph Henkel, who, prior to the wedding, robs the family of money and jewelry, allowing the suspicion to fall upon Lossenwerder, a sad sack of a clerk in the Dollinger firm, who had slipped into the house to bring flowers to the secretly admired Clara; Lossenwerder dies of a wound incurred from a suicide attempt on the way to jail, and his sister Hedwig becomes Clara's servant. In America, Clara, incapacitated by the shock of the discovery of her husband's villainy and generally incapable, must be managed by Hedwig; thus the relationship of mistress and servant is reversed in the less class-ridden environment, where the steamboat firemen may be "Grafen und Barone, Referendare und Lieutenants," where the son of a minister of justice has been a coal miner, steamboat cook, baker, and cigar maker, and where a high-born lad, a newsboy who hopes to rise to street sweeper, converses about the relationship of industrious labor to success (NA, 3:143; 4:205–18). Hedwig's responsibility, in turn, makes her a more self-reliant person (NA, 4:111–12). Throughout the remainder of the novel Henkel is pursued until he is finally exposed and run to ground, but this is nothing but a primitive narrative armature, of no significance or importance, and it is not certain that Gerstäcker himself took it seriously, for Henkel, who travels in America under an assumed name, actually manages to convince some of the others that an evil twin was responsible for his deeds. Second, Gerstäcker attempts to impose coherence by having his episodically separated characters encounter one another in one coincidence after another, as though they were the only human beings on the continent. Verisimilitude of plotting was not one of his mimetic resources, but the point is trivial and has no bearing on the interest of the novel.

Apart from the family situations set out at the beginning, there are elaborate scenes in taverns in which the emigration question is debated back and forth. A passing band of emigrants ignites an argument between one man who notes their poverty and downtrodden condition, and another who believes they have it good enough where they are and resents the emigration "als eine indirekte Beleidigung gegen den Staat, gewissermaßen als eine Grobheit, die man ihm geradezu unter die Nase sage—: 'ich mag nicht mehr in Dir leben und weiß einen Platz, wo's besser ist.' . . . Der Staat hätte auch eigentlich den Skandal gar nicht dulden sollen; hunderte von Menschen, reine Deserteure aus ihrem Vaterland, liefen da frank und frei vorbei, Anderen noch obendrein ein böses Beispiel gebend, und er begriff die Regierung nicht, wie sie dem Volke nur noch einen Paß gestatten konnte" (NA, 1:25–26). There are arguments over bad reports about America and whether they are credible or not, over motivations and whether they are sufficient. Thus people do try to think things out, but they are woefully uninformed. The horror tales about emigration and the hostility of the newspaper are countered by a shopkeeper, Weigel, who has become an emigration agent and gets a taler a head for anyone he can inveigle; he is a great extoller of America, which he knows only from books, and distributes brochures, which, as the author comments, poison the minds of families with excessive expectations, unfitting them for real experience: "fanden sie sich jetzt plötzlich in den wilden extravaganten Ideen, die sie durch solche Lectüre eingesogen, enttäuscht, fanden die Hoffnungen nicht realisirt, die man ihnen gemacht, so hielten sich für schlecht behandelt und unglücklich, und verfielen nun oft in das Extrem trostloser und eben so unbegründeter Verzweiflung" (NA, 1:103). Weigel sells not only tickets but also land grants. A letter he receives from a client denouncing him as a crook and complaining that his land and tickets were no good he naturally suppresses.

Gerstäcker evaluates motivation and susceptibility largely by social gradation. At the bottom of the scale are criminals and other evaders of responsibility, who fade into the underclass in America. A brutal butcher, a poacher and suspected murderer, and his disorderly, unwomanly wife, in order to emigrate, abandon their children to communal care, under which they eventually die; he changes his name in America, but his abused wife succumbs to sorrow and guilt. Before the emigration ship leaves its harbor, a pilot puts criminals on board who are being forcibly expatriated to New Orleans with letters of reference and five dollars for the first weeks (NA, 3:109); the dumping of criminals from European countries on American shores became in time an irritant of nativist politics. A step up is a shifty wine salesman named Steinert, a know-it-all and sharper, a type to which Gerstäcker prophesied doom in America; at the end of the novel, after his schemes have failed, he is reduced to selling smuggled cigars on the streets of New Orleans. Three Oldenburg peasants, whose doltishness becomes a kind of leitmotif, emigrate for no good reason but an expectation of boundless free land where peasants, according to a song they know, ride in carriages dressed in velvet and silk and eat meat three times a day (NA, 3:340); when they get to America, they sit down and wait for someone to take care of them. Despite his training as an agriculturalist, Gerstäcker evinced a rather bourgeois condescension toward peasants, and he does not show much empathy here for the land hunger that churned the hopes and fancies of European farmers.[4] He is more sympathetic to a weaver who is driven in sorrow to emigrate from the poverty of technological obsolescence; although he is wrong to think he will escape the machines in America, he will turn out, owing to his character and skill, to be a type of the successful immigrant. An actuary named Ledermann is desperate to flee his squabbling and grasping family; he pretends suicide to escape his wife and turns up working in a New Orleans lawyer's office under the assumed name of "Fortmann." He is shocked to hear that she and the rest of the family are planning to emigrate (*NA*, 6: 152–55).

In the emigration group there turns up a "Literat" named Theobald; he is not, however, a persona of the author but a figure of fun. In New Orleans, where he is thrashed for attempting to protect a slave girl from a beating, he announces that he will destroy this injustice with the power of his pen, ignoring the assurances of others that he does not have the slightest chance of doing so. His book on improving America cannot be published. Though he knows no English, he plans to plunge "in den Strudel der sich hier vor uns öffnet, in die Charybdis dieses weiten Reiches . . . , ein kühner Schwimmer" (*NA*, 3:97). To a German newspaper he offers manuscripts that will make a furor, but is told the paper must cater to the Whigs, who have the money; the editor is not likely to print abolitionist tracts, as he does not want the mob to smash his press or kill him. The editor is willing to accept dreadful verse or stories forbidden by the censor in Germany, but is astonished to hear that Theobald expects to be paid for them (*NA*, 4:144–60). The "Literat" is a superfluous hanger-on, endlessly complaining about the lack of opportunity in America for a man of *Geist*. Eventually he attempts to foist a sheaf of awful poems (possibly Gerstäcker's own?) on a musician, so that the latter will not be reduced to setting the texts of Heine and Freiligrath (*NA*, 6:175).

This musician, a violinist named Eltrich, is one of Gerstäcker's model immigrants. Robbed of all his belongings by a Negro porter immediately upon his arrival in New Orleans, he does not allow himself to be thrown into despair, but resolutely works his way back, hoisting casks on the waterfront with his delicate hands, gradually obtaining pupils, and eventually becoming *Kapellmeister*. Similarly, Georg Donner, a pastor's son and physician, does not attempt to practice in America, competition with the quacks being hopeless, but makes his way initially as a sailor on the Mississippi; he is undoubtedly the ideal figure in the novel, though not a very colorful one. For a time he is associated with Professor Lobenstein, a classic case of the notorious "Latin farmer," the man of culture and learning who will show the Americans how to do it. The actual stand-in for the author in the novel may be an ebullient adventurer named von Hopfgarten, who is disappointed that America does not match the images he brought with him—including imagined adventures with horse thieves and crooked gamblers that look as though they had been acquired from Gerstäcker's early novels (*NA*, 2:171–72)—but he adapts in good spirits, as American food and air make him more practical (*NA*, 5:155–57). Because he is free from family ties and, like Gerstäcker, a traveler rather than an emigrant, it is he who is able to dash about in pursuit of the wily villain Henkel, thus tenuously holding the plot together as the agent, so to speak, of the narrator.

Following upon the elaborate process of consciousness formation among the would-be emigrants, the novel falls into three unequal segments. The first of them deals with the process of embarkation, encompassing the gathering of the group in Bremen, its transport to Bremerhaven, and the actual boarding and departure of the ship. These apparently straightforward matters fill four substantial chapters, as Gerstäcker makes every effort to show how difficult it is to get from one point to another and how ill-prepared the travelers are, for Germans are the least practical people in the world (NA, 2:26–27). The main difficulty is the transport to Bremerhaven, which the cabin-class passengers achieve in three hours by steamer, but the remainder must traverse on an uncomfortable, jam-packed, unroofed boat that moves when the tide is right or the captain feels like it and takes two days to cover the twenty miles. Many a passenger is losing his romantic notions of America even before embarkation (NA, 2:53).[5] The next part covers the actual sea journey, with its attendant discomforts and abrasions, to the landing in New Orleans. Here, more than anywhere, Gerstäcker stresses the absurd side of the emigration. Most of the emigrants have no defined purpose. They do not speak English; they do not know where to go; no one looks out for them; advice, when available, is unreliable, for there is always the chance of being cheated; work is very difficult to find and there is nativist hostility against immigrants for depressing wages; they are easily cheated and robbed; and they are sitting ducks for an unscrupulous German innkeeper, who takes them in, confident that he will eventually be able to confiscate the belongings he has taken as security and sell them off. The most helpless arrivals find themselves on the shore of their dreamland "rathlos—trostlos, verzweifelnd... zerknirscht, gebrochen, mit jeder Hoffnung geknickt" (NA, 3:261–62).

The remaining and largest segment of the novel becomes completely episodic as the characters fan out from this chaos to their various endeavors and fates. One of the more important strands is the effort of Professor Lobenstein to establish himself as a farmer in a nondescript Indiana town which, as it turns out, has no future because it is to the side of main transportation routes. An authority in his household, outside it he has failed in his endeavors in Germany and is easily flustered by adverse circumstances but impervious to sound advice; not knowing what to do, he lets the criminal Henkel decide for him. Like so many of Gerstäcker's characters, he is induced to purchase land of little value.

He employs the poor weaver, who does not like going into service but is inhibited by the "Schüchternheit sich gleich von vorn herein ein selbständiges Handeln zuzutrauen, die unseren armen Klassen nur zu sehr eigen ist" (NA, 3:191–92); he turns out to be a competent and steady worker, who after a time leaves and thrives on his own farm. But otherwise Lobenstein hires too many Germans who lack an American work ethic, must have a German maid because he cannot get along with the American one, and insists on farming out of German books rather than observing American experience. Theobald the "Literat," having found work to be beneath his dignity, loafs in Lobenstein's household, teaching the son to paint. Lobenstein wastes time and resources on planning a "Lusthäuschen," a project suggesting that he is trying to build a European landed estate rather than an American farm. Like Theobald, he belongs to what a character in the novel calls the most useless class among the immigrants, "die mittellose gebildete Klasse" (NA, 4:212–13).[6] He quarrels with Donner, who has come to work for him, for being practical rather than theoretical; he disapproves of the facility Donner has acquired with the American ax, which for Gerstäcker is a highly positive signal (NA, 5:167–69). After an argument, Lobenstein orders Donner off the property. The result, naturally, is disaster: the son dies in a hunting accident, the farm fails, and in the end a contrite Lobenstein must accept Donner as a son-in-law and let him take over the farm. The property, to be sure, is rescued by the discovery of coal, a rather maladroit novelistic device, especially in view of Gerstäcker's normal predilection for farming.

Many subsidiary characters make Gerstäcker's various points. A Baron von Benkendorff is on a private trip to observe the "nichtswürdigen republikanischen Zuständen"; he knows what he will find and has already written his articles; he is merely going in order to reinforce his views (NA, 2:156–57). After six months in a New Orleans hotel, spending his time with whist and claret and having seen and done nothing, he finds all his prejudices confirmed (NA, 5:145–50). A young aristocratic lady, Fräulein von Seebald, is on her way to visit her sister, who has married a Polish count named Olnitzki in order to live the pastoral life in the Edenic Arkansas wilderness. She finds her, of course, ill and nearly starving in a miserable hut and abused by the cynical Polish barbarian, whom the locals call "Old Nitzki" and who turns out to be a pal of the villain Henkel. One suspects that Gerstäcker may have known this man in Arkansas, though it is likely that the characterization reflects the German liberal disillusionment with the aristocratic Polish revolutionaries of the 1830s. The German tavern keeper from the first part of the novel has moved his establishment to "Milwaukie in Michigan" (*NA*, 5:211),[7] where he has become his own best customer and is sinking into a degradation for which his ill wife blames the emigration agent at home (*NA*, 5:248–49); he is easily swindled by Henkel. It can also turn out that self-confidence and *chutzpah* lead not to comeuppance but to success. This is the case with Gerstäcker's two favorite professions, the medical and the clerical. An incompetent barber-surgeon, who travels at half fare as the emigration ship's "doctor," in America confers an M.D. upon himself and sets up a thriving practice in Milwaukee in principled opposition to American quackery. The disreputable scissors-grinder, later tinker and jack-of-all-trades, Zachäus Maulbeere, a comic clown who shocks the passengers with a mildly sacrilegious mock sermon on the redemptive benefits of schnapps, turns up at intervals in the novel as a crafty picaro and, no doubt inevitably, discovers a fine living as a Methodist preacher called Mulberry.

More than most of Gerstäcker's works set in America, *Nach Amerika!* is focused on German rather than American characters. In Arkansas, Fräulein von Seebald is shocked by an Americanized German's earthiness—"Tschisus Etsch Dobbeljuw Kreist" (*NA*, 4:6)—which she interprets as materialism. An exemplary Arkansas backwoodsman prevents Henkel from driving the widow of a man killed by Olnitzki off her farm; with thirty of his fellows, he intimidates the townspeople from interfering when he has the widow's granddaughter bid a quarter for the property at auction. In general, however, Americans are extras on the stage of this novel. Here it must be agreed that there is no larger political context. Only an improvised but fair and effective jury that renders justice to a Polish Jew, whose pocket has been picked on a steamboat, is an index to democratic institutions (*NA*, 3:172–78). Slavery is a presence, an unalterable one, as we have seen, but is not otherwise much addressed; the theft of the violinist's belongings by a Negro is only a moment. However, the attitude toward slavery is clear. The omniscient narrator tells us that a slave, whose tears cannot be seen from the riverboat, has suffered the sale of one grandchild to another state, while another has been beaten to a pulp for refusing to cut the switches with which his mother was to have been whipped. The narrator cites the opinion of travelers that the slaves are better off than the European poor, but adds: "*ein* Elend wird nicht durch das andere gehoben" (*NA*, 3:136). Since, as I pointed out earlier, Gerstäcker himself had earlier ventured this view, the passage may be a self-revision. It is observed disapprovingly that no Negroes, no matter how rich, would be permitted in cabin class on a steamboat, but they are allowed to travel with the cattle in steerage (*NA*, 3:204–6). The violinist Eltrich is in the process of freeing a slave, as usual nearly white in color, having paid half her price and letting her work off the other half (*NA*, 6:162).

The treatment of Jews is also more evenhanded than elsewhere. There is, to be sure, the hardhearted Polish Jew, Veitel Kochmer, who exploits his son's beautiful voice for money; he pretends to be lame in order to avoid loading his own belongings, and no one on board wishes to share a cabin with him; later, a Pennsylvanian offers to find the boy a refuge if he wishes to run away, and in the end the boy grows ill, can no longer sing, and dies (NA, 2:18–22, 38; 3:197–200; 6:86). Hopfgarten accuses Veitel of having made the boy sing himself to death; Veitel shrugs off the charge and with implacable persistence tries to sell him something, including the stolen jewels, a coincidence that leads to Henkel's capture (NA, 6:210–14). But another Jew named Wald is a positive character. When a desperate boy turns up who lacks the money for passage, Wald takes up a collection for him; he has to squeeze the Polish Jew, but otherwise it is a good thing that there were so many Jews among the passengers, for they give freely, without inquiring about details, "so geizig sie sonst sein mochten," while the Christians quibble and stint (NA, 2:41). (The young man, Berger, turns out to be a deserter; the passengers hide him from capture by the harbor police, but he later dies in a steamboat explosion. Whether the patriotic Gerstäcker is ambivalent about him is undecidable.) Later Wald pays for milk for the children of a stranded family in New Orleans, pretending that he has found the money on the ground (NA, 3:73). He meets an acquaintance who speaks a horrible mixture of Judeo-German, English, French, and Spanish, who could not find work and was reduced to street peddling, to which he is adapting (NA, 3:375–76). This turns out to be prophetic, for Wald himself must adapt to peddling, in which role he is cordially received by a farmer and his wife who recall his kindness in New Orleans (NA, 6:77–79). Jews on board stick up for themselves; one makes Steinert get off his mattress (NA, 2:72–73). The "Literat" Theobald causes one seasick Jew to vomit by holding a plate of food under his nose, but when Theobald himself gets queasy, the Jew returns the favor (NA, 2:118–19). Hopfgarten when traveling must take refuge in a Jew's house, a scary place with an evil dog and an ugly old woman; he suspects the Jew of trying to poison his grog and cannot sleep for fear of being murdered, but when he awakes, the Jew is only cutting bread; he is perfectly kind and hospitable, refusing any money for lodging. Hopfgarten (as Gerstäcker's persona?) realizes his fears were all in his imagination and is ashamed of himself (NA, 4:262–63; 5:1–20).

Toward the end of the novel, Hopfgarten, who has been home to Germany and has returned for a visit, mulls with Eltrich the sadness of a carpenter who has made money supplying coffins during the fever, but lost all his family to it, so that his activity no longer has a purpose. His wife had already gone insane in a storm and died at the end of the voyage, so that he begins his American experience in remorse at his selfishness, which has murdered her (NA, 2:245–46). "Das Amerika," he says, "ist ein rechter guter Platz, Geld zu verdienen, wenn man fleißig ist, aber das ist auch Alles; ja, wenn es mir in Deutschland schlecht gegangen wäre" (NA, 6:165). Hopfgarten, picking up on this, blames the man for emigrating when he had no need to do so. But Eltrich will not accept this severity and replies that everyone carries in his breast the desire to improve himself. He goes on to say that if Germany would do more for the happiness of the people and recognize that the grace of God is not properly restricted to one crowned head, many fewer would be driven away: "Die Noth treibt vielleicht nur zwei Drittheile aller Auswanderer über das große Wasser, der Ekel das andere—und das gerade thut Deutschland weh—unendlich weh, denn was für wackere Kräfte sind ihm dadurch verloren gegangen!" To this Hopfgarten replies: "Ja, die Geheimräthe wandern nicht aus." Eltrich then asks Hopfgarten how he found Germany. He replies that, after the freedom of America, it seemed so artificial, constricted, petty, bureaucratic, and obsequious that it is a wonder the people don't all emigrate and leave officialdom behind; yet it is home, the fatherland; he wept to see it again. Eltrich understands but says he will never return, though Hopfgarten predicts that he may (NA, 6:165–68). In this passage is concentrated the ethos of the novel; for all the turmoil, suffering, and loss the emigrants experience, American freedom is what it is, a magnetic value to oppressed people, and some component of it a necessity for Germany if the drain on the nation is to be reversed.

The novel ends in the German town where it began. The previous tavern keeper has returned, reduced to beggary. The emigration agent has fled, exposed as a swindler. Hopfgarten marries Clara, widowed by the villainous Henkel when he shot himself to avoid arrest. It is learned that the son of the swindling innkeeper in New Orleans, who has protested his father's immoral dealings, has prospered after marrying Hedwig and offered the city half his fortune if it will match it to build a place for the proper care of immigrants (NA, 6:248–49). All the threads are tied in the conventional manner, but it is a curiously unstable ending, because the larger dynamic that has put the novel into motion has in no way come to rest.

## *Gold! Ein Californisches Lebensbild*

Readers who have encountered Gerstäcker's novel of the gold rush, originally published in 1857–58, have often come away with a good opinion of it. Even a critic generally disposed against his novels judged it the most perfect of his works on account of the unity of "Stoff und Erzähler."[8] It has, however, generally been numbered among the adventure novels rather than the emigration works. But if one of Gerstäcker's most fundamental concerns is the occupation of consciousness by yearnings, images, and fantasies attracting the susceptible to America, surely nothing else in American history, before or since, so spectacularly and extensively occupied consciousness as the discovery of gold in California. It was a kind of hyperbolically charged pressure cooker of the emigration; the forty-eighters became forty-niners. Of course, Germans were only a fraction of the forty-niners, and *Gold!* is not as exclusively focused on them as *Nach Amerika!* was, but they continue to be Gerstäcker's main concern.

Gerstäcker arrived in California, providentially, one must say, in August 1849 and, after first going bear hunting, just to stay in character (R, 2:22), headed for the mines. For some reason that has so far escaped me, he had a connection with "Captain" John Sutter (1803–80), the dubious Swiss adventurer on whose land, to his ultimate misfortune, the gold was originally discovered. To Cotta, Gerstäcker gave as a possible California address "care of Capt. Sutter" (*Br.* 2, 26), and he visited Sutter at his farm, bringing him a box of books from a friend of his youth (R, 2:133–34); later he described Sutter's conflict with radical egalitarians claiming squatter's rights on his property, who are treated as immature rowdies mouthing democratic slogans about the flag and the forefathers (R, 2:150–53). Gerstäcker remained in California until December 1850. Unlike some of the characters in his novel, he did not imagine he would obtain riches; as he put it to Cotta: "auf Californisches Gold darf ich doch verständiger Weise nicht zu viel rechnen" (*Br.* 2, 22). It was miserable, hard work that drove him against the limit of his endurance—after all the miseries came the bad luck that an Indian stole his gun (R, 2:98–124, 273)—but one must say that his fortune was not bad; he estimated that he had averaged about fifty dollars a week after expenses.[9] However, as has been mentioned earlier, it was an El Dorado for writing. The experience generated a long string of publications, fictional and nonfictional. As luck would have it, he landed in Australia in time for the gold rush of 1851, which he took to be a reprise of the Californian drama (R, 4:242) and which generated a further sequence of writings.

With impressive promptness he managed to get published during 1849 a booklet for emigrants consisting of translations of items from a California newspaper.[10] Another project had a more curious history: a translation of J. Tyrwhitt-Brooks, *Four Months among the Gold-Finders in*

*Alta California*, published in London in 1849.[11] This book was a hoax, concocted by the English writer Henry Vizetelly (1820–94), who never left London. The fraud was remarkably successful. The book was enthusiastically reviewed in England and, as the perpetrator cheerfully noted, "was instantly reprinted in a cheap form on the other side of the Atlantic, where it met with a large sale, and was translated into several foreign languages."[12] Gerstäcker was not aware of this, nor are his indefatigable bibliographers, but he smelled a rat: though he believed the author had been in the mines, he found the work "in vieler Hinsicht eine Erdichtung" and "die nicht üble Speculation eines englischen Buchhändlers"; Californian Indians do not take scalps as the book claimed, and Sutter assured him that, despite a detailed account of a visit to his farm and family, he had never seen the man (*R*, 2:246–47). Here, again, Gerstäcker's realistic instincts were at work.

The aspect of *Gold!* as adventure fiction does not appeal to me as much as it has to others, and I would prefer to leave its actual plot aside, which is, again, a matter of crimes perpetrated and exposed; there is a kind of armature in the troubles of a man named Hetson, who has married a woman who had been engaged to an English sailor believed lost but who has turned up again and whom Hetson fears, quite unnecessarily, as it turns out. His worries are exploited by the novel's villain, a crooked gambler and schemer named Siftly, and his quondam associates, though there is no honor among thieves in this novel. They are brought to justice in another of Gerstäcker's rough and ready but ultimately effective courtroom scenes. All of this, and more, is complicated and conventional; I shall restrict myself to some general observations.

Gold-rush California, including San Francisco, is a place more primitive, closer to the precivilized, brutish nature of man, than the backwoods of Arkansas. There are even, to my surprise, coyotes howling in San Francisco (*G*, 1:156–57). Here men are truly liberated into the combat of all against all, associating with one another for purely pragmatic and temporary reasons. The solidarity of the passengers shatters upon landing like mercury thrown to the ground (*G*, 1:60–61). Crime, cheating, chiseling, deception, and betrayal abound; there are cases of arson and murder (in his travel memoir, Gerstäcker indicated less crime and reported that theft was interdicted by regulators [*R*, 2:26–27]; the fiction is more sensational). A nugget is planted to trick men into buying a claim. Men leave their families and jobs to go into the mines; sailors desert as soon as their ships dock; the U.S. Navy must keep a watch on warships to prevent the seamen from deserting (*G*, 1:258). In a short story Gerstäcker remarked that the gold seekers have neither past nor present, only a future ("Die beiden Doppelgänger," *Z3*, 34;

cf. G, 1:130). Yet at the gateway to all this there is a fascinating magic place, a city of Oz: San Francisco, "die wunderlichste *Stadt* der Erde" (G, 1:45); arriving there was like entering a *Märchen* (R, 2:5–6). Having grown in a year from an unprepossessing adobe village to a bustling market city (G, 1:246–48), it is destroyed overnight by fire, rebuilt the next day, and so on; in his travel memoir Gerstäcker remarked that the fires were seen as regular, expected events (R, 2:240). After a fire destroys the city, a sign is put up reading:

> Go ahead young California!
> Who, the hell, cares
> for a fire!

This, the narrator observes, expresses the spirit of the Californian people; "'Who cares!' könnte das Motto für ganz Californien sein" (G, 1:183–84). But changes were visible even during the time he was away at the mines: the streets are now paved with wood and the city is becoming more North American, less Spanish; Gerstäcker notes the celebration of Californian statehood (R, 2:449–51). He makes a point that, when all of this is over, there will be a great future in this place (G, 2:293–94, 3:154).

Naturally, he is concerned to show how Germans behave under these conditions. Some suffer from the familiar emigrant pipe dreams, though cranked up to a higher pitch by the lure of gold. One, expecting his fiancée in three months, is confident of being able to mine an ounce a day until then, while another, a pharmacist, skeptical of such hopes, looks forward to exploiting the fools who get sick in the mines (G, 1:13–14); yet another is in a hurry because he must get back home in ten months with 20,000 talers in order to buy a farm; he is later discovered working alone, completely wild and in despair (G, 1:98–99; 3:103–9). Some, influenced by sensationalistic reports that exaggerate the lawlessness of California, arm themselves and form a militaristic fortress (G, 1:105–7), refusing to allow a countryman to join them because he is unarmed; they are treated as comic figures who have little success. An authoritarian, lazy *Justizrath* succeeds for a time in imposing his class authority on "biedere Deutsche" who could not shake off "den alten Unsinn" of deference toward his pompous title, but in the long run he fails because his self-estimate does not correspond to the reality around him; eventually he is dismissed as a "Holzkopf" (G, 3:325, 335). On the other hand, a baron makes his way by waiting on tables in a San Francisco hotel, completely shedding his aristocratic attributes; he eventually marries a poor Hispanic singer after rescuing her from the villains, one of whom he chivalrously brains with a plate (G, 1:233). Some do well but lose their earnings to crooked gamblers and gouging merchants. Some fail, while a few succeed in finding enough gold to meet their expenses. It would be hard to say that the Germans are very different from anyone else. It is said of them, however, that while the Americans are galvanized by the fire into rebuilding, the Germans, anxious and less resilient, flee the city: "die Amerikaner waren von Haus aus an ein bewegteres, von Wagnissen begleitetes Leben gewöhnt, während der Deutsche hier plötzlich Alles über den Haufen geworfen fand, was er bis dahin zu einer bürgerlichen Existenz als unumgänglich nöthig erachtet, nämlich: Ruhe und Sicherheit!" (G, 1:194). Typically unpolitical, they ignore the election of a new alcalde (G, 2:118).

Race problems are exacerbated in these conditions; there is a great deal of intergroup hostility and some belligerent nativism, a hatred of the English, Irish, and Mexicans (G, 2:88). The Indians, whom Gerstäcker portrays here with greater sympathy than anywhere else in his work since Assowaum in *Die Regulatoren*, are dignified but hopelessly marginalized. Dismissed by the *Justizrath* as "schwarze Heiden—Lumpenpack" (G, 1:296), they can get no hearing from the local, corrupt alcalde against a rapist because they have no gold, so they cut the rapist's ears off in desperate vigilantism. The alcalde is too busy selling quitclaims to give them justice against a murderer. The Americans stick together against the Indians. A big, broad-shouldered free Negro trying to help fight a fire is accused of arson and trampled to death by the mob (G, 1:174–77). The state attempts to impose a tax of twenty dollars a head on all foreign miners (G, 2:19); the French and Mexicans rebel against it and are put down by force; later, the Mexicans are attacked on a wholly unfounded suspicion of murder. The Chinese, whose industriousness (and restaurants) Gerstäcker praised in his memoir (R, 2:239), are attacked and abused because they are suspected of secretly finding gold. On the other hand, one of the characters forms a partnership with a Jew, "ein braver, ordentlicher Mann, der allerdings auf seinen Nutzen sah, dabei aber auch den seines wackern und unermüdlich thatigen Gehülfen wahrte" (G, 3:304).

All the turbulence destabilizes Gerstäcker's conventional notions of the American character. He wants to argue, as he does elsewhere, that the pursuit of money is the Americans' only motive—"hier galt weder Rang noch Stand—nur Gold" (G, 1:116); that life is cheap to Americans—"Menschenleben waren das Billigste in ganz Californien" (G, 1:251); and that they are oblivious to the beauties of nature where there is no gold (G, 1:253), valuing the environment only for exploitation—"Die Amerikaner sind ein praktisches Volk, und wo sie speculiren, geschieht das ohne alle Phantasie. Ein Amerikaner wird sich nie eine reizende Gegend zum Wohnort aussuchen, wenn er nicht seinen ganz besonderen Zweck dazu hat. Er liebt den rauschenden Wald—wenn er seine Stämme zu Brettern und Pfosten benutzen kann—er freut sich der murmelnden Quelle—wenn sie stark genug läuft, eine Mühle zu treiben—sonst nicht" (G, 1:262). A chapter is ironically called "Das Paradies" after the name of a town in the midst of God's temple of nature, defiled by the moiling for gold (G, 1:271-72). The speed of recovery after the fire, the opening of a bar in the midst of the ruins, is ascribed to the Yankee obsession with selling (G, 1:182). The first structure rebuilt is the Parker House with its gambling hell (G, 1:192-93). But how can this view be maintained? The gold rush is an international event; everyone behaves alike. What we see is not American but human behavior. And so the realistic *Geist der Erzählung* intervenes to counter the cliché. A German who shoots his ass's foal because it was causing its mother to move too slowly is whipped by an American despite his claim that he can do as he pleases with his own property (G, 1:278-80). The reformed baron says that, from what he had read, he expected to find the Americans "ein rohes, tabakkauendes, immer blos speculirendes, krämerhaftes Volk," but he has learned better:

> Gesindel genug giebt es unter ihnen, das ist wahr—und vielleicht auch nicht mehr wie bei uns in Deutschland, nur daß es hier nicht in so feinen Röcken und mit Glanzstiefeln umherläuft; aber ein Unternehmungsgeist steckt dafür in den Burschen, eine Kraft und Ausdauer, eine Zähigkeit in einmal Begonnenem, und ein Muth, das Tollköpfigste, Riscanteste zu unternehmen, vor dem man wirklich Respect haben muß. Ich verlange nicht, daß wir ihnen ihr ekles Tabbakkauen nachmachen sollten, aber wenn wir uns ein Beispiel an ihrem nationalen Gefühl, an ihrem National*stolz* nehmen, und das nur einmal bei uns *pflanzen* wollten, dann könnte das ein großer Segen für uns werden, und wir gewönnen vielleicht auch einen Platz dabei, auf dem es *wachsen* möchte.
>
> (G, 3:118-19)

That Gerstäcker later observed exactly the same behavior in Australia would seem considerably to modify the charge against the Americans and make it relevant, at best, to a mid-nineteenth-century development in socially determined consciousness.

Even in the Californian turmoil Gerstäcker finds occasion to draw a contrast with German unfreedom. When the American flag flies in the attack on the Mexicans, the narrator breaks out into an eloquent expression of yearning for a flag of the fatherland that would protect its citizens with force and symbolize an effective diplomacy: "Oh, im

Geiste seh' ich die beiden Menschen vor mir—den Amerikaner in seinem schlichten Rocke, das gehobene Banner seines Vaterlandes in der Linken, nur den *Versuch* zu züchtigen, seine Flagge zu beleidigen, und müßte er ihn mit dem eigenen Leben zahlen—und dagegen den geschmeidigen Diplomaten mit gesticktem Frack, dreieckigem Hut und seidenen Strümpfen, die Brust mit Orden bedeckt, die er bei Geburtsanzeigen und Hoffesten bekommen, höflich und rücksichtsvoll gegen die ganze Welt, nur das eigene Volk, die eigene Flagge unter die Füße tretend, die daheim in Winkeln und auf Böden modert" (G, 3:41–42). Rarely do we see in such concentrated form how the vision of American independence feeds Gerstäcker's nationalism and his bourgeois resentment and ambition simultaneously.

## *In Amerika. Amerikanisches Lebensbild aus neuerer Zeit. Im Anschluß an "Nach Amerika"*

*In Amerika*, which, as the subtitle and other comments of the author clearly indicate, was intended as a sequel, was the last book-length work of Gerstäcker's lifetime. While it was serialized in the *Hamburgische Nachrichten* beginning in the fall of 1871, he evidently did not live to see the book version, for he suggested to Costenoble that it be postponed to the fall of 1872, and in his last letter to his publisher of April 22, 1872, a little over a month before his death, he was still giving instructions for its division into volumes (*Cost. Corr.*, cols. 1200–4). Even by the standards of his spotty reception history, it was stillborn and forgotten. Even his champion Ostwald feels obliged to say that its execution was "lustlos," that figures turn up and disappear without any characterization, and that the links to *Nach Amerika!* "bestehen teilweise überhaupt nicht oder können nur erahnt werden."[13] Indeed, certain aspects of the novel suggest failing powers. The plot lines are stringy, tangled, and jumpy; once again crimes, pursuits, and punishments are plugged in, but to no cohesive avail. At the end of the novel there is no obvious reason why it could not just keep going on.

A number of characters from the earlier novel do recur, among them the colorless hero Donner, now a prosperous but simply-living coal mine owner recovering in his Indiana town of Donnersville from a Civil War wound. The actuary Ledermann, still fearful of being discovered by his wife and still under the name "Fortmann" from the first novel, now seems to express some of the views of the author. The medical and clerical professions continue to receive familiar treatment. Along with impressive American quacks, the barber from the emigration ship has now set himself up as a pompous physician employing un-German, American advertising practices by placing a skeleton in his show window, while a genuine M.D. from Germany, a new character named Rosswein, has become a barber in America. Rosswein drives the fraud from the field by parodying him with a skeleton drawn on the front of his own house; it turns out he is serving a self-imposed penance for having lost his wife in childbirth, and, instead of returning to medical practice, he determines to found a chemical factory. The picaresque Maulbeere has returned to the redemptive benefits of brandy; he has founded a tavern called "Zum Methodistenprediger," and is able to frustrate the protesting Methodist preachers by proving that he is certified as one himself. He seems to have defrauded the denomination, but nothing can be done about it, as he knows too much (*IA*, 2:81–82). Thus the novel is not without humor and invention, but much of it, including some would-be comic episodes, seems labored and reinforces the impression that Gerstäcker was wringing it out of himself.

However, qualitative considerations aside, the novel has its interest for the purposes pursued here because it attempts to evaluate continuities and discontinuities in the immediate post–Civil War situation. It is also more overtly political than its predecessor or the American novellas and stories. It begins in Georgia during the last phase of the war at the time of Sherman's march (the narrator says "December des Jahres 1863," *IA*, 1:3, but this is obviously a mistake for 1864). As we have seen, Gerstäcker became acquainted with General Sherman, for whom the fourth chapter of *In Amerika* is named. Gerstäcker, normally averse to heroization, had described him with admiration in his travel book as "ein guter Mensch" and here makes a hero of him; he splits the South "mit einer Zähigkeit und Kühnheit, die ihres Gleichen suchte," gives a "short and sweet" reply to planters who seek an audience with him, and is described with a footnoted excerpt from a German history of the Civil War (*IA*, 1:61, 63, 66–67). Although Sherman himself was apolitical, his heroization here is nevertheless a symptom of the political outlook of the novel, a punitive attitude toward the postwar South that locates Gerstäcker, for the only time in his career, within an American political discourse to a degree distantly comparable with that of Sealsfield. That is, with respect to postwar policy and Reconstruction, Gerstäcker aligns himself with the Radical Republicans, though he does not quite do so on all issues, as we shall see. The alignment is exhibited most explicitly in recurrent expressions of contempt for President Andrew Johnson as a betrayer of the cause, an ineffectual evader of responsibility, and an appeaser of the resurgent planter aristocracy, which interprets his weakness as cowardice. He is referred to as "Schneider

Johnson" (*IA*, 2:77); this contempt for his working-class origins, of which he himself was proud, is completely inconsistent with the positive view of American equality in the novel—for example, the observation that often the lowest work is done by educated people, who are admissible to society if their *Bildung* allows it, or the willingness of one of the characters from the predecessor novel, a count named Wolf, to cast off title and privilege (*IA*, 1:79, 83). The inconsistency suggests that the condescending view of Johnson is taken in an unmediated way from American political discourse.[14]

The most specific delinquency with which the novel charges Johnson is his failure to take energetic steps to suppress the Ku Klux Klan. The depiction of the Klan is the one particular of the novel that has occasionally caught the attention of scholars. Gerstäcker sees the Klan in class terms: it is one of the devices of the southern aristocrats, who have not learned how to work and are at a loss without slave labor, to reverse as far as possible the verdict of the war. In the process they are descending into degeneration and brutality; bringing them to justice takes considerable effort. Before the defeat of the Confederacy, these men despise the Yankee slave catcher, who regards himself as a republican and therefore in turn despises them as aristocrats and monarchists. The narrator interprets their disdain for blacks as a subset of a general class arrogance: "Verachteten jene südlichen 'Herren' doch grundsätzlich die arbeitende Klasse, welcher Farbe sie auch angehörte" (*IA*, 1:11–12, 15). Gerstäcker is aware that the southern gentry thought of themselves as republicans, but remarks that few actually were (*IA*, 1:15). Quite in the Radical Republican line, he comments that the South is being shown too much kindness, "so daß das arme Land gar nicht zu Ruhe kam und die volle Ordnung selbst bis zu diesem Augenblick (1872) noch nicht wieder hergestellt werden konnte" (*IA*, 3:65). Georgians hope for a war between the United States and Mexico in which the South would ally itself with France and the Mexican Emperor Maximilian, of whose lugubrious fate Gerstäcker naturally knew at the time of writing (*IA*, 2:134).

With regard to slavery and blacks the situation in this novel is more complicated than ever before. On slavery, Gerstäcker has come to a clear view of it as an unmitigated evil. In a footnote he describes again the separation of families at auction, the agents of which are slave dealers from the North, called "cooper-heads" (*IA*, 1:7; the error is perhaps the typesetter's rather than the author's). In another, long footnote he denounces the defenders of slavery—"Selbst hier in Deutschland"—and dismisses the argument that the slaves are better off than European workers by asking if even the most miserable proletarian would *choose* slavery, a point that may be an echo of Abraham Lincoln himself. Again he talks of the separation of families, adding remarks on their treatment as domestic animals and their enforced illiteracy. He concludes by thanking God for slavery's abolition in the United States and demanding its abolition in other countries (*IA*, 1:54). In another place, the narrator denounces the "dickköpfige deutsche 'Gelehrte'" who defend slavery and dismisses the southern preachers who defend it from the Bible, since anything can be proven from the Bible (*IA*, 1:141); elsewhere, Rosswein, too, curses those in Germany who defend slavery (*IA*, 2:31).

The potential of slave rebellion and black resistance is also present. Gerstäcker finds occasion to quote Schiller's "Worte des Glaubens": "vor dem Sclaven, wenn er die Kette bricht—vor dem freien Menschen erzittere nicht" (*IA*, 1:63). Sherman's invasion brings turmoil to slaves and slaveholders alike. The novel begins with the pursuit and capture of a free black preacher who is bringing the slaves the news of the emancipation, which the slaveholders have tried to keep secret for fear of an uprising; he is subsequently freed from lynch justice by other blacks. Gerstäcker cites in this connection the "self-evident" truth "that all Men are created equal," ascribing it, however, to the Constitution rather than the Declaration of Independence (*IA*, 1:17). The slaves are skeptical that this war is intended to free them, since they know that families were broken up by northerners as well (*IA*, 1:35). While the southern blacks are still intimidated by the master, a northern black teases him and must be prevented from shooting him when threatened with a whipping. Something like an uprising actually occurs on the plantation liberated by Sherman's troops. The slaves, who turn violently against both their detested mulatto slave driver and one of the worst of the slaveholders, "waren plötzlich *Menschen* geworden" (*IA*, 1:58); they kill the former and throw the latter out a window, trampling him to death. In New Orleans, however, unemployed, dangerous blacks, led by an evil-looking rascal who knocks out two policemen, become a mob that must be quelled by soldiers, with some loss of life (*IA*, 1:147–50). Still, when they arm themselves to demand the right to use the streetcars, the occupying soldiers support them out of hatred of the cotton barons (*IA*, 1:168). At the end of the novel the slave catcher of the first scene is found hacked to pieces in Donnersville, apparently by the black preacher he had nearly caused to be lynched (*IA*, 3:203–5). At the same time, the fears of a slave rebellion, which are alleged to account for Lincoln's hesitation, much commented on by German observers, to issue the Emancipation Proclamation, are said to have been overwrought (*IA*, 2:77–78).

There are admirable blacks in the book, among them a blacksmith and his wife, whose children, two pretty girls, have been taken from them; the restoration of this family is one of the detective-story plot lines of the novel. The freed slaves who come to Donnersville are praised as good workers (*IA*, 2:2). The freed slaves on the plantations, on the other hand, are feckless because they have never had to think of the future. They have rhythm, however, and their musicality shows that the race is not bloodthirsty or vengeful (*IA*, 1:47). A vignette of the free black community in Cincinnati may strike the contemporary reader as less humorous than Gerstäcker meant it to be. He had earlier set a story, entitled "Ein Nachmittag in Cincinnati" (originally 1855), in this milieu, in which a fight breaks out between drunken whites and a black, "der arme Teufel, der keinen Menschen beleidigt hatte" (*AmT*, 2:157), who is chased into the house of a black doctor, which is wrecked by the mob.[15] Now, however, the blacks have become mildly comic figures, the fat women speaking in bass voices the idiosyncratic dialect that separates blacks from the white community; the freedmen take on incongruously dignified white names; and they dress with tasteless imitativeness (*IA*, 1:111–14, 126). In a comparable scene in Savannah, the incongruous names are "Euphrosine, Julie, Adelaide, Sidonie, Feliciana, Franciska, Eugenie, Rosa..., Guidos, Georges, Williams, Victors, Leos, Charles..., Washington, Jefferson, Franklin, Lincoln, Grant, Sherman" (*IA*, 1:205–6).

It is in this connection that "Fortmann" appears as a persona of the author: to a pronounced racist he replies that the blacks cannot be expected to take responsibility for themselves at once, and, if they cause trouble to whites in the future, it will be deserved as "der Fluch der bösen That" (*IA*, 1:120–21). At least they are not as drunken and disorderly as the Irish (*IA*, 1:125), a motif that recurs several times, clearly absorbed from the environment; Maulbeere turns up in such a slovenly condition that he is taken for an Irishman (*IA*, 3:175). But "Fortmann," like Gerstäcker, admits that he finds blacks an unpleasant race and comments on their imitativeness: "Der Neger hat etwas Affenartiges in seinem Nachahmungstrieb"; being denied schooling, they can only choose the most stupid things (*IA*, 1:121, 127). But aping is not only a metaphor; the blacks really do look like monkeys—as do the Irish and the Germans once in a while, and even Maulbeere (*IA*, 1:201–2; 2:83). The narrator finds it an incongruity that Americans crush the Indians at the same time as they have freed "die äthiopische Race" (*IA*, 3:88).

On the matter of suffrage Gerstäcker begins to deviate from the Radical Republican line. With the election of Grant—the novel here looks ahead to 1868—the Republicans begin to misuse their power, "wie das leider so häufig geschieht" (*IA*, 2:77). The suffrage was a device to punish the South, but a bad idea, for the blacks have become shiftless, dirty, and alcoholic without their masters, especially since Sherman has taken the youngest and strongest with him; they are not ready for responsibility and should have had a literacy test; some blacks when voting forget their names, since so many of them are the same, and they are easily misled (*IA*, 2:80–81, 87, 110). The plantations are becoming abandoned. Gerstäcker elaborated these points at considerable length in his postwar travel book. He tells of a plot to make a black vice-president; what if he were to become president! It would lead to revolution (*NR*, 1:109–10, 308–9, 327–29, 348). But even in the novel, where he seems to be moving in the direction of post-Reconstruction sophistries, he tries to put his observations in a less racially defined, more anthropologically comparative context: "Sie wollten jetzt gern zeigen, daß sie freie, unabhängige Menschen wären, und wußten das in keiner andern Weise fertig zu bringen, als daß sie unverschämt wurden—genau so, wie es in den Staaten nur zu häufig unsere deutschen Bauern machen, wenn sie sich als freie, unabhänige [*sic*] Amerikaner zeigen wollen und das dann *auch* in keiner andern Weise darzuthun wissen" (*IA*, 2:122). The familiar uneasiness about race and color is still evident. The brave preacher is "kein ächter Vollblutneger mit breit gedrückter Nase und wulstigen Lippen, sondern ein Mulatte, von ziemlich dunkler Färbung allerdings, aber mit einem sonst [!] ganz intelligenten . . . Gesicht" (*IA*, 1:4). A footnote explains that Creoles are not, as people suppose, "eine Mischlingsrace" but "Vollblut-Weiße" (*IA*, 1:27). Again we have the beautiful black girl who is really white, an orphan named Hebe with blond hair and blue eyes, racially identifiable only by her fingernails; she is rescued from a murderous mob by Wolf, who, as a German, is free from prejudice, and she will be taken to unprejudiced Germany as the wife of a young painter (*IA*, 1:134, 142–43; 3:166, 168–69).

Whether the claims that Germany is without prejudice are consistent with the strictures on German defenders of slavery is perhaps an idle question, but they indicate a certain shift in the depiction of Germans in this novel, which is the consequence of the tour Gerstäcker made in 1867, when he found the Germans in much improved circumstances. He even moved toward a sense of superiority toward other Americans that became typical of the German American community, although he never abandons his admiration for American ingenuity and efficiency, and he flatly denies pipe dreams of a future German hegemony in America (*NR*, 1:29, 95, 245–46, 382–83). Both Donner and Wolf in the novel are thinking of returning to Germany. To be sure, some of the older attitudes remain. Once again it is said that the emigrant must lose the last cent brought with him before he can earn his first dollar (*IA*, 1:108). German swindlers, loafers, and incompetents are still in evidence;

a fat-headed *Freiherr* and his stupid wife are objects of satire. Echoing a complaint of many commentators on the German American community, the narrator deplores their aloofness from politics carried over from the petty particularism of the homeland (*IA*, 2:3–4). They have also retained their obsequious respect for the police (*IA*, 2:30). The emigration issue arises again in a curious way, in an effort to lure German peasants to a despoiled plantation as replacements for the lost slave labor; even the knavish emigration agent from the beginning of *Nach Amerika!* turns up in this connection. Donner warns the peasants that they will be hated in the South because of the German sympathies for the Union as well as despised as working men (*IA*, 1:107). However, although Donner worries that the peasant blockheads will be easily fooled, Gerstäcker now connects their vulnerability to his obsession about schooling. When asked why the Irish, who are much more stupid than Germans, do not fall for such tricks, Donner replies that it is because German peasant communities starve their schools so that their youths are deprived of learning (*IA*, 1:93). The Germans to whom the desolated plantation is sold are called "weiße Nigger" (*IA*, 2:115). Other Germans are sold land by planters that actually belongs to the United States government and must be paid for again; the neighborliness Gerstäcker remembers from the wilderness has disappeared; a Klansman agitates for the extirpation and outlawing of all Germans (*IA*, 3:52–53, 67).

But in other places Germans are beginning to show signs of superiority in the American environment. In a footnote Gerstäcker refers with pride to the engineer John Roebling, who designed the bridge across the Ohio River at Cincinnati as well as the Brooklyn Bridge (*IA*, 1:110; repeated 2:54–55 and note and *NR*, 1:91–93). Cincinnati is no longer a place of unemployment and deprivation, but a thriving center of German life and at the same time more the real America than New York (*IA*, 2:41). While Gerstäcker earlier had consistently argued that Germans should not insist upon their traditional customs and equipment, now, in Indiana, they are warmer in winter because they heat with German stoves instead of wasteful American fireplaces (*IA*, 3:139). Yet it is just here that Gerstäcker, in the person of the normally sarcastic Rosswein, places his most eloquent statement of the capacity of American freedom for enabling Germans to achieve their human potential:

> Wir hier in Amerika sind ein ganz anderes Volk wie daheim, wir haben uns nicht allein körperlich, sondern wohl auch geistig hier geändert, und zwar auf eine ganz wunderbare Weise. Was wir nämlich in Deutschland selber nie waren, das sind wir plötzlich

hier Alle miteinander geworden: wirkliche Deutsche, und die alten, elenden Vorurtheile der Heimath konnten gleichfalls das Seewasser nicht vertragen. Wir wurden nicht allein Deutsche, sondern auch Menschen, mit dem Bewußtsein der Gleichberechtigung bei Allen, die auch etwas leisten, und damit erwachte, was Viele daheim kaum dem Namen nach gekannt: unser Selbstgefühl.

(*IA*, 3:145)

Here and there Gerstäcker cannot refrain from clichés about the American fixation on earning money. An innkeeper in Georgia hates blacks, but does business with them anyway, "ein Amerikaner durch und durch, und wenn er nur Geld verdiente—von wem, blieb sich vollkommen gleich" (*IA*, 2:113). But he acknowledges that this commercial energy is bringing the great Union Pacific Railroad into being (*IA*, 2: 173–74). As a kind of valedictory, he provides a panorama of the whole expanding nation: he imagines himself in a giant balloon, surveying the busy, industrializing North, the desolate South, full of hate and passion, the struggle of wilderness and civilization in the West, the progress of the telegraph and the railroad, the cities blooming on the West Coast, and the great forests; in regard to the lawlessness of the West, he observes, quite like the Alkalde in Sealsfield's *Cajütenbuch*, that such ruffians are necessary to conquer the land (*IA*, 3:86–89). Thus there is still strength of vision in this last of Gerstäcker's emigration novels.

## A Postscript on Mimesis

With a certain wiliness, the narrator of *In Amerika* recurs to the venerable trope that his book is not a novel. Of a marriage of two characters brought together by his customary recourse to coincidence, he remarks: "Die ganze Sache hatte allerdings nicht das geringste Romanhafte oder Abenteuerliche; keine Schwierigkeiten waren zu überwinden, keine Intriguen zu spielen, und kein langer und vielleicht ungewisser Brautstand lag vor ihnen" (*IA*, 3:139). But, if the novel is not like a novel, real life can be, as the author's persona "Fortmann" explains, "Sie glauben gar nicht, welche wunderlichen Schicksale mancher einzelne Mensch durchzumachen hat und wie sich oft in unserer unmittelbaren Nähe, ja unter unseren Augen und bei den unscheinbarsten Menschen wirklich romanhafte Zustände abspielen, ohne daß wir eine Ahnung davon haben" (*IA*, 3:156). Of course, these gestures are devices of fiction, but in Gerstäcker's case they are meant literally, to account for the artlessness of which, as a widely read man, he was doubtless well aware. The difficulty bedeviling "realism" in literary criticism is not only epistemological, but also a practical problem of aesthetics. Art is inimical to mimesis, and vice versa, because art accentuates the shaping and organizing purpose that is present in all discourse but is refined and elaborated in literature to the point that, "realistic" or not, literature comes to be bounded from common experience and thus absorbs mimesis into form. Whatever our theoretical views may be on the possibility of mimesis in literature nevertheless somehow surviving, one thing is clear: mimesis was Gerstäcker's *intention* in his fiction about America. That he claims so in his texts (e.g., *Reg*, 3; *NA*, 1:viii–ix), is, of course, no proof that it is so, for it might be a literary convention, especially as he subtitles one of his fantastic ghost stories "Nach einer wahren Begebenheit" (*AzW*, 1:83). More compelling are the relatively seamless transitions between his fiction and nonfiction. The reader of his emigration manual is in the same realm of perception as the reader of his emigration novels.

He was not an author who aspired to art and failed; he aspired to be useful to people by transmitting true images, and a case can be made that he achieved much of what is possible in such an endeavor. I do not hold with arguments that see him as an essentially Edenic and romantic writer submerging mimesis in mythography.[16] Gerstäcker sought in America a realm of freedom and love, of untouched nature (*Br. 1*, 11, 172), but that is not what he found, and not what he reported; instead, as the editor of his correspondence with Schultz observes: "Seine romantischen Vorstellungen von der 'weiten Welt,' geprägt durch Romane Coopers und Defoes, Bulwer-Lyttons und später Melvilles, wurden zerstört" (*Br. 1*, 277). It is more accurate to say that, from a literary point of view, his realism "limits the scope of his art," that he was too dependent on experience, not enough on imagination.[17] Yet such a judgment ignores his purpose. The historian Miller observes that Gerstäcker, as "a man of action, not a contemplative intellectual," is misunderstood by ignoring "the extent to which ... these works ... were based in reality without mythopoeic intent," and acknowledges that "he put more energy into ensuring that his descriptions of physical and social institutions were accurate than he did into other aspects of fiction."[18] In fact, historians have used his account in *Nach Amerika!* of the boat connection from Bremen to Bremerhaven as a source.[19] Gerstäcker requires to be measured by his own standards of mimesis. By those standards, he achieved an excellence hardly matched in the two hundred years of writing about America from Germany.

# Excursus II. Anti-Americanism? Talvj, Ferdinand Kürnberger, Reinhold Solger

The negative discourse about America has a long history. There seems to have been a need among Europeans to repel the implications of a vast New World. The eighteenth century developed a peculiar set of quasi-scientific ideas about the diminishment and stunted growth of nature on the American continent. Elaborated by the French naturalist George-Louis Leclerc, Comte de Buffon, and a Netherlander in Prussia, Cornelius de Pauw, they had a long life in various guises.[1] The refusal of American reality to be congruent with the utopian image of it sometimes called forth a sharp reversal into disappointment and defamation. As early as 1797, a frustrated speculator, Dietrich von Bülow, wrote an extremely critical book, *Der Freistaat von Nordamerika in seinem neuesten Zustand*, in which several long-lived themes are already present: lack of culture, lawlessness, religious fanaticism, and, above all, the enduring motif of German anti-Americanism: the distortion of the moral life by crass commercialism. In 1820 the by now determinedly counterrevolutionary Friedrich Schlegel emphasized the sinister flaw that more than anything else inhibited German acceptance of the claims of American democracy: slavery. The emigration was also in many quarters an irritant, for it seemed a reproach to nationalist fidelity. In the German discourse about America, anti-Americanism became a kind of subgenre.[2]

The term "anti-Americanism," however, is sometimes applied indiscriminately. A discourse critical of America is not necessarily anti-American, since we have a discourse critical of ourselves. I should like to see the term restricted to assaults on the core of American experience and self-understanding, bearing the characteristic markers of prejudice, cliché, and tendentiousness. An example of an author who might be exempted from the charge of anti-Americanism in this sense is Talvj, the pen name of Therese Albertine Luise *von* Jakob Robinson (1797–1870).[3]

I venture my comments on her in a tentative spirit, however. Talvj was until quite recently an almost totally forgotten writer. Most of the contemporary work on her has been accomplished by a single person, Martha Kaarsberg Wallach of Central Connecticut State University, without whose assistance I could not even have approached the topic.

Not having had access to the German original of Talvj's novel *Die Auswanderer* (1852), I have been obliged to work from the translation (probably Talvj's own), *The Exiles*, published in the following year.[4] On the strength of her career as a whole, if not so much of this novel alone, Talvj is a worthy beneficiary of the revived interest in women writers and intellectuals. For although she lived an almost completely domestic life, first with her parents, then with her American husband, Edward Robinson (1794–1864), a learned, well-regarded biblical scholar, she was a philologist of major accomplishment.[5] Having lived in Russia in her youth, she became competent in Slavic languages and, at the suggestion of Goethe, who was very interested in Serbo-Croatian poetry, translated Serbian folk songs, which appeared in 1825–26. According to Talvj, "Goethe considered it as an advantage, that the work of translation had fallen into the hands of a lady. Only a female mind, the great poet thought, was capable of the degree of accommodation requisite to clothe the 'barbarian poems' in a dress, in which they could be relished by readers of nations foreign to their genius."[6] That passage appeared in the learned work in English on the history of Slavic languages and literatures she published in 1850. She had earlier written a book on Germanic folk songs and, more importantly, in 1840 she produced the demonstration that the renowned songs of Ossian had been concocted by James Macpherson. She also wrote an extensively researched history of the colonization of New England in the seventeenth century and translated novels of Sir Walter Scott, a study of American Indian languages, and several volumes of her husband's researches in the Holy Land. For these achievements alone she deserves to be remembered.

Of her several stories and novels, *The Exiles* is the only one that takes place in America, but it is grounded in extensive experience. After her marriage in 1828 she lived in Andover, Massachusetts, then in Boston, where she met the radical refugee Karl Follen and his wife, then in New York City, where her husband became professor at the Union Theological Seminary and where she became acquainted with Washington Irving and Margaret Fuller. After her husband's death she settled in Hamburg; her American experience encompassed, with interruptions for travel in Europe and Palestine, thirty-six years. But it is doubtful whether she ever fully acclimated herself. The semantic shift in title from *Die Auswanderer* to *The Exiles* is telling, and the novel is full of the stress imposed upon German consciousness and identity in an alien environment.

The heroine of *The Exiles*, Clotilde Osten, is an almost saintly young woman who is engaged to Franz Hubert, an idealistic young man who has been imprisoned for participation in the abortive revolutionary attack on the Frankfurt arsenal in 1833. After six years, he is pardoned on condition that he leave for America. (The chronology is a little unclear; later, Talvj has young men disputing with one another about Jackson, Nicholas Biddle, and the Bank [E, 230], issues that had become considerably less current by the time the action of the novel must take place; in any case, Hubert is not a forty-eighter, as he is sometimes called in the criticism.) The departure is so rushed that they do not have time to be married. On the other side of the Atlantic, the ship burns and sinks; each believes the other is lost. Clotilde washes up on the Florida coast, where she is rescued by a fiery, darkly handsome young planter of obscure half-Hispanic origins, Alonzo Castleton. After having her nursed back to health, Alonzo places her as governess in the family of his cousins in Charleston, South Carolina, whose beautiful, willful, and high-strung daughter Virginia, "a literary ancestor of Scarlett O'Hara,"[7] Alonzo is rather unsuccessfully courting. For Virginia is infatuated with a "Polish nobleman" called Berghehof, who is being prosecuted for abolitionist activity. The experienced novel reader will have guessed early that this is, in fact, Hubert, who had rather implausibly been rescued by a passing vessel and taken to Maine. There he had been nurtured by a picture-book Yankee merchant, who would not lend him a hundred dollars but otherwise showed him every hospitality. How Hubert got to South Carolina is too complicated and implausible to explain; however, after he has been sentenced to ten years in prison for abetting a slave escape, there is an implausible recognition scene with Clotilde, who has brought him a message from Virginia; Clotilde implausibly springs him from jail and they flee northward, get married, and eventually settle in rural tranquility in Vermont. However, Alonzo, incited by a raging Virginia, pursues them there. Hubert refuses to duel with him, having learned that Alonzo is his implausible half-brother, Hubert's father having had an illicit dalliance with a passionate but otherwise unsatisfactory Hispanic woman. Alonzo, who does not know this, murders Hubert; Clotilde gives birth to a stillborn baby and dies herself; Alonzo travels the world in grief and remorse; Virginia marries a wealthy planter she despises and lives with him in Europe, where she is likely to turn Catholic.

Thus this is not one of your American success stories. Ten years later, a German American writer, Georg Willrich (?1805–61), named the heroine of his much more optimistic novel, *Erinnerungen aus Texas. Wahrheit und Dichtung*, Bertha von Osten, very likely to highlight the contrast with Talvj's novel.[8] But it is not an American tragedy, either, because its interests lie elsewhere. First and foremost, the novel, characteristically for Talvj, is concerned with woman's fate. This aspect need not be recapitulated in detail here, as it has recently received a thorough if quite disapproving feminist analysis.[9] The author's basic outlook is one of moderate and enlightened but quite firm conservatism. Clotilde, centered and sure in herself, is the touchstone of propriety and value. She wishes to learn and expand, and in matters of thought and feeling to be on a footing of mutuality with her man, but she is fully committed to the domestic role; her ambition in life is to be the head of a household, a comfort and support to a husband and a nurturer of children. Hubert, who is kindly and considerate as well as loving, nevertheless often pays no attention to her wishes and ideas, a preoccupation with himself that Clotilde notes but accepts in silent obedience. The beautiful, passionate, independently wealthy, and freedom-loving Virginia is given short shrift by the author; indeed, she is the main source of the catastrophe in the novel. Clotilde tries but fails to persuade her that "Berghehof" appears to be avoiding her because a poor immigrant of culture and conscience could not honorably pursue a liaison with a wealthy young woman, while Virginia supposes she may declare this distinction to be of no importance. Her view that she may choose a man without her father's approval and blessing meets with Clotilde's implacable disapproval; indeed, it is this circumstance that gives Clotilde permission to run off with Hubert.

The most central and deeply rooted element of identity in the novel is religious. Nothing isolates Clotilde more in the American environment than her affective commitment to conventional German Protestantism, a direct, uncomplicated, and undisturbed relationship to God. Though she has learned some English before her emigration, she feels that it is *"a language in which she could not pray"* (*E*, 25; Talvj's emphasis). In the Castleton family there is a history of Catholic bigotry that continues to have disruptive effects in the current generation. The daughter Sarah, an exact opposite to her freethinking sister Virginia, is a fanatical evangelical, who eventually, in obedience to the sect's elders, renounces a missionary she likes in order to marry another she does not care for. Clotilde is dismayed by this, as she is by Sarah's relentless religious activity, her rigidity, and her mechanical devotions, yet, because she is pious, honest, and in service to her highest principles, Clotilde thinks better of her than she does of Virginia. A northern woman, a "great-granddaughter of the celebrated Dr. Cotton Mather" (*E*, 133), who comes to South Carolina to dispose of her slaves more advantageously, harasses Clotilde with absurd, literalist theological questions while complaining of the "infidels and atheists among the learned men of Germany," one of whom, the celebrated theologian Tholuck, is even reputed to be a "Universalist" (*E*, 135). In Vermont, Clotilde does not like the dry Congregationalists and finds that the Methodist church is attended mostly by blacks, ministered to by a stagecoach driver (*E*, 343).

But the real threat to her equilibrium lurks in Hubert, who in religious matters is a *Vormärz* liberal. Even before leaving Germany, she finds that his pantheism conflicts with her "simple Christian morality," even though he believes in God with awe and avoids the horrors of materialism (*E*, 38–39). When they are reunited, he shocks her with his wish to transcend "superannuated prejudices" by getting married without benefit of clergy, since "the mere religious ceremony is of no account." He yields the point, but the ceremony turns out to be unpropitious; the Lutheran pastor is a farmer who, interrupted in his milking, gets through the ceremony as quickly as possible, not even calling out the couple's names. Clotilde, who felt a "drop of poison" corroding her heart at Hubert's attitude, is "inwardly frozen" at the ceremony, while Hubert regards it with "contemptuous indifference" (*E*, 206–7, 209). Although the loving couple is able to negotiate these differences, one imagines seeds of trouble for the future, which, however, their early deaths turn into a blind motif.

It is evident from this development of the theme that Clotilde's religious displacement is not fundamentally a critique of America but a function of the conservative ethos of the novel. Other areas of criticism can also be found to be not strictly anti-American. Clotilde, to be sure, is horrified at the culture of slavery that surrounds her in Florida and South Carolina, but must keep silent because she has learned that one cannot criticize slavery and northern "lukewarmness" without the "reproach of arrogantly meddling with their domestic affairs" (*E*, 122). Virginia's professed antislavery position is treated as merely contrariness toward her family, for she lacks empathy with blacks, and when a maid breaks one of her favorite objects, she has the girl given thirty lashes. Sarah, on the other hand, is unhappy with slavery, but regards obedience to constituted authority as obedience to God; she teaches her slaves about the Gospel, though not reading, as that is against the law. But it would seem plain that antislavery sentiment should not be equated with anti-Americanism, since America itself was so divided by it, unless slavery is identified with the essence of America, as it sometimes is.

Furthermore, it is clear that Talvj was quite conventionally racist herself, or, as Wallach has put it more gently: "Die Einstellung der Autorin den schwarzen Sklaven Nordamerikas gegenüber ist durch Mitleid und Unbehagen gekennzeichnet."[10] The blacks who rescue her from her shipwreck speak "jargon" and are grotesque in appearance, with lips that seem swollen from blood and enormous, scary teeth (*E*, 42–44). On

New York streets there are "negroes of all shades, from a coal-black to a pale, dirty brown. . . . And in the afternoon, when the cooks and chambermaids have leisure to walk and shop, there peeps out from many a white satin plumed bonnet, from many a pink or sky-blue dress-hat, an African face, which seems to belong to the monkey tribe rather than to the human race" (E, 304). The abolitionist agitator with whom the hapless Hubert has become associated is represented as something close to a maniac, and Hubert himself says he disapproves of the methods of the abolitionists (E, 183, 274). On other matters, such as the Irish, or the new wave of European immigrants, Talvj has absorbed American prejudices. Among the elegant ladies of New York "many a wild-looking, bandit-like fellow saunters along, fresh from 'Erin's green isle'"; the Irish are "a thoroughly raw, uneducated people" denationalizing New York but still held in check by the respectable people of Boston. Even German immigrants are a pitiful sight: "For the immigration of the last twenty years has inundated New York with the plague of most large European cities, the troublesome brood of insolent beggar children of all nations, an abandoned race, in whom the thinking American sees, with alarm, the curse of his favored land growing up" (E, 304, 305). Women's emancipation does not fare much better; Hubert observes complacently that such attempts "never excited any sensation but a good-natured ridicule" (E, 232); a prison matron in a Bloomer hat, a "moral female physician" and "priestess of philanthropic socialism," who regales her fellow stagecoach passengers with chatter about substituting reform for punishment, reveals herself to be a crackpot phrenologist (E, 317–23).

The one feature of America that disturb's Clotilde's complaisance most is the absence of class distinctions. Talvj was, after all, a *von* Jakob, even though that status was only a Russian service nobility that had been conferred upon her father. Except for Clotilde, all her female heroines are aristocrats.[11] Clotilde's guardian, a baron who is in love with her, warns her off Hubert and emigration to America; from time to time she has occasion to recall the warning, and the baron reappears to mourn at the end of the novel, perhaps a sign that she had chosen the wrong course. In one place, Clotilde marvels at Alonzo's preoccupation with his genealogy: "what an undue importance this son of a democratic republic attached to a noble descent, and distinguished family-connections. A longer residence in the United States taught her that there is no land in the world where high birth, and consequential, fashionable connections, are more valued than in democratic America"; it is also noted how susceptible American women are to European impostors whom they take to be titled (E, 59, 182). However that may be,

Clotilde and Hubert do not value American egalitarianism. Both see a lack of reverence as the negative side of self-esteem (*E*, 222, 246). The whole matter comes to a head in the much discussed servant problem. In scenes that could have been comic had Talvj had a sense of humor, Clotilde, whose neighbors wonder why she cannot do the work herself, has insuperable difficulties finding and keeping a servant girl, who expects to be treated as a member of the household and be introduced to guests. Neither she nor her mother

> had any idea that there existed between them and Clotilde any other than the accidental difference that the latter had a little more money than they, and could *pay* for a girl. They were themselves not cultivated enough to comprehend the immense chasm which education, culture, delicacy of feeling, refinement of manners, had laid between them; consequently Mrs. Wheeler and her daughter saw in Clotilde's reproofs only the pride and arrogance of the wealthy, and deemed it right to make as much opposition as possible, and to abase this pride. . . .
> Clotilde felt how impossible it was for the individual to bring about, in a country where no difference of *rank* exists, where there is legally but *one* class, a general recognition of that distinction in society, without which no scientific culture can be attained, no art can be practised to perfection, without which no grace of manners can exist, no refinement of domestic life can take place—the distinction between master and servant, between those who labour and those who pay. Custom and habit alone can affect a recognition of this difference—as it has done, for instance, in all the large American *cities*—and draw the delicate limit, beyond which it may not extend, without degenerating into exclusiveness and a spirit of caste.
>
> (*E*, 338–39)

One would like to read this as authorial irony, but there is no warrant to do so. If this be anti-Americanism, let us make the most of it.

Talvj employs Hubert's account to Clotilde of his experiences after having been rescued to fill a couple of chapters with a general critique of America. We need not concern ourselves here with the nuances, which are not remarkable within the general discourse about America of the time. Much effort is applied to weighing things evenhandedly, and if many of the observations are critical, they are no more anti-American than Tocqueville's. It is never forgotten that America, for all its faults, is free, and that Germany, for all its virtues and homeyness, is not. In the letter in which he urges Clotilde to emigrate with him,

Hubert says "Germany is nothing but a huge prison with thirty-eight cells" (E, 18); later, with a degree of irony, Virginia's father, who holds the then by no means eccentric opinion that slavery is *necessary* to freedom,[12] scoffs at the German abolitionist: "To come from a country where they have thirty or forty tyrants, and preach liberty here in democratic America!" (E, 165). In the preface for the American reader, Talvj acknowledged her European perspective, but laid claim to a "heart which beats for the free native land of the dearest which it possesses on earth, and the home of its voluntary adoption" (E, vi).

It has been said that "Clothilde's [sic] raison d'être lay in the perpetuation of an ideal *German* womanhood,"[13] and there is certainly something to this; when she is reunited with Hubert, "how sweetly did the pure, sonorous *German*, so long unheard, fall upon her listening ear from the lips of her beloved" (E, 204). But the privileged status of German *culture* is not as clear as it usually is in anti-American discourse. Clotilde is engaged to teach the Castleton daughters German. Sarah, naturally, wishes to read hymns and "Young Stilling" (E, 84), but Virginia's infatuation with "Berghehof" has inspired a wistful admiration for German poetry; she wishes to read Goethe and Schiller, and it turns out she has heard from "Berghehof's" lips "a divine poem of Heine's" (E, 97, 113–14). That looks like a bad sign, and later it is observed that German love poetry only excites her passions the more (E, 150). At the very end of the novel, after the catastrophe, we are told that Virginia has "banished all German books from her library" (E, 399). Are we, then, to accept the view, expressed by Americans in the novel, that German literature is to be deplored for its excess of sentiment and for condoning infidelity? Yet Clotilde is implicitly identified with Goethe's Iphigenie: she gazes upon the sea, "seeking the land of the German with her soul's eye" (E, 71). The heroine of another of her novels, *Heloise* (English 1850, German 1852), is said to be modeled on Iphigenie, as well as the Princess d'Este in *Tasso* and Schiller's Thekla from *Wallenstein*.[14] Yet Talvj does not maintain these allegiances at the expense of American literature. Hubert, after finding himself obliged to praise American painting and sculpture, especially singles out "Bryant, Longfellow, Whittier, Hawthorne" as "names which would be acknowledged as important in the literature of *every* country" (E, 242). Hollyday has observed that *The Exiles* "is the only German novel of the pre-Civil-War period that mentions the excellence of American sculptors and compliments individual American authors," a possibly rash generalization, but one I am unable to refute from my experience.[15] Perhaps, then, this novel does not fully belong in Hollyday's category of anti-Americanism at all.

For the real thing, we must go forward two or three years to *Der*

*Amerika-Müde*, published in 1855 by the Viennese liberal Ferdinand Kürnberger (1821–79). The title is an allusion to Ernst Willkomm's novel of 1838, *Die Europamüden*, which ends in a prospect of rescue by emigration to America. Willkomm's bizarre work is one of the last gasps of the Young German movement, of which Kürnberger himself was a late descendant. His purpose was to refute Willkomm's utopian vision and, by extension, the whole current discourse of American attractiveness. He wanted the novel explicitly understood as "antiamerikanisch" and "von der Auswanderung abschreckend."[16] In this endeavor he was quite in harmony with official Austrian policy, which, fearful of democratic infection, had remained aloof from the United States since the Revolution; discourse about America played less of a role in nineteenth-century Austria than in Germany: "Österreichische Zeitungen berichteten nicht nur vornehmlich über US-amerikanische Rohheit, Primitivität, Trunksucht und Verbrechen, sie wurden von der Regierung in Wien auch zum Kampf gegen die Auswanderung eingesetzt. Negative Berichte österreichischer Diplomaten über die schlechte Behandlung und schamlose Ausbeutung der Emigranten in den USA wurden immer wieder in die Zeitungen plaziert, um die Auswanderung zu stoppen."[17]

Kürnberger's protagonist, a young aristocrat traveling under the name of Moorfeld, bursts out in an exclamation of hope and enthusiasm when entering New York harbor. But he is soon filled with disgust at everything he sees. He is pained by New York journalism and Cincinnati society; he is disgusted by zigzagging rail fences because they are not straight German hedges and by the grid pattern of Philadelphia streets because they are not zigzagging, and he describes Pennsylvania as practically a desert where he encounters miserable people helplessly starving to death. Travelers offend his ears with dirty jokes and babies upchuck on him; Pittsburgh is polluted and Ohio, where he is cheated in a land swindle, swampy; Negroes play music incorrectly in public and people look at him oddly when he tries to straighten them out; on the Sabbath violin playing is forbidden but people love to watch houses burn; religion is fanatic and medicine quackery; women lack subservient domesticity; schools annoy him because they teach the trivial history of America instead of important things like the Battle of Leipzig; the very trees depress him because they differ from European species. There is no style, nor manners, nor culture. Though he is doubtless meant to incorporate European superiority, one observer has remarked how he "passagenweise seine eigene bürgerlich-philiströse Natur—wohl unfreiwillig—verrät."[18]

The overriding antipathy of the book is directed toward the commercial atmosphere, which is presented as one of insatiable, obsessive, knavish moneygrubbing displacing and obscuring all other human relationships. Consciousness is governed by the opportunistic, materialistic maxims ascribed to Benjamin Franklin by Kürnberger's manipulation, which misled even Max Weber.[19] However, it is clear that the objection is against the *earning* of money. Moorfeld has no financial worries of any kind and is able without difficulty to put three thousand dollars on the table for the purchase of his ill-fated Ohio farm. This attitude has remained a cliché of German and, indeed, European anti-American discourse up to the present day.[20] More ominous is that the novel is a tract in the interest of German nationalism, thus articulating an attitude of superiority that has a long history among German observers as well as German Americans, that for some decades was characteristic of the teaching of German language and literature in the United States,[21] and that culminated in the quasi-official Nazi doctrine of Colin Ross's *Amerikas Schicksalsstunde* (1935) and *Unser Amerika* (1936). When the Constitution causes the country to collapse in anarchy and military dictatorship, Germany will send its fleet and colonize the United States through its German population; the whole world will then become German: "Deutschland erwacht" (*A-M*, 176). However, Kürnberger does not seem wholly optimistic about this prospect. At present Americans scorn and oppress Germans because "das Volk fürchtet instinctiv die deutsche Geistesüberlegenheit" (*A-M*, 366). Even his model German American, Benthal, comes to be assimilated to the pervasive corruption. The trouble is that the German character is too tender and sensitive to thrive in a crude and brutal environment: "Wir sind wahrhaftig unter den Lügnern, wir sind aufopfernd unter den Selbstlingen, wir sind zart unter den Ungeschlachten, wir sind keusch unter den Frechen, wir sind tiefsinnig unter den Stumpfen, wir sind fromm unter Heuchlern, wir haben Herzen unter Ziffern, wir sind Menschen unter Bestien!" (*A-M*, 399) The hero's final departure from New York takes place amid a phantasmagorical pogrom against the German population of the city by the non-German barbarians.

Kürnberger, of course, was never in America; he cobbled his novel together from various sources. As he indicates at the end, and as has been long recognized, the most important of these is the correspondence of Nikolaus Lenau from his ill-fated excursion to Ohio in 1832.[22] He was an eminently poor source, however. A fantastic and unworldly man, he was wholly unprepared for his undertaking and ignored all advice. Although he appears to be one of those alleged, perhaps partly apocryphal victims of Gottfried Duden's optimistic memoir of his Missouri settlement, in fact he paid no attention to Duden's warnings. He knew almost no English and therefore was unable to understand newspapers or other printed information. Although he paraded an ethereal sensibility, he was actually in search of wealth and leisure, hoping to turn a quick dollar in land speculation and perhaps become some sort of Hungarian magnate on American soil. Numerous people tried to help him. On a riverboat he met the cosmopolitan vice-president Martin Van Buren, who offered him assistance. With instinctive incompetence he found his way to the most barren land in all of Ohio. Naturally he failed, and naturally he concluded that a poet could not survive in a land without nightingales, an ornithological fact he discovered after eight days in Baltimore, in October. The claim of Lenau, who was not in the United States in the spring and summer, that there are no songbirds in American forests, maintained a surprising tenacity in the anti-American discourse. Strubberg remarked of this: "Es ist unbegreiflich, daß in ganz Europa der Glaube herrscht, in Amerika tragen die Vögel zwar sehr schöne Farben, könnten aber nicht singen, während unbestritten mehr Arten von Singvögeln und schöner singende auf diesem Continent leben als in Europa."[23] The belief, incidentally, was international; it goes back to the eighteenth century and even Jefferson shared it.[24] Keats wrote in a poem of 1819: "There bad flowers have no scent, birds no sweet song"; and Oliver Goldsmith in "The Deserted Village" imagined "matted woods where birds forget to sing."[25] However, the notion had already been opposed by Duden himself.[26] Gerstäcker commented on this matter in several places. He observed in Louisiana that the mockingbird, the American nightingale, "flötete, besonders Nachts, wenn auch nicht so schwermüthig und bezaubernd als die unsere, doch sanft und lieblich," and spoke in another place of "die wunderbaren Laute ... der Whiz [sic] poor Will (die amerikanische Nachtschwalbe)" (SJ, 2:284; ZS, 38). Travelers seem to have felt obliged to address the question; one made a point of having heard songbirds in Virginia in 1833;[27] while another in 1844 found the birds colorful but without song.[28]

Kürnberger had various other sources. One that is likely is Charles Dickens's *Martin Chuzzlewit* (1843–44), which, like all of his works, was translated immediately into German.[29] As anti-American as Kürnberger may have been, he was also pronouncedly Anglophilic. In his political journalism he repeatedly contrasted British liberties to Austrian oppression and pettiness. For example, he praised the Magna Charta on its eight-hundredth anniversary on June 15, 1866; asserted that, while Ludwig Börne had been preoccupied with the provincial political debates in Hesse and Baden, Goethe had seen "auf die Erdkugel die angelsächsische Kulturbewegung sich ausbreiten"; and praised England, "welches trotz aller menschlichen Unvollkommenheiten der unbestrittene Musterstaat ist" (SR, 24–28, 107, 470). Hardly any attention is paid to the United States in his political journalism, apart from a reference to the satires of Sam Slick, a sardonic citation of a Frenchman's remark that the most progressive nation in the world is governed by a tailor (i.e., Andrew Johnson), another ironic reference to America as "dem besseren Jenseits," a passing glance at "die Rowdies in Newyork und San Francisco," and, for once, a respectful citation of an American work of scholarship, *History of the Intellectual Development of Europe* (1863) by John William Draper (1811–81) (SR, 40, 49, 132–33, 267, 376–78). Another source is Sealsfield, from whom he borrows in several places. One of these borrowings fits rather poorly, a scene about a villainous German farmer taken from *Morton*.[30]

Another source that he used, or rather misused, as I was able to show some years ago, was the autobiography of Lorenzo Da Ponte.[31] Kürnberger depicts Da Ponte as a broken-down derelict in New York, victimized by the barbaric absence of culture and sensibility in the United States. As Kürnberger could easily have seen from the memoirs, Da Ponte, though he had his troubles in America, as he did in all countries, many of which he brought upon himself, nevertheless had much good to say of his American life and especially of New York, a place he loved and that may have been the happiest environment of his life. He makes it altogether clear, and the historical record supports him, that he was recognized, patronized, and encouraged by highly cultured people, especially Clement Moore, the poet of "The Night before Christmas," to whom Da Ponte is generously grateful in his memoirs. He lived in a fairly grand style in a fine house on Broadway and always kept servants and a horse. One of his sons became a professor at the University of Maryland and New York University, and married into President Monroe's family. The version of the memoirs that Kürnberger used does not reach the point of Da Ponte's appointment as professor of Italian at Columbia College, of which Moore's father had been president, and which made him the founder of Italian studies in the United States, or of an enthusiastically received New York performance of his own *Don Giovanni*, but it should have been clear from what Kürnberger could read that Da Ponte did not regard America as a locus of desolate misery. The case shows quite clearly the unscrupulous tendentiousness of the novel.

In recent times there have been efforts to redirect attention to the proletarian-born Kürnberger as a midcentury dissident writer. Even though he was not notably sympathetic to the proletariat and the working-class movement, some of these efforts have emanated from the left, particularly from the former German Democratic Republic, where *Der Amerika-Müde* was published in 1973 as a warning against "die Abgründe des Phänomens Amerika" and an exhibit, in the figure of Da

Ponte, of "die tragische Entfremdungssituation des Künstlers, ja des Individuums in der kapitalistischen Welt."[32] This sort of outlook was not unknown in the West.[33] But the more common practice has been to put the novel to one side and call attention to the remainder of Kürnberger's career. Even Hans-Joachim Lang, who finds much to praise in the book, nevertheless treats it as caricature and fantasy, and acknowledges its "ludicrous and at times actually silly details."[34] It is true that the novel was written on the run, in Frankfurt am Main, where Kürnberger was a more or less underground refugee from the Revolution of 1848. It seems to have been conceived as a potboiler—like so many other nineteenth-century German writers, he was mesmerized by the prestige of the drama and was seeking fame by that route—and he was apparently as surprised as anyone at the ten thousand copies the novel sold. Years later he acknowledged in a semisheepish and convoluted way that such a novel written from armchair experience was a violation of his own realistic principles:

> Schreiber dieses hat . . . mit der ganzen deutschen Unart, von Reflexionen anstatt von Anschauungen auszugehen, seinen Roman "Der Amerika-Müde" auf einem streng idealistischen Standpunkte und zwar in seiner Poetenstube zu Frankfurt am Main, mitnichten aber zu Newyork am Hudson geschrieben. Wenn sich nun trotzdem sein Buch just in einen guten *realistischen* Kredit gesetzt hat und der Autor des Buches wohl nach siebzehn Jahren noch gelegentlich die Frage vernimmt, nicht ob, sondern bloß wie lang er in Amerika gewesen: so ist das ein literarhistorisch nicht zu unterschätzendes Symptom, daß der deutschen Stubenpoesie wenigstens das Licht der Selbstkenntnis aufgegangen, womit sie ihre Mängel zu decken und ihren Idealismus in realistische Zucht zu geben gelernt hat.
>
> (LH, 510)

Nevertheless, he planned, though did not carry out, a novel about Aaron Burr, "dem Catalina von Nord Am."[35]

Of greater recent interest has been Kürnberger's literary and political journalism. Unquestionably, his was a pungent dissident voice against church and state, especially in the 1860s and 1870s, full of irony, transparent allegory, and satire; he risked arrest, exile, and the shutdown of his periodicals. Because he mounted a critique of public and journalistic language usage in his time, he was praised or republished by Karl Kraus on more than thirty occasions, which in some quarters amounts to a beatification.[36] He was admired also by Wittgenstein, Max Weber, and, later, by Hermann Bahr and by Adorno, who took a motto from Kürnberger, "Das Leben lebt nicht," for his *Minima moralia*.[37] His literary-critical principles, though firmly anchored in the classicism of Goethe and Schiller—from 1866 to 1869 he was the director of the Schiller Foundation—tended increasingly to a realism bordering on naturalism. He particularly admired Gottfried Keller and wrote an impressive review of *Sieben Legenden* in 1876, asserting that Keller was something new, "satirisch wie Voltaire, naiv wie Homer, graziös wie Heine, humoristisch wie Jean Paul" (*LH*, 223). Keller was pleased and wrote him a letter of thanks.[38] He admired Ferdinand von Saar, Leopold von Sacher-Masoch, and Marie von Ebner-Eschenbach, to whom he mediated Turgenyev.[39]

There is no doubt that Kürnberger developed into a relentlessly crusading, confrontational journalist, perhaps the leading feuilletonist in the Vienna of his time.[40] He was sometimes effective, as when he helped prevent the deforestation of the Vienna Woods by profiteers (*SR*, 6–8). Not all of his interventions were progressive in the strict sense. In some ways he was antimodern, deploring "the erosion of older genuine values," in particular opposing the urban renewal surrounding the building of the *Ringstraße*.[41] But what tends to be somewhat elided by modern commentators is his very intense nationalism, the same affect that informs *Der Amerika-Müde*. It is perhaps not surprising that, apart from a certain sympathy with the Hungarians, he was rather dismissive of the aspirations of the "Asian" nationalities within the Austrian Empire and downright hostile to Italian claims on the South Tyrol, demanding its "Zurück-Germanisierung" (*SR*, 45–46). More striking is the *German*, indeed, especially at the time of the Franco-Prussian War, *Prussian* character of his allegiance. In fact, he was publicly attacked as a Prussian agent (see *SR*, 150–51). As a historian observed: "In dem Ringen zwischen Österreich und Preußen ist Kürnberger nicht auf Seiten Habsburgs gestanden."[42] He fumed that the Prussian king had begun to create an invisible imperial crown while the Austrian one was moldering in the hands of Jesuits, and he called for the slogan: "Preußen *in* Deutschland und Österreich *mit* Deutschland!" (*SR*, 94–95). This stance is also apparent in the peculiar tone of his essays on Franz Grillparzer in January and February 1871, during the war, and on the occasion of his death and burial in 1872, where Kürnberger, all affection and admiration for him notwithstanding, appears to see him as having missed his vocation by having been an Austrian rather than a German writer, for whom appearance came to matter more than substance (*LH*, 259–75).

Kürnberger deplored Austria's position as bystander during the war, poured fanatical venom on the French, especially Victor Hugo, and celebrated the German victory. He always, incidentally, viewed England as Germanic, a natural, potential ally of the Germans; against French pretensions to liberty, equality, and fraternity, he asserted: "und doch sagt nur der germanische Angelsachse 'self-government,' was die wirkliche Freiheit bedeutet; der keltische Franzose dagegen sagt 'gouvernement fort,' worin wenig Freiheit, dagegen viel Tyrannei steckt" (SR, 127). In the process he developed a diction that reminds us of the worst German tirades at the time of World War I. No other nation has writers like Goethe and Schiller, able to think about the beautiful (LH, 144). As in Der Amerika-Müde, the Germans are traditionally innocent, pure victims: "Du warst in der Geschichte von jeher nur da, armes deutsches Opferlamm, um geschoren zu werden," though now, at last, they do not hesitate to conquer; as for the French, he asserted, "Die Partei ist nicht gleich, denn der Deutsche ist ein höheres Wesen als der Kelte. Es ist der *wirkliche* Pionier der Kultur," and "Dem Deutschen ist nichts verschlossen, dem Franzosen ist vieles verschlossen. Das ist die Formel zwischen den beiden Völkern" (SR, 134, 147). Austria, in fact, is not German, but infected by the Asiatic character of the East: "Deutsch ist der Vortritt der *Sache* vor der Person, die selbstlose Hingebung der Person an die Sache, das Verschwinden und Aufgeben des persönlichen Momentes im Interesse und im Dienste der Sache. Just umgekehrt herrscht bei uns wie bei allen Ostvölkern die Neigung vor, alles Persönliche zuerst und zumeist zu berücksichtigen, die Person beständig vor die Sache und über die Sache zu stellen" (LH, 302). Such an utterance anticipates the jargon of the Third Reich. There is something substantially racist about this discourse, because Kürnberger, like many others before the heyday of systematic race theory, subsumed nationality and ethnicity along with what we might call race under the term *Rasse*.

It is this manner of thinking that got Kürnberger into paradoxical confusions about the Jews. When I first encountered a comment about "his vicious and slightly paranoid anti-semitism"[43] I was very surprised, because I was prepared to claim that, for a man in his time and place, he was notably free of anti-Semitism. But this is the paradox, for a naturally and instinctively unprejudiced attitude toward Jews, especially in the individual case, is subverted by the racist habits of discourse. In one place he described a vision of a ghetto in Rome at the time of Hanukkah; the Christ Child comes and is kindly received; the children invite him to play with their dredel—"In der Mitte der Judenkinder feierte sein Weihnachtsfest—der Knabe aus der Fremde!"—and if they grow up to gather the treasures of the earth, at least they do not do it in Christ's name (SR, 331–32). He regularly wrote admiringly of Jewish writers, notably Leopold Kompert, whom Kürnberger praised for combating stereotypes by displaying the dignity of the Jews and whom he compared favorably, opposing fashion as usual, to the more successful Berthold Auerbach (*LH*, 395–403).⁴⁴ He wrote an admiring obituary of the originally Jewish August Lewald, stressing, however, an inability to share the undemocratic and ultramontane views of the zealous Catholic convert (*LH*, 211–16). Kürnberger's views on Heine shifted some; in one place he remarked sarcastically of Gustave Doré's illustrations that we now know that the Song of Songs is not an allegory of the bride of Christ but "ein Gedicht von Heine, nämlich ein sinnlich brünstiges Liebeslied; für mich wenigstens leidet es gar kein Zweifel, daß es der jüdische Ahnherr vor Heinrich Heine gedichtet hat"; if that is the case, why not add one of Heine's satirical poems to the Bible (*LH*, 39)? But in another place he defended Heine from an anti-Semitic attack (*LH*, 64), and in general he appears as a successor to him as a model realist.⁴⁵ He indicates Heine's influence when he numbered Jews and Germans among "den seelenhaftesten Völkern der Erde" or says of monasticism that it is neither Jewish nor Christian, but Egyptian (*SR*, 165, 291). He quite specifically echoes Heine, if perhaps not quite exactly, when he remarks in an obituary of Moritz Hartmann that there are Jewish Jews and Hellene Jews and that Hartmann was, apart from Heine and Lewald, the purest type of the latter. The Jew touched by the Greek spirit is one of the most beautiful mixtures; Kürnberger harks back, as Heine often did, to medieval Spanish Jewry, and observes that Hellene Semites are "die wirklichen Kirchenväter der europäischen Humanität." The language here, to be sure, is not free from reproach. He sees the Jewish Jews as stubborn in their chosenness and defines Semitic form as "das Zerstreute, Zerfahrene, Formlose und Phantastische" (*LH*, 217–22). He might also make a relatively harmless joke about the Jews from time to time, such as his remark: "Ein katholisch Getaufter, wie ich, hat zum Juden zu wenig und zu viel. Zu wenig Ahnen, aber zu viel—unskalpiertes Material" (*SR*, 11). Nevertheless, when one considers the sorry standards of the time, Kürnberger's comments on the Jews might strike us as generally friendly.

However, there are other moments that are more troubling. He accuses the Jewish "Ruhmes-Hyänen" of crowding about Grillparzer's coffin at his funeral in order to make themselves important (*LH*, 279–80). It is true that this passage occurs in connection with a more generalized lament over the hypocrisy of celebration at the demise of an isolated and nonconforming writer, but its specifically anti-Semitic tone is nevertheless disconcerting. Even more troubling is an 1876 review of a novel by one Erwin Schlieben, *Das Judenschloß*; Kürnberger begins with a citation from Max Müller to the effect that racial (including national and ethnic) hostility is universal and unavoidable in the whole world.

But as he goes on, he clearly begins to approach the diction of the more systematic racism developing in his time. Now he will no longer distinguish between Jews and Christians, but "zwischen Semiten und Ariern" (*LH*, 203). He then goes on about Jewish exclusivity toward Christians, while no Christian ritual lords it over the Jews; about claims of anti-Semitism being used as a weapon against "Aryans": though Jews have been emancipated, they now want to be coddled, while the hands of "Aryans" who want to make the most justified racial observations are tied; although four of the novel's six Jews are virtuous, Jewish critics complain about the other two. At the end Kürnberger takes the side of the cultured Westernized Jew against capitalists and *Ostjuden*: "mancher jüdischer Ehrenmann auf der Höhe arischer Bildung und Ethik [hegt] gegen Gründer-Juden und Kaftan-Wucherer dieselben Gefühle ... wie nur der Beste der Arier selbst" (*LH*, 209). From a historical point of view there is nothing particularly strange about an utterance like this. But in the context of Kürnberger's attitudes generally it shows how a supposed objectivity and liberality are corrupted by racist habits of thinking. When we extrapolate to nationalism as belonging to the same pattern, a similar charge can be made against *Der Amerika-Müde*.[46]

When we turn to Kürnberger's later fiction, we find something rather different: the satirical bite of *Der Amerika-Müde* has turned into a drastic unconventionality that has not yet been estimated in its true dimensions or employed as a retrospect on *Der Amerika-Müde* itself. Of his numerous novellas, the one that has been declared the most interesting is *Die Last des Schweigens* of 1878.[47] It is a first-person inner monologue of a Hungarian nobleman on the eve of his execution for having murdered his rival in love by substituting poison for medicine being brought to him by an innocent Jewish peddler. The murderer in no way repents his crime, which he sees as an act in fulfillment of his sovereign self; before the murder, he tests whether he can get along without love by killing his faithful dog. But he finds that the need to keep silent about his act does, in fact, limit his freedom. He cries out an admission on the open plains and is overheard by accident; after having been charged, he makes no claim of innocence, for a gentleman does not lie.

This narrator has been thought to prefigure Dostoyevsky's Raskolnikov and, more particularly, to reflect the author's strong interest in Schopenhauer. In fact, however, the protagonist's principled amorality goes well beyond anything in Schopenhauer, perhaps beyond Nietzsche also. It is difficult to say whether we are meant to see the murderer suffering from delusion in his denial of conscience, which he unconsciously obeys, but there are no clear signals in the text that this is the case, except that the contemplation of the murder causes him attacks of depression and anxiety. At the end of the story, he thinks of his immortal self continuing in his son, but at the same time he wonders if there *are* any other people: "Auch das Ich ist ein Aberglaube!" (255). The tone of totally amoral narcissism points toward the decadence of the fin de siècle. Kürnberger's place in this development, which contrasts interestingly with his allegiance to Goethe and Schiller, to Keller, Stifter, and Grillparzer, has never, to my knowledge, been discussed.

Considerably more drastic is the novel *Das Schloß der Frevel*, which resembles no other contemporary German-language novel of my acquaintance. Kürnberger began publishing it in a newspaper in 1875, but the Austrian authorities, rather unsurprisingly, seized the copies. It finally appeared posthumously in 1903, but the wholly unexpurgated text was not published until 1912.[48] The convoluted plot, such as it is, concerns the search for a collection of lascivious nude paintings for which Italian society ladies (and, for unclear reasons, the protagonist's fiancée) have been induced to pose. We are here in darkest, most lawless, conspiratorial, Jesuitical Italy, to which the protagonist Baum attempts to adapt, though his native German virtuousness wins out in the end. He is, however, a fierce proponent of the double standard; while he takes Italian mistresses, more or less condescendingly, he summarily rejects his fiancée when he recognizes her in one of the paintings; she, however, effects a reconciliation by an abject display of German-maiden selflessness and devotion. There is an unusual amount of illicit sex in the novel—the most elegant femme fatale among Baum's mistresses yields to a burly warehouseman, after which she is burned to death together with the paintings—along with quite explicit homosexuality, presented as a higher, "Greek" realization of the self transcending bourgeois and Christian morality. Interspersed are lengthy dialogues on religion and aesthetics, which appear to make the novel a successor to Wilhelm Heinse's *Ardinghello* and Friedrich Schlegel's *Lucinde*. But much in it—impenetrable conspiracies, secret family relationships, underground imprisonments, and whatnot—remind one inexorably of Eugène Sue: it might as easily have been titled *Les mystères de Rome*. Although to my knowledge Kürnberger mentions Sue in only one place, rather dismissively as a writer whose evil Jew, in contrast to Stifter's, is a caricature (*LH*, 207), it seems to me that Kürnberger here is even more than Strubberg under Sue's influence. Yet for all the novel's lewdness and depravity, Kürnberger's German nationalism is still intact in it.

Kürnberger was a writer who combined vigor, a colorful, sprightly style, and a sometimes weird sense of humor with sensationalism and subliterary instincts. These characteristics apply to *Der Amerika-Müde* also. I have occasionally been chided for taking too censorious a view of that novel, of not appreciating its wit and satire. But I do not think I have been mistaken. A book like this pollutes the discourse, reinforcing prejudices and ill will for long decades. How it does this is evident in a review in the *Blätter für literarische Unterhaltung* in September 1856, which, while recognizing the novel's tendentiousness and exaggeration, nevertheless praised it for drawing together and making plausible what we already know of "all den Roheiten und Herzlosigkeiten, den Absurditäten und Lächerlichkeiten, den Prellereien und Gaunereien, welche in Amerika dominiren, und namentlich mit den Gefahren, Verfolgungen und Leiden, denen der eingewanderte Deutsche dort ausgesetzt ist."[49] Such an endorsement of Kürnberger's informational value could be found a century later in one of the more fanatical anti-American tracts of today's Germany.[50]

Readers of Gustav Freytag's best seller *Soll und Haben*, which appeared in the same year as *Der Amerika-Müde*, 1855, will recall that the clever if somewhat disreputable renegade aristocrat Fritz von Fink, who threatens to steal the novel from its boring protagonist, gets involved in a dubious commercial enterprise in America. Anton Wohlfart's moral outrage provides Fink with the backbone to torpedo the enterprise by publicly exposing his partners; on another occasion Fink makes over to Anton an "estate" on Long Island, which turns out to be a sand bog with a duck blind. Some seven years later Reinhold Solger (1817–66), the nephew of the romantic aesthetician Karl Wilhelm Ferdinand Solger, wrote in the United States a sequel, *Anton in Amerika*. An amusing, confusing, and perhaps somewhat deceptive book, it won a prize in a contest sponsored by a New York newspaper for the best serial novel of German American life.[51]

Born in Stettin, Solger, like Möllhausen and Gerstäcker, lost his father at an early age and was shunted among various relatives. He studied at Halle, where he became attached to Arnold Ruge and the Hegelian left, and he completed a doctorate in 1842 at Greifswald. In the following year he took off for America, but in England, so the story goes, he obtained a counterfeit boat ticket and remained stranded—for four years!—supporting himself as a house tutor in a comfortable home and perfecting his English. There he began but did not complete a mock epic satirizing Prussian militarism, modeled on Byron's *Don Juan*. He then lived in Paris for a while, where he made the acquaintance of such revolutionaries as Bakunin, Herzen, and Georg Herwegh; returned to Germany, where he made friends with Feuerbach; and quite naturally became involved in the Revolution of 1848, after which he was obliged to flee to Switzerland, where he began a satirical, somewhat risqué, perhaps partly autobiographical mock epic on Prussian cadet life, later published in the United States.[52] In 1850 he wrote a truly funny one-act comedy about the revolution, *Der Reichstagsprofessor*. Solger cheerfully exploits all the conventions of popular comedy: young love balked by stuffy elders, escapes through windows, switched identities, and a saucy housemaid smarter than anyone else, in this case equipped with a markedly proletarian consciousness. What is genuinely comical is the unremitting sequence of sardonically displaced allusions to the political jargon of the failed Frankfurt Parliament and the fatuities of Friedrich Wilhelm IV.

Solger returned to England in 1852, where he was encouraged by Carlyle and Bulwer-Lytton, and by Dickens, who helped him to a lecture series, which, however, did not succeed. After a year he emigrated to the United States and settled in Roxbury, Massachusetts; he gave well-regarded lectures on German philosophy and the new critical historiography in Lowell as well as in Cambridge, where the Harvard president and faculty listened admiringly. Despite the fact that he shared one series with our native sage, Emerson, Friedrich Kapp's view of this activity was that Solger was bringing the German light to the barbarians: "Die Vereinigten Staaten stehen in dieser Beziehung noch auf den Standpunkt, welchen Deutschland vor zweihundert Jahren einnahm, als die Land-Pastoren die Stützen der Literatur wurden."[53] In 1859 he became active in the nationwide commemoration of Schiller's centennial; he won a prize for a poem from the New York committee and gave the keynote address for the celebration in Boston, in which he deplored the absence of *Gedankenfreiheit* in America.[54] In 1860 he became involved in Lincoln's presidential campaign; he stumped for Lincoln in Indiana but is said to have been too abstract and ironic to be an effective political orator. He tried to adapt *Der Reichstagsprofessor* to an attack on the proslavery Democrats under the title of *The Hon. Anodyne Humdrum or the Union Must and Shall be Preserved*, but it could not be performed in New York because it had a black character on an equal footing with whites.[55] As a reward for his political work, the Lincoln administration in 1863 appointed him as "assistant register" in the Treasury Department. But in the following year, at the age of forty-six, he suffered a stroke; he died in January 1866. Kapp's summary judgment on him was that he was the most gifted, learned, and widely effective of all the forty-eighters in America.[56]

*Anton in Amerika* purports to relate the American adventures of the son of Freytag's Anton "Wohlfahrt" (respelled thus by Solger as by many an inattentive commentator), called "Antonio" by his doting mother, the domestically virtuous Sabine Schröter now become socially ambitious. Generically the novel is somewhat composite. Like *Soll und Haben*, it is a novel of commerce, though the commercial transactions described in it are less detailed and, to me, in my ignorance of such things, rather difficult to follow, but the adventures in it are picaresque. As in Strubberg's autobiographical fictions, commercial success and failure fluctuate wildly and, as in Kürnberger's *Der Amerika-Müde*, the original stake the "europamüde" (*AA*, 1:61) Antonio brings with him, in this case ten thousand dollars, is eventually lost. The capitalist speculator Dawson, whom Antonio meets shortly after arrival, is the type of thin-lipped, bloodless Yankee who was becoming a cliché in the America novels. He appears to lose his entire fortune, thus illustrating the chaos of capitalism, but it turns out that this is a rumor he has put into circulation, allowing him to buy up his own shares at distress prices, so that he winds up richer than ever. The dollar is "der Stein der Weisen, die Wahrheit des Yankeelebens" (*AA*, 1:83).

But Solger replicates Kürnberger's satirical tone less uncompromisingly. For example, there is a comic portrait of a feminist and otherwise progressive busybody, Mrs. Parsons, who, among other projects, wants to make Antonio president of the University of Iowa, but she is much more kindly treated than Sealsfield's Big Lady in *Die Deutsch-amerikanischen Wahlverwandtschaften* or Talvj's Bloomer woman. Like Sealsfield, however, Solger divides his moral landscape into urban and rural segments: Solger's first volume, full of commercial shenanigans, is entitled "Stadt"; the second, more Edenically, "Land," though some fairly gruesome things happen out there, also. As in Möllhausen's novels and some of Gerstäcker's, the plot turns on the suspenseful but ultimately successful exposure of heinous crime. The guileless Antonio brings complications upon himself by rescuing a beautiful beggar woman who had been forced into prostitution by an abusive French husband, now masquerading in society as a count. For reasons too complex to relate briefly, she is eventually murdered by the Frenchman and his helpless debtor, Dawson's depraved son. Antonio, naturally, is convicted of the murder, but is rescued from hanging at the last moment by Dawson's brave daughter Mary, who serves in this case as the traditional *reitende Bote*, although the reader's expectation that they will marry soon is frustrated. Some of this plotting is not badly executed for those who like that kind of writing. There may also be a touch of Dickens, especially in Antonio's steadfastness in allowing himself to be hanged rather than offer an explanation that he believes would compromise Mary. The more he tries to be noble, helpful, and good, the more trouble he gets into. There are other literary echoes. For example, Antonio's ruthlessly commonsensical friend and quondam associate

Wilhelmi may be modeled on the character of the same name in Karl Immermann's novel *Die Epigonen*.

Solger's novel, in contrast to Kürnberger's, shows signs of having been written out of American experience. He became a naturalized United States citizen; the novel is reportedly based in part on letters he wrote in French to his wife.[57] He is able to set scenes plausibly in New Haven, in North Conway, New Hampshire, and in the Five Points slum of New York City. He shows something of the corrupt grip on New York politics maintained by Tammany Hall, or rather, as he prudently writes: "........ Hall" (*AA*, 1:48). There is a fair amount of skirmishing, mugging, and shooting in the streets. Blacks are not conspicuous. The phony French count's Negro servant grins and gestures like a monkey, but Solger makes it clear that the wily black is parodying the swindler out of contempt for him (*AA*, 1:59, 64). In one place Solger parodies race theory (*AA*, 1:17). Solger's Irish, on the other hand, may remind us at first of Sealsfield's. The O'Shea family, with whom Antonio places the fallen woman he is trying to rescue, is a pugnacious, uncouth bunch; during one epic brouhaha, the grandmother attacks a miscreant and digs out one of his eyes with a toast fork (*AA*, 1:87). However, Paddy, the son of this tribe, is a bright and capable fellow with whom Antonio makes friends; he sets up a newsstand on Wall Street, where he picks up enough investment information to make his own eventual fortune. "*Smart* ist das Wort," he tells Antonio, who is failing in the hardware business and otherwise in difficulty (*AA*, 1:120). There are numerous Americanisms in the text: Antonio is asked if he is "nicht süß auf die allmächtig feine junge Lady"; a servant is called "die 'Hülfe,' wie man die Dienstmädchen hierzulande tituliert"; a man wears an "Ofenröhre," that is, a stovepipe hat; more comically, "ich will mich einen 'Spruch' setzen"—"sit a spell," no doubt—or "es thut kein gut" (*AA*, 2:12, 16, 27, 58, 71). These and many other examples are signs of genuine intimacy with the American language.

It is an index of the deceptiveness of Solger's novel that the two contemporary interpretations of it have come to quite opposite conclusions. Horst Denkler sees it as a "kühles Votum für den amerikanischen Kapitalismus" in the interest of progress, acknowledging but accepting oppression and exploitation.[58] Certainly one can find support for this view in the text. Antonio's friend Wilhelmi at one point says: "der Geist . . . [ist] die treibende Kraft in der Geschichte . . . , aber er wirkt nicht plötzlich, sondern nur Zellen bildend. Die Zellen sind wir Geschäftsleute, der Geist seid Ihr Gelehrte, Philosophen, Poeten, Propheten. Die Gegenwart gehört uns, die Zukunft gehört Euch" (*AA*, 2:94). Jerry Schuchalter, on the other hand, finds much more negative implications:

A society steeped in materialism is ruthlessly waging a war to destroy art and sensibility. . . . The "Yankee-Geist" is then the incarnation of America in *Anton in Amerika*. The "Dollar" paradoxically becomes the highest good, replacing other compelling and meaningful ideals such as literature, culture, community, virtue, civic duty, all those values that were previously thought to belong to the *Kulturstaat* and the *Rechtsstaat*. The world has been turned on its head in America. Not only has the material corrupted the ideal, but, even more absurd, it has become tantamount with the ideal itself. In such a world then everyone is fallen.[59]

The explanation for such contradictory responses may lie in a certain universality of irony in the novel. Solger is a wit. For all his devotion to Schiller, he will apply a Schillerian tag as insouciantly as any other German humorist: "Antonio gedachte einen langen Schlaf zu thun" (*AA*, 2:42). He tends to lampoon and satirize wherever he can, but he does not necessarily sustain a position. An example is what seems to be a lack of consistency in his postfiguration of Freytag's novel. At first it looks like a burlesque. Solger begins with an ironic synopsis of *Soll und Haben*, with which Freytag "mit Recht die besten Geschäfte macht." He treats the story of Anton and Sabine as a fairy tale, "nicht bloß lehrreich für Bürgerliche, sondern auch für Adlige," by teaching everyone his place. The son Antonio, however, does not seem to inherit the habits of "dieser Gewürzkrämerfamilie," but develops a dandified, retrograde lust for social climbing (*AA*, 1:1, 3, 5). Wilhelmi at one point is abandoned by Antonio's uncle Schröter in a business crisis (*AA*, 1:117). Antonio even says of himself, "die moderne deutsche Dichtkunst, welche das Volk bei seiner Arbeit aufsucht, würde ein unwürdiges Subjekt an mir finden" (*AA*, 2:94), an obvious allusion to Julian Schmidt's well-known motto to *Soll und Haben*. Sabine is made to look like a rather silly woman. But when she dies it is said of Antonio that she had represented an ideal for him and his whole purpose in life had been to be worthy of her (*AA*, 2:81–82). Antonio himself, without exactly "developing" in a *Bildungsroman* sense, turns out to be a nobly brave and highly moral character who escapes from crassly commercial America into Near Eastern studies and explorations.

The solution lies once again in nationalism. Solger's is not as fanatic as Kürnberger's; he weighs German virtues and faults against one another, and against American virtues and faults, but the German allegiance is an ultimately superintending principle. With German friends and conversation Antonio finds himself once again at ease, "gerade wie zu Haus im lieben Vaterland. Es war ein eigenes Heimathsgefühl, das den schon so tief ins Amerikanische verwickelten Antonio bei diesem plötzlichen Auftauchen in deutscher Luft überkam; längst begraben geglaubte Gefühle erwachten in aller Stärke, Sehnsucht und Heimweh, und eine drängende Ungeduld, keinen Tag mehr zu weilen, schon morgen an Bord und übers Meer zu gehen" (*AA*, 2:93). Antonio is able to succeed and amaze as a lecturer not because he is particularly intellectual or learned, but because German *Bildung* and commonplace knowledge of world affairs are far superior to American crudity and provinciality. The climactic scene of the novel is Antonio's trial for murder, which turns into a clash of American attitudes toward Germans. Popular opinion has already condemned him as an evil European aristocrat and adventurer offending American modesty. His defense lawyer praises the Prussian system of education and seeks sympathy for Antonio as a refugee from monarchism in a democratic land. But the prosecution cranks up all the prejudices and clichés of American nativism. The defense attorney is scorned as a foreigner from the West, where Germans may be influential, but not here; the defense is "deutscher Mondschein." The "Abschaum" of Germany comes to America. The Prussian educational system is a "Pflanzschule des Despotismus" producing "senile Beamten, unpraktische Träumer und infame Atheisten"; American girls should flee the blandishments of German atheists (*AA*, 2:110–16). This last point is the salient one; Antonio shows no sign of religious allegiance. The judge urges the jury to protect American morality and religion; with such a charge, the verdict must turn against Antonio, who can be rescued only by a conventional fictional device.

Nativist contempt for German immigrants is a theme often encountered in the German discourse about America. At an intellectual level, scorn for German philosophy as impractical and dreamy, and fear of it as subversive of religion, as Heine, after all, eloquently insisted it was, are frequently adduced. The successes of German philosophy, from New England Transcendentalists to St. Louis Hegelians, or the growing prestige of German literature and thought in the American educational system, are less noticed. Sometimes these complaints degenerate into a whiny ethnic self-pity occasionally encountered even today among German American spokespersons, a somewhat incongruous affect, considering that the German Americans have been among the most successful of all immigrant groups. Solger does not go that far; he repeatedly makes efforts at evenhandedness. While his narrator complains that deep German philosophy has become degenerate phrasemongering in a Universalist clergyman, he soon afterward acknowledges that Americans are honest, helpful, and tolerant (*AA*, 1:69–70). Wilhelmi explains that Germans are among the dirtiest and vilest business men in

America, but also among the most liberal and high-minded. He continues: "Wenn es Gemeinheit gilt, so ist der Yankee mehr Schuft und der Deutsche mehr Schubiak; wenn die andre Seite gilt, so ist der Yankee mehr 'gentleman,' und der Deutsche mehr 'nobleman'; der Yankee mehr anständiger Mann, der Deutsche mehr edler Mensch" (*AA*, 2:96). This strikes me as fairly muddy; it is, perhaps, one of Solger's efforts to remain within the realm of universal satire. But it turns out that his irony and satire find their limits in a fundamental, nationalist conviction of German superiority, so that the image of America in the novel, while not relentlessly anti-American, is ultimately dismissive. It seems that Solger, like Antonio, was less an immigrant than an exile.

# Part III. Fantasy: Karl May

# 10. Germany's Americans: Old Shatterhand and Winnetou

When the president of Germany, Roman Herzog, was asked what film role he would have most liked to play, he replied without hesitation: "Winnetou."[1] The anecdote encapsulates the extraordinary pervasiveness of Karl May's works in the consciousness of the German people. While the phenomenon may be in decline among younger generations, it still retains astonishing dimensions. Few other features of contemporary German life give me, as a tolerably sympathetic American student of German literature and culture, more of a sense of foreignness. In this condition I have felt long hesitant about attempting to engage Karl May, for, although there has been a vast amount of analysis of the phenomenon, I still do not fully understand how an evidently meretricious and, as it seems to me as it eventually did to May himself, psychopathological writer could achieve such a commanding presence among the *Volk der Dichter und Denker*. I suspect that the phenomenon escapes final analysis, because it is overdetermined and, perhaps, to some degree accidental. I draw no conclusions about the "German mind" from it, because I have always doubted that literature or even literary reception reflects a common social consciousness with any fidelity or that even huge best sellers occupy a commanding place in the mental economy of their readers. In the current environment of literary studies, I am obliged to inquire of myself whether my resistance to May is chargeable to exclusive and discriminatory preoccupation with aesthetic value or indifference to literature in its social significance and as an expression of the anxieties and hopes of the inarticulate majority. I think not, but I may be laboring under a deficiency, for it is perhaps comparable that I have never been able to understand how serious and cultivated adults can devote a large amount of interest and attention to the works of Sir Arthur Conan Doyle. On one occasion some years ago, while trying to do my part in an interdisciplinary literature course, I was obliged to deal with Sherlock Holmes for the first time since my boyhood. I was surprised at how ungratifying I found this reacquaintance. The paperback we employed cited the critic who accounted for the enduring popularity of Sherlock Holmes by saying that in his world "it is always 1895."[2] That would suit me fine, but it did not seem to me to be 1895 or any other time; the setting is thin and perfunctory, at least by the standards of Victorian realism. As for the vaunted ratiocination, it struck me as manipulative and shallow, and therefore tedious, so that I was obliged to conclude that the Sherlock Holmes cult, though it involves a surprising number of intelligent people, has no intelligible literary dimension. As near as I can tell, the tone of the cult is generally one of play, playacting, or even campiness. Karl May, however, is regularly regarded with the greatest earnestness: massive scholarly tomes are written about him; he is placed into elaborate moral-philosophical, even religious contexts.

Although my failure to appreciate these endeavors may, from the German perspective, number me as one of the descendants of the crass Yankees in *Winnetou IV*, busy in their inaccessibility to everything elevated and spiritual, the whole complex seems monstrously out of proportion to May's slender if obsessive talent and suffocatingly commonplace mind. To be sure, he was not without a certain primitive skill in narration. At any given point in his best writing one might find something positive to say of it. When reading the first volume of *Winnetou* I found myself noting that some episodes were not badly designed by the standards of adventure writing. But over his thousands of pages, May becomes monotonous. His vocabulary has been estimated at around 3,000 words,[3] which is approximately that of a tabloid newspaper. Retrospectively, he disclaimed any concern for style.[4] He had a vivid imagination but little inventiveness. Scenes, narrative devices, characterizations, and preoccupations undergo some shifts of emphasis but not much evolution in his career. He has the pedantry of the mimetic realist without the richness of observation. The reason for this, of course, is that his experiences were fabricated and their details cobbled together from books. May's research abilities in geographic, ethnographic, technological, and linguistic matters were unquestionably prodigious; source seeking in his oeuvre has become a minor industry in its own right. But, as the one American monograph on May's American novels has remarked, "these facts, however thick they may be, do not lead to literary realism."[5] However justified my resistant response may or may not be, it is in one sense quite conventional, as it is consistent with the almost total lack of interest in May on the American side, a matter to which I shall return in the next chapter.

May's Westerns lie somewhere between Cooper and comic book. Like Cooper, he is able to drive an adventure narrative through more or less preposterous circumstances in a way that can absorb the reader's attention even against one's own better judgment. May's feeling toward the Indian is, like Cooper's, one of tragic sympathy—Winnetou is the ultimate German reduction of Uncas—rather than commitment to the

Indian cause. Neither writer, of course, takes the red man's side against the white; in order to generate conflict, both divide the Indians into good tribes, associated with the virtuous white protagonists, and bad tribes, and do so with equal arbitrariness: what for Cooper are the Delawares versus the "Mingos" are for May the Apaches versus the Kiowas. This pattern, as Billington has shown, was employed by novelists for a long time.[6] While May's plotting is much simpler than Cooper's, both rely largely on the same collage of innumerable variations of the same tactical elements: reconnaissance, ambush, siege, the stalking movement, capture and release, the commando strike. His characteristic plot structure, clearly taken over from Cooper, has been recognized as "die Handlungsprogression von 'flight' und 'pursuit,' von Auf-der-Flucht-Sein und wiederum Selbst-hinter-etwas-her-Sein, womit Cooper in Durchschnitt 400 Seiten pro Roman zu füllen in der Lage ist."[7] To this might be added a specific Cooperian plot device that struck me: of a trio of protagonists, one goes off on a separate mission and disappears from the narrative and the reader's consciousness for a time; he can then reemerge to rescue the others from a pickle, such as being burned at the stake. It is easy to see how May's works could become the inspiration for generations of children's games, played anywhere there was, or could be pretended to be, a field, a hill, or a ravine.[8]

His comic-book aspect resides in his peculiar handling of his narrator, which is very different from Cooper's thoughtful and sometimes philosophical treatment of his protagonists. This side of May's strategy appeals less to the communal make-believe of game playing than to private, Walter Mitty–like fantasies. The first-person narrator—presented as identical with the author—is superman. Although at the opening of *Winnetou* he is an inexperienced German boy—the first section of the novel is entitled "Ein Greenhorn"—he can from the beginning outshoot, outride, outsurvey, and outthink the most experienced trapper or scout, outstalk and outwit the most skillful Indian. The old Western hands try to patronize him, but he teaches them one lesson after another. He is of bionic strength. The blow of his fist is irresistible and earns him the early nickname of "Old Shatterhand," a name May gave to the luxurious villa he built with the proceeds of his achievements, which today houses the Karl May Museum in Radebeul near Dresden. The narrator's knowledge of everything, from the habits of buffalo to the psychology of Indians, from trail reading to taming mustangs, is superior to anyone's. He has nothing more to learn and makes no mistakes.

And how has this greenhorn acquired all this knowledge and skill? By reading German books in his homeland, as he repeatedly assures his understandably incredulous companions. Thus, by a recursive, literal duplicity, the author builds into his narration salesmanship for his own product. For naive shamelessness there is probably nothing quite like it in the history of popular literature. This is the author who, in *Winnetou IV*, poured scorn on the crass commercialism of American publishers' representatives.

The magnitude of the phenomenon never ceases to amaze. It is well known that May is by a large margin the best-selling imaginative writer in the German language. Not only his stunning success during his career, but his endurance in German cultural life to the present day is beyond compare. Since the expiration of his copyright in 1962, it seems hardly possible to count the number of copies published with any accuracy; estimates are approaching one hundred million, and annual sales a decade ago continued at around two million, though they have dropped off since to about a quarter of a million.[9] There have been and continue to be societies of admirers, museums if not shrines, films and summer theater festivals, and a whole publishing house devoted to this one author. His writings became one of the main inspirations for children's games in Germany for a century if not more, and made the American Indian an iconic figure in German culture. As for the Near Eastern stories, Arno Schmidt asserted plausibly in the 1950s that even seventy-year-olds were still able to recite the full twelve-part name of Kara Ben Nemsi's Muslim companion Halef.[10] May seems to have infiltrated every level of society with any sort of reading habit; he turns up in the boyhood, and, more frequently than one might suppose, girlhood memories of a remarkable number of Germans prominent in public life and the arts.[11] In fact, I would find the phenomenon easier to comprehend if, instead of generating fantasies of power and competence in frustrated intellectuals, which I take to be the function of the Sherlock Holmes phenomenon, he had remained a writer of stories for children, "als Symptom für die Problem- und Interessenlage einer bestimmten Alters- und Entwicklungsstufe aufgefaßt."[12]

To be sure, the complex is enriched by a psychological fascination with the author himself, surely one of the most bizarre personalities ever to appear in the literature of any nation. His story has been often told: his birth on February 25, 1842, among deeply impoverished, technologically obsolescent weavers in the Erzgebirge of Saxony; his blindness during the first few years of his childhood, to which he ascribed his inward turn to the imagination; the dilettantish efforts of his father to force-feed him with unsystematic rote learning, undoubtedly in the hope that the son might better himself socially; the self-sabotage of his incipient career as a teacher on the lowest rung of prestige by a series of petty thefts and swindles, resulting in prison terms totaling some eight years; the plan developed in prison of becoming a writer of fiction; and the subsequent career, first as an author of subliterary pulp, an episode that later was to cause much embarrassment, then, rather rapidly as it turned out, his progress to fame and fortune in his fictive personae of Kara Ben Nemsi and Old Shatterhand.

But it is not these matters, as interesting as they may be, that make May the unique figure he became. Many writers have come out of impoverished origins; there have been others who have suffered or overcome physical disabilities; writers who have spent time in prison are not unknown to literary history. The peculiarity in May's case is the apparent disappearance in his own mind of the boundary between reality and fiction, the increasing meld of the narrative persona with the empirical author, to the point where May had himself portrayed in Western and Near Eastern costume and began to display locks of Winnetou's hair (subsequently discovered to be horsehair) and other relics of adventure such as his famous weapons, which he had secretly manufactured for him by a gunsmith (one of which, the fourteen-shot Henry Rifle, he probably learned of from Gerstäcker [NR, 1:224]). The plain if outlandish truth of the matter is that May, who first visited the Near East in 1899 and America in 1908, at the ages of fifty-seven and sixty-six respectively, presented himself to the public as the actual, virtually superhuman hero of his adventure tales; even his publisher believed this. To a degree these pretenses appear as a way of drawing a veil over his unsavory past, especially, as in his heyday, he became muscularly Christian, patriotic, and conservative. But they went deeper; his odd character collapsed the ancient distinction between fiction and lying. He solemnly claimed to know dozens if not hundreds of exotic languages, though in fact he seems not to have known any foreign language well; he pretended to have a doctoral degree, eventually acquiring one from a mail-order diploma mill in Chicago. The impostures were eventually exposed, as one would think they were bound to be. Doubts about his claims began to surface on several sides, and a malevolent journalistic hooligan dredged up his criminal past. May fought back fiercely but hopelessly against an attack that quickly degenerated into a witch hunt, and these squabbles, along with endless litigation over the rights to his early writings and the complexities of a disagreeable domestic situation, embittered his latter days until his death in 1912; indeed, the disputes outlived him by many a year.

His conduct presents us with a fascinating psychological riddle. It would be inappropriate to respond to it with postmodernist or deconstructionist glee as a paradigmatic case of the dissolution of reality and the authorial self into language and fiction; May was a victim, ultimately a tormented one. His case has been viewed psychoanalytically as one of profound narcissism, and sociopsychologically as the acting out of the nearly hopelessly deprived proletarian's needs for recognition and authority, enabled in this instance by an uncommon vivacity and density of the imagination and a talent for narrative—just as May's swindles, also designed, one would think, for inevitable exposure and punishment, involved role playing of figures of authority such as a doctor or detective; as late as 1879, when he was thirty-seven years old and his writing career had already begun, he served three weeks in jail for impersonating a detective. The authorial self-praise and self-congratulation in his texts can be extremely aggressive and in places can reach nearly lunatic proportions; other characters are made to chime in with it. He can do anything, from driving a locomotive to teaching other westerners how to sew (W, 3:5–66; OS, 3:405–6). He makes constant propaganda for his own books, especially in the late works. To me he rather resembles the television evangelists of our time, who may superficially appear to be mere charlatans and hypocrites, but who, like Sinclair Lewis's Elmer Gantry, may have been self-hypnotized by the force of their own rhetoric, salesmanship, and psychological need into a form of belief in their masquerade. May himself, in his late autobiography—to my mind by far the most interesting book he ever wrote—attempted a self-diagnosis with some psychoanalytic ideas he had picked up, with a result that sounds like a form of schizophrenia, seeing himself as a congeries of several selves in dramatic conflict with one another and claiming to have heard voices; he blamed society and, rather paradoxically, the pulp literary reading of his youth for leading him astray.[13] It seems at least plausible that this elaborate fraud contributed initially to his immense popular success, in that he invited an identification with the imagined selves of his readers in a shared environment of fantasy.

As is the case with other cultic literary figures, such as Wilhelm Raabe, there has been an effort to capture and elevate the phenomenon by cleansing it of obnoxious ideological complicities, subjecting it and its reception history to critical inquiry, and illuminating it with conscientious research and sophisticated scholarship. In recent decades, this endeavor has reached quite substantial proportions. There are, first of all, daunting philological problems. Even more than Gerstäcker's works, May's, as a possession of the public domain, have been raw material for editors and publishers, so that what is commonly available is in many cases quite different from what May originally wrote and published; one of the older guardians of the legacy explicitly required the reworking of May's earlier, less pure texts in order to make them congruent with the later writing.[14] Restoring at least the original published versions is a major project of May scholarship, and a critical edition has generated several volumes, though whether it will continue to be feasible is not clear, as it has for the present become a victim of infighting among publishers. Both the encyclopedic character of May's synthesis of sources and the vastness of the reception history should provide an inexhaustible fountain of research for the foreseeable future. His dialectical embeddedness in Wilhelminian culture and society invites elaborated speculation. There is an evident need to upgrade May evaluatively, to gain him admission to an expanded literary canon and justify the expenditure of major institutional resources of literary scholarship on him.

Since there is little that can be said on his behalf under the traditional critical categories—style, structure, coherence, subtlety of vision, and the like—the revision has been pursued, on the whole, in three ways. First, in the context of a broad revaluation of what has been traditionally regarded as subliterature, he has been seen as a vessel and articulator of the utopian imagination of the masses deprived under capitalism of plenitude and gratification. Obviously a project of the neo-Marxist left, this approach is explicitly traceable to Ernst Bloch, the theoretician of utopian hope.[15] A second direction, somewhat connected to the first, has been to see in May certain significantly countercultural impulses. These concern mutual respect among cultures and nations with an at least implicit antiimperialism and an increasingly explicit pacificism, along with a repudiation of racism, especially toward the latter part of May's career. In these respects, he seems to be resisting Wilhelminian ideological trends that can appear retrospectively as protofascist and thus ominously premonitory of the worst calamities of our century.[16] However, the claim made in the former East Germany that the campaign against May late in his career was a conspiracy of reactionary circles opposed to his pacifism, antiracism, and anticolonialism has been rightly rejected.[17] Third, there has been an effort at aesthetic revaluation by shifting the critical perspective from the popular best sellers to the late mystical-prophetic, allegorical-symbolic works, especially volumes three and four of *Im Reiche des silbernen Löwen* (book publication 1902, 1903), the two volumes of *Ardistan und Dschinnistan*, and the fourth volume of *Winnetou* (1910). This initiative, which is growing into a sizable industry of criticism, is largely traceable to a series of essays and radio documentaries produced by Arno Schmidt from 1956 to 1963. Even those of us who may find Schmidt's excesses and obsessions a little irritating must give him credit for his persistent efforts to expand the constricted German literary canon, to urge us to read some *other books* for a change.

May reception has not, of course, been unremittingly positive. The outrage over the discovery of his imposture intersected with and intensified a campaign against his works as trash corrupting the youthful imagination. This campaign is of no further interest today, except as a chapter in the recurrent efforts to exert social control by controlling reading, especially of young people. Such efforts are, apart from their obnoxiousness from a civil-rights point of view, of dubious utility, since, despite the immense efforts of literary sociology, we still have no idea of to what extent reading fiction affects moral consciousness, individually or collectively, or even if it does at all. But the evaluation of culturally prominent Germans has also not been unanimous, either; a number have recalled boredom or hostility in their experiences of reading May. These form a not undignified list of quite various ideological provenance, e.g., Max Brod, Oskar Maria Graf, Manfred Hausmann, Helmut Heissenbüttel, Hans Egon Holthusen, and Erich Kästner.[18] Rudolf Huch remarked in his autobiography that he could not see how May could be named in the same breath with Gerstäcker: "May gibt ein Gemengsel dick aufgetragener Abenteuer, von wahrer Anschaulichkeit ist nicht die Rede."[19] However, Huch (brother of the better known Ricarda Huch) was a nephew of Gerstäcker's son-in-law, a connection with effects perhaps similar to the ban on mentioning May's name in the family of Balduin Möllhausen.[20] I have found, however, little trace of the parody and satire he would seem to invite. The only genuinely funny comment on May I have encountered is Oskar Panizza's straight-faced claim that there was no such person as Karl May and that his works had been written under a pseudonym by Kaiser Wilhelm II.[21] An extremely witty, quotation-drenched fantasy of May meeting Kafka on a ship to America, *Vom Wunsch, Indianer zu werden*, by the Austrian writer Peter Henisch has appeared recently.

As for the effort to upgrade May aesthetically or philosophically by reference to his last works, I can only say that it has left me totally unmoved: I find them tedious, morally simpleminded, in no intelligible literary-historical dimension "mystical," and, like all his works, oppressively self-indulgent. They would be most fairly evaluated in the context of popular fantasy writing, the magical-occult counterpart to science fiction. One must observe in any case that his basic narrative habits have not changed in the late works: the chain of adventures based upon capture and liberation, the astonishingly easy solving of difficulties by the hero's amazing skills and reasoning powers, the unrelenting self-praise and self-advertisement, and especially the apparent identification of the narrator with the empirical author, despite the public chastisement he had suffered from the exposure of his imposture and despite the quite plain assertion in his autobiography that his personae were fictive.[22] The device is put under an almost ironic strain in the fourth volume of *Winnetou*, where May not only appears in his own right as author and traveler but brings in his (second) wife, "das Herzle," as a most improbably resolute, skilled, and resourceful companion in the Wild West. Bernd Steinbrink has rightly warned against overlooking May's consistency and continuity:

> Die strikte Trennung von "unliterarischen" Vorarbeiten und "ästhetischem Spätwerk," die auch in späteren Arbeiten anklingt, der von Schmidt beschriebene Bruch also, scheint mir allerdings einen wesentlichen Aspekt des Gesamtwerks in den Hintergrund zu rücken. Mays Schriften bauten von Beginn an eine Gegenwelt zur real erfahrenen Wirklichkeit auf, und das Spanien, das hinter den Bergen Ernsthals liegt, ist identisch mit jenem Dschinnistan, dessen Berge im Spätwerk am Horizont aufleuchten; thematisiert ist in allen Schriften Mays ein "Pilgerzug," der ebenso ein Ausbruch wie ein Initiationsprozeß des Helden (und mit diesem auch des Autors und Lesers) in die Gegenwelt ist, die May "Wunscherfüllung, Ergänzung und Überhöhung seines Ich" bedeutete.[23]

Although he allowed in his autobiographical confession that it had been a mistake to attempt to solve the whole of the human problem, at virtually the same time he devised for an unwritten novel, *Abu Kital*, the subtitle *Ein Versuch zur Lösung der Menschheitsfrage und zur Aussöhnung des Morgenlandes mit dem Abendlande*.[24]

As to May's ideological virtues, the best case can be made for pacificism. If there is any evolution in his oeuvre, it is from the rather conventional blood and thunder in certain episodes of his early works to an increasing commitment to nonviolence, until in *Ardistan und Dschinnistan* whole military operations are undertaken with the purpose of preventing fighting and bloodshed. It is not improbable that May, if he had not died in 1912, might have been numbered among the opponents of the war, a posture that would have further diminished his already impaired popularity at that time. The claim of antiimperialism needs to be relativized by acknowledgment of his intense German nationalism, but it does appear that, at least after his depressing Near Eastern journey of 1899–1900, he disapproved of the colonial enterprises of the Wilhelminian era and, by extension, of colonialism in general. His smuggling of an antiimperialist story, *Et in terra pax* (1901), into a volume intended to celebrate Kaiser Wilhelm's imperialistic designs on China is one of the most appealing feats of his odd career.[25] Since we know that Bismarck pursued colonial enterprises without conviction, out of pure opportunism in domestic politics, May might be thought of as a consistent Bismarckian in this matter. In his ambivalence in this regard he might invite a comparison with Kipling.

With regard to racism, however, the record is a good deal less clear. If racism is understood as a systematic doctrine attempting to discover, define, and, in some cases, evaluate differences among human races, then there seems to be little trace of it in May's writings. As to whether there is an underlying Darwinistic discourse, opinions have differed. George L. Mosse has ascribed social Darwinism to May's view (not consistently held, by the way) that the Indians must inevitably perish;[26] as we have seen, however, this position is in no way unusual and need have nothing to do with Darwin. Martin Lowsky interprets May's advocacy of the Indians in Wilhelminian Germany as anti-Darwinistic, adding that on account of his defense of the Kurds his novels may not be imported into Turkey.[27] Even in regard to the Indians, however, there are moments when racial distinctions are applied. In *Winnetou II* it is asserted that the superiority of white men over the Indians is owing to the formers' cold-blooded willingness to face death, and in *Winnetou III* there is an often noted passage in which Old Shatterhand explains why he can't save himself from being tortured to death by marrying an Indian girl: "Daß ein gebildeter Europäer nicht seine ganze Zukunft dadurch preisgeben kann, daß er ein rotes Mädchen heiratet" (*W*, 2: 532; *W*, 3:575). In an early story, even working-class whites are superior to Indians in a fight: "es zeigte sich da allerdings, daß bei gleichen Waffen der zähere und intelligentere Weiße meist im Vorteile steht" (*OS*, 2:163). However, this passage occurs just before one where Winnetou scalps an enemy and waves the trophy around with a victory cry (*OS*, 2:168), a scene that interpreters unanimously regard as belonging to a primitive phase when May's concept of Winnetou had not yet matured. Still, observers have also noted that the most admirable Indians tend to have Caucasian features (examples in *OS*, 2:223; *OS*, 3:52). There are other signs that he thought in racial categories conventional for his time; for example, he wrote in a letter to his publisher that "Surehand ist unter den Weißen, was Winnetou unter den Rothen war, die Verkörperung des Rassenideales" (*OS*, 1:N 7). However, in the novel itself, the narrator mounts an impassioned lecture against racism (*OS*, 1:241–42). An answer to this question would have to be sought on the surface of popular discourse. May was not educated or intelligent enough to make use of philosophical resources; he would most likely have learned about Darwinism from family magazines rather than from, say, Ernst Haeckel. The result is an unsystematic confusion, which yields even to the friendliest gaze "ein zwiespältiges Bild."[28]

As for blacks, Lowsky recognizes that May regularly portrayed them as comic figures.[29] May probably never saw a black person before his visit to the United States in 1908, if then. The best that can be said for his portrayal of blacks is that it is condescending. A Negro is said to be "zwar ein Schwarzer, stand aber an Begabung viel höher als gewöhnliche Leute seiner Farbe"; he is helpful and friendly, a good rider and observer, and he is delighted when Old Shatterhand tells him that "dein Verstand heller ist als deine Hautfarbe" (W, 2:177–78, 181). The Negro Bob in *Old Surehand* speaks ungrammatically, cannot count above ten, cannot be a westerner "bei seiner geistigen Bescheidenheit," and is thrilled to be treated as "grad so Gentleman wie weißer Gentleman" notwithstanding "die geistigen Schwächen seiner Rasse" (OS, 1:283, 297, 317). The incorrigible scoundrel Old Wabble has a countenance "mit starken Niggerlippen" (OS, 1:14). It has, to be sure, been pointed out on May's behalf that his prejudices were moderate compared with those of others, notably Sealsfield's.[30] As with Sealsfield, however, mixed race is almost always a pejorative sign in May's stories; half-breeds, it is observed in *Winnetou IV*, inherit the worst characteristics of both parents (W, 4:306). Here, too, however, he is not consistent. The racial mixture of whites and Indians in the family of Old Surehand has positive results (W, 4:11–12).

However, May's most significant failing in the area of race is an absence rather than a presence. The greatest need for tolerance, understanding, and reconciliation in May's environment was toward Germany's Jewish citizens, as much of his career was contemporaneous with a rising tide of anti-Semitism. His contribution toward the relief of this pestilence may be fairly estimated at zero. Jews are not very prominent or common figures in his stories, and their portrayals tend to be neutral with a faintly pejorative coloration.[31] On the strength of his characterizations, his allegiance to classical German *Humanitätsphilosophie*, and his high regard for Lessing's *Nathan der Weise*, his commitment to tolerance in regard to the Jews has been defended.[32] His closest friend of his late years, Richard Plöhn, was of partly Jewish origin, and May married his widow (who, however, became a Nazi partisan in later years). It is possible that his views on this as on other matters mellowed as he grew older. Some of his earliest writings are mildly protective of the Jews; anti-Semitic clichés appear in the 1880s; more positive attitudes appear again later on, especially at the end of his career.[33] In *Winnetou I* the narrator expresses a quite conventional view of Jewish religion when he remarks that the Indians have a defective understanding because, like the people of Israel, they can think of redemption only as external, not as internal (W, 1:419). The passage has been interpreted, not very convincingly to my mind, as expressive of tolerance and fraternity.[34] But in the 1890s, in his three-volume novel *Satan und Ischariot*, published only in abridged form, a seductive, vain, and greedy Jewish woman is paralleled to a highly moral Christian hero. This parallelization appears to be a variation on the contrasted Jewish and Gentile figurations in Gustav Freytag's *Soll und Haben* and Wilhelm Raabe's *Der Hungerpastor*. May is said to have been the only writer to replicate the pattern with a female Jewish figure.[35]

Yet in 1906, May wrote a quite remarkable letter to a Jewish boy who had been inspired by his books to convert to Christianity. May endeavors to dissuade him from this course on the grounds of filial piety: "der Glaube Deiner Väter ist *heilig, ist groß, edel und erhaben*. Man muß ihn nur kennen und verstehen. Einen solchen Glauben wechselt man nicht einiger Bücher wegen und noch viel weniger des Geldes oder des Geschäftes wegen."[36] But this document appears to be unique, and the argument is, in any case, grounded in May's by then pervasive social conservatism. The record in the texts is indifferent at best. In *Winnetou III*, among the various nationalities observed in San Francisco there is a dirty Polish Jew (W, 3:286).[37] In an early story, also set in San Francisco, there appears one Jonathan Livingston, identified in May's imaginary English as a "Horse-haggler..., dem der Pferdejude auf tausend Schritten Entfernung anzusehen war" (OS, 2:507). He is an unpleasant person who haggles and tries to cheat, though he is not too bad and he does not speak in jargon, as many fictional Jews in German literature did. One must measure this thin material against the magnitude of the issue in May's time. His Near Eastern setting strikes me as, in this respect, an evasion, for it allows him to deal with "Semites"—Muslims, Arabs— while avoiding Jews. When the editor of the *Mitteilungen der Karl-May-Gesellschaft* praises May for having made the Germans immune to hatred of the Indians but adds: "Die Juden jedoch... haben bis heute keinen Autor gefunden, der es fertig gebracht hätte, einer breiten Masse die seit Jahrhunderten aufgestaute Voreingenommenheit... zu nehmen," he implicitly admits that May has contributed nothing in this area.[38]

Apart from pacifism and cross-cultural tolerance, the general ideological tone of May's writings is compliantly conservative, and becomes more so as he goes on. Schmiedt has suggested that the unpolitical, apparently antiauthoritarian attitude reflects the German citizen's avoidance of politics at that time and creates a new authoritarian hierarchy led by the hero, whose total superiority displaces such verbal allegiance to liberalism and democracy as may be present, reflecting the authoritarian welfare state of Bismarck's time.[39] One of the less bedazzled of the May scholars has argued that he met a need for a reconstituted feudal order in a public disoriented by the complexity of modern social processes and industrialization.[40] In *Ardistan und Dschinnistan*, everything, including the creation of peace, is accomplished through relations among feudal rulers; the results are merely announced to the people. The narrator of *Winnetou II* asserts forthrightly: "Ich bin ein Deutscher und bekümmere mich nicht im mindesten um Eure Politik" (*W*, 2:81). May certainly did not extrapolate from his proletarian origins and experiences a sympathy for revolution or for working-class politics. Quite early in his career he created and edited a magazine for miners designed to turn them away from Social Democratic politics.[41] Near the beginning of the first *Winnetou* volume we encounter a German forty-eighter, who has now become an Apache named Klekih-petra. But, far from having carried the spirit of liberty to America, as many forty-eighters did, Klekih-petra is a contrite former university instructor who condemns himself for his allegiance to the Enlightenment, for having robbed people of their faith, and for having not even regarded the king as sacred (*W*, 1:128–30). In the second volume, the narrator polemicizes directly against the Revolution of 1848 (*W*, 2:501–2).

The sentiment is repeated in May's autobiography, where he asserts his complete disapproval of revolution and claims to have learned early that happiness lies in allegiance to "Gott, König und Vaterland."[42] In *Ardistan und Dschinnistan*, even a well-meaning revolutionary is chastised, for it is wrong to attempt to overthrow the bad Mir; reason and persuasion should be applied instead: "Es wäre jedenfalls vorteilhafter gewesen, euch einander zu nähern, euch einander zu erziehen, euch einander zu bessern." In the process of the development from the "Gewaltmensch" to the "Edelmensch," it is the "Empörer in uns" that must be destroyed (*AuD*, 2:484, 544). In *Winnetou IV* the sullen workers on the ill-conceived monument to Winnetou are hostile to Old Shatterhand, and their crude, violent, half-Indian, half-black leader is known as "der Nigger": "Einen treffenderen Typ der Brutalität als ihn konnte man sich wohl kaum denken!" (*W*, 4:560)—another example, incidentally, of mixed race as a pejorative sign. Eventually the leader, in a drunken state, attempts to take power by force. The fourth volume is, if anything, even more explicitly conservative than the earlier ones. We get a lecture on the obligation of the young to honor the old—even artists are not specially privileged in this regard—and an Indian woman is rather pointlessly praised for having no interest in the right to vote: "Die ist wahrlich nicht nach dem Mount Winnetou unterwegs, um dort Suffragettenreden zu halten! Die weiß, was sie will!" (W, 4: 443, 320). Judging from some passages in *Ardistan und Dschinnistan*, May also became a temperance enthusiast (*AuD*, 1:302–3, 350–67), a position that, in itself, would not have endeared him to the German American community.

His most pervasive ideological instrument is religion. His Christianity may well appear heterodox and incoherent—for example, he is consistently hostile to Mormons, though this is an element that he probably inherited from his literary predecessors[43]—but it certainly is vigorously obtrusive, overriding both his heroizing of the Indian and his apparent respect for Islam, and it continues to be aggressively stressed by his Christian partisans today.[44] Klekih-petra finds consolation for his political regrets in religion (W, 1:129–30). In the first volume of *Old Surehand*, the religious preaching becomes relentless, taking on qualities of obscurantism, authoritarianism, and repression. Old Shatterhand confesses that learning ancient languages to read biblical texts in the original had led to skepticism by way of scholarly criticism, "Aber Gott war barmherzig gegen den Thoren und führte ihn auch auf dem Wege des Studierens zu der Erkenntnis, daß jene fromme Kinderglaube der allein richtige sei." A corollary to this "Kinderglaube" is that fathers have the right and obligation to beat sons, who have no right to demand justification (*OS*, 1:407, 411). In one of the early stories a westerner who ran away from his aunt because she beat him too much now sees that she was actually kind to do so, and he wants to reward her with money (*OS*, 2:608–9). In the third volume of *Old Surehand*, the narrator, after a disquisition on the reality of guardian angels, declares: "ich trete mit dieser meiner Anschauung nur deshalb vor die Oeffentlichkeit, weil in unserer materiellen Zeit, in unserer ideals- und glaubenlosen *fin de siècle* nur selten jemand wagt, zu sagen, daß er mit diesem Leugnen und Verneinen nichts zu schaffen habe" (*OS*, 3:151–52). In that same work, the militant atheist Old Wabble is converted while dying by prayer and the singing of "O Ewigkeit, du Donnerwort" (*OS*, 3:494–97).

There is a good deal of hymn singing in the third volume of *Winnetou* also. Old Shatterhand and his companions come upon a church in the Rocky Mountain wilderness and find the German pioneers singing an "Ave Maria" of Old Shatterhand's own composition (W, 3:414–15). Winnetou, who has become dissatisfied with Indian religion and longs for Christian universalism, is told: "Der Glaube der roten Männer lehrt Haß und Tod. Der Glaube der weißen Männer lehrt Liebe und Leben!" He too, in his famous dying scene, is converted to Christianity by that same hymn (W, 3:424–25, 427–28, 473–74). Even in *Winnetou IV* (imaginary) Indian architecture is criticized for being earthbound, for not striving upward like a Christian church tower or Islamic minaret (W, 4: 417). This rhetoric of soaring idealism came to be supported by the illustrations of Sascha Schneider, with whom May became associated late in his career, and whom he praises explicitly in *Winnetou IV* as a creator of "die wahre Kunst" (W, 4:501). A good deal has been written about these paintings, which are currently being revived as cover illustrations for one series of the reprint edition. My own, doubtless not entirely qualified opinion is that they represent monumentalized neo-Nazarene and conceivably protofascist kitsch, and are in any case quite dreadful.[45] The effect, like much else in May, seems polemically antimodern.

The question as to the degree to which May's fiction engages the modern world leads, like so much else in him, to a mixed result. The action in *Winnetou II* is dated "mitten im Bürgerkriege" (W, 2:5). Since May was only nineteen at the outbreak of the Civil War, the identification of the author with the hero implies a very precocious youth indeed. However, the appearance later in the novel of the Ku Klux Klan (said to be, by the way, an enemy of "Deutschtum" [W, 2:130], not the issue for which the Klan is best remembered) indicates a period after the war; the source here is probably Gerstäcker. The one modern element that is present from the beginning is the railroad. This may remind us of those many paintings of the Old West in which the railroad is the single modern image in a landscape that is otherwise virtually prehistorically Edenic. The motif of a fire in an oil field was used by May several times—also taken from Gerstäcker, as we shall see in a moment. In Winnetou-City, where the vulgar monument is to be erected, oil has been found, and a waterfall is to be "chained" to gain electricity, but these enterprises are criticized on ecological grounds (W, 4:398). X-rays are mentioned in *Old Surehand III* and there is an allusion to the honking of an automobile horn in *Ardistan und Dschinnistan* (OS, 3:189; AuD, 1:73). Sometimes May's technoscientific knowledge is rather spurious. Old Shatterhand can see underwater at night because water retains daylight just as a diamond does (OS, 1:143). One unsurpassed moment of involuntary comedy is provided with the invention of a flying machine by the Indian "Junger Adler" in *Winnetou IV*. This appears to be a body suit with mechanically operated wings, designed on the model of bird flight (W, 4:458, 577–78)—foisted upon the reader a half-dozen years after the Wright brothers demonstrated how flight was to be achieved. May knew this perfectly well; in 1909 he attended the first German air show where he saw a flying demonstration by Louis Blériot.[46] Like everything else, the scene in the novel is only symbolic.

This unevenness is again owing to May's dependence on sources, including literary ones reaching well back in the century. Gerstäcker is a prominent example. The previously mentioned scenes of the burning oil field seem quite clearly taken from Gerstäcker's story, "Im Petroleum" (*KENS*, 1:483–534). For his early serial novel, *Der Schatz im Silbersee*, May took passages about tree-poaching gangs verbatim from Gerstäcker's "Rafters,"[47] and in *Winnetou III* a man telling of his adventures speaks of having known "die Flußpiraten des Mississippi" (*W*, 3:303). The villain Santer in the *Winnetou* novels bears the pseudonym of a criminal in *Die Flußpiraten*. May's description of the Mission of Santa Lucia near Sacramento during the gold rush reminds one of Gerstäcker's account of the Mission Dolores (*OS*, 2:83; cf. *R*, 2:163–224), and the various bear fights may also owe something to him, though, as we have seen, they were a staple of German Westerns. May worked variations on texts of Sealsfield and Möllhausen also.[48] It has been suggested that Sealsfield's Tokeah is one of the ancestors of Winnetou.[49] It is clear, however, that May domesticates and normalizes the naturalistic wildness of Sealsfield's language; like Old Shatterhand himself, it is now "sauber, korrekt, gewandt."[50]

There are a large number of motifs from general literary reading.[51] The influence of Cooper is beyond doubt.[52] The piratical Miss Admiral in May's sea stories may be a descendant of Milady in Dumas's *Three Musketeers*, though to set Dumas's witty novel side by side with May seems especially unfair.[53] Here and there one senses echoes of Goethe and Schiller, though these may come out of the pervasive atmosphere of *Bildung*, for example, when it is said that everything offered by our present world is "weiter nichts als nur ein Gleichnis" (*W*, 4:64). The wise woman Marah Durimeh in *Ardistan und Dschinnistan* seems to owe something to Makarie in *Wilhelm Meisters Wanderjahre*, and the verses of the smithy on Sitara that smelts the new self echo Goethe's "stirb und werde" (*AuD*, 1:342–43). There is a sudden allusion to Schiller's "Das Mädchen aus der Fremde" in *Old Surehand III*, and the claim that the Mir of Ardistan may be a tyrant and have become contemptuous of the people because he never encountered a person of true value may be an echo of *Don Carlos* (*OS*, 3:182; *AuD*, 2:98). However, these are just probes into a great mass of *gesunkenes Kulturgut* that struck me in unsystematic reading.

As far as the tradition of fiction about America goes, it would not be accurate to see May, despite all his borrowings, in its succession. In important ways he stands in contrast to both Sealsfield and Gerstäcker: he replicates neither the confrontational anarchism of the former nor the inquiring spirit of the latter. Despite the exotic, constantly excited tone of adventure, bounding from one crisis to another, May forms a utopia of conventional and substantially conservative values that have no detectable American dimension and contain very little challenge to the unexamined presuppositions of the German majority. From this point of view, it is a question whether May's fiction is in any intelligible sense about America at all, and whether the provincial introversion underlying its superficial exoticism accounts to some degree for the American lack of interest in it, doubts that will be addressed in the following chapter.

# 11. On the Absence of Germany's Americans in America

Every author discussed so far, except Kürnberger, had a presence in the United States. Sealsfield, Gerstäcker, Talvj, and Solger were published here. Möllhausen played a significant role in the exploration of the West and Strubberg in the German colonization in Texas; the books of both are easily found in American libraries. But Karl May, by a large margin the most widely published and widely read writer of fiction in the German language, is hardly known in the United States. Proportionately to the millions of copies of his works in circulation, he is not conspicuously represented in American libraries. The narrator of *Winnetou IV*, coincidentally named Karl May, asserts "Es sind viele tausend deutsche Exemplare des 'Winnetou' hier in den Vereinigten Staaten verbreitet" (W, 4:79), but there is no direct evidence of this or of much notoriety in America. His one public appearance in the United States, on October 18, 1908, in Lawrence, Massachusetts, is said to have been enthusiastically received.[1] The composition of the audience is not known; my guess is that it consisted largely of recent immigrants. Given the magnitude of the German American community at that time and its efficient communication media, it is noteworthy that May did not have other opportunities to lecture. The Lawrence appearance was arranged through a personal connection, by an immigrant from May's birthplace in Saxony. He has rarely been published in German in the United States; to be sure, the major part of his career postdated American acknowledgment of international copyright. Before that, one pirated edition appeared in Philadelphia; however, it was not one of his Westerns in the specific sense, but the detective novel *Auf der See gefangen*.[2] There were a couple of efforts to edit May texts for language instruction, but they have disappeared.[3] The writer Frederic Morton, born in Vienna in 1924, was astonished to discover as a young immigrant that his schoolteacher had never heard of Old Shatterhand.[4]

This absence is so striking and so disproportionate to the magnitude of the Karl May phenomenon in German culture, as well as to the notable burgeoning in recent decades of May scholarship in Germany, that it seems in itself to beg for explanation. His popularity has by no means been restricted to German-speaking countries. He is said to be the most translated German author, and into so many languages that their number is uncertain; one source gives twenty, another thirty-nine.[5] In 1962, when May's copyright expired, *Der Spiegel*, evidently worried about a new subliterary deluge, reported that a Polish translation of *Winnetou* published immediately after World War II sold 450,000 copies in two weeks.[6] There was also a large public for May in Italian translation.[7] According to the *National Union Catalogue*, even several Hebrew translations appeared in Israel in the 1950s. What we do not find in the *NUC* is large numbers of American editions.

English translations have been few and, for the most part, insignificant. An adaptation of *Winnetou I, II,* and *III*, put out in two volumes by a semiofficial Catholic publishing house in 1898, has remained obscure because in libraries it is cataloged not under May's name but under that of the adapter, Marion Ames Taggart (1860–1945), a Catholic convert who otherwise specialized in books for girls.[8] The collective title of both volumes is *Jack Hildreth among the Indians*: the Jesuit-educated young American Hildreth is the narrator identical with Old Shatterhand; thus May has vanished, and with him the German-centered ethos of the work.[9] May's nearly 2,000 pages have been cut back to 223 and 231 respectively, but, apart from some deviations necessary for continuity, the translation is more or less literal, except that the generally nondenominational Christianity of the original is made more specifically Catholic; naturally, May's "Ave Maria" is prominently featured. Most of the best-remembered highlights have been retained, and the result is quite fluent and readable, so that one might conclude that *Winnetou* profits from compression. However, the books have left no detectable trace; they have become rarities, obtainable only with difficulty via interlibrary loan.

An effort undertaken around 1977 by the Seabury Press to produce a comprehensive May edition in English foundered and vanished after a half-dozen volumes. It began with three representative texts: *Winnetou I* and *III*, one of the Near Eastern novels, and the "mystical" *Ardistan und Dschinnistan I* and *II*.[10] I well recall that, at a Modern Language Association convention at that time, a representative of the publishing house assured me that Karl May would become the new Hermann Hesse. This was not, to be sure, the best way to appeal to me, and in any case the result was to be otherwise; despite an effort at paperback publication, the project had to be abandoned. The few reviews, mostly in library journals, were not encouraging. The reviewer for public libraries demurred: "Academic libraries may want to consider these volumes as phenomena of popular culture, but they are not likely to have a wide enough appeal to the general reading public to justify purchase by the average public library."[11] The reviewer for academic libraries thought the opposite:

"... can hardly be recommended for an academic library, but the tired academic might well enjoy escaping with it."¹² The reviewer for the publishing industry complained: "May's old-fashioned narrative style and his stilted dialogue ... convey a simplicity bordering on naiveté. His practice of infusing social and religious dogma may prove tedious to the reader."¹³ No one seemed to think that the books had anything to say about America. In the *New York Times Book Review,* under the headline of "Cowboys for the Kaiser," Walter Laqueur, who was born in Breslau in 1921 and had had, like the great majority of Germans, boyhood experiences of May, was skeptical of his success in English, and remarked of *Ardistan und Dschinnistan* that "I found it unreadable as a schoolboy, and still do today."¹⁴

A compendium of reception materials published in 1980 tried to suggest some American echo by quoting a passage from Ernest Hemingway's novel *Islands in the Stream,* in which a man is said to be throwing a grenade as though he had learned the gesture from Karl May, and by repeating a magazine report of an interview with a "Cherokee Indian chief" and "Schriftsteller" named Iron Eyes Cody, who is alleged to have asserted that May is superior to all American literature put together and if published in the United States would surely be a hit.¹⁵ However, it turns out upon inspection that Hemingway's original referred to the famous baseball pitcher of the 1920s, Carl Mays;¹⁶ the translator doubtless substituted a more accessible allusion for German readers. As for Cody, he is neither a chief nor, except for essays and children's introductions to Indian lore, a "Schriftsteller," but has been a self-styled "Hollywood Indian" practically since the inception of the movies. He appeared in hundreds of films and organized Indians for many others, but is perhaps best remembered as the Indian weeping a tear at the polluted landscape in the environmental advertisements on television in 1971. In his highly entertaining autobiography he does not mention May, though he does comment that, while traveling with a Wild West show in Germany in the 1920s, he observed: "Of all the Europeans we encountered, I would have to say the Germans were the most enthusiastic Injun lovers.... Germany still has a fascination with Indians; they read about them, their generals (especially in World War Two) studied Indian guerilla tactics, and they all go to Western movies regularly. In fact, the Germans regularly crank out Westerns themselves. They have their own Duke Waynes and everything.... German commanders ... knew a great deal about Indians.... Probably the average German schoolboy knew more about Indians that [sic] his American counterpart."¹⁷ It is fascinating to read this observation from someone who did not at that time know the *reason* for all this German identification with American Indians, on which topic it has been reported that an Indian soldier in the U.S. Army who kidnapped a German couple attracted sympathizers to the "redman's plight, theorizing on how terrible it must have been for the son of the wild prairie to be torn away from the wigwams of his tribe and the playground of the wide open spaces." There were pleas for mercy, even from the kidnapped couple, and a committee of support was founded.[18] I suspect that the alleged comment on May by Cody was a product of his well-developed sense of drollery and was probably generated as publicity for the ill-fated Seabury Press edition.[19]

Another question concerns the Karl May films of the 1960s, in which the former Tarzan, Lex Barker, achieved a new career as Old Shatterhand and the role of Winnetou made a star out of a French actor, Pierre Brice. They were distributed in the United States, but how successfully I do not know; a few years ago I caught sight of one on cable television in the wee hours of the morning, but they do not seem to be available on home video. Notices of the films appeared in *Variety*;[20] they are all positive, but, as they are dated from Berlin (signed "Hans"), they were probably sent in by the distributor in order to draw attention to the films in the United States. The notices stress the exceptional commercial success of the films in Germany. *Motion Picture Guide* remarked with regret that the distributed copy of *Der Schatz von Silbersee* (*The Treasure of Silver Lake*, 1965) had met with little interest because of poor continuity and inaccurate dubbing; it is suggested that one of the European versions be seen instead. The comments on *Winnetou II* (*The Last of the Renegades*, 1966) and *Old Shatterhand* (1968) are noticeably cooler.[21] Renata Adler dismissed the latter in the *New York Times* in half a sentence as a "gory, Italian-made Western" (*sic*) of which no one would want a review.[22] In reply to an inquiry as to what had become of Lex Barker, an informant supplied exact data on the Karl May films but without any commentary.[23] None of the reviewers, with the exception of "Hans," seems to have had the faintest notion of May's import in German culture.

Things are little different in the area of secondary literature. The astonishing fact is that there is only one American monograph devoted entirely to May, an unpublished master's thesis from the University of Utah dating from 1963; part of a University of California dissertation of 1994 deals with the Near Eastern novels.[24] At a time of the expansion and propagation of German studies in the American academic world, a serious scholarly engagement with the May phenomenon would seem long overdue. Most of the few articles written about him have appeared in general-audience magazines or journals of western associations, and are without exception ironic and superior in tone.[25] The number of American scholarly articles can be counted on the fingers of one hand. Billington was evidently deserted by his customary accuracy and perspicuity when it came to May, of whom he asserts that his "Messianic-inflated egotism vastly appealed to his imperialistic-minded countrymen" and that his popularity was not ended by the "fall of Hitlerism."[26] This judgment may have been influenced by the curious tendency of the exiles from fascism to turn against May; this seems to have been the case even with Ernst Bloch, who, as we have seen, earlier assimilated May's utopian vision to his principle of hope.[27]

The most notorious of these assaults to appear in America was undoubtedly Klaus Mann's attack on May as a forerunner of Hitler, which appeared in two different periodicals in 1940. "It is hardly an exaggeration to say," Klaus Mann exaggerates, "that Karl May's childish and criminal fantasia has actually—though obliquely—influenced the history of the world. . . . The Third Reich is Karl May's ultimate triumph, the ghastly realization of his dreams. It is according to ethical and aesthetic standards indistinguishable from his that the Austrian housepainter, nourished in his youth by Old Shatterhand, is now attempting to rebuild the world."[28] Given Karl Kraus's great influence on the intellectuals of that generation, it is possible that his remark that Hitler's "Weltbild nicht so sehr durch Freud als durch Karl May geformt scheint"[29] lies behind Klaus Mann's diatribe. While Mann's essay is cited from time to time,[30] few informed people take it seriously today. There may be an echo of it in William H. Gass's recent novel in an ill-founded speculation of the narrator, a historian who is puzzlingly and perhaps pathologically preoccupied with Nazi Germany: "The fascist salute looks borrowed from one of Karl May's awful books about American Indians."[31] It is, to be sure, well established that Hitler devoured Karl May in his youth; he said so in his conversations.[32] In 1933, it was observed that the majority of books in his house were by May—doubtless a symptom of Hitler's arrested adolescence—and in 1940 he asserted that his hesitant general staff officers "should have read more Karl May!"[33] But it has been more than once observed that if Hitler had absorbed more of May's true spirit, the world might have been spared much calamity. Anyway, *everyone* read May, from Albert Schweitzer to Albert Einstein. It has recently emerged that Winnetou was the moral inspiration for the Nicaraguan revolutionary Tomás Borge: "No one should attempt the impossible task of writing better westerns than the novels written by Karl May. His characters seem to be within arm's reach in the next room. They reproduce the virtues we ourselves would like to possess, imitate what we are in our dreams; they shake our hands and depart with the implicit promise of returning."[34] We are not likely to find the key to Hitler in this place.

Persuasive reasons for May's absence from the American scene are not easily found. From time to time it has been suggested that Americans resist May because of his partisanship for the Indian cause.[35] But this is a judgment that is itself fed by anti-American clichés. Peter Uwe Hohendahl has rightly observed that this can hardly have been the explanation, "denn diese kritische Einstellung ist der zeitgenössischen amerikanischen Indianerliteratur nicht fremd," and in any case it was not the settlers but the eastern "Yankees," so scornfully depicted by May, who were most sympathetic to the Indian plight.[36] It might be argued in addition that May never became visible enough to be rejected in the first place. Nor is it easy to argue that the indigenous American Western left no room for May. Of course, there had been Western stories and dime novels in the nineteenth century, but May actually antedates the classical American Western, which is a more recent genre than one might think; of those works regarded as the generic ancestors, Owen Wister's *The Virginian* appeared in 1902 and Zane Grey's *Riders of the Purple Sage* in 1912; both writers were much younger than May.

But perhaps some element of American culture might be found that would aid a comparison. The tireless reader of the noncanonical, Arno Schmidt, proposed *Tarzan*.[37] But, though anachronistic by about half a century, the most apt item of comparison seems to me to be *The Lone Ranger*, which began to be broadcasted in January 1933 and became the most successful serial that radio had yet known. It would not be surprising to discover that one or another of the creators of *The Lone Ranger* had some knowledge of May, given the continuing presence of things German in the American cultural memory despite the depredations of World War I, but there is no evidence of it. Parallels, however, emerge easily. Like May's works, *The Lone Ranger* is also said to have been in the succession to Cooper.[38] The Lone Ranger's identity is secret, and we know only one of his names, though, unlike Old Shatterhand's, it is his last rather than the first. He is closely bonded with an Indian companion who has great skills in healing, and each is in possession of an exceptionally talented, once wild horse. The Lone Ranger never shoots to kill, and Tonto never kills anybody. As in May's tales, plot resolutions frequently turn on information obtained from conversations overheard in hiding, though here it is Tonto who likes to go into town in disguise to spy on the villains. The Lone Ranger, gifted with rational thought and deductive reasoning, readily grasps puzzling situations before anyone else. The moral standing of characters is generally, though not in every instance, determinable from their external physiognomy.[39] In one of the Lone Ranger novels, Tonto reminds us of Old Shatterhand by stunning a villain with one blow of his fist.[40] Given the millions of listeners, members of Lone Ranger Clubs, public appearances of the masked man, and so forth, it is not surprising that there were some who were unable to grasp the Lone Ranger's fictional status, writing to him and in other ways perceiving him as a real person, though this was a side effect, not a hoax perpetrated by the creators as in May's case.

In regard to differences, two things spring at once to the eye. The first is that *The Lone Ranger*'s homiletic dimension is much more elementary and subdued. Of course the implications are strictly moralistic and supportive of conventional values. But the moral aspects are simple, unproblematic, and tersely expressed; there is no sign of May's inveterate sermonizing. Furthermore, *The Lone Ranger*, in keeping with its commercial character, explicitly avoids controversy and maintains strict abstinence in political and religious matters; script writers were instructed to avoid "controversial subjects of today."[41] May's relatively explicit and certainly persistent political and religious contentiousness is naturally absent. While there may be large mythical implications of Manifest Destiny and American uniqueness in the background, the Lone Ranger's overt purpose is to assist justice; he is not engaged in an enterprise of reforming mankind and refounding civilization. There is no sign of May's mystical-utopian, allegorical-symbolic dimension. The second point is perhaps too obvious even to mention, but is relevant to our purposes: *The Lone Ranger*'s frontiersmen are not primarily Germans.

May's device of making the most capable westerners, starting with Old Shatterhand himself, men and, occasionally, women of German origin has, of course, been much commented upon. The question is whether it must not necessarily make the whole fictional enterprise seem somewhat parochial in an American context. But it is hard to know; during May's career German culture was prestigious in the United States and the German American community was large and significant. The more sensitive question is whether the foregrounding of the German spirit in the Wild West does not have anti-American implications that might have found an echo among some German Americans but not, I suspect, with a majority of them. There is some external evidence that May can be seen in such a light. In 1936, May's works were recommended to the readers of the *American German Review* by a visitor, who had been introduced to the shrine by May's now Nazified widow, on the grounds that "they remain so essentially un-American."[42] Klaus Mann, from a contrasting point of view, declared May "decidedly anti-American."[43] The sudden shift in the policy of the German Democratic Republic toward him in 1982 from rejection and prohibition to acceptance and encouragement seems to have been in part justified by an understanding of him as a fighter against American capitalism and the alleged extermination of the Indians.[44] A monograph of 1985 by Harald Eggebrecht shows clearly how an enthusiasm for Karl May can be associated with academic anti-Americanism.[45]

If we look at May's texts themselves, the result is somewhat confusing owing to the blurriness of his focus on an America existing only in his imagination. Since he drew substantially from the extant German literature on America, it is not surprising that he reproduces its clichés. That the Americans proper, unlike Germans, are interested only in moneymaking is a note struck early in the first volume of *Winnetou* and often thereafter; American newspapers, on the other hand, do not write about the thousands who fail (e.g., W, 1:37; W, 2:20). That America is overrun by medical quacks is a notion quite likely taken over from Gerstäcker (W, 2:13). In 1893 May asked the printer to remove the phrase, "Der rote Gentleman," from the titles of the first three *Winnetou* volumes, saying that "eine Idealgestalt wie Winnetou" should not be sullied by the "Terminologie Onkel Sams"; this was not done, however, until 1904 (W, 3:[ii]).[46] The image of the German as an honest and pure victim of a crude and heartless land oppressing him as a "damned Dutchman" is, of course, familiar from the tradition. But May hyperbolizes the specialness of the German in America, gives it unusual thematic weight, and recurs to it repeatedly to the end of his career. "Die Krieger der Germani," Old Shatterhand tells the Comanches, should be differentiated from the palefaces, for they have never done any harm to the Indians (W, 3:237). In the stories that originally formed the second volume of *Old Surehand*, the tavern of Mutter Thick is more comfortable because it is "mehr deutsch als amerikanisch" and she herself praises the Germans for drinking beer instead of brandy like the Yankees (OS, 2:4). In the same book, some men encountered in the wilderness are so kind that they cannot be Yankees; they turn out to be Germans and Austrians (OS, 2:226). Even as late as *Ardistan und Dschinnistan* it is asserted that only the Germans and the red men, unlike all other peoples, have the ineffable quality of "Gemüt": "Dieser rote Mann stirbt nicht. Kein Portugiese, kein Spanier, kein Englischmann, kein Yankee hat die Macht, ihn auszurotten. Und der Deutsche geht nicht hinüber, um des Indianers Feind zu sein. Sie haben Beide das, was wohl kein Anderer hat, nämlich Gemüt, und das wird sie vereinen. Der sogenannte 'sterbende' Indianer wird wieder aufstehen. . . . Der gegenwärtige Yankee wird verschwinden, damit sich an seiner Stelle ein neuer Mensch bilde, dessen Seele germanisch-indianisch ist" (AuD, 1:18–19).

It is true that, here and there, more indulgent comments on America appear. May evidently read something about the dedication of Yellowstone National Park in 1872 that greatly impressed him. In *Winnetou III* he praises it as a wonderland and gives its history, pointing out that Congress has preserved it from "dem gemeinen Schacher" (W, 3:354–55). When he finally visited America for the first and only time in 1908, he made some positive observations that are reflected in the fourth *Winnetou* volume. He praises American "Genialität" in the design of cemeteries, comments on the charity of the rich that allows the poor equal burial—"Das tut der Yankee. Wer tut es noch?"—and admires the comfort of railroad cars (W, 4:57–58, 87). Some of this, to be sure, may have been lifted from Gerstäcker (cf. NR, 1:101–2, 37–38). He waxes even more eloquent about the landscape than he had previously; the narrator assures his wife "daß die Schönheiten des Harzes, des Schwarzwaldes, ja sogar der Schweiz sich unmöglich mit den landschaftlichen Wundern der Vereinigten Staaten vergleichen könnten" (W, 4:138). But these are just moments within the superintending condescension. The absurd Yankees who are attempting to buy the American rights to May's works in order to suppress them are suffering from "amerikanischer Unsinn" when they attempt to pay for his time in an interview (W, 4:30). The corrosive cash nexus is everywhere. It has temporarily corrupted the young artists, the son of Old Surehand and his Indian nephew, who have been "in echt amerikanischer Weise auf den Abweg der Busineß hinübergeleitet"; it is not credible that Old Surehand himself has become capable of competing "mit der geschäftlichen Smartneß eines geriebenen, amerikanischen Pfiffikus" (W, 4:12–14). The meretricious project of erecting a giant, vulgarized statue of Winnetou as an urbanized tourist attraction has been supported by Congress (W, 4:432).

However, it is not these more or less cranky critiques that constitute the real problem of anti-Americanism. That problem, like the Jewish problem, is one of an absence rather than a presence, an absence of any sense of what makes America significant in the course of human affairs: the great experiment in creating a democracy, in balancing the often conflicting claims of liberty, equality, and justice, an effort often frustrated, distracted, tarnished, yet taken up ever again in theory and practice, in subtle doctrine and complex politics, the world-historical endeavor that as early as 1864 had wrung from such a basically uncongenial observer as Heinrich von Treitschke the admission: "Man male die Schattenseiten des amerikanischen Lebens noch so schwarz: auf diesem Boden hat die Demokratie ihre größten Wunder vollbracht."[47] Writers like

Sealsfield and Gerstäcker knew that this is what mattered about America for Germany and Europe; Karl May seems to have lacked any sense of it. To be sure, in one of the stories in the original second volume of *Old Surehand*, it is remarked that Americans do not condemn a man until his guilt is fully proven (OS, 2:66); but this sort of moment is conspicuous by its rarity. In the same work Abraham Lincoln makes an appearance as a brave frontiersman, "ein Kerl, der es noch zu etwas bringen kann!" In a reflection of the typical German American view of Lincoln's career and assassination, it is said that he "hat es bis zum Höchsten gebracht, was ein braver *self-man* werden kann.... Fluch dem Schurken, der ihn abfeuerte!" (OS, 2:44, 73). One might compare, incidentally, the praise of Lincoln by Julius Goebel, one of the founding fathers of German studies in the United States, as "ein echt germanischer Gemütsmensch."[48] But May's tales are both anachronistic and fantastic, and, in fact, Old Shatterhand himself calls the veracity of the narrator into question.

May was not a democrat in any intelligible sense. Helmut Schmiedt has identified in him traditional German ideas of aristocratic, elitist thinking that counter a superficially antiaristocratic affect, calls attention to the fact that, from his apparently antiauthoritarian position, he has his completely superior, invincible, and illiberal hero create a new hierarchy under his leadership, and connects him with concepts of the authoritarian German welfare state and, in general, with the Bismarckian atmosphere.[49] May's antipathy to social democracy is on record. In a possibly forged reader's letter he has his admirer give the assurance that "wir [sind] keine Sozialdemokraten mehr."[50] In the substratum of May's adventure discourse lurks a social, moral, and increasingly religious discourse of pronounced conventionality, despite his peculiarities in regard to imperialism and militarism.

Whether his parochialism within what superficially appears to be a cosmopolitan discourse accounts for the failure of his works to obtain a footing in America is difficult to say, but it does suggest a continuing irrelevance. The relentless denunciation of moneygrubbing and mammon worship is actually an evasion of democratic issues, as it continues to be today among the German intellectual left, and, as has been pointed out, it shows certain structural similarities with anti-Semitism.[51] So thoroughly did he seem to represent these conventions that, after World War II, personnel stationed in Germany "were urged to become familiar with Karl May in order to better understand the German concept of the United States."[52] May's evolution of a mystical-utopian vision of human redemption is merely a further digression, suggesting that he had no real interest in America despite his American settings, and that he diluted and dissipated a potential interest in America in his readership. Thus I would categorize him only nominally as an anti-American writer, but, more fundamentally, as one devoid of any larger significance in German-American cultural relations.

# Outlook

The transition from Friedrich Gerstäcker's mimesis to Karl May's fantasy is symptomatic of a turn away from the empirical United States in German fiction. I know of no major nineteenth-century German novel primarily about America after *In Amerika*, and its indifferent reception was probably also a sign that the time for such things was past. Germans were more preoccupied with themselves, and many were more confident and hopeful with the founding of the Reich; in the mid-1880s the emigration began to decline and ceased to be a prominent topic of public discourse. Overall, however, there were many more books than those I have discussed. Mikoletzky, who, incidentally, also noted the move away from realism in the last third of the century, came up with 162 titles from 1835 to 1905; almost half of these, however, were written by what she calls the "classic" authors: Sealsfield, Gerstäcker, Ruppius, Strubberg, and Möllhausen, along with Karl May in a class by himself.[1] It is not unusual to mention the forty-eighter Otto Ruppius (1819–64) in this connection, and some attention might have been given here to his America novels, *Der Pedlar* (1857) and *Das Vermächtnis des Pedlars* (1859).[2] I decided not to attempt it, partly because I did not have easy access to good texts, and partly because I did not think that, despite his extensive, authentic experience in the United States, they developed any particular perspective of their own. Ruppius was, however, peculiar in one respect. On the one hand, his two best-known novels of America are distinctly philo-Semitic, for the title character (though not the protagonist) is a Jewish peddler whose reiterated claim that he does nothing without profit to himself is but an ironic mask for his kindness, generosity, and wisdom. With regard to blacks, however, Ruppius was, or came to be, one of the most racist of our writers, arguing that slaves were better off than white workers, blacks were lazy, emancipation was unwise, miscegenation dangerous, and segregation necessary; he replicated the American view that the principle of the equality of all men was never meant to include blacks.[3]

American scenes were, of course, also attempted by authors who had never been there, and the results did not have to be as disagreeable as Kürnberger's. An early example in the spirit of the late Enlightenment is Heinrich Zschokke's (1771–1848) *Prinzessin von Wolfenbüttel* of 1804, which was made into a drama in 1820 and an opera in 1829. In it a mistreated princess, the wife of the tsarevitch, pretends to die and begins a new life of hard work on the Côte des Allemands in Louisiana.[4] The best-known writer to have attempted depiction from afar is Theodor Fontane, whose novel *Quitt* (1891), though belonging to his middle period, as he was approaching his maturest work, is not regarded as one of his most successful novels, largely because the second part takes place in a milieu with which he was not familiar and that has appeared implausible to some.[5] In it a young man, Lehnert, who is morally insecure because his environment lacks integrity, comes to shoot an evil forester and escapes to America, where he knocks about as a California miner, a bankrupt, and a carpenter; on a train he meets a German Mennonite, whose community provides Lehnert with a utopia of nurturance, tolerance, and the dialogue of contrasting opinions, where he can heal his damaged soul and die under circumstances of poetic justice, in some degree shriven. *Quitt* is regularly seen in succession to Schiller's story, *Der Verbrecher aus verlorener Ehre*, but other literary influences are likely. In chapter 25 there is a debate as to whether Bret Harte's *The Luck of Roaring Camp* and *Outcasts of Poker Flat* present too euphemistic a picture of the California mines. But that the community has a dog named "Unkas" is an unmistakable sign that Cooper maintained a presence in Fontane's consciousness. In any case, it has been shown that Fontane, by reading and oral inquiry, obtained extensive knowledge of the geographical setting and the historical personages he depicts.[6] *Quitt* belongs to a kind of subgenre of novels split more or less evenly between German and American settings. Möllhausen has been mentioned in this connection; another example is Wilhelm Raabe's early *Bildungsroman*, *Die Leute aus dem Walde* (1862–63), in which the protagonist solves his personal and practical problems by finding gold in America. As in Fontane's *Quitt*, the American scene shows signs of having been constructed at second hand from other books. But in his more mature novel, *Alte Nester*, Raabe avoids this pitfall; he does not try to depict a setting foreign to him, but shows a character greatly strengthened in competence and self-esteem from his experience of farming in America.[7]

Particularly interesting in this regard is Berthold Auerbach (1812–82), whose once international reputation has all but disappeared. As a militant liberal and democrat, he maintained a lively and earnest interest in America. His novel, *Das Landhaus am Rhein* (1869), is, despite its title, much concerned with American slavery and the Civil War, in which the protagonist eventually serves on the Union side. The novel praises the Unitarian sage Theodore Parker and virtually apotheosizes Abraham Lincoln,[8] but its presiding genius is Benjamin Franklin, whom Auerbach regarded as the model of the modern, free, self-determined, benevolent citizen. In the eighteenth century Franklin was the recipient of many honors in Germany and widely admired, especially by Herder.[9] In the nineteenth century, as we have seen in connection with Kürnberger, Franklin came in some quarters to be misunderstood as the avatar of soulless pragmatism and naked greed for profit. But not so for Auerbach, who published a biography of Franklin in 1876 and, upon having been introduced to Franklin's granddaughter, said that he felt as though he had met a descendant of Aristides.[10] Auerbach's preoccupation with America has been discussed now and again, but its contextual significance and its representation in his elaborate novel have yet to receive detailed attention.

There were, of course, a vast number of other works, fictional, semifictional, and nonfictional, about America during the nineteenth century.[11] Of late an understandable interest has developed in the reportage of women, such as Friedrich Hebbel's quondam mentor Amalie Schoppe (1791–1858), who settled in Schenectady in 1853 and developed a close connection to Union College; Mathilde Anneke (1817–84), who is often treated as a German American writer but was born in Westphalia and came to the United States as the wife of a forty-eighter at the age of thirty-two; and the redoubtable Ottilie Assing (1819–84), Varnhagen's radical niece, whose reports from New York for the Stuttgart *Morgenblatt* from 1853 to 1865 have been cited earlier.[12] Among those who had the training and understanding to ignore the clichés about moneygrubbing and perceive instead the dynamics of progress was a contemporary of Sealsfield, the Austrian railroad pioneer Franz Anton Ritter von Gerstner (1795–1840). In 1838 he undertook a journey to examine American transportation. Unfortunately he fell ill and died in Philadelphia in 1840, but the two volumes of his findings, illustrated with large, foldout charts, were edited by his widow and an assistant; like Möllhausen's travel works, they are printed in Roman type rather than German black letter, a sign of their scientific and progressive character. They cover the settled parts of the United States region by region, giving statistics and technical information on railroads, steam shipping on the Great Lakes, and canals—especially the Erie Canal, which when extended will be "gewiss die grossartigste Communication dieser Art in der Welt."[13] The account is animated by the most sincere respect and admiration for the technological achievements of the Americans who, although they started later, are now overtaking the rest of the world. An implicit message to hidebound Austria is probable.

After the turn of the century, nonfiction works, especially travel memoirs, became more prevalent. The prominent historian Karl Lamprecht (1856–1915) made a journey for a few months in 1904, allowing him to form tenaciously provincial generalizations on "Yankee" culture and its superfluousness for the world at large, on indigestible food, the intractability of the "Negro problem" owing to the high proportion of race mixing, and the resistance of Jews to physical labor. In a diary entry, he kills two birds with one stone: "Die englische Sprache ein fürchterliches Werkzeug der Weltherrschaft, namentlich als gesprochene Sprache. Man kann sich in ihr leicht verständlich machen. Jeder Neger lernt das binnen kurzem." Highly entertaining is his complacent remark: "Wiederholt habe ich Leuten aus guter Gesellschaft bald leise, bald in unmißverständlicher Entschiedenheit klarmachen müssen, welche Behandlung ich als deutscher Professor gewöhnt bin."[14] One can easily imagine these scenes. Initially more flexible and rather more charming is the memoir of the Munich humorist and cabaret director Ernst von Wolzogen (1855–1934), who made a lecture tour from November 1910 to February 1911 as guest of the Germanistic Society of America and endeavored, apparently, to inculcate Americans with a sense of humor. At the Harvard-Yale football game he professed to detect "eine höchst eindrucksvolle Auferstehung der Antike." He admired coeducation and advised Germans to send their daughters to American institutions, though, somewhat like Gerstäcker, he was surprised to see a professor pushing a baby carriage or hear that he did housework. But his account is disfigured by a racism now become systematic, even theoretical. "Die unwiderstehliche Kraft des Yankeetums liegt ohne Zweifel in seinem unbeugsamen Rassestolz. Dem Yankee ist es so heilig ernst damit, daß er sich nicht einmal im Spaß, d. h. im freien Verhältnis, viel weniger in der Ehe, mit den Angehörigen der zahlreichen anderen Rassen, die seinen riesigen Kontinent bevölkern, vermischt." Race mixing leads to degeneration: "Solches Menschenmaterial ist kaum durch Schrecken zu regieren, viel weniger durch friedliche Mittel zu einer höheren Kultur emporzuführen, denn *Mischmasch-Menschen nehmen eben keine Vernunft an*; das Beispiel so mancher südamerikanischen Republik beweist es." At the end of the concomitant nationalism breaks through: he urges greater German American chauvinism and begs the German Americans to remember that they have a finer and deeper culture than their hosts.[15] A book that, given Wolzogen's literary reputation, one might take in hand with cheerful expectation comes to be a sour reading experience.

A curious work of uncertain genre was published during World War I. It purports to be letters home to Mecklenburg detailing the experiences of an immigrant farmer. Written in places in a macaronic German English and sufficiently rustic in style and content, it suddenly, in the last chapter, breaks out into pro-German war hysteria, advising immigrants to return to Germany and take land instead that will be conquered in Eastern Europe.¹⁶ At a 1993 conference on the book in Mecklenburg some well-founded doubts concerning its authenticity were raised, and it looks as though it should be counted among the fictional works.¹⁷ After World War I, German responses to America became, not surprisingly, rather high-strung; the lost war and the distress caused by the imposition of reparations were major irritants. One scholar has written: "With no distinction between people and their government, or men and their machines, Americans were the Shylocks of the Weimar republic."¹⁸ In some quarters Woodrow Wilson was almost hysterically detested as a sanctimonious hypocrite and masked economic imperialist.¹⁹ The anticapitalist affect allowed the hostility to be shared by left and right. Much attention has been given to the radical "speeding reporter" Egon Erwin Kisch, whose book of 1930, *Beehrt sich darzubieten: Paradies Amerika*, endeavored to expose the oppression and suffering imposed by the moronic rich.²⁰ However, this attitude was not universal. The prominent theater critic Alfred Kerr, who claimed to be the first German to visit New York and London after the war (1922), fairly bubbled with enthusiasm: "Ich glaube nach wie vor an Amerika. Nur, nur, nur an Amerika," and, although he worried about the decline of *Deutschtum*, he asked how a country could be without soul that had Germans, Celts, Russian Jews, Latins, and Slavs among its population.²¹ Another well-meaning observer was the young Manfred Hausmann (1898–1986), whose novelized, third-person account of his meander through the United States in 1929 has been characterized by a historian as "a charming and exotic, but hardly accurate portrayal of American life."²² Very striking, however, is the degree to which the humorous, gentle-spirited Hausmann, who was to evolve into a Christian existentialist, exhibits deep-seated racist instincts, especially in his account of a service in a Harlem church, which he describes as a barbaric and manic ritual of animalistic savages.²³

At the end of the interwar period there appeared two books by a Viennese of Scottish descent, Colin Ross (1885–1947), *Amerikas Schicksalstunde* (1935), and *Unser Amerika* (1936), that have been curiously neglected. It appears that Ross was ambitious to be the expert on America for the Nazi movement, but it is unclear to what extent he succeeded; in any case, he was commissioned by the army high command to write an informational booklet, *USA*, for German soldiers to carry in their knapsacks. The title *Unser Amerika* was the motto of the German-American Bund, which was an organization not so much of German Americans as of German nationals resident in the United States and was a front for the Nazi Party in Germany.²⁴ Ross was a cosmopolitan author of many travel books; his works on America are curiously incoherent mixtures of tolerant goodwill and cranky ideas. He strives for a tone of sweet reasonableness, opposing the view that America is merely a land of moneygrubbers; praises Roosevelt as exhibiting the same facial features of toil and responsibility as Hitler; strives to be kind about blacks, though he was clearly immersed in race theory and declared the voice of the racist demagogue Father Coughlin to be like that of Christ; he commiserated with American worries about immigration in view of the "den furchtbaren Rassenmischmasch in Newyork"; insisted that German Americans should not be regarded as Germans even if America was a creation of the German spirit; praised the German Americans for their opposition to slavery, their contribution to preserving the Union, and their support of Lincoln; puzzled over the American willingness to exclude Jews while resisting anti-Semitism and race theory; and prophesied the end of democracy to be brought about by the rise of a German Tom Paine.[25] Even if Ross was not influential, he was thematically symptomatic, and I have been surprised not to have found any detailed discussion of him.[26] This is evidently a task yet to be undertaken.

World War II with its appalling atrocities naturally created a chasm in German-American cultural relations. It has often been remarked that the exiles produced relatively little notable fiction about America.[27] Exiles, after all, are not travelers and, for the most part, are not immigrants. They tend to be preoccupied with their spiritual and, often, material deprivations and commonly continue to live emotionally in their homeland; in any case, many of them knew in advance that America was a spiritual desert, devoid of culture, and obsessed with material gain to the exclusion of all other considerations. Joachim Maass, a voluntary exile, had thought of America as the land "nach dem ich weniger Sehnsucht verspürte, als nach irgendeinem anderen in dieser Welt."[28] The degree of refusal of perception is in some cases quite astonishing, for example, in the journals of Brecht, whom apparently no amount of experience and observation could lever out of his fixed opinions.[29] The Karl Kraus disciple Berthold Viertel contemplated with mixed feelings Californians on the beach, "Hellenen ohne Hirn," while Alfred Werner admitted that "ohne Liebe werdet ihr nie / eindringen in die Zementpalastwunder ... in die lächelnden Zirkusreiterseelen."[30] The knowledge that there was no culture naturally preserved the strangers from encountering any; it is curious, for example, how far one has to seek for any awareness of the vigor and qualitative level of the contemporary American literary scene.

An impressive achievement of some exiles was to write novels of America in which there are practically no Americans. An example commanding respect is Oskar Maria Graf's *Die Flucht ins Mittelmäßige*, subtitled *Ein New Yorker Roman* (1957), in which New York, Chicago, and even the wilds of New Jersey are exclusively populated by Germans.[31] Similarly in *Lisas Zimmer* (1965) by Hilde Spiel (who was in English exile, but set the novel in New York), the only prominent American character is Lisa's husband Jeff, an inarticulate, incompetent, sodden drunk, whom, for reasons I did not fully understand, the Latvian narrator marries after Lisa's death. Here one exile writer says to another: "Sie leben nicht in diesem Land. Keiner von euch." Whether in Boston, Washington, or New York, they make "eine europäische Stadt in irgendeinem unbestimmten Land. Macht euch doch nichts vor. Keiner von euch hat Europa je verlassen." But that is not a reproach, for it cannot be helped: "wie kann man da in einer fremden Welt der Kaugummi und Popcorn und Baseball existieren?"[32] A special case is Carl Zuckmayer, who, alone among the exiles, to my knowledge, took up actual dirt farming in Vermont and achieved genuine contact with neighbors. The experience enabled him to overcome the clichés that he had absorbed from Karl May and to urge others to do so also.[33]

Zuckmayer turns up as a peripheral character in a novel that is another and even more significant exception to my generalization about exile writing: Johannes Urzidil's *Das Große Hallelujah* (1959), to some degree a roman à clef of modern American life, in which the author portrays himself quite exactly in the figure of Josephus Weseritz, content to accept his fate of exclusion from intellectual and literary life as he makes a modest living with leatherwork. In that persona, Urzidil displays a number of conservative Central European parochialisms, among them an obsessive animosity toward emancipated American women and permissively raised children.[34] Personally he longs for an "America" of his youth, which turns out to be compounded of images from Cooper, old Westerns, Gerstäcker, and even Karl May: "Die Planwagen. Die Indianer auf dem Kriegspfad. Die Goldgräber am Sacramento. Die reitenden Sheriffs. Die Flußpiraten des Mississippi. Die Regulatoren am Arkansas. Winnetou. Das blutige Blockhaus."[35] The novel has visionary aspects, especially toward the end, and built into the mosaic of narration is a criminal story with a ruthless, elegant, and intellectual protagonist, which looks more like a literary exercise than an effort at mimetic representation. On the other hand, most of the characters are Americans for once, and they, their lives, and their environments are depicted with an accuracy of detail, custom, manners, and even of language that is without compare in the exile writing of my acquaintance.

After the war, German-American literary relations got off to a somewhat rocky start owing to the at least partial failure of the ambitious reeducation campaign in the U.S. prisoner-of-war camps, which has been much criticized.³⁶ Antifascist intellectuals and writers were gathered in special camps to protect them from the Nazi spirit that governed the POW camps generally and were encouraged to support the spirit of democracy as Americans understand it through a systemwide newspaper, *Der Ruf*. But when *Der Ruf* moved to Munich after the war, it soon came into conflict with the U.S. military government and was banned; the consequence was the formation of the most seminal circle of postwar German writers, the *Gruppe 47*.³⁷ The central figure of the group, Hans Werner Richter, was left with a rather bitter streak of anti-Americanism, as one can see from his novelized account of the experience, *Die Geschlagenen* (1949). The other major writer who addressed it most directly, Alfred Andersch in *Die Kirschen der Freiheit* (1952) and, retrospectively, *Mein Verschwinden in Providence* (1971), was less hostile but still more disoriented than edified by the experience.³⁸ The recalcitrance of the intended beneficiaries of the program may have been owing to traditional German convictions about the inferior level of American culture, but some part of it was a feeling of absurdity that they were to be instructed in political philosophy by people who were not even socialists.

Nevertheless, the postwar atmosphere was not without positive elements. Germans began to catch up on American literature, especially Hemingway, who for a time exerted a strong influence on German prose style. A habit developed of publishing translations "aus dem Amerikanischen," as though Americans wrote in some language other than English. Josef Eberle, one of a group of German journalists invited to a tour in 1948, sent back virtually ecstatic reports. He was even able to take a humorous view of the kitschy time capsule of Yorkville, which has given many German observers the willies: he described it as "Über-oberbayrisch" where "das Deutschland von 1911 fröhliche Auferstehung [feierte]."³⁹ Essayistic and journalistic works meditating on America proliferated over the years. One of the most perceptive of these in my experience is Robert Jungk's *Die Zukunft hat schon begonnen* (1952), because he tried to put the imprinted images to one side and actually look at things. What he looked at particularly was science and technology in their military purposes; he visited the atomic weapon center at Alamogordo, the White Sands rocket testing range, Edwards Air Force Base, uranium mines in Colorado, Los Alamos, and other installations. He observed the beginnings of robot technology and computers, recognizing their importance despite his romantic melancholy about them. He experimented with a lie detector and worried about the erosion of democratic traditions. He listened to a Du Pont executive predict non-freezing motor oil for 1965 and synthetic food for 2010, and met J. Robert Oppenheimer at the Institute for Advanced Studies in Princeton.

The verdict is critical, yet grounded in understanding: "Ich habe Angst um Amerika: Angst, daß es sein Bestes, die Achtung der Freiheit und Menschheit, in seinem Streben nach fast göttlicher Allmacht verlieren könnte."[40] The postwar writer who probably spent the most time in the United States, Max Frisch, also developed a critical but thoughtful understanding. Like Zuckmayer, he wrote an early essay renouncing the stock responses of European anti-Americanism.[41] At least superficially friendly and tolerant, if perhaps slyly subversive, is *Amerikafahrt* (1959), originally conceived as a radio program by the most mysterious German writer since Sealsfield and Traven, Wolfgang Koeppen, who achieves a form of authenticity with a kind of subjective realism, reflecting on his response rather than merely asserting judgments.[42]

From the German Democratic Republic there was, naturally, relatively little of interest, since few East German writers could travel to the United States and, in any case, their views were prescribed in advance. The only interesting effort of my acquaintance is Günter Kunert's *Der andere Planet* (1975), the product of a visiting professorship at the University of Texas in the fall term of 1972. Despite a number of clichés and stock responses, the book gains a degree of complexity from what was probably already at that time an inner process of alienation from the GDR. Like Koeppen, Kunert accepts his subjectivity as unavoidable; it has been said that he radically breaks with every effort to represent objectively.[43] While some of his observations and criticisms retain a generalized Marxist coloration, they may also be motivated by the fundamental misanthropy that was liberated to the surface after his escape to the West in 1979.[44]

Contemporary German fiction with American motifs tends in varying degrees to be dreamlike, even hallucinatory, as though it were following the precept of academic imagologists that there is no possibility of representing an accurate image of the foreign other. I have a suspicion that behind much of this writing stands, at a greater or lesser distance, the ghostly presence of Franz Kafka's *Der Verschollene*, long known under the imposed title of *Amerika*. Kafka's source, insofar as he needed one, was Arthur Holitscher's *Amerika heute und morgen* (1913), a rather unfriendly, otherwise fairly typical travel work of its time.[45] While Kafka takes motifs and images directly from Holitscher, from the moment his protagonist catches sight of the Statue of Liberty brandishing a sword until he vanishes on the way to what may or may not be the utopia of the "Naturtheater von Oklahama" (Kafka's original spelling, derived from Holitscher), the apparent referentiality of Kafka's images, as everywhere in his writing, dissipates under any effort to fix them interpretively. Mimesis is displaced by metonymy, and the consequence is the evanescence of a genuinely dialogic interest in America. The perspective, in fact, is relentlessly Eurocentric; as has been observed, Kafka's America "retains a curious Old World ambience . . . the most successful characterizations are European."[46] One might contend that this is a modernist victory of the mode of fantasy, implying that Karl May was the pioneer after all. But this would be an unjust and misleading suggestion, for the meretriciousness of pretended mimesis is absent from Kafka as it is from the contemporary writers. Nevertheless, the distinction between an imitation of imitation on the one hand and the frankly imagined or imaginary on the other can be subtle. One work that makes the succession to Kafka fairly explicit is Joachim Seyppel's *Columbus Bluejeans oder Das Reich der falschen Bilder* (1965). Seyppel, an exile who had attended Harvard and taught at Bryn Mawr, returned to Berlin and in 1973 fled to freedom in the GDR, where he did not find it. His novel, in part a parodistic imitation of Kafka's, follows an innocent German simpleton from a Harvard education to a professorship at a small college in the South, through a phantasmagoria of American commercialism, racism, brutality, and delusion, until he finds his death seeking a true utopia in India.

However, in my experience, the most ingenious and elusive work of what one might call magic realism is Peter Handke's *Der kurze Brief zum langen Abschied* (1972). The novel exhibits an unusual geographical specificity; the front and back covers unfold into maps of the United States indicating the route of the journey structuring the narrative—an exactitude of reference that, in a modern novel, ought perhaps to arouse initial suspicion. The narrative begins on a specifically named street in Providence. As it happens, I lived in that neighborhood for a couple of years, and it turned out upon inspection that the description is *close*, but not *exact*. Similarly with other details: one can match the route numbers given with a road map, but when Handke puts toll booths at intervals on the Pennsylvania Turnpike rather than at the exits, the knowledgeable reader may become disoriented, while the less knowledgeable will not notice anything, and the imagologist will say that the whole question of referentiality is irrelevant. I have discussed Handke's example of the theoretical problem of varying extrinsic referentiality in the text and in the reader elsewhere and cannot go it into further here.[47] But it seems evident that when the novel's journey ends in Bel Air, California, in an extensive colloquy with the film director John Ford, it not only privileges fantasy over mimesis with so emphatic an interest in film and, particularly, the Western, but it also turns, once again, Eurocentric, as film has been the carrier of American images abroad.[48] Introversion is even more noticeable in the novel of Handke's countryman Michael Scharang, *Auf nach Amerika* (1992), which, despite its title and a quasi-picaresque American adventure, is really about Austria. In 1993, an Austrian visitor found the United States at once exotic, childish, and annoying. He was particularly put off by the "Unterhaltungspogrom" on television. However, it is clear that he is a universal satirist; in reference to the colossal wine-adulteration scandal in Austria several years earlier, he praised the Austrian embassy in Washington as the only place where one could still get wine containing antifreeze.[49]

Because Handke makes a rather public display of an alleged aloofness from political and ideological commitments, there is a tendency to compare him to Uwe Johnson, whose vast *Jahrestage* (1970–83) I regarded during its genesis as one of the truly outstanding works of German literature in its time. However that may be, it exhibits Johnson's obsessively probing preoccupation with matters of history and politics. An important aspect of his technique might be compared with Sealsfield's as a mimesis of discourse. But, while we must recover the discourse Sealsfield imitates with historical research, Johnson sets out for us verbatim the texts of the *New York Times* from which he takes his cues. As Sealsfield identifies with but also implies distance from his first-person narrators, so Johnson achieves both identification with and distance from the consciousness of his protagonist Gesine Cresspahl, whose personal history and outlook are both similar to and, especially as a woman, different from his. But he also generates alternative voices, particularly that of Gesine's increasingly Americanized daughter Marie, voices that are not meant, as with Sealsfield, to be overrun and scorned from the fixed ideological center, but represent a genuine polyphony. There is no space here for an adequate commentary on *Jahrestage*, nor would I be competent to undertake it, but, whether or not one agrees with or accepts all of Johnson's perspectives and judgments, I believe that it is a work of an earnestness and integrity rarely encountered in the German fiction about America, surpassing in this regard even Gerstäcker.[50]

For all of Johnson's skepticism about omniscient narration and generic conventions, he appears a downright classical realist when set against the imaginative creations of other writers. For example, the Swiss author Jürg Federspiel's *Museum des Hasses* (1969) is an impressionistic, sometimes surreal, apparently disordered sequence of images and implausible events. Uwe Johnson appears in it as a golem wandering the catacombs of Grand Central Terminal, obsessively formulating his sentences. Federspiel's imagination does not prevent him, however, from replicating familiar received opinion, for example, in a view of Fifth Avenue: "In keiner Straße der Welt sind die Ellbogen der Vorübergehenden so stählern wie in dieser. . . . Gold im Herzen und im Mund, Eisen in den Knochen, Blei in der Seele, Silber am Handgelenk und Quecksilber im Blut";[51] only the murder of Martin Luther King brings about a brief pause for reflection among Americans. The narrator has visions of blacks threatening to mutilate him with razors and exhibits an odd fascination with the clever Jews who dominate the city. Gruesome atrocities are culled from the daily news. A preoccupation with Swiss matters regularly supervenes. A German version of this black-comic, antagonistic satire is the novel *Das große Knock-out in sieben Runden* (1972) by Herbert Heckmann, who was a visiting professor at Northwestern University from 1965 to 1968. His pop-picaresque German visitor engages in a seven-round boxing match with America, ultimately to be knocked out as a commercialized doll and dispatched by rocket into outer space. The graphics of the Statue of Liberty before each round grow steadily more faded and fuzzy. Somewhat akin to Handke's novel is Gerhard Roth's *Der große Horizont* (1974). Here the neurotic Austrian protagonist suffers from anxiety and violence in the United States. He is constantly beset by dangerous-seeming blacks and fears being beaten by them; he imagines that he is witness to a murder; a woman with whom he has sex dies immediately afterward, so that he flees across the country, expecting to be charged with murder and contending with a mysterious antagonist whom he attacks and holds at gunpoint, then pays for his tooth repair by a huge-nosed Jewish dentist; finally he learns that the woman had died of a bad heart so that he is exonerated. Apparently the reason all these things happen to him is that his consciousness is occupied by Raymond Chandler's detective fiction; he constantly imagines himself to be, and on one occasion pretends to be, Philip Marlowe. Thus again the European imported image balks mimesis and the essentially introverted imagination revolves within itself. One might categorize as unintentional fantasy Angelika Mechtel's ill-tempered roman à clef of a journey through the German departments of American universities, *Gott und die Liedermacherin* (1993). Another disappointment, to me at least, though more in a traditional realist mode, is Martin Walser's attempt at a campus novel, *Brandung* (1985). It is rather dispiriting to compare this humorless, pale, curiously adolescent work with the English classics of the genre.

It is unmistakable that within many of these imaginings a recrudescence of anti-Americanism has been developing. While it has repeatedly been shown that the German people as a whole are not predominantly hostile to the United States, the affect is well established among intellectuals and writers. Doubtless there are a number of reasons for this, among them insecurities about postwar German identity and a secular religion of anticapitalism among intellectuals.[52] But certainly the most important cause of the intensification of a hostile attitude is to be found in dismay at American practices and policies. One German academic has listed these irritants as repression and exploitation in Latin America, imperialism in Iran, the murder of Martin Luther King, and the Vietnam War.[53] Of these, Vietnam was undoubtedly the most important.[54] At the time it was never adequately perceived in the United States how much harm the Vietnam War was causing to the standing of our nation among our most natural democratic allies abroad. This is one of the reasons why a closer monitoring of German-American cultural relations by observers in the German studies field would be of practical value.

At the same time, we have an obligation to be alert to wretched excess and the propagation of ignorant superstitions about America that in rhetorical structure and argumentative strategy bear an exact resemblance to racism. A notorious example is a widely known book by a half-educated charlatan of uncertain experience in the United States, L. L. Matthias, *Die Kehrseite der USA* (1964), which presents the United States as corrupted by the lust for gain from its very founding in its fraudulent revolution and as a land having been throughout its history without indigenous culture, science, social theory, technology, religion, military honor, or democracy, far beneath the moral, prejudice-free, and humanistic level of Europe and Russia but representing in its arrogated power a threat to mankind.[55] Such books are not without influence. The Simple Simon of contemporary German letters, Rolf Hochhuth, found that his eyes had been opened to the truth about America by Matthias and dedicated the ludicrously anti-American drama *Guerillas* to him.[56] They also generate clones, such as two vicious books published recently by a journalist named Rolf Winter, who is particularly fond of ticking off the incompetence, wickedness, and hypocrisy of all our presidents beginning with George Washington.[57]

Because such phenomena pollute the international atmosphere, it would seem to belong to the responsibilities of Americans working in the field of German studies to monitor and analyze them more closely than they have been inclined to do in recent times. An interest in the quality of mimesis in fictional representations serves such a purpose. It is a relative quality, the evaluation of which does not have to be committed to untenable mirroring theories. Ulrich Ott has observed wisely that it is not a matter of "naive Abbildästhetik, wenn . . . von der Annahme einer Wechselwirkung von fremder Realität und literarischer Darstellung ausgegangen wird." As the examples from contemporary writing illustrate, one can make distinctions according to intention: "Es gibt Texte, die bewußt imagotype Strukturen transportieren; und es gibt Texte, die autoreflexiv dem Sog imagotyper Mechanismen zu entrinnen suchen, indem sie eine neue Wirklichkeitssicht konstituieren."[58] Sara Markham has warned: "Critics who stress myth over reality in their analyses... tend to obscure the observer's actual ability to perceive and respond creatively to a given historical situation, thereby obviating, to a great degree, a consideration of authorial cognitive factors in image portrayal."[59] My own view is that assumptions of mimesis tend to occupy much reader reception, regardless of what literary theoreticians may argue; Karl May, after all, was taken by many German readers to have formed his works, the fantastic dimensions of which are apparent to any American, mimetically out of lived experience. Evaluating and contextualizing the mimetic dimensions of fictional representations of the foreign would therefore seem to be one of the tasks of the literary historian as a possible contribution to the comity of nations and peoples.

# Notes

## Chapter 1

1. Castle, *Der große Unbekannte* (1952), p. 175.
2. See Arndt, "The Louisiana Passport of Charles Sealsfield."
3. All references to Sealsfield's works are cited from *Sämtliche Werke*, ed. Arndt et al., with volume number, original volume number where necessary, and page number, a procedure required by the circumstance that organization by volume of the edition does not always correspond to that of the reprinted originals.
4. Castle, *Das Geheimnis des grossen Unbekannten*, p. 296.
5. I found nothing relevant in a search of every Louisiana parish on the Red River (which runs practically through the whole state from northwest to southeast) in the manuscript record of the U.S. Census for 1830, but this is not surprising. We do not know under what name Sealsfield might have been living; the census taker might have encountered and recorded the name of an overseer (the census reports of that time list only names with no other information); and Sealsfield may well have left Louisiana before the 1830 census was taken.
6. See Arndt, "Charles Sealsfield and the *Courrier des Etats-Unis*."
7. For an evaluation, see Wilhelm Kreutz, "Zeuge der Revolution: Sealsfields europäische Korrespondentenberichte 1830–1832," in Schüppen, ed., *Neue Sealsfield-Studien*, pp. 135–56.
8. Jerry Schuchalter, "Morton oder die Große Tour: A Book in Search of an Interpretation," in Brancaforte, ed., *The Life and Works of Charles Sealsfield*, p. 246.
9. Immermann, *Münchhausen*, chaps. 13 and 14 (actually the third and fourth chapters, as the novel begins with chapter 11), *Werke*, 3:20–40. The connection was made by Castle, *Der große Unbekannte* (1952), p. 429.
10. For an argument that *Das Cajütenbuch* as a whole is symmetrically structured, see Sehm, *Charles Sealsfields Kajütenbuch*, pp. 28–34 and passim. A claim that Sealsfield's adaptation of the Irish anecdote is not only more colorful and vivacious than Lover's original, but is significantly related to theme and structure of *Das Cajütenbuch*, is mounted by Joseph P. Strelka, "'Kishogues Fluch': Zur Sprachkunst und Romankomposition von Sealsfields 'Kajütenbuch,'" in Schüppen, ed., *Neue Sealsfield-Studien*, pp. 293–306.
11. See Peter, *Charles Sealsfields Mexiko-Romane*, esp. pp. 84–111. *Süden und Norden* continues to baffle me. The most promising study of it is Renner, "Arbiträre Zeichen."
12. See Emmel, "Vision und Reise bei Charles Sealsfield," pp. 117–23. Emmel told me that she had made a journey to view the landscape of Oaxaca and

persuaded herself that Sealsfield must have been there. The Mexican Germanist Marianne de Bopp, though critical of Sealsfield's knowledge and understanding, is also certain that he had been in Oaxaca (18:XXXI*). Other scholars have been skeptical. Friesen, "'Sealsfield's Unrealistic Mexico,'" is agnostic on the question.

13. Information via Internet from Chris Dolan, University of Wisconsin. For a welcome if possibly overoptimistic effort to bring some interpretive order into the undoubtedly crucial landscape imagery of the novel, see Klaus Weissenberger, "Das Landschaftsbild in Sealsfields mexikanischen Romanen von der exotischen Kulisse zur Poetisierung im magischen Selbstbezug," in Schüppen, ed., Neue Sealsfield-Studien, pp. 307–29.

14. Walter Grünzweig, "Mariquitas Rache: Charles Sealsfield und die Psychologie des Expansionismus," in Brancaforte, ed., The Life and Works of Charles Sealsfield, pp. 254–69.

15. See Rolf Günter Renner, "Das Eigene im Anderen: Zur psychologischen Inschrift in Sealsfields Texten," in Brancaforte, ed., The Life and Works of Charles Sealsfield, pp. 38–57.

16. Mundt, Geschichte der Literatur der Gegenwart, pp. 425–26.

17. See Ashby, Charles Sealsfield.

18. See Gerhard K. Friesen, "Sealsfield's British Pirates and Promoters" (with the letters of the pirates, Joseph and Frederick Hardman), in Schüppen, ed., Neue Sealsfield-Studien, pp. 391–440.

19. Arndt, "Newly Discovered Sealsfield Relationship Documented."

20. The riddle has by no means been solved by Arndt, "Sealsfield's Command of the English Language."

21. Sebald, "Ansichten aus der Neuen Welt," p. 39.

22. Schüppen, "Wirtschaftlicher Optimismus."

23. Castle, Der große Unbekannte (1952), pp. 636–37.

24. See my effort to bring some reason into the matter, "Charles Sealsfield und das Freimaurertum. Mehr Fragen als Antworten," in Schüppen, ed., Neue Sealsfield-Studien, pp. 31–52. There persists an argument that Morton systematically alludes to Masonic practices and symbols. See Spaude, "Das Foucaultsche Pendel." A different argument that derives Sealsfield's republican ideas from Masonic sources in parallel to and possibly in contact with Ludwig Börne has been adumbrated by Zeman, "Ein Mitteleuropäer sieht Amerika."

25. Katz, Jews and Freemasons, p. 172.

26. See the introduction by Günter Schnitzler to the republication of Castle's Der große Unbekannte as a supplement volume to Sealsfield, Sämtliche Werke, p. 5*.

27. Sengle, "Karl Postl/Charles Sealsfield," p. 753. On this major essay, see Paul Gerhard Klussmann, "Friedrich Sengles Sealsfield-Deutung im Kontext seiner Biedermeierzeit," in Schüppen, ed., Neue Sealsfield-Studien, pp. 53–71.

28. See Grünzweig, "'Niemals verging sein deutsches Herz.'" Grünzweig acknowledges Castle's persecution but remarks, perhaps somewhat too gently, that his biography exhibits "noch deutlich der Einfluß von in der nationalsozialistischen Periode oftmals wiederholten Flachheiten" (p. 42).

29. Schuchalter, *Frontier and Utopia*, pp. 86, 304. Schuchalter has also provided what strikes me as the most subtle discussion of the whole question: "Charles Sealsfield's Polyvalent Novel: Der Dichter zwischen zwei Hemisphären," in Schüppen, ed., *Neue Sealsfield-Studien*, pp. 73–100.

30. Grünzweig, "'Where Millions of Happy People Might Live Peacefully,'" p. 236; see also Ritter, "Charles Sealsfield: Politischer Emigrant," p. 55.

31. Sengle, "Karl Postl/Charles Sealsfield," p. 762.

32. Schnitzler, *Erfahrung*, pp. 12, 128. See also Michelsen, "Americanism and Anti-Americanism," p. 277.

33. See Fritz, *Die Erzählweise*.

34. Sengle, "Karl Postl/Charles Sealsfield," p. 809.

35. Gutzkow had published a, by his standards, reasonably friendly if brief review of *Morton* in 1835. Text in Spiess, *Charles Sealsfields Werke*, p. 58. The author is identified as Gutzkow by Houben, *Zeitschriften des Jungen Deutschlands*, 2: col. 156.

36. On Paulding, Sedgwick, Child, and Simms, see Nirenberg, *The Reception of American Literature in German Periodicals*, pp. 75–81, 84–85.

37. See Heller, "Some Sources of Sealsfield," pp. 587–92; Castle, *Der große Unbekannte* (1952), pp. 451–53. On the sources of imagery and episodes in the Texan memoir, see Glen E. Lich, "Das Kajütenbuch and Texas," in Brancaforte, ed., *The Life and Work of Charles Sealsfield*, pp. 224–27.

38. Schüppen, *Charles Sealsfield*; Grünzweig, *Das demokratische Kanaan*.

39. For more detail on these points, see my essay, "Charles Sealsfield: Innovation or Intertextuality?"

40. Rahv, "Paleface and Redskin," pp. 251–52.

41. See Arndt, "Plagiarism: Sealsfield or Simms?"

42. Ritter, "Charles Sealsfield," p. 51. Ritter also comments on Sealsfield's dubious literary judgments in "Charles Sealsfields 'Madonnas of(f) the Trails,'" p. 92.

43. Schuchalter, *Frontier and Utopia*, p. 36. We do not certainly know that Sealsfield went bankrupt or even that he actually was a planter.

44. Cf. Ritter, *Darstellung*, pp. 235, n. 1, 314; Grünzweig, *Charles Sealsfield*, p. 42; Schuchalter, *Frontier and Utopia*, p. 56; Schnitzler, *Erfahrung*, p. 359. Sengle, "Karl Postl/Charles Sealsfield," p. 739 n., in keeping with his thesis of 1848 as a caesura in literary history, argues that Sealsfield was incongruent with the programmatic realism. But the documents suggest that the hindrance to the publication of his proposed later works was political and that publication was held up by the publisher Metzler (*Briefe*, 235, 246).

45. Suleiman, *Authoritarian Fiction*, p. 7. Suleiman's reiterated insistence that the authoritarian novel be unambiguous in meaning and interpretation (pp. 54, 59, 67, 71) would not apply to Sealsfield.

46. Fuerst, *The Victorian Age of German Literature*, pp. 44–45.

47. Ritter, *Darstellung*. Fischer, "Baumwolle und Indianer," p. 86, opposes Ritter's aesthetic evaluation, at least for *Der Legitime*.

48. Schnitzler, *Erfahrung*, passim. He was preceded by Jahnel, *Charles Seals-*

*field und die Bildende Kunst*, who compared Sealsfield's landscape descriptions to the paintings of the Hudson River School.

49. Schuchalter, *Frontier and Utopia*, pp. 215, 308–9.

50. Ibid., p. 56.

51. Put into circulation by the literary historian Johannes Scherr in 1875; see Castle, *Das Geheimnis des großen Unbekannten* (1952), pp. 297–98. The source of the notion seems to have been an ill-willed former fellow monk, who spread derogatory rumors about Sealsfield (ibid., p. 514).

52. On the Traven case, see Guthke, *B. Traven*.

## Chapter 2

1. Reviews are collected in Spiess, *Charles Sealsfields Werke*. See Steinecke, *Romanpoetik von Goethe bis Thomas Mann*, pp. 124–29, and Schuchalter, "Charles Sealsfield's 'Fable of the Republic,'" pp. 20–21.

2. Steinecke, *Romanpoetik*, p. 33.

3. Riederer, afterword to his edition, *Gesamtausgabe der Amerikanischen Romane*, 5:449; Hildegard Emmel, "Recht oder Unrecht in der Neuen Welt. Zu Charles Sealsfields Roman 'Der Legitime und die Republikaner,'" in Bauschinger et al., eds., *Amerika in der deutschen Literatur*, p. 76; Sengle, "Karl Postl/Charles Sealsfield," p. 759; Grünzweig, *Das demokratische Kanaan*, p. 225; Michelsen, "Americanism and Anti-Americanism," p. 277; Schnitzler, *Erfahrung und Bild*, p. 12.

4. Grünzweig, *Das demokratische Kanaan*, pp. 219, 223.

5. Remini, *The Life of Andrew Jackson*, p. 304. The stolen election is referred to explicitly in a note to *Ralph Doughby's Esq. Brautfahrt* (12:115).

6. Castle, *Der große Unbekannte* (1952), pp. 218, 209.

7. See esp. Grünzweig, "'Where Millions of Happy People Might Live Peacefully,'" pp. 219–36.

8. Hans Jörg Fürst, "Charles Sealsfield, Painter of Indian Manners: The Ethnographic Content of the Novel 'Tokeah and the White Rose'" [in German], in Brancaforte, ed., *The Life and Works of Charles Sealsfield*, pp. 270–90.

9. Meinig, *The Shaping of America*, p. 89.

10. Cf. Emmel, "Recht oder Unrecht," pp. 75, 78; Grünzweig, *Charles Sealsfield*, pp. 14–15.

11. Rozwenc, ed., *The Meaning of Jacksonian Democracy*, p. 2.

12. For a comparison of the two versions, see Fischer, "Baumwolle und Indianer," esp. p. 88.

13. The substantial role played by Creoles in the defense of New Orleans was neglected or denigrated in the myths that grew up around the battle. See Ward, *Andrew Jackson*, p. 26 and n. 38.

14. Schlesinger, *The Age of Jackson*, pp. 320–21.

15. Bemis, *John Quincy Adams and the Union*, p. 18.

16. Remini, *The Life of Andrew Jackson*, p. 307; Remini, *The Legacy of Andrew Jackson*, p. 89.

17. For this episode, see Remini, *The Life of Andrew Jackson*, pp. 109–10. The critical events occurred after the battle, not before and during it, as Sealsfield places them to heighten the effect. Jackson was fined $1,000, not, as Sealsfield has it, $2,000.

18. Jefferson, *Notes on the State of Virginia*, p. 163; see Grünzweig, *Das demokratische Kanaan*, p. 157.

19. Sellers, *The Market Revolution*, p. 90.

20. Grünzweig, *Das demokratische Kanaan*, pp. 160–62; Emmel, "Recht oder Unrecht," p. 80.

21. See Pessen, *Jacksonian America*, pp. 296–98, and Sellers, *The Market Revolution*, pp. 308–12. On Jackson's claim that the Indians had to be rescued *for* civilization by removing them *from* civilization, see Ward, *Andrew Jackson*, p. 41.

22. Bernd Fischer, "Zum historischen Gehalt von Charles Sealsfields Indianerromanen," in Schüppen, ed., *Neue Sealsfield-Studien*, pp. 175–93.

23. Zantop, "Dialectics and Colonialism: The Underside of the Enlightenment," pp. 314–15.

24. Tocqueville, *Democracy in America*, 1:346, 356–57.

25. See Steinecke, *Romanpoetik*, p. 124.

26. Ritter, "Charles Sealsfield: Politischer Emigrant," p. 47; Steinbrink, *Abenteuerliteratur des 19. Jahrhunderts in Deutschland*, p. 6.

27. Kriegleder, "Die 'Prosa unserer Union' und 'die Poesie des deutschen Gemüthes,'" pp. 108–9. Kriegleder rightly rejects Günter Schnitzler's argument that Sealsfield became virulently anti-American.

28. Schnitzler, "Erfahrung und Erfindung," p. 15, points out that Sealsfield's Virey in Mexico is also described as having a hanging lower lip. I continue to think that such details cannot bear the weight Schnitzler ascribes to them.

29. Spiess, *Charles Sealsfields Werke*, p. 20.

30. Steinecke, *Romanpoetik*, pp. 127–28.

31. Ritter, "Charles Sealsfield: Politischer Emigrant," p. 51.

# Chapter 3

1. Mikoletzky, *Die deutsche Amerika-Auswanderung*, pp. 286, 288. In the 1860s, Balduin Möllhausen bitterly attacked German supporters of slavery. See Barba, *Balduin Möllhausen*, p. 88. Möllhausen may have had Sealsfield in mind.

2. For an account of this matter in a somewhat debunking spirit, see Rippley, *The German-Americans*, pp. 58–71.

3. Trefousse, "Friedrich Hecker and Carl Schurz," p. 39.

4. See, e.g., Fischer, "Form und Geschichtsphilosophie," p. 249; Grünzweig, *Das demokratische Kanaan*, pp. 138–43; Schnitzler, *Erfahrung*, p. 167.

5. The most straightforward treatments of the issue are to be found in Schuchalter, *Frontier and Utopia*, pp. 188–213, in Hartley, "Society and Politics," pp. 154–82, and in Sehm, *Charles Sealsfields Kajütenbuch*, p. 3; Sehm may have been made more sensitive to the issue from his South African vantage point.

6. Frederickson, *The Black Image*, p. 3.

7. Kennedy, *Swallow Barn*, 2:227. Sealsfield may have known Kennedy personally; see Arndt, "Newly Discovered Sealsfield Relationships," p. 458.

8. Frederickson, *The Black Image*, pp. 2–5; Jefferson, *Notes on the State of Virginia*, p. 143.

9. Frederickson, *The Black Image*, p. 23; cf. Tocqueville, *Democracy in America*, 1:370–97.

10. At least one historian has argued that northern abolitionism was a device to ascribe virtue to capitalist entrepreneurs and distract attention from working-class suffering, and that working-class radicals saw abolitionists as agents of their capitalist oppression: Sellers, *The Market Revolution*, pp. 128, 388–89, 404–05.

11. Woodward, *The Old World's New World*, p. 121.

12. Frederickson, *The Black Image*, p. 68. Schuchalter, *Frontier and Utopia*, p. 142, speaks of *Herrenrassenmoral*.

13. Arndt, "Newly Discovered Sealsfield Relationships," p. 461.

14. Ritter, "Charles Sealsfield (1793–1864): German and American Novelist," p. 637.

15. Frederickson, *The Black Image*, 150–51.

16. The first to have noticed this was Schuchalter, *Frontier and Utopia*, pp. 189, 192.

17. Schmidt, *Amerikanismen bei Charles Sealsfield*, p. 24.

18. On the possible influence of Turner's *Confessions*, see Grünzweig, *Das demokratische Kanaan*, p. 140.

19. See Schuchalter, *Frontier and Utopia*, pp. 232–52; Frederickson, *The Black Image*, p. 49.

20. Schuchalter, *Frontier and Utopia*, p. 246.

21. Ibid., p. 198.

22. Taylor, *Cavalier and Yankee*, p. 300.

23. Kennedy, *Swallow Barn*, 1:117, 2:58, 73.

24. Ibid., 2:227–31.

25. Ibid., 2:258. Schuchalter, *Frontier and Utopia*, p. 192, also calls attention to the figure of Abe.

26. On Paulding's evolution, see Taylor, *Cavalier and Yankee*, pp. 67–94.

27. Paulding, *The Dutchman's Fireside*, p. 44.

28. Paulding, *Westward Ho!*, p. 4.

29. Ibid., pp. 58, 64–65.

30. [Simms], *The Yemassee*, pp. 204, 217, 225, 229, 231.

31. Remini, *The Life of Andrew Jackson*, p. 92.

32. Ridgley, *William Gilmore Simms*, p. 97.

33. Simms, *Woodcraft*, p. 509.

34. Ibid., pp. 121, 154, 183.

35. [Simms], *The Yemassee*, pp. 106–7.

36. Grünzweig, *Das demokratische Kanaan*, pp. 150, 143–44; see also Schnitzler, *Erfahrung*, pp. 167–68.

37. Anneliese Duncan, "Der fingierte Autor: George Howard and Charles Sealsfield," in Schüppen, ed., *Neue Sealsfield-Studien*, pp. 211–25; Grünzweig, *Das demokratische Kanaan*, p. 152.

38. Grünzweig and N'Diaye, "Voodoo im Biedermeier," pp. 147–66; for a further effort in this spirit, see Grünzweig, "Die wunderlichen Weisen der Methodisten: Sklavenreligion und Subversion bei Charles Sealsfield," in Schüppen, ed., *Neue Sealsfield-Studien*, pp. 227–44. In order to make the position plausible, Grünzweig is driven to postmodernism and deconstruction, as he confesses in "Der lüsterne Sklavenhalter."

39. Fritz, *Die Erzählweise*, p. 30; Sengle, "Karl Postl/Charles Sealsfield," pp. 982–84. Schüppen, *Charles Sealsfield*, pp. 396–97, also raises the possibility of irony through Howard as an unreliable narrator, only to reject it.

40. Schuchalter, *Frontier and Utopia*, p. 30.

41. Osterweis, *Romanticism and Nationalism in the Old South*, pp. 17, 26, 47; Horsman, *Race and Manifest Destiny*, pp. 39–41.

42. Osterweis, *Romanticism and Nationalism in the Old South*, p. 38.

43. Ibid., pp. 29–30, 114.

44. Grünzweig, *Das demokratische Kanaan*, p. 192, doubts that the anti-Catholic affect is to be interpreted biographically. Schnitzler, *Erfahrung*, p. 27, argues on the other hand that Sealsfield's identity as a Catholic priest determined his perceptions at all times.

45. Billington, *The Protestant Crusade*, pp. 380–429. On the burning of the convent, see pp. 68–95. Charles Godfrey Leland, in a characteristically irrelevant note to his translation of Heine's *Französische Zustände* (*Works*, 7:308), commented amusingly on a general unwillingness to admit to membership in the Know-Nothings, "the native American party in the United States, of which it was perfectly proved that 'nobody whatever had ever belonged to it at any time. . . .' There was but one Lodge of them left in Pennsylvania, and it was accustomed to meet in a cavern or a hole in the ground in a secluded spot. After the defeat of their candidate Fillmore, they once more assembled and *drew the whole in after them*, and so disappeared for ever."

46. See Grünzweig, *Das demokratische Kanaan*, pp. 98–105.

47. See Oppel, "Die deutsche Siedlung in Louisiana," pp. 18–38, and Kondert, *The Germans of Colonial Louisiana*.

48. Grünzweig, *Das demokratische Kanaan*, pp. 97–105; see also Grünzweig, "'The Italian Sky in the Republic of Letters,'" p. 15. This view is held also by Franz Schüppen, "Nationale Charakteristiken und liberales Weltbürgertum. Zu Sealsfields Kritik der Deutschen," in Schüppen, ed., *Neue Sealsfield-Studien*, pp. 355–56. A contrary interpretation, which sees Sealsfield's Jemima as the conventionalized shrew, but also as an ironic representation of the ethnocentrism of the white man, is given by Gabriela Scherer, "Die doppelte Jemmy: Sealsfield und Flint," in ibid., pp. 245–57.

49. A welcome abstract of the Alkalde's long monologue, making it, however, sound perhaps more democratic and statesmanlike than it is, will be found in Ritter, "Die texanische Revolution," pp. 98–100.

50. Taylor, *Cavalier and Yankee*, p. 15.

51. See Osterweis, *Romanticism and Nationalism in the Old South*, pp. 6, 48; Horsman, *Race and Manifest Destiny*, p. 164.

52. Flint, *Francis Berrian*, p. 103.

53. Ibid., p. 104.

54. Ibid., p. 266.

55. Ganilh, *Mexico versus Texas*, pp. 157–58. Ganilh, incidentally, was clearly, if ironically and obliquely, opposed to slavery; one of his characters is a learned and philosophical escaped slave of considerable wit and dignity. According to Gaston, *The Early Novel of the Southwest*, p. 35, n. 4, Ganilh was a Catholic priest of French origin; Gaston ascribes to him "strong pro-Catholic attitudes," but Grünzweig, *Das demokratische Kanaan*, pp. 201–2, calls him an anticlerical priest and judges his novel to be anti-Catholic.

56. Meinig, *The Shaping of America*, p. 190.

57. Bolzano is discussed in greater or lesser detail in almost every comprehensive treatment of Sealsfield and in numerous specialized studies. See particularly Ritter, "Charles Sealsfields gesellschaftspolitische Vorstellungen"; Ritter, *Darstellung*, pp. 53–57; Schnitzler, *Erfahrung*, passim; Alois Hofmann, "Karl Postls Flucht im Lichte der Polaritäten zwischen dem josephinisch-frühliberalen Fortschrittsstreben und der österreichisch-katholischen Restauration," in Brancaforte, ed., *The Life and Works of Charles Sealsfield*, pp. 10–17.

58. Schüppen, *Charles Sealsfield*, pp. 270–75.

59. I have relied largely upon Winter, *Die Sozial- und Ethnoethik Bernard Bolzanos*, and Christian, ed., *Bernard Bolzano*.

60. Sermon of 1818, Winter, *Die Sozial- und Ethnoethik Bernard Bolzanos*, p. 103.

61. On Bolzano's political and economic views and their philosophical foundation, see esp. Jaromír Loužil, "Bernard Bolzanos Sitten- und Gesellschaftslehre," in Christian, ed., *Bernard Bolzano*, pp. 5–28.

62. See on this matter Winter, *Die Sozial- und Ethnoethik Bernard Bolzanos*, and Stern, "Language Consciousness and Nationalism." Stern does not mention Sealsfield.

63. For a comparison, see Bernd Fischer, "Europäische Blicke auf die Neue Welt: Ein ideologiekritischer Vergleich von Charles Sealsfields und Alexis de Tocquevilles Amerika," in Brancaforte, ed., *The Life and Works of Charles Sealsfield*, pp. 153–71.

64. Schuchalter, "Charles Sealsfield's 'Fable of the Republic,'" p. 14.

65. See especially Sehm, *Charles Sealsfields Sprache im "Kajütenbuch."*

## Chapter 4

1. Schuchalter, *Frontier and Utopia*, pp. 267–68; Ward, *Andrew Jackson*, pp. 133–34. *Das Cajütenbuch* has been called "an allegory of Manifest Destiny" by Glen E. Lich, "'Das Kajütenbuch' and Its Relation to Texas Affairs," in Brancaforte, ed., *The Life and Works of Charles Sealsfield*, p. 222.

2. See Ward, *Andrew Jackson*, pp. 30–35.

3. On the priority of civilization over nature, see Schüppen, "'Der Amerikaner lebt in und durch Stürme,'" and Ward, *Andrew Jackson*, pp. 37–40. See also, for a thoughtful, differentiated analysis, Karl W. Doerry, "Nature in the New World: Sealsfield's Civilized Wilderness," in Brancaforte, ed., *The Life and Works of Charles Sealsfield*, pp. 208–20.

4. Cf. Lacour-Gayet, *Everyday Life in the United States*, p. 147: "Cowboys, settlers, trappers were not particularly disposed to authority. Authority was useful, they felt, only in a local and strictly limited context. Somewhat in the manner of the Germanic tribes, they made personal loyalty the basis for all authority and all obedience."

5. Tocqueville, *Democracy in America*, 1:413–14.

6. See, as a recent example in a long line, Winter, *Ami go home*.

7. Neitzel and Cargill, "'Stay at Home and Live with Integrity,'" pp. 72–73.

8. After his writing career was over, Sealsfield had lost his taste for violence and assumed a more conventional view. In 1854 he reports from Chicago: "Der gegenwärtige Zustand in den V. St. ist ein gräßlicher." Murders abound, twelve in one day in New York, no one is punished, people shoot down table companions in cold blood. He claims he is collecting newspaper articles, "denn es thut Noth, daß eine ehrliche Feder über diese horriblen Auswüchse unserer Democratie und Demagogie endlich ihr Urtheil abgiebt" (*Briefe*, 295), but nothing came of it, so far as we know.

9. See Lacour-Gayet, *Everyday Life in the United States*, p. 55; on the fragility of steamboats and their tendency to explode, without reference to racing, see Larkin, *The Reshaping of Everyday Life*, p. 230.

10. Source in Krumpelmann, "Sealsfield and Sources."

11. Weiss, "Der Zusammenhang zwischen Amerika-Thematik und Erzählkunst," p. 108. Weiss is frequently acknowledged in Sealsfield studies as a pioneer.

12. Cf. Schüppen, *Charles Sealsfield*, pp. 301, 304.

13. Schnitzler, *Erfahrung*, pp. 290–91, for example, takes the Conde as a spokesman for Sealsfield's views.

14. See, e.g., Magris, "Der Abenteurer und der Eigentümer," p. 158; Fischer, "Form und Geschichtsphilosophie," p. 245.

15. Sellers, *The Market Revolution*, p. 36.

16. Magris, "Der Abenteurer und der Eigentümer," p. 156.

17. Schuchalter, *Frontier and Utopia*, p. 265.

18. Ritter, "Geschichten aus Geschichte." p. 133. See also Ritter, "Die texanische Revolution," pp. 91–92, where the backgrounding of the Alamo is seen as a device to highlight the narrator's role.

19. Palmer, *The Age of the Democratic Revolution*, pp. 187–88.

20. Schuchalter, *Frontier and Utopia*, p. 12.

21. For some not wholly systematic and occasionally speculative observations on Sealsfield's views of and connections with the French, see Peter Krauss, "Zwischen Achtung und Verachtung: Sealsfield und die Franzosen," in Schüppen, ed., *Neue Sealsfield-Studien*, pp. 375–89.

22. Meinig, *The Shaping of America*, pp. 15, 18, 19, 189.

23. Fischer, "Form und Geschichtsphilosophie," p. 248, speculates plausibly that, in his obsession with sexual purity, "seine eigenen Ängste mitschwingen." Numerous commentators have noticed the combination of prudishness and sexual fascination, even salaciousness; it would deserve a separate study. Perhaps the strangest, most unexpected moment is Bohne's lecture in *Süden und Norden* (where there is also much sensuous, seductive dancing) on the exceptionally large noses on Mexican statues of God and Christ, which he interprets in a strikingly modern way as a representation of male potency (18:251).

24. Schuchalter, *Frontier and Utopia*, p. 316.
25. Ward, *Andrew Jackson*, pp. 45, 78.
26. Grünzweig, *Das demokratische Kanaan*, p. 97.
27. The epithet of "Flying Dutchman" was commonly applied to Van Buren. See Schlesinger, *The Age of Jackson*, p. 292.
28. Schuchalter, *Frontier and Utopia*, pp. 13–14.
29. See Pessen, *Jacksonian America*, p. 305 and passim.
30. Sellers, *The Market Revolution*, pp. 6, 17.

# Chapter 5

1. Spiess, *Charles Sealsfields Werke*, pp. 94–100.
2. Ashby, *Charles Sealsfield*, pp. 18–19. A review of the English translation is reprinted in Grünzweig, *Das demokratische Kanaan*, p. 265.
3. Grünzweig, *Charles Sealsfield*, p. 39; cf. *Das demokratische Kanaan*, p. 235.
4. Heine, *Historisch-kritische Gesamtausgabe der Werke*, 5:372.
5. On Menzel's evolution, see Hermand, "'Was ist des Deutschen Vaterland?'"
6. Campbell, *Edward Bulwer-Lytton*, p. 27; Zipser, *Edward Bulwer-Lytton and Germany*, pp. 183–85.
7. Zipser, *Edward Bulwer-Lytton and Germany*, p. 44.
8. Grünzweig, *Das demokratische Kanaan*, pp. 121–25.
9. Reynolds, *James Kirke Paulding*, p. 14; Grünzweig, *Das demokratische Kanaan*, pp. 124–25.
10. See Grünzweig, *Das demokratische Kanaan*, pp. 118–21.
11. Billington, *The Protestant Crusade*, p. 196.
12. Schlesinger, *The Age of Jackson*, pp. 408–10, 490–91.
13. Grünzweig, *Das demokratische Kanaan*, p. 111.
14. Curiously, a feminist manifesto patterned on the Declaration of Independence appeared a few years later, in 1848 (Lacour-Gayet, *Everyday Life in the United States*, p. 78).
15. Fischer, "Form und Geschichtsphilosophie," pp. 237, 254; cf. Magris, "Der Abenteurer und der Eigentümer," p. 165.
16. Ritter, *Darstellung*, p. 261.
17. Fischer, "Form und Geschichtsphilosophie," p. 253.
18. For a more metaphorical and literary-historical interpretation, see Lars-

Peter Linde, "Schiffahrt als Motor und Metapher im Romanwerk Charles Sealsfields—unter besonderer Berücksichtigung der 'Deutsch-amerikanischen Wahlverwandtschaften,'" in Schüppen, ed., *Neue Sealsfield-Studien*, pp. 259–76.

## Excursus I

1. Hans-Otto Hügel, *Untersuchungsrichter, Diebsfänger, Detektive. Theorie und Geschichte der deutschen Detektiverzählung im 19. Jahrhundert* (Stuttgart: Metzler, 1978). My review appeared in *Germanic Review* 54 (1979): 46–47.
2. Grünzweig, *Das demokratische Kanaan*, pp. 65–66.
3. Ritter, "Nachwort," in Sealsfield, *Das Kajütenbuch*, ed. Ritter, p. 499.
4. Billington, *Land of Savagery, Land of Promise*, p. 32.
5. Apart from Billington, some of the most informational current sources are Mikoletzky, *Die deutsche Amerika-Auswanderung*; Brenner, ed., *Der Reisebericht in der deutschen Literatur*, pp. 519–34, 609–28; and Brenner, *Reisen in die Neue Welt*.
6. Biesele, *The History of the German Settlements in Texas*, p. 39. I am grateful to Glen E. Lich for this reference.
7. Henry Moellhausen, *Die in Texas und Virginien gelegenen . . . Ländereien*. The publisher was a vanity press. Here he identified himself on the title page as "vormaligen Major der Artillerie der Republik Texas."
8. Correspondence in Graf, *Der Tod der Wölfe*, pp. 377–80.
9. On Paul Wilhelm, see Spahn, "German Accounts of Early Nineteenth-Century Life in Illinois," pp. 479–80.
10. There is no such place today, but it has been identified as "a small tributary of the Big Blue, and located in present Gage County, Nebraska, close to the Kansas border" by Miller, "Balduin Möllhausen," p. 58, n. 33.
11. Graf, *Der Tod der Wölfe*, p. 206.
12. The case has been persuasively made by Graf (ibid., pp. 110–20). The relationship was long suspected and was mentioned as a possibility by Dinkelacker, *Amerika zwischen Traum und Desillusionierung*, pp. 37–38, and Schegk, "Balduin Möllhausen," pp. 136–37.
13. Miller, "Balduin Möllhausen," pp. 90, 109.
14. Ibid., pp. 199, 236.
15. Letter in Barba, *Balduin Möllhausen*, pp. 173–74.
16. Graf, *Der Tod der Wölfe*, p. 70.
17. For a comparison, see Hartmann, *George Catlin und Balduin Möllhausen*.
18. Miller, "Balduin Möllhausen," pp. 217–18.
19. "The Crusoe of the Snowy Desert," *All the Year Round* 1, no. 2 (May 7, 1859): 44–48; see Graf, *Der Tod der Wölfe*, p. 184, where the year is given as 1858.
20. *Cost. Corr.*, letter of July 6, 1862, col. 1110. At this time Gerstäcker can only have known, besides Möllhausen's sketches in *Die Gartenlaube*, the first novel, *Der Halbindianer*, and possibly the second, *Der Flüchtling* (1862), both published by Costenoble.

21. Dinckelacker, *Amerika zwischen Traum und Desillusionierung*, p. 76.
22. Graf, *Der Tod der Wölfe*, pp. 132–33, 136–41, 160.
23. Barba, *Balduin Möllhausen*, pp. 71, 59.
24. Ibid., p. 88.
25. Möllhausen, "Die Tochter des Häuptlings (Scenen aus dem Urwalde)," *Palmblätter und Schneeflocken*, 2:1–102. That the old chief who is the princess's father comes ultimately to look benignly on this union seems odd.
26. On the belief in the hardness of Negroes' skulls, encountered also in others of our writers, see Frederickson, *The Black Image*, p. 57.
27. Cf. Dinkelacker, *Amerika zwischen Traum und Desillusionierung*, pp. 136–37.
28. See Ashliman, "The Image of Utah and the Mormons," pp. 209–27. Ashliman remarked in "The American West in Nineteenth-Century German Literature," p. 196, on Möllhausen's "most sinister image" of Mormons.
29. One peculiarity is Möllhausen's confused use of Spanish genders. He regularly treats "rancho" as a feminine noun; "cañon" also is construed as a feminine. In one place a girl is referred to as "muchacho." The "Llano estacado" quite confusingly appears as masculine, feminine, and plural. One would think a traveler in the West would have learned *that* much Spanish from observation.
30. See Dinkelacker, *Amerika zwischen Traum und Desillusionierung*, pp. 142–46; Graf, *Abenteuer und Geheimnis*, pp. 116, 119–22.
31. In *Der Mayordomo* there is a positive if inscrutable Chinese character, another example of Möllhausen's lack of focus in these matters.
32. Brenner, *Reisen in die Neue Welt*, p. 135.
33. Möllhausen, *Palmblätter und Schneeflocken*, 2:137.
34. Graf, *Der Tod der Wölfe*, pp. 129–32, 170–72.
35. The *Adelsverein* still awaits its modern historian. Its official documents have been published by Klotzbach, *Die Solms-Papiere*. Its archives are now preserved in the Western Americana Collection of the Beinecke Rare Book and Manuscript Library, Yale University. One segment, known as the "Strubberg papers," appears to have been abstracted from the archive at one time to support a defense of Strubberg's conduct. See Lich, Moltmann, and Womack, "'New Crowns to Old Glory.'" For corroboration of Strubberg's account of conditions in the colony, see Mikoletzky, *Die deutsche Amerika-Auswanderung*, p. 216, n. 194.
36. Barba, *The Life and Works of Friedrich Armand Strubberg*, pp. 27–61.
37. A thorough critique has been undertaken by Märtin, *Wunschpotentiale*, pp. 89–114. Useful information on the Friedrichsburg episode is given by Huber, "Frederic Armand Strubberg," although Huber still continues to be too credulous about other aspects of Strubberg's life; on the episode of the medical studies, Huber substitutes St. Louis for Louisville.
38. Steinbrink, *Abenteuerliteratur des 19. Jahrhunderts*, p. 145.
39. Arndt, "Sealsfield and Strubberg at Vera Cruz," found a German-born officer Seafield or Seefeld who was in Vera Cruz at the time and whom he be-

lieves Strubberg met. The suggestion is persuasive, providing Strubberg was ever in Vera Cruz at all.

40. Penniger, ed., *Fest-Ausgabe*, pp. 51–53, 72, 81.
41. Gillespie County Historical Society, *Pioneers in God's Hills*, pp. xvii–xviii.
42. King, *John O. Meusebach*, p. 107.
43. On this episode, see Huber, "Frederic Armand Strubberg," pp. 61–68.
44. Barba, *The Life and Works of Friedrich Armand Strubberg*, p. 79: "in good taste never permits himself as a character to enter into matrimony."
45. *AJR*, 116. A previous reader of the copy I used penciled three exclamation points into the margin at this point.
46. Barba, *The Life and Works of Friedrich Armand Strubberg*, p. 90.
47. *AJR*, 141, 433. The previous reader placed a question mark next to the first item. The second item is accompanied by one of Strubberg's drawings. Sometimes his illustrations do not correspond exactly to the text. For example, one on p. 101 shows Strubberg's dog, who is a prominent character in the book but was not taken on the outing in question.
48. *AJR*, 4, 11, 314. The first and third scenes are accompanied by illustrations.
49. On the parallel, see Märtin, *Wunschpotentiale*, pp. 112–13.
50. Ashliman, "The American West," p. 167.
51. Barba, *The Life and Works of Friedrich Armand Strubberg*, p. 97.
52. Woodson, *American Negro Slavery*, p. 76. Woodson does not quite see the importance of the mixed race.
53. Hollyday, *Anti-Americanism in the German Novel*, p. 142.
54. *BW*, 2:125; cf. 2:268–72, where the beauties of the Hudson and the fine sights of New York harbor are praised, but Americans are too busy following the god of wealth.
55. See "Die Mormonen-Ansiedlung bei Friedrichsburg," in Penniger, ed., *Fest-Ausgabe*, pp. 108–9, and Gillespie County Historical Society, *Pioneers in God's Hills*, p. xviii: "Prosperity was provided for young Fredericksburg by the thriving colony of Zodiac nearby (1847–1853).... The Mormons supplied the settlers with meal and lumber for their mills and showed them how best to cultivate their land."
56. Armand, "Die Amerikaner in Mexico," and "Der Sturm von San Antonio," in *Scenen aus den Kämpfen der Mexicaner und Nordamerikaner*, pp. 104, 124. These stories are banal Westerns, dime-novel stuff, perhaps with the exception that the second ends not with an access of poetic justice but in unappeased horrors, doubtless also a commentary on America.
57. Woodson, *American Negro Slavery*, pp. 130–46.

## Chapter 6

1. See the "Nachwort" to *Eck*, 4:vii, xii–xvi, and Postma, "Hagenmarkt und Mississippi."
2. Kolb, "Friedrich Gerstäcker and the American Frontier," p. 63.

3. Schleucher, *Das Leben der Amalia Schoppe und Johanna Schopenhauer*, p. 364. How widespread this notion was appears in Mikoletzky, *Die deutsche Amerika-Auswanderung*, pp. 245–47 and n. 410.

4. [Rattermann], "Zwei . . . Deutsch-amerikanische Pioniere." Rattermann was a kind of professional German American of highly conservative views, and it is not known whether his account derives from his own observations.

5. Gerstäcker, *In the Arkansas Backwoods*, ed. Miller, p. 29; on the honorary citizenship, see p. 1. The historian who instigated it, Clarence Evans, has researched the accuracy of Gerstäcker's depictions: "Friedrich Gerstäcker, Social Chronicler of the Arkansas Frontier"; "Gerstaecker and the Konwells of White River Valley." See also Bukey, "Friedrich Gerstaecker and Arkansas."

6. Steeves, "The First of the Westerns." Steeves does not inspire confidence at all points. Without a clear reference, he praises even more a third novel, *Die Moderatoren*, which is not by Gerstäcker as far as I know and is probably an imitation. He also suggests that during the ten months of Gerstäcker's time in Texas that he left unreported, he might have had direct experience with a band of criminals, an allegation I consider altogether inconceivable. In *SJ*, 2:254, Gerstäcker tells of joining a posse to capture horse thieves; the episode is probably the source of *Die Regulatoren* (see n. 79 in *SJ*).

7. See Walker, *Germany and the Emigration, 1816–1885*; Rippley, *The German-Americans*, chap. 6, tables on p. 75; Moltmann et al., eds., *Deutsche Amerikaauswanderung*, p. 201.

8. Roth, *Die Darstellung der deutschen Auswanderung*, p. 59.

9. Gerstäcker was not alone with this suggestion; such plans were much discussed after the Revolution of 1848. See Walker, *Germany and the Emigration*, pp. 106, 148.

10. Gerstäcker, *Die Deutschen im Ausland*, pp. 1–2.

11. Brenner, *Reisen in die Neue Welt*, p. 69. However, Gerstäcker is not negative enough for Brenner, who becomes discontented with friendly reports on America (pp. 118–19).

12. See Roth, *Die Darstellung der deutschen Auswanderung*, pp. 42–43.

13. On the unfortunate consequences of emigration to Brazil, the scandal it aroused, and Prussia's ban on emigration to Brazil in 1859, see Walker, *Germany and the Emigration*, pp. 38, 119, 178.

14. Gerstäcker, *Die Colonie*. See also "Deutsche Colonisation in Brasilien," Z3, 51–53.

15. Gerstäcker, *In the Arkansas Backwoods*, ed. Miller, pp. 18–19. Miller provides a quotation here that I have not been able to verify—he may have left out the reference—but he refers appositely to Mikoletzky, *Die deutsche Amerika-Auswanderung*, who gives a good account of the economic and educational state of the reading public, pp. 75–105.

16. Reitzel, *Adventures of a Greenhorn*, p. 12.

17. On the circumstances of the grant, see Moltmann, "Überseeische Siedlungen."

18. On the Australian episode, see Corkhill, *Antipodean Encounters*, pp. 73–102.

19. A photograph of this party will be found in Postma, "Hagenmarkt und Mississippi," p. 217, and in Ostwald, *Friedrich Gerstäcker*, between pp. 108 and 109.
20. The poem, "Tristia," is included in *Herweghs Werke*, ed. Tardel, 3:122–23.
21. Roth, "Friedrich Gerstäcker und Georg Herwegh."
22. O'Donnell, "Gerstäcker in America," p. 1042.
23. Prahl, "America in the Works of Gerstäcker," p. 214; Gerstäcker, *In the Arkansas Backwoods*, ed. Miller, p. 20.
24. Cazden, *A Social History of the German Book Trade*, p. 312.
25. See Garzmann, Ostwald, and Schuegraf, *Gerstäcker-Verzeichnis*, which contains Gerstäcker's own lists.
26. Gerstäcker, *China, das Land und seine Bewohner*. For the circumstances of this publication, see the "Nachwort."
27. See Karsen, "Friedrich Gerstäcker in South America." The article is purely descriptive of the novels set in Ecuador.
28. Neuhaus, *Der zeitgeschichtliche Sensationsroman in Deutschland*, p. 200.
29. Postma, "Hagenmarkt und Mississippi"; Brenner, *Reisen in die Neue Welt*, pp. 163–68.
30. See Tatum, *The Reception of German Literature in U.S. German Texts*, pp. 141–43 and the annual tables in appendix F. Tatum remarks (p. 142) that a textbook version of it was still advertised at the time of his study. Ostwald has provided a commentary to his reprint of the original edition of *Germelshausen*.
31. Private communication from Mr. Joseph C. Zamenick, Belfast, Maine, May 1, 1984.
32. Krumpelmann, "Gerstaecker's 'Germelshausen' and Lerner's 'Brigadoon.'"
33. Weber, *America in Imaginative German Literature*, p. 157.
34. Ashliman, "The American West in Nineteenth-Century German Literature," pp. 32–33.
35. Cf. Heine, *Historisch-kritische Gesamtausgabe*, 5:369.
36. Reproduced in Hollyday, *Anti-Americanism in the German Novel*, p. 138.
37. Kolb, "Friedrich Gerstäcker and the American Frontier," p. 19; Gerstäcker, *In the Arkansas Backwoods*, ed. Miller, p. 11; Pagni, "Friedrich Gerstäckers 'Reisen.'"
38. Postma, "Hagenmarkt und Mississippi," p. 219.
39. He is not usually seen in this light, but cf. the perspicacious observation by Rippley, *The German-Americans*, p. 168: "Cynical in some respects, Gerstäcker nevertheless lauded American pioneer virtues."

## Chapter 7

1. Gerstäcker, *Waidmanns Heil!*
2. Steinbrink, *Abenteuerliteratur des 19. Jahrhunderts*, p. 48.
3. In 1926 a blockhouse serving as an Indian museum, called "Villa Bärenfett," was built in the yard of the May museum, "Villa Shatterhand," in Rade-

beul. The name was transmitted via May's children's novel, *Der Ölprinz* (Stuttgart: Union Deutsche Verlagsgesellschaft, 1897).

4. On the reception of the translation, see Nirenberg, *The Reception of American Literature in German Periodicals*, pp. 82–83. Francis Grund reported to the Augsburg *Allgemeine Zeitung* in 1845 that Hoffman was "der beste amerikanische Scenendichter" with "keine Spur einer krankhaften Phantasie": Wagner, ed., *Was die Deutschen aus Amerika berichteten*, p. 30.

5. Hoffman, *Wild Scenes in the Forest*, p. 43. An American edition did not appear until 1843, so Gerstäcker's translation was fairly prompt. See Barnes, *Charles Fenno Hoffman*, p. 121.

6. Sullivan, *In Praise of Blood Sports*, pp. 106, 112, 118.
7. Rubin, "William Elliott Shoots a Bear."
8. Elliott, *Carolina Sports*, p. 100.
9. Ibid., pp. 165–66, 163.
10. *The Faulkner Reader*, pp. 253–352.
11. Elliott, *Carolina Sports*, p. 151.
12. Brenner, *Reisen in die Neue Welt*, pp. 155–56, 184; on p. 155 Brenner cites a passage from *AWS*, 1:40, where Gerstäcker asserts his preference for bear because it is not the kind of game that turns and flees.

13. This must have occurred in 1839, the year in which the originally 160-mile-long "Great Raft" was cleared after six years of labor. See Meinig, *The Shaping of America*, p. 234. The clearing process must have been well advanced when Gerstäcker went down the river. He does not give this impression, however, indicating that the raft still consisted of forty miles of debris.

14. The behavior concerns a claim by another woodsman, which Gerstäcker tries to verify by observation, that bears chew bark as high as they can reach in order to show other bears how big they are and to enable them to decide whether to fight or not. The editor of the reprint edition, Thomas Ostwald, recalls (n. 43) a description of this behavior in one of the Disney nature films.

15. See, e.g., Kolb, "Friedrich Gerstäcker and the American Frontier," p. 94, who denominates Assowaum as "the Rousseauistic noble savage," and the critique of Brenner, *Reisen in die Neue Welt*, p. 201, who apparently knows more about Indians than Gerstäcker did.

16. The best-informed and most thoughtful examination of this topic is Di Maio, "Borders of Culture." She touches on our exemplary story on p. 70.

17. Ostwald, *Friedrich Gerstäcker*, pp. 121–22. For a commentary on Gerstäcker's analysis of the council, see Di Maio, "Borders of Culture," pp. 61–66.

18. Landa, "The American Scene," p. 245.
19. Di Maio, "Borders of Culture," p. 72.
20. Billington, *Land of Savagery, Land of Promise*, p. 105; see also Landa, "The American Scene," p. 250.
21. Di Maio, "Borders of Culture," pp. 55–56.
22. Cf. the chapter "Die Railtroublers," in May, *W*, 3:354–96.
23. Di Maio, "Borders of Culture," p. 53, grounds this point theoretically.
24. Ibid., p. 71.

## Chapter 8

1. Walter D. Kampfhoefner, "Dreissiger and Forty-eighter: The Political Influence of Two Generations of German Political Exiles," in Trefousse, ed., *Germany and America*, p. 91.
2. Wagner, ed., *Was die Deutschen aus Amerika berichteten*, pp. 167–68. Assing is misspelled "Assig" throughout the book.
3. Meinig, *The Shaping of America*, pp. 191, 300, 311.
4. Ostwald, *Friedrich Gerstäcker*, p. 186. The novel was *The Wigwam and the Cabin* (1845–46). It is not certain whether anything is to be made of its absence, as Gerstäcker's lists of his publications are not perfect. On the positive reception of the translation, see Nirenberg, *The Reception of American Literature*, p. 84.
5. Woodson, *American Negro Slavery*, p. 181, notes this point but adds that Gerstäcker later changed his mind, as we shall see also. On the elaborated comparisons with peasants and proletarians, see Genovese, *Roll, Jordan, Roll*, pp. 58–64.
6. Brenner, *Reisen in die Neue Welt*, pp. 371–73.
7. Landa, "The American Scene," pp. 137, 230. However, an incongruously dressed free black in Ecuador is portrayed as a dignified figure ("In den Manglaren," *Z6*, 197).
8. On "Jazede" see Woodson, *American Negro Slavery*, pp. 186–90.
9. Gerstäcker liked the grave-robbing motif so well that he recycled it, once in a story called "Im Grabe," set in Valparaiso, in which a young man, reluctantly obliged by a doctor to obtain the cadaver of a crippled man, turns out to be the murderer—his own retarded brother, a friend of the crippled man, springs out of the grave and stabs him in revenge (*KENS*, 1:207–27)—and again in a story set in Ecuador, "In den Manglaren" (*Z6*), in which the outraged Indians trick the would-be grave robbers, a French doctor and an Italian adventurer, into a mangrove swamp from which they only escape from the rising water by the skin of their teeth. This last story is one of several that may remind us a little of Joseph Conrad, though without Conrad's tragic sensibility. Another episode set in Valparaiso shows a narrator fascinated by a graveyard, to which he keeps returning (*R*, 1:415–32).
10. See Postma, "Hagenmarkt und Mississippi," p. 228.
11. Ostwald, *Friedrich Gerstäcker*, p. 139.
12. See Billington, *Land of Savagery, Land of Promise*, pp. 184–86; Larkin, *The Reshaping of Everyday Life*, pp. 278–81. Cf. Ottilie Assing to the *Allgemeine Zeitung* in 1858: "Jeder gebildete Europäer beklagt hier bekanntlich das Vorherrschen des Sektenwesens, wodurch Heuchelei und Verdummung hervorgerufen und der geistige Fortschritt gehemmt wird": Wagner, ed., *Was die Deutschen aus Amerika berichteten*, p. 6.
13. See Brenner, *Reisen in die Neue Welt*, pp. 337–38.
14. Gerstäcker, *In the Arkansas Backwoods*, ed. Miller, p. 74.
15. Larkin, *The Reshaping of Everyday Life*, pp. 89–90.

16. Lacour-Gayet, *Everyday Life in the United States*, p. 96; see also Sutherland, *The Expansion of Everyday Life*, pp. 195–96; and Mikoletzky, *Die deutsche Amerika-Auswanderung*, p. 263, who argues that the claim of quackery had a real basis.

17. Pessen, *Jacksonian America*, pp. 64–66.

18. See on this point Landa, "The American Scene," p. 274.

19. Gerstäcker, *In the Arkansas Backwoods*, ed. Miller, p. 24.

20. Larkin, *The Reshaping of Everyday Life*, p. 261.

21. Stuecher, *Twice Removed*, pp. 18–20.

22. A close competitor would be Francis Grund, whose reports to Cotta's publications in the 1840s correspond closely to Gerstäcker's views; he is, if anything, even more sardonic about the German immigrants. See Wagner, ed., *Was die Deutschen aus Amerika berichteten*, passim.

23. To Gottfried Duden's optimistic *Bericht über eine Reise nach den westlichen Staaten Nordamerika's* (1829), has been ascribed, at the time and in later studies of the emigration, a deleterious influence, luring emigrants into catastrophe, to the point where Duden himself felt obliged to a self-criticism in 1837. It is possible that Duden's influence has been overestimated and that he became a kind of straw man in the emigration debate. On Duden, see Brenner, *Reisen in die Neue Welt*, pp. 102–20, and Peter Mesenhöller, "'Auf, ihr Brüder, laßt uns reisen fröhlich nach Amerika.' Reisebericht und Reiseliteratur im Kontext der deutschen Amerikaauswanderung des frühen 19. Jahrhunderts," in Brenner, ed., *Der Reisebericht*, pp. 368–74; on Gerstäcker and Duden, see Durzak, *Das Amerika-Bild*, p. 54.

24. In a note, Gerstäcker explains that "cayoten" is a Mexican word meaning to dig like a coyote. News to me.

25. Roth, *Die Darstellung der deutschen Auswanderung*, p. 127, n. 21, doubts, partly on chronological grounds, that this can have been the case; if it was not, it is a particular political point of the author.

26. Gerstäcker, *Die Deutschen im Ausland*, pp. 12–16.

27. Pagni, "Friedrich Gerstäckers 'Reisen,'" p. 283.

28. Brenner, *Reisen in die Neue Welt*, p. 163.

29. Durzak, *Das Amerika-Bild*, p. 212, n. 26.

30. Tocqueville, *Democracy in America*, 1:198.

31. A scene comparable with this is Möllhausen's cornhusking bee, *Palmblätter und Schneeflocken*, 2:187–88.

32. Tocqueville, *Democracy in America*, 1:3.

33. Durzak, *Das Amerika-Bild*, p. 41, thinks that Gerstäcker meant with his incompetent aristocrats to satirize the hapless Lenau's American fiasco.

34. Kolb, "Friedrich Gerstäcker and the American Frontier," p. 50.

35. Hollyday, *Anti-Americanism in the German Novel*, pp. 129–39.

36. See Landa, "The American Scene," p. 215.

37. Brenner, *Reisen in die Neue Welt*, p. 286; Pagni, "Friedrich Gerstäckers 'Reisen,'" p. 282.

38. Billington, *Land of Savagery, Land of Promise*, p. 190, who takes his ex-

ample from Dickens's *Martin Chuzzlewit*; Lacour-Gayet, *Everyday Life*, pp. 44 and 86, with reference to Mrs. Trollope; Sutherland, *The Expansion of Everyday Life*, p. 72.

39. Billington, *Land of Savagery, Land of Promise*, p. 76; see also p. 271: "This was utter nonsense, for there is no evidence that such affairs ever took place."

40. Larkin, *The Reshaping of Everyday Life*, p. 258; Lacour-Gayet, *Everyday Life*, p. 82.

## Chapter 9

1. Seyfarth, *Friedrich Gerstäcker*, p. 39. The dissertation gives an impression that the topic was imposed on an unwilling candidate, who came actively to dislike it.

2. Durzak, *Das Amerika-Bild*, pp. 45–46.

3. Bade, "Trends and Issues," pp. 15–16.

4. When the Homestead Act was passed in 1862, granting 160 acres free to anyone promising to cultivate it, a Norwegian newspaper refused to believe the news but others were electrified: Semmingsen, *Norway to America*, pp. 121–22.

5. A very similar account is given by Thran, *Meine Auswanderung nach Texas*, pp. 21–22. The details are so close that this may have been a source for Gerstäcker.

6. Cf. in Wagner, ed., *Was die Deutschen aus Amerika berichteten*, p. 217, Francis Grund's observation to the Augsburg *Allgemeine Zeitung* in 1843: "Von den deutschen Gelehrten die sich hieher verirren, will ich gar nicht reden. Die können hier ebensowenig den Hund aus den Ofen locken als in der Heimath, und sind verglichen mit den Eingeborenen so wenig anstellig, und so sehr bescheiden, daß man sie ihrer idealen Liebenswürdigkeit wegen eher bemitleidet als ihnen die Leitung großartiger gemeinnütziger Pläne überläßt." This may be a prejudice, however. Mikoletzky, *Die deutsche Amerika-Auswanderung*, pp. 243–44, indicates that, historically, the educated were often flexible and successful.

7. This geographical identification—the next chapter, set in Milwaukee, is entitled "In Michigan"—makes it unclear when the novel is supposed to be taking place. Since a character in that chapter speaks of the large number of Germans in Wisconsin (*NA*, 5:235), Gerstäcker knows where he is, but the Wisconsin territory separated from Michigan in 1836; it is hard to understand why he would set the novel nearly twenty years in the past, at a time before he had even arrived in America. It is probably just an error; Olnitzki is said to have fled the Polish revolution ten years before (*NA*, 4:54), which would place the action of the novel in the early 1840s.

8. Seyfarth, *Friedrich Gerstäcker*, p. 40.

9. A good, succinct account of his experiences in California is given by Ostwald, *Friedrich Gerstäcker*, pp. 38–58.

10. Friedrich Gerstäcker, *Kaliforniens Gold- u. Quecksilber-District. Nach: the California Herald* (Leipzig: Jurany, 1849), reprinted in Gerstäcker, ed., Tyrwhitt-Brooks, *Vier Monate unter den Goldfindern*.

11. The somewhat abridged translation was published by Weber in Leipzig in 1849 as *Vier Monate unter den Goldfindern in Ober-Kalifornien. Tagebuch einer Reise von San Francisco nach den Golddistrikten*; it went through four editions. A much shorter version by an unknown translator is reprinted in the item cited in the previous note.

12. Vizetelly, *Glances Back through Seventy Years*, 1:347. See also Braunsdorf, "Gerstäcker at the California Gold Rush."

13. Ostwald, *Friedrich Gerstäcker*, pp. 147–48. The judgment is not much different from that of the exasperated doctoral candidate: "Als Ganzes ist das Werk haltlos und uneinheitlich, eines der schwächsten aus Gerstäckers gesamtem Schaffen" (Seyfarth, *Friedrich Gerstäcker*, p. 40).

14. Cf., however, Ottilie Assing's fierce denunciation of Johnson to the *Allgemeine Zeitung*, in Wagner, ed., *Was die Deutschen aus Amerika berichteten*, pp. 195–97.

15. Gerstäcker begins this story by saying that it took place in the summer of 1838 or 1839 on the day of a total eclipse of the sun, which would date the event on September 18, 1838 (I am grateful to Yale astronomers Bradley E. Schaefer and Paolo Coppi for information on this point). I have not been able to find confirmation of the event, but a quite similar incident (without eclipse) occurred in September 1841; see Dabney, *Cincinnati's Colored Citizens*, pp. 41–42, and the *Daily Cincinnati Enquirer*, n. s., 1, nos. 124, 125, 126, 129, September 3, 4, 6, 9, 1841, all [p. 2]. The *Enquirer*, a Jacksonian paper, blamed the disturbances on the abolitionists and complained: "We were overrun with negroes [who] obtruded their miscreated visages, like Milton's devils, where they had no business" (no. 129, September 9). It is in such places that we see the American source of the discourse on race that is sometimes replicated in German writing.

16. This is the position of Kolb, "Friedrich Gerstäcker and the American Frontier," pp. 11, 77, 79; while I owe useful insights to this study, I cannot support its superintending thesis.

17. Landa, "The American Scene," pp. 4, 41.

18. Gerstäcker, *In the Arkansas Backwoods*, ed. Miller, pp. 15, 16, 19. Miller also points out, p. 22 and n. 52, that the historian Clarence Evans managed to prove that a number of Gerstäcker's characters and events were based in reality, results that build confidence in the oeuvre as a whole.

19. Roth, *Die Darstellung der deutschen Auswanderung*, p. 81.

## Excursus II

1. See the definitive study, Gerbi, *The Dispute of the New World*.
2. See Hollyday, *Anti-Americanism in the German Novel*; Durzak, *Das Amerika-Bild*.

3. She is featured in Hollyday, *Anti-Americanism in the German Novel*, pp. 49–54, yet he points out that, at least in the northern section of her novel, she "emphasizes favorable characteristics" (p. 51).

4. Even for access to this version I owe thanks to Professor Wallach.

5. For exact bibliographical references to the following works, see Wallach, "Talvj (Therese Albertine Luise von Jakob Robinson)," pp. 280–82.

6. Talvi [sic], *Historical View of the Languages and Literatures of the Slavic Nations*, p. 321. There are no such remarks in the drafts of Goethe's letters to Talvj, on which see Milović, *Talvjs erste Übertragungen für Goethe*, pp. v–ix.

7. Wallach, "Women of German-American Fiction," p. 332.

8. Lang, *The Process of Immigration in German-American Literature*, pp. 67–68 and n. 4.

9. Stuecher, *Twice Removed*, pp. 53–69. This book's potential usefulness is sabotaged by typographical anarchy; apart from the now customary disorder in the text, the page numbers in the table of contents have no relation to those in the book, and the superscript numbers come to have none to the notes.

10. Wallach, "Die Erfahrung der Fremde," p. 86.

11. Stuecher, *Twice Removed*, p. 56.

12. On this view, see, for instance, Woodward, *The Old World's New World*, p. 121.

13. Stuecher, *Twice Removed*, p. 68.

14. Wallach, "Talvj (Therese Albertine Luise von Jakob Robinson)," pp. 285–86.

15. Hollyday, *Anti-Americanism*, p. 54. Sealsfield certainly admired some contemporary American writing, but nowhere does he allude to it explicitly in his fiction.

16. Letter to his brother Matthias, September 10, 1855, in Kürnberger, *Briefe eines politischen Flüchtlings*, p. 198.

17. Wagnleiter, *Coca-Colonisation und Kalter Krieg*, p. 45. Kürnberger's novel was written at a time of negative news about emigration and a significant number of disappointed returnees; in that year of 1855 the volume fell to one-third of that of the previous year. See Walker, *Germany and the Emigration*, p. 174.

18. Kriegleder, "Die 'Prosa unserer Union,'" p. 104. Kriegleder points out, pp. 106–7, that Willkomm and Kürnberger, despite their opposite evaluation of America, both believed that American prose was in need of spiritualization by European poesy.

19. Pütz, "Max Webers und Ferdinand Kürnbergers Auseinandersetzung mit Benjamin Franklin." See on this also Schuchalter, "Literature, Representation, and the Negotiation of Cultural Lacunae," pp. 34–35.

20. Lengauer, *Ästhetik und liberale Opposition*, p. 204, suggests, rather overingeniously, that the anticommercial affect is Kürnberger's expression of chagrin that in entering upon a commercial contract for the novel he was sacrificing poesy to the market. Lengauer treats Moorfeld, who just *has* money, as a capitalist (pp. 230–31); this seems to me a confusion of class identity.

21. See Spuler, *"Germanistik" in America*.

22. Mulfinger, *Ferdinand Kürnberger's Roman "Der Amerikamüde"*; see also Manfred Durzak, "Nach Amerika. Gerstäckers Widerlegung der Lenau-Legende," in Bauschinger et al., eds., *Amerika in der deutschen Literatur*, pp. 135–53. Some modifications to Durzak's hard view appear in the sensible article by Crichton, "'And No Birds Sing.'" On Lenau's adventure, see Gladt, "'Es ist ein Land voll träumerischem Trug....'" Gladt has photographs of the house and room where Lenau lived in the United States, which seem quite nice.

23. *AJR*, p. 358. On the tradition of the absence of songbirds, see Brenner, *Reisen in die Neue Welt*, pp. 325–27 and n. 240.

24. Gerbi, *The Dispute of the New World*, pp. 160–65.

25. Briggs, "Keats, Robertson, and That Most Hateful Land," p. 184; Honour, *The New Golden Land*, p. 190.

26. Weber, *America in Imaginative German Literature*, p. 116.

27. Lange, *Briefe aus Amerika von neuester Zeit*, p. 71; again they are mockingbirds.

28. Grisson, *Beiträge zur Charakteristik der Vereinigten Staaten von Nordamerika*, p. 12.

29. Ashliman, "The American West in Nineteenth-Century German Literature," p. 85, remarks that *Der Amerika-Müde* follows *Martin Chuzzlewit* "much too closely to be coincidental."

30. Compare *A-M*, 288–92, with Sealsfield, *Sämtliche Werke*, ed. Arndt, 10: 63–72. Kürnberger seems to have believed that Sealsfield had also invented his America "aus dem Tintenfaß einer deutschen Studierstube": (*LH*, 2:511).

31. *Memoiren von Lorenz da Ponte von Ceneda. Von ihm selbst in New-York herausgegeben* (Stuttgart: Franck, 1847). See my essay, "The Lorenzo Da Ponte Episode in Kürnberger's *Der Amerika-Müde*."

32. Kürnberger, *Der Amerikamüde*, ed. Berger, pp. 565, 572.

33. See, e.g., Rüdiger Steinlein, "Ferdinand Kürnbergers 'Der Amerikamüde.' Ein 'amerikanisches Kulturbild' als Entwurf einer negativen Utopie," in Bauschinger et al., eds., *Amerika in der deutschen Literatur*, pp. 154–77. Steinlein seems to draw most of his knowledge of America from the writings of Marx and Engels.

34. Lang, "Ferdinand Kürnberger One Hundred Years Later," p. 54.

35. Lengauer, *Ästhetik und liberale Opposition*, p. 235.

36. Stenger, "Ferdinand Kürnberger," p. 183. Lengauer, *Ästhetik und liberale Opposition*, pp. 32–33, points out that the increasingly conservative Kraus came to distance himself from the antifeudal and anticlerical Kürnberger.

37. Kürnberger, *Feuilletons*, p. 7; Kühnel, *Ferdinand Kürnberger als Literaturtheoretiker*, pp. 1–2.

38. Gottfried Keller to Kürnberger, January 3, 1877, in Keller, *Leben, Briefe und Tagebücher*, 3:204–5; see Kühnel, *Ferdinand Kürnberger als Literaturtheoretiker*, pp. 105–8.

39. Kühnel, *Ferdinand Kürnberger als Literaturtheoretiker*, pp. 34, 117–18, 123.

40. For a sound account, see Müller, "Ferdinand Kürnbergers Siegelringe."

41. Bailey, "Ferdinand Kürnberger, Friedrich Schlögl and the Feuilleton," p. 160.

42. Müller, "Ferdinand Kürnbergers Siegelringe," p. 344.
43. Lang, "Ferdinand Kürnberger One Hundred Years Later," p. 65. Lang's note gives no support for this statement, only the observation that some of Kürnberger's best friends were Jews (p. 69, n. 36).
44. See Kühnel, *Ferdinand Kürnberger als Literaturtheoretiker*, pp. 115–16.
45. Ibid., p. 57.
46. For comments on both the *Judenschloß* review and the essay on Grillparzer's funeral, see Scheichl, "Franz Grillparzer zwischen Judenfeindschaft und Josephinismus," pp. 133–34.
47. Kürnberger, *Novellen*, pp. 221–56; republished in Brandstetter, ed., *Österreichische Erzählungen des 19. Jahrhunderts*. See also Kürnberger, *Feuilletons*, p. 181.
48. Kürnberger, *Das Schloß der Frevel*, prefatory note.
49. Zeisig, [review of *Der Amerika-Müde*], reprinted in Estermann, ed., *Literaturkritik*, 4:371.
50. Matthias, *Die Kehrseite der USA*, p. 169.
51. The novel was originally published in the newspaper, Rudolf Lexow's *New Yorker Criminal Zeitung und Belletristisches Journal*, from March to September 1862 and pirated in Bromberg in Germany the same year. Cited here (as *AA*) will be the U.S. book edition. Almost everything known about Solger is derived from an essay, originally of 1866, by his friend Friedrich Kapp, "Reinhold Solger."
52. Solger, "Aus Hanns von Katzenfingen."
53. Kapp, "Reinhold Solger," 1:367.
54. Ibid., 1:373. A detailed analysis of the German American spirit of this address is given by Schuchalter, "Reinhard Solger's *Bildungsreise*," pp. 16–23. On the magnitude of the Schiller celebration in the United States, see my essay, "The Schiller Centennial," pp. 5–6. Solger's Schiller poem, along with a contemporary English translation, is reproduced in Dickie, "Reinhold Solger," pp. 64–65.
55. According to Dickie, "Reinhold Solger," p. 35, it was published by Steiger in New York in 1860.
56. Kapp, "Reinhold Solger," 1:380.
57. Dickie, "Reinhold Solger," pp. 18, 39.
58. Denkler, "Die Schule des Kapitalismus," p. 120.
59. Schuchalter, "Reinhold Solger's *Bildungsreise*," pp. 43, 45.

# Chapter 10

1. Augstein, "Weiter Weg zu Winnetou," p. 130.
2. Baring-Gould, *The Annotated Sherlock Holmes*, 1:34, citing James Montgomery. For a comparison, see Volker Neuhaus, "Old Shatterhand und Sherlock Holmes," in Arnold, ed., *Karl May*, pp. 146–57. Like Conan Doyle, May became interested in spiritism for a time; see Ueding and Tschapke, eds., *Karl-May-Handbuch*, p. 100.

3. Schmiedt, *Karl May*, p. 202. The estimate is repeated in Ueding and Tschapke, eds., *Karl-May-Handbuch*, p. 166, in a passage that offers some analysis of his style. Whether "das nüchterne präzise Papierdeutsch" ought to remind us of Kafka (p. 190) is another question.

4. May, *Mein Leben und Streben*, p. 228.

5. Cracroft, "The American West of Karl May" (1963), p. 125.

6. Billington, *Land of Savagery, Land of Promise*, pp. 110–24.

7. Rossbacher, *Lederstrumpf in Deutschland*, p. 52.

8. On the importance of Indian games in German children's play, see Ashliman, "The American West in Nineteenth-Century German Literature," pp. 9–10.

9. Lowsky, *Karl May*, pp. 138, xi; Augstein, "Weiter Weg zu Winnetou," p. 140. Some twentieth-century, prewar figures for individual texts are given by Richards, *The German Bestseller in the 20th Century*, pp. 184–87.

10. Schmidt, "Vom neuen Grossmystiker," p. 100. Berman, "Orientalismus, Kolonialismus und Moderne," p. 95, n. 92, tells of having met two Brazilians who could recite all of Halef's names in Portuguese.

11. See Heinemann, ed., *Über Karl May*.

12. Bröning, *Die Reiseerzählungen Karl Mays*, pp. 12–13.

13. May, *Mein Leben und Streben*, pp. 212, 121, 92.

14. Franz Kandolf, "Der werdende Winnetou," in *OS*, 3:A32. The philological problems are unmanageable for anyone but the deep specialist. I have opted for the reprints of the original editions in the *Freiburger Erstausgaben*, ed. Schmid (see bibliography).

15. Bloch, "Die Silberbüchse Winnetous" (1929).

16. This position is adumbrated by today's outstanding student of the nineteenth-century German novel, Steinecke, in *Romanpoetik von Goethe bis Thomas Mann*, pp. 143–45.

17. Heermann, *Der Mann, der Old Shatterhand war*, p. 318; see the review by Helmut Schmiedt in *Jahrbuch der Karl-May-Gesellschaft* (1990): 330–31.

18. Heinemann, ed., *Über Karl May*, pp. 22, 45, 50, 51, 56, 61.

19. Ibid., p. 60.

20. Ibid., p. 80.

21. Ibid., p. 88. This canard was naturally repeated by Schmidt, "Vom neuen Grossmystiker," p. 101.

22. May, *Mein Leben und Streben*, pp. 144–45.

23. Steinbrink, *Abenteuerliteratur des 19. Jahrhunderts*, p. 218.

24. May, *Mein Leben und Streben*, p. 300; *AuD I*: N2.

25. See Ueding and Tschapke, eds., *Karl-May-Handbuch*, pp. 301–8; Berman, "Orientalismus, Kolonialismus und Moderne," pp. 125–30. Berman finds the Near Eastern novels, written before the journey, totally conformed to the colonialist discourse in Germany of the time and to the European dismantlement of the Ottoman Empire.

26. Mosse, "Was die Deutschen wirklich lasen," p. 104. Mosse's carefully balanced judgment in this matter interestingly ascribes liberal tolerance to all the subliterary writers of this period, including May: "Die Trivialliteratur

dieser Ära ist überhaupt Ausdruck eines unveränderten Liberalismus, und zwar nicht nur in ihrer Arbeitsethik, sondern auch in ihrem Eintreten für Toleranz und Menschenwürde. Eine Welt, in der Schönheit und Harmonie herrschen soll, kann weder auf Rassenhaß noch auf religiöser Heuchelei oder Klassengebundenheit beruhen" (pp. 112–13).

27. Lowsky, *Karl May*, pp. 86–87.

28. Eckehard Koch, ". . . die Farbe der Haut macht keinen Unterschied. Betrachtungen zum angeblichen Rassisten Karl May," in Ilmer and Lorenz, eds., *Exemplarisches zu Karl May*, p. 108. Dueling with quotations does not get us any further in this matter; the problem would have to be examined in the total historical and sociological context.

29. Lowsky, *Karl May*, p. 87.

30. Schmiedt, *Karl May*, pp. 147–48.

31. Examples cited in Ueding and Tschapke, eds., *Karl-May-Handbuch*, pp. 260, 264, 368, 499, 529. On the Near Eastern novels, see Berman, "Orientalismus, Kolonialismus und Moderne," pp. 97–98.

32. Stolte, "Auf den Spuren Nathans des Weisen."

33. Jeglin, "Karl May und der antisemitische Zeitgeist," p. 128, observes that, given the environment and May's defective education, it is noteworthy that his record is not worse.

34. Claus Roxin, "'Winnetou' im Widerstreit von Ideologie und Ideologiekritik," in Sudhoff and Vollmer, eds., *Karl Mays "Winnetou,"* p. 294.

35. Krobb, *Die schöne Jüdin*, pp. 191–92 and n. 125.

36. Stolte, "Auf den Spuren Nathans des Weisen," p. 18. The episode is also discussed by Heermann, *Der Mann, der Old Shatterhand war*, p. 159.

37. In this scene, by the way, the Chinese are described much more pejoratively. It has several times been noted that the Chinese lie outside May's universe of tolerance, a prejudice that he may have picked up from some American sources.

38. Hansotto Hatzig, cited in Heermann, ed., *Old Shatterhand läßt grüßen*, pp. 168–69.

39. Schmiedt, *Karl May*, pp. 124–30.

40. Frigge, *Das erwartbare Abenteuer*, p. 319.

41. See "Karl der Deutsche," p. 59; on the origin of the journal, *Schacht und Hütte*, one of his projects with the subliterary publisher Heinrich Gotthold Münchmeyer, see Ueding and Tschapke, eds., *Karl-May-Handbuch*, pp. 89–90.

42. May, *Mein Leben und Streben*, p. 46.

43. See Cracroft, "The American West of Karl May" (1967), p. 258.

44. This is the tone of Wohlgschaft's monumental, appropriately named *Große Karl May Biographie*. Wohlgschaft is a Roman Catholic priest whose intensely Christian view of May, which has received the explicit imprimatur of the Karl-May-Gesellschaft, is, in my view, correct, but I put a less positive valuation on it.

45. There is an essay by E. A. Schmid, originally written in 1928, on Schneider and his illustrations in the appendix to the reprint of *Winnetou IV*. While they seem to reinforce May's evangelistic aspect, it is interesting that Schnei-

der himself is said to have been antireligious: Stolte, "Auf den Spuren Nathans des Weisen," p. 27. The illustrations have also been interpreted as homoerotic, as May's figures have been; see Berman, "Orientalismus, Kolonialismus und Moderne," pp. 41–47.

46. Wohlgschaft, *Große Karl May Biographie*, p. 585.

47. *MB*, 3:209–34. See Ostwald, "Friedrich Gerstäckers ethnographischen Realien," p. 22.

48. For comparisons, see Jürgen Wehnert, "... *und ich das einzige lebende Wesen in dieser Wildnis*. Zur Innovation des Ich-Helden bei Karl May," in Arnold, ed., *Karl May*, pp. 5–38; Graf, "'Habe gedacht, Alles Schwindel!'"

49. Christoph F. Lorenz, "Von der Vaterfigur zum Indianermythos: Charles Sealsfields Tokeah als literarischer Ahnherr von Karl Mays Winnetou," in Brancaforte, ed., *The Life and Works of Charles Sealsfield*, pp. 291–302. Without giving a reason, Lorenz refers to the English version of the novel, whereas May more probably would have had read the German version, as he does not seem to have known English well. The endnotes to Lorenz's article have no connection to the text and look as though they belong to a different paper altogether.

50. Schüppen, *Charles Sealsfield, Karl Postl*, pp. 177–78. In his research report, "Charles Sealsfield," p. 318, Schüppen found that Sealsfield's influence on May is not yet well understood.

51. On his literary reading, see Schmiedt, *Karl May*, pp. 52–61.

52. Cracroft, "The American West of Karl May" (1963), pp. 51–62.

53. Wohlgschaft, *Große Karl May Biographie*, p. 55, thinks it probable that May read *The Count of Monte Cristo* in his youth. Wohlgschaft mentions the names of many authors in May's reading experience without weighing their particular influence.

## Chapter 11

1. Wohlgschaft, *Große Karl May Biographie*, pp. 520–21.

2. Andreas Graf, "Winnetou im *Criminalroman*. Aspekte zeitgenössischer Aktualität in Karl Mays frühem Roman 'Auf der See gefangen,'" in Arnold, ed., *Karl May*, p. 39. A pirated American translation of *Waldröschen*, of which I caught sight in the Karl May Museum in Radebeul, I have not been able to identify further.

3. May, *Der Pfahlmann*, ed. Russum, in which there is not one single word about the author or the provenance of the text, and an abridgment from *Winnetou III*: May, *Winnetou*, ed. Sharp and Donhauser.

4. Morton, "Tales of the Grand Teutons: Karl May among the Indians," *New York Times Book Review*, January 4, 1987, p. 15.

5. Schmiedt, *Karl May*, pp. 65–71; Ueding and Tschapke, eds., *Karl-May-Handbuch*, p. 646. If these figures are correct, he is certainly not the most translated author, being outstripped by Heine, for one.

6. Anon., "Karl der Deutsche," p. 73.

7. Noether, "As Others Saw Us," p. 123.
8. On Taggart, see Hoehn, ed., *Catholic Authors*, pp. 725–26.
9. *Winnetou, The Apache Knight; The Treasures of Nugget Mountain*. On the first of these, Benziger is identified as "Printers to the Holy Apostolic See." The second volume is subtitled: *Adapted for Our Boys and Girls from C. May*; there is no mention of May in the first. For first calling my attention to these books I am obliged to Dr. René Wagner, director of the Karl May Museum in Radebeul. A further effort by Taggart, which I have not seen, *Jack Hildreth on the Nile* (New York: Benziger, 1900), is also identified as adapted from May.
10. May, *Winnetou; In the Desert; Ardistan and Djinnistan* (all in *Collected Works*, ed. Haeberle). For information about this project I am grateful to Dr. Haeberle.
11. Melanie Axel-Lute, *Library Journal* 102 (1977): 2386.
12. *Choice* 15 (1978): 404.
13. *Publishers Weekly* 212, no. 12 (September 19, 1977): 142.
14. Walter Laqueur, "Cowboys for the Kaiser," *New York Times Book Review*, January 29, 1978, p. 7.
15. Heinemann, *Über Karl May*, pp. 51, 25.
16. Hemingway, *Islands in the Stream*, p. 424.
17. Cody, *Iron Eyes*, pp. 53, 215.
18. Stadler, "Karl May: The Wild West under the German Umlaut," p. 295.
19. The comment is taken from Bernd Deck, "Ein Indianer an der Schreibmaschine," *Bunte Wochen Zeitung*, no. 28 (July 14–20, 1979): 4. For this reference I am grateful to Erich Heinemann. Cody's remark is no longer contained in Heinemann's new edition, *Dichtung als Wünscherfüllung*.
20. *Der Schatz in Silbersee, Variety*, January 23, 1963, p. 6; *Winnetou I*, December 25, 1963, p. 6; *Old Shatterhand*, July 22, 1964, p. 6; *Winnetou II*, November 4, 1964, p. 18; *Winnetou III*, January 19, 1966, pp. 6, 28; *Winnetou und sein Freund Old Firehand*, April 5, 1967, p. 6.
21. Jay Robert Nash and Stanley Ralph Ross, *Motion Picture Guide, 1927–1983* (Chicago: Cinebooks, 1985–87), 8:3535; 5:1615; 6:2239. The other films noted briefly are *Winnetou I* (*Apache Gold*, 1965) and *Winnetou III* (*Desperado Trail*, 1965), 1:82–83; 2:628.
22. *New York Times*, June 6, 1968, p. 54.
23. *Films in Review* 18 (1967): 60, 190.
24. Cracroft, "The American West of Karl May" (1963); Berman, "Orientalismus, Kolonialismus und Moderne," pp. 13–130.
25. A list, not perfectly accurate and somewhat out of date, will be found in Cook, "Germany's Wild West Author," p. 70.
26. Billington, *Land of Savagery, Land of Promise*, p. 318.
27. Augstein, "Weiter Weg zu Winnetou," p. 135.
28. Mann, "Karl May," pp. 393, 400.
29. Karl Kraus, *Die Dritte Walpurgnisnacht* (Munich: Kösel, 1967), p. 42.
30. E.g., Ruland, *America in Modern European Literature*, p. 20.
31. William H. Gass, *The Tunnel* (New York: Knopf, 1995), p. 299.
32. *Hitler's Secret Conversations: His Private Thoughts and Plans in His Own*

*Words, 1941–1944,* ed. H. R. Trevor-Roper (New York: Farrar, Straus and Young, 1953), p. 257. The passage is dated February 17, 1942. On the Hitler issue, see Schmiedt, *Karl May,* p. 243; Scholdt, "Hitler, Karl May und die Emigranten," pp. 60–91; Heinemann, ed., *Über Karl May,* pp. 54–55.

33. John Toland, *Adolf Hitler* (New York: Doubleday, 1976), pp. 317, 604.

34. Tomás Borge, *The Patient Impatience. From Boyhood to Guerilla: A Personal Narrative of Nicaragua's Struggle for Liberation* (Willimantic: Curbstone, 1992), pp. 10–11, 32. See the review by Stephen Kinzer in *New York Review of Books,* December 3, 1993, pp. 17–18. Borge's information about May is grossly erroneous.

35. E.g., Kremer, "Edle Wilde im 'Dritten Reich'?," p. 450.

36. Hohendahl, "Von der Rothaut zum Edelmenschen," pp. 230, 235.

37. Schmidt, "Old Shatterhand und die Seinen. Eine Darstellung vom Leben und Werk KARL MAY's," *Das essayistische Werk,* 4:154.

38. Billington, *Land of Savagery, Land of Promise,* p. 107.

39. See David Rothel, *Who Was That Masked Man? The Story of the Lone Ranger* (South Brunswick, N.J.: Barnes; London: Yoseloff, 1976).

40. Fran Striker, *The Lone Ranger and the Mystery Ranch* (New York: Grosset and Dunlap, 1938), p. 37.

41. Rothel, *Who Was That Masked Man?,* p. 86.

42. Read, "Karl May: Germany's James Fenimore Cooper," p. 6.

43. Mann, "Karl May," p. 397.

44. Gerber, "Old Shatterhand Rides Again!," pp. 243–44. On the situation in the GDR see also Ueding and Tschapke, eds., *Karl-May-Handbuch,* pp. 644–45.

45. Eggebrecht, *Sinnlichkeit und Abenteuer.*

46. See also Ueding and Tschapke, eds., *Karl-May-Handbuch,* p. 205.

47. Fraenkel, *Amerika im Spiegel des deutschen politischen Denkens,* p. 119.

48. Goebel, *Der Kampf um deutsche Kultur in Amerika,* p. 109.

49. Schmiedt, *Karl May,* pp. 80, 85, 128–30, 134.

50. "Dr." Karl May, "Freuden und Leiden eines Vielgelesenen," in Wollschläger, *Karl May. Eine philologische Streitschrift,* p. 23.

51. See Hennigsen, *Der Fall Amerika,* p. 82.

52. Cracroft, "The American West of Karl May" (1963), p. 2, n. 2.

## Outlook

1. Mikoletzky, *Die deutsche Amerika-Auswanderung,* pp. 234, 312–14, 36, 50.

2. See Graevert, *Otto Ruppius und der Amerikaroman;* Hering, "Otto Ruppius, der Amerikafahrer."

3. See Woodson, *American Negro Slavery,* pp. 249–92.

4. See Oppel, "Die deutsche Siedlung in Louisiana."

5. For a quite dismissive critique, see Demetz, *Formen des Realismus,* pp. 100–12. A more positive view is taken by Aust, *Theodor Fontane: "Verklärung,"* pp. 189–228. Aust argues that the American part of the novel should not be judged on realistic principles. See also Keune, "Das Amerikabild in Fontanes

Romanwerk." The occasional comparisons of Fontane with Sealsfield suggested by Schüppen, *Paradigmawechsel*, are thin and speculative.

6. Ziegelschmidt, "Truth and Fiction and Mennonites."

7. See my comments on Raabe's differentiated view of America in *Wilhelm Raabe: The Fiction of the Alternative Community*, p. 95.

8. Auerbach, *Das Landhaus am Rhein*, part II, book 8, chaps. 1, 6, 8; part III, book 15.

9. See Schmitt, *Herder und Amerika*, pp. 148–77; see also Victory, *Benjamin Franklin and Germany*, pp. 117–19, on Herder; pp. 122–24, on Auerbach.

10. Zwick, *Berthold Auerbachs sozialpolitischer und ethischer Liberalismus*, p. 119. This was originally a Columbia University dissertation.

11. For observations on several, see my article, "Germans Assessing America."

12. On Schoppe, see Schleucher, *Das Leben der Amalie Schoppe und Johanna Schopenhauer*; on Anneke, *Die gebrochenen Ketten: Erzählungen und Reden (1861–1873)*, ed. Wagner; Wallach, "Women of German-American Fiction"; Stuecher, *Twice Removed*, pp. 115–65; and Roethke, "M. F. Anneke"; on Assing, Felden, *Frauen Reisen*, pp. 105–32, with a list of Assing's reports from the United States, pp. 141–54; also Felden, "Ottilie Assing's View of America." As noted earlier, some of the reports are reproduced in Wagner, ed., *Was die Deutschen aus Amerika berichteten*, where she is misspelled "Assig."

13. Gerstner, *Die Innern Communicationen*, p. v.

14. Lamprecht, *Americana*, pp. 44, 89.

15. Wolzogen, *Der Dichter in Dollarica*, pp. 44, 59–60, 102, 105, 23–24 (emphasis in original), 270. In 1922 Wolzogen expressed his bewilderment at Fontane's tolerance in racial matters. Fontane's biographer speaks in this connection of the "zum borrnierten Fanatiker gewordene *Ernst v. Wolzogen*" (Reuter, *Fontane*, 2:743).

16. Gillhoff, *Jörnjakob Swehn der Amerikafahrer*.

17. Reppmann, "Jürnjakob Swehn Symposium."

18. Hammond, *American Paradise*, p. 104.

19. See Fraenkel, "Das deutsche Wilsonbild."

20. On Kisch, see Hammond, *American Paradise*; Markham, *Writers, Women, and Afro-Americans*, pp. 236–49; Ott, *Amerika ist anders*, pp. 194–242.

21. Kerr, *Newyork und London*, pp. 47, 88. On Kerr see Hammond, *American Paradise*, pp. 83–87, Ian C. Loram, "Alfred Kerr's America," in Ritter, ed., *Deutschlands literarisches Amerikabild*, pp. 468–75, and Ott, *Amerika ist anders*, pp. 169–91.

22. Gatzke, *Germany and the United States*, p. 96.

23. Hausmann, *Kleine Liebe zu Amerika*, pp. 102–21. On Hausmann's racism, see Hammond, *American Paradise*, p. 91.

24. See Diamond, *The Nazi Movement in the United States*. On Ross's connection to the Bund, see pp. 224–25.

25. Ross, *Amerikas Schicksalstunde*, pp. 27, 92, 221; *Unser Amerika*, pp. 15, 26, 173, 215–32, 284–88, 300.

26. Beck, "Colin Ross in South America" provides some useful information

on him but, as the title indicates, deals with a different matter. For the possibility of an influence on Ezra Pound, see Symington, "Eine deutsch-amerikanische literarische Freundschaft," p. 19, and Hans Galinsky, "Wechselbeziehungen zwischen der deutschen und der amerikanischen Literatur mit Einschluß ihrer 'Bilder vom anderen Volk,'" in Krampikowski, ed., *Amerikanisches Deutschlandbild und deutsches Amerikabild*, pp. 56–57.

27. See Pfanner, *Exile in New York*, p. 85, and Ott, *Amerika ist anders*, pp. 278–79.

28. Gong, ed., *Interview mit Amerika*, p. 163.

29. See Lyon, *Bertolt Brecht in America*, and Thomas O. Brandt, "Das Amerikabild Brechts," in Ritter, ed., *Deutschlands literarisches Amerikabild*, pp. 451–67; on Brecht's preexile conceptions, see Ruland, *America in Modern European Literature*, pp. 115–36.

30. Gong, ed., *Interview mit Amerika*, pp. 249, 162.

31. On Graf, see Pfanner, *Exile in New York*, pp. 86–90.

32. Spiel, *Lisas Zimmer*, pp. 128, 130.

33. Carl Zuckmayer, "Amerika ist anders," in Gong, ed., *Interview mit Amerika*, pp. 381–412 (first published in the *Neue Schweizer Rundschau* in 1948). See Siegfried Mews, "From Karl May to Horace A. W. Tabor: Carl Zuckmayer's View of America," in Ritter, ed., *Deutschlands literarisches Amerikabild*, pp. 476–94.

34. See Schwarz, "Urzidil und Amerika," esp. nn. 6 and 19. Schwarz indicates that the novel exhibits more balance and sympathy than Urzidil's novellas with American themes, which are more anti-American in tone.

35. Urzidil, *Das Große Hallelujah*, p. 374.

36. An almost contemptuous view of the program as a project of careerist, unworldly humanists is given by Robin, *The Barbed-Wire College*. See also Gansberg, *Stalag: U.S.A.* The most important study from the German perspective continues to be Wehdeking, *Der Nullpunkt*. Neither Robin nor Gansberg seems to have a good command of German. Neither cites Wehdeking; Gansberg cites no German-language sources, Robin very few. A more integrated view of this topic would be desirable.

37. For an overview, see Richter with Mannzen, eds., *Almanach der Gruppe 47*, and Schwab-Felisch, ed., *Der Ruf*. For an account of the conflict less friendly to the group than most, see Mandel, *Group 47*, pp. 1–31.

38. For samples of the views of Richter and Andersch, see Gong, ed., *Interview mit Amerika*, pp. 351–61.

39. Eberle, *Die Reise nach Amerika*, p. 43.

40. Jungk, *Die Zukunft hat schon begonnen*, p. 311. Other examples in this genre are the conservative if not to say aristocratic admonitions of von Borch, *Amerika. Die unfertige Gesellschaft*, and the more tolerant and differentiated observations of Harpprecht, *Der fremde Freund*. Borch was U.S. correspondent of *Die Welt* and Harpprecht of German television.

41. "Unsere Arroganz gegenüber Amerika," in *Max Frisch in Amerika*, ed. Hage, pp. 5–14 (originally in the *Neue Schweizer Rundschau* in 1953).

42. On Koeppen, see Manfred Koch, "Wolfgang Koeppens 'Amerikafahrt,'"

in Ritter, ed., *Deutschlands literarisches Amerikabild*, pp. 495–24; Ott, *Amerika ist anders*, pp. 315–55.

43. Ott, *Amerika ist anders*, p. 379.

44. See the interview by Osterle, "Ansichten von Amerika," republished in Osterle, ed., *Bilder von Amerika: Gespräche mit Schriftstellern*, pp. 137–56. An extremely critical view of Kunert's perceptions as distorted through an irrelevant lens of East German preoccupations is given by Futterknecht, "Noch einmal: Der andere Planet."

45. See Ott, *Amerika ist anders*, pp. 127–60, and Fingerhut, "Erlebtes und Erlesenes."

46. Ruland, *America in Modern European Literature*, p. 110.

47. Sammons, *Literary Sociology and Practical Criticism*, pp. 138–39.

48. See Durzak, *Das Amerika-Bild in der deutschen Gegenwartsliteratur*, pp. 180–84, Nägele, "Die vermittelte Welt," and, more briefly, "Amerika als Fiktion und Wirklichkeit."

49. Gruber, *Einmal Amerika und zurück*, pp. 35, 60.

50. There is, of course, a large body of scholarly literature on Johnson and *Jahrestage*. See Krätzer, *Studien zum Amerikabild*, because of her comparative dimension, even though her study was written before Johnson's more problematic fourth volume appeared; see also Krätzer, "To Want the Unthinkable: Uwe Johnson's *Anniversaries*," in Osterle, ed., *Amerika! New Images in German Literature*, pp. 149–73; Lennox, "Die *New York Times* in Johnsons *Jahrestagen*"; and Lennox, "History in Uwe Johnson's *Jahrestage*."

51. Federspiel, *Museum des Hasses*, pp. 117, 32.

52. For an overview of German anti-Americanism in the twentieth century, see Ott, *Amerika ist anders*, pp. 95–102.

53. Ekkehart Krippendorf, "Die westdeutsche Linke und ihr Bild von den USA," in Adams and Krakau, eds., *Deutschland und Amerika*, pp. 39–46.

54. See David Large, "America in the Consciousness of the Germans," in Krampikowski, ed., *Amerikanisches Deutschlandbild und deutsches Amerikabild*, p. 206.

55. On Matthias, see my lecture at the 1995 congress of the Internationale Vereinigung für Germanische Sprach- und Literaturwissenschaft, "Zu den Grundlagen des Antiamerikanismus in der deutschen Literatur," esp. pp. 34–40. Matthias, has, of course, been much criticized by competent observers. See Hennigsen, *Der Fall Amerika*, pp. 32–36; Christoph Eykman, "Zwischen Zerrbild, Schreckbild und Idealbild: Die Auseinandersetzung mit dem Asylland im Exilschriftum," in Pfanner, ed., *Kulturelle Wechselbeziehungen im Exil*, pp. 35–37; Diner, *Verkehrte Welten*, pp. 21–29; Ott, *Amerika ist anders*, p. 306.

56. Hochhuth, *Guerillas*, pp. 7, 12. See Hennigsen, *Der Fall Amerika*, 32–33.

57. Winter, *Ami go home* and *Gottes eigenes Land?* On Winter, see my Harold Jantz Memorial Lecture, "The German Image of America," pp. 12–13. Another recent work in this spirit is Riedl, *Leere Räume, laute Stimmen*.

58. Ott, *Amerika ist anders*, pp. 25, 47.

59. Markham, *Workers, Women, and Afro-Americans*, p. 2.

# Bibliography

Adams, Willi Paul, and Knud Krakau, eds. *Deutschland und Amerika. Perzeption und historische Realität*. Berlin: Colloquium, 1985.
Amlinger, Lore, ed. *Germany and the United States: Changing Perceptions—Danger and Hope. The University of Virginia and Roanoke College Symposia 1985*. Stuttgart: Heinz, 1987.
Andersch, Alfred. *Die Kirschen der Freiheit. Ein Bericht*. Frankfurt am Main: Frankfurter Verlagsanstalt, 1952.
———. *Mein Verschwinden in Providence. Neun neue Erzählungen*. Zurich: Diogenes, 1971.
Anneke, Mathilde Franziska. *Die gebrochenen Ketten: Erzählungen, Reportagen und Reden (1861–1873)*. Edited by Maria Wagner. Stuttgart: Heinz, 1983.
    Roethke, Gisela. "M. F. Anneke: Eine Vorkämpferin für Frauenrechte in Deutschland und in den Vereinigten Staaten." *Yearbook of German-American Studies* 28 (1993): 33–51.
    See also Wallach, "Women of German-American Fiction" under Talvj.
Armand. *See* Strubberg, Friedrich Armand.
Ashliman, D. L. "The American West in Nineteenth-Century German Literature." Diss., Rutgers University, 1969.
Assion, Peter. "Fremdheitserwartung und Fremdheitserfahrung bei den deutschen Amerikaauswanderern im 19. Jahrhundert." In *Kulturkontakt, Kulturkonflikt: zur Erfahrung des Fremden*, edited by Ina-Maria Greverus, 1:157–67. Frankfurt am Main: Institut für Kulturanthropologie und Europäische Ethnologie, 1988.
Auerbach, Berthold. *Das Landhaus am Rhein*. In Auerbach, *Schriften*, 2nd ser. Stuttgart: Cotta, 1871.
    Zwick, M. I. *Berthold Auerbachs sozialpolitischer und ethischer Liberalismus. Nach seinen Schriften dargestellt*. Stuttgart: Kohlhammer, 1933.
Augustin, Siegfried, and Walter Henle, eds. *Vom Old Shatterhand zum Sherlock Holmes*. Munich: Ronacher, 1986.
Bade, Klaus J. "German Emigration to the United States and Continental Immigration to Germany in the Late Nineteenth and Early Twentieth Centuries." In *Labor Migration in the Atlantic Economies: The European and North American Working Classes during the Period of Industrialization*, edited by Dirk Hoerder, pp. 117–42. Westport, Conn.: Greenwood Press, 1985.
———. "Trends and Issues of Historical Migration Research in the Federal Republic of Germany." *Migration* 6 (1989): 7–28.
Baring-Gould, William S. *The Annotated Sherlock Holmes*. New York: Potter, 1967.
Bauschinger, Sigrid, Horst Denkler, and Wilfried Malsch, eds. *Amerika in der deutschen Literatur. Neue Welt—Nordamerika—USA*. Stuttgart: Reclam, 1975.

Beck, Earl R. *Germany Rediscovers America.* Tallahassee: Florida State University Press, 1968.
Behrmann, Günter C. "Antiamerikanismus in der Bundesrepublik: 1966–1984." *Amerikastudien/American Studies* 31 (1986): 341–52.
———. "Geschichte und aktuelle Struktur des Antiamerikanismus." *Politik und Zeitgeschichte.* Beilage zum *Das Parlament* B 29–30 (1989): 3–19.
Bemis, Samuel Flagg. *John Quincy Adams and the Union.* New York: Knopf, 1956.
Berg, Peter. *Deutschland und Amerika 1918–1929. Über das deutsche Amerikabild der zwanziger Jahre.* Lübeck: Matthiesen, 1963.
Biesele, Rudolph Leopold. *The History of the German Settlements in Texas, 1831–1861.* Austin: von Boeckmann-Jones, 1930.
Billington, Ray Allen. *Land of Savagery, Land of Promise: The European Image of the American Frontier.* New York: Norton, 1981.
———. *The Protestant Crusade, 1800–1860: A Study of the Origins of American Nativism.* Gloucester, Mass.: Peter Smith, 1963.
Boerner, Peter. "America in European Eyes—An Amalgamation of Images." *Ethnic Literatures since 1776: The Many Voices of America. Proceedings of the Comparative Literature Symposium* 9, pt. 2 (1978): 607–20.
———. "Amerikabilder der europäischen Literatur: Wunschprojektion und Kritik." *Amerikastudien/American Studies* 23 (1978): 40–50.
———. "Das Bild vom anderen Land als Gegenstand literarischer Forschung." *Sprache im technischen Zeitalter* 56 (1975): 313–21.
———. "Utopia in der Neuen Welt. Von europäischen Träumen zum American Dream." In *Utopieforschung: Interdisziplinäre Studien zur neuzeitlichen Utopie,* edited by Wilhelm Vosskamp, 2:358–74. Stuttgart: Metzler, 1982.
Borch, Herbert von. *Amerika. Die unfertige Gesellschaft.* Munich: Piper, 1961.
Brecht, Bertolt. *Arbeitsjournal.* 3 vols. Edited by Werner Hecht. Frankfurt am Main: Suhrkamp, 1973.
  Lyon, James K. *Bertolt Brecht in America.* Princeton: Princeton University Press, 1980.
Brenner, Peter J. *Der Reisebericht in der deutschen Literatur. Ein Forschungsüberblick als Vorstudie zu einer Gattungsgeschichte.* Tübingen: Niemeyer, 1990.
———. *Reisen in die Neue Welt. Die Erfahrung Nordamerikas in deutschen Reise- und Auswandererberichten des 19. Jahrhunderts.* Tübingen: Niemeyer, 1991.
———, ed. *Der Reisebericht. Die Entwicklung einer Gattung in der deutschen Literatur.* Frankfurt am Main: Suhrkamp, 1989.
Briggs, Harold E. "Keats, Robertson, and *That Most Hateful Land.*" *PMLA* 59 (1944): 184–99.
Bülow, Dietrich von. *Der Freistaat von Nordamerika in seinem neuesten Zustand.* Berlin: Unger, 1797.
Campbell, James L., Sr. *Edward Bulwer-Lytton.* Boston: Twayne, 1986.
Cazden, Robert E. *A Social History of the German Book Trade in America to the Civil War.* Columbia, S. C.: Camden House, 1984.
Christian, Curt, ed. *Bernard Bolzano. Leben und Wirkung.* Österreichische Akademie der Wissenschaften Philosophisch-historische Klasse Sitzungs-

berichte, vol. 391. Vienna: Österreichische Akademie der Wissenschaften, 1981.
Cody, Iron Eyes, as told to Collin Perry. *Iron Eyes: My Life as a Hollywood Indian*. New York: Everest House, 1982.
Crichton, Mary C. "'And No Birds Sing': Lenau's Desolate *Urwald*." *Michigan Germanic Studies* 1 (1975): 152–64.
Dabney, Wendell P. *Cincinnati's Colored Citizens: Historical, Sociological and Biographical*. Cincinnati: Dabney, 1926.
Diamond, Sander A. *The Nazi Movement in the United States, 1924–1941*. Ithaca: Cornell University Press, 1974.
Diner, Dan. *Verkehrte Welten. Antiamerikanismus in Deutschland. Ein historischer Essay*. Frankfurt am Main: Eichborn, 1993.
Dippel, Horst. *Americana Germanica 1770–1800. Bibliographie deutscher Amerikaliteratur*. Stuttgart: Metzler, 1976.
———. *Germany and the American Revolution, 1770–1800: A Sociohistorical Investigation of Late Eighteenth-Century Political Thinking*. Translated by Bernhard A. Uhlendorf. Foreword by R. R. Palmer. Chapel Hill: University of North Carolina Press, 1977.
Doerry, Karl W. "Three Versions of America: Sealsfield, Gerstäcker, and May." *Yearbook of German-American Studies* 16 (1981): 39–49.
Durzak, Manfred. *Das Amerika-Bild in der deutschen Gegenwartsliteratur. Historische Voraussetzungen und aktuelle Beispiele*. Stuttgart: Kohlhammer, 1979.
———. "Perspektiven des Amerikabildes, historisch und gegenwärtig. Reisen in der Zeitmaschine." *Sprache im technischen Zeitalter* 56 (1975): 297–310.
Eberle, Josef. *Die Reise nach Amerika. Eindrücke Beobachtungen Erlebnisse*. Stuttgart: Turmhaus, 1949.
Eggebrecht, Harald. *Sinnlichkeit und Abenteuer. Die Entstehung des Abenteuerromans im 19. Jahrhundert*. Berlin: Guttandin und Hoppe, 1985.
Elliot, Wm. *Carolina Sports by Land and Water*. Charleston: Burges and James, 1846.
    Rubin, Louis B., Jr. "William Elliot Shoots a Bear." In Rubin, *William Elliot Shoots a Bear: Essays on the Southern Literary Imagination*, pp. 14–27. Baton Rouge: Louisiana State University Press, 1975.
Erhart, Walter. "Fremderfahrung und Ichkonstitution in Amerika-Bildern der deutschsprachigen Gegenwartsliteratur." *Orbis Litterarum* 49 (1994): 99–122.
Faulkner, William. *The Faulkner Reader: Selections from the Works of William Faulkner*. New York: Random House, 1954.
Federspiel, Jürg. *Museum des Hasses. Tage in Manhattan*. Munich: Piper, 1969.
Felden, Tamara. *Frauen Reisen. Zur literarischen Repräsentation weiblicher Geschlechterrollenerfahrung im 19. Jahrhundert*. Frankfurt am Main: Peter Lang, 1993.
———. "Ottilie Assing's View of America in the Context of Travel Literature by 19th-Century German Women." *German Quarterly* 65 (1992): 340–48.
Fingerhut, Karlheinz. "Erlebtes und Erlesenes—Arthur Holitschers und Franz Kafkas Amerika-Darstellungen. Zum Funktionsübergang von Reisebericht und Roman." *Diskussion Deutsch* 20 (1989): 337–55.

Flint, Timothy. *Biographical Memoir of Daniel Boone.* Edited by James K. Folsom. New Haven: College and University Press, 1967.

———. *Francis Berrian or the American Patriot.* Boston: Cumming, Hilliard, 1826.

———. "Jemima O'Keefy—A Sentimental Tale." *Western Monthly Review* 1 (1827): 384–93.

Fontane, Theodor. *Quitt.* Berlin: Hertz, 1891.

    Aust, Hugo. *Theodor Fontane: "Verklärung." Eine Untersuchung zum Ideengehalt seiner Werke.* Bonn: Bouvier, 1974.

    Demetz, Peter. *Formen des Realismus: Theodor Fontane. Kritische Untersuchungen.* Munich: Hanser, 1964.

    Keune, Manfred E. "Das Amerikabild in Fontanes Romanwerk." In Ritter, ed., *Deutschlands literarisches Amerikabild,* pp. 338–62.

    Loewen, Harry. "From Prussianism to Mennonitism: Reality and Ideals in Theodor Fontane's Novel 'Quitt.'" *Journal of German-American Studies* 15, no. 2 (June 1980): 25–38.

    Reuter, Hans-Heinrich. *Fontane.* Munich: Nymphenburger, 1968.

    Ziegelschmidt, A. J. F. "Truth and Fiction and Mennonites in the Second Part of Theodor Fontane's Novel 'Quitt': The Indian Territory." *Mennonite Quarterly Review* 16 (1942): 223–46.

    See also Schüppen, *Paradigmawechsel,* under Sealsfield, Charles.

Fraenkel, Ernst. *Amerika im Spiegel des deutschen politischen Denkens. Äußerungen deutscher Staatsmänner und Staatsdenker über Staat und Gesellschaft in den Vereinigten Staaten von Amerika.* Cologne: Westdeutscher Verlag, 1959.

———. "Das deutsche Wilsonbild." *Jahrbuch für Amerikastudien* 5 (1960): 66–120.

Franz, Eckhart G. *Das Amerikabild der deutschen Revolution von 1848/49. Zum Problem der Übertragungen gewachsener Verfassungsformen.* Heidelberg: Winter, 1958.

Frederickson, George M. *The Black Image in the White Mind: The Debate on Afro-American Character and Destiny, 1817–1914.* New York: Harper and Row, 1971.

Friesen, Gerhard K., and Walter Schatzberg, eds. *The German Contribution to the Building of the Americas: Studies in Honor of Karl J. R. Arndt.* Hanover, N. H.: University Press of New England for Clark University Press, 1977.

Frisch, Max. *Max Frisch in Amerika.* Edited by Volker Hage. Frankfurt am Main: Schöffling, 1995.

    See also Krätzer, *Studien zum Amerikabild.*

Galinsky, Hans K. "America's Image in German Literature: A Neglected Field of American-German Literary Relations in Critical Retrospect." *Comparative Literature Studies* 13 (1976): 165–92.

Ganilh, Anthony. *Mexico versus Texas, A Descriptive Novel, Most of the Characters of which Consist of Living Persons, by a Texian.* Philadelphia: Siegfried, 1838.

Gansberg, Judith M. *Stalag: U.S.A. The Remarkable Story of German POWs in America.* New York: Crowell, 1977.

Gaston, Edwin W., Jr. *The Early Novel of the Southwest.* Albuquerque: University of New Mexico Press, 1961.

Gatzke, Hans W. *Germany and the United States: A "Special Relationship"?* Cambridge, Mass.: Harvard University Press, 1980.
Genovese, Eugene D. *Roll, Jordan, Roll: The World the Slaves Made.* New York: Pantheon, 1974.
Gerbi, Antonello. *The Dispute of the New World: The History of a Polemic, 1750– 1800.* Revised and enlarged edition, translated by Jeremy Moyle. Pittsburgh: University of Pittsburgh Press, 1973.
Gerstäcker, Friedrich. *Das alte Haus.* Leipzig: Costenoble, 1857. Reprinted Braunschweig: Friedrich-Gerstäcker-Gesellschaft, 1989.
———. *Amerikanische Wald- und Strombilder.* Dresden and Leipzig: Arnold, 1849. Reprinted Braunschweig: Friedrich-Gerstäcker-Gesellschaft, [1980].
———. *Arbeiten für "Das Ausland."* Reihe Zeitschriftenveröffentlichungen Friedrich Gerstäckers, vol. 7. Braunschweig: Friedrich-Gerstäcker-Gesellschaft, 1994.
———. *Arbeiten für "Das Buch der Welt."* Reihe Zeitschriftenveröffentlichungen Friedrich Gerstäckers, vol. 6. Braunschweig: Friedrich-Gerstäcker-Gesellschaft, 1992.
———. *Arbeiten für die "Gartenlaube," Band I.* Reihe Zeitschriftenveröffentlichungen Friedrich Gerstäckers, vol. 3. Braunschweig: Friedrich-Gerstäcker-Gesellschaft, 1991.
———. *Arbeiten für das "Illustrirte Familienbuch," Band I.* Reihe Zeitschriftenveröffentlichungen Friedrich Gerstäckers, vol. 5. Braunschweig: Friedrich-Gerstäcker-Gesellschaft, 1992.
———. *Arbeiten für das "Pfennig-Magazin," Band I.* Reihe Zeitschriftenveröffentlichungen Friedrich Gerstäckers, vol. 4. Braunschweig: Friedrich-Gerstäcker-Gesellschaft, 1992.
———. *Aus meinem Tagebuch. Gesammelte Erzählungen.* Leipzig: Arnold, 1863. Reprinted Braunschweig: Friedrich-Gerstäcker-Gesellschaft, 1982.
———. *Aus zwei Welttheilen. Gesammelte Erzählungen.* Leipzig: Arnold, 1854. Reprinted Braunschweig: Friedrich-Gerstäcker-Gesellschaft, 1984.
———. *China, das Land und seine Bewohner. Aus dem Englischen.* Leipzig: Wigand, 1848. Reprinted Braunschweig: Friedrich-Gerstäcker-Gesellschaft, 1985.
———. *Die Colonie. Brasilianisches Lebensbild.* Jena: Costenoble, 1864.
———. *Der deutschen Auswanderer Fahrten und Schicksale.* Leipzig: Brockhaus, 1847.
———. *Die Deutschen im Ausland. Vorlesung gehalten von Friedrich Gerstäcker im Saale der Kaiserlichen Militär-Akademie.* Rio de Janeiro: Winter, 1861. Reprinted Braunschweig: Friedrich-Gerstäcker-Gesellschaft, 1989.
———. *Erzählungen für die "Fliegenden Blätter," Band I.* Reihe Zeitschriftenveröffentlichungen Friedrich Gerstäckers, vol. 1. Braunschweig: Friedrich-Gerstäcker-Gesellschaft, 1991.
———. *Erzählungen für die "Hausblätter," Band I.* Reihe Zeitschriftenveröffentlichungen Friedrich Gerstäckers, vol. 2. Braunschweig: Friedrich-Gerstäcker-Gesellschaft, 1991.
———. *Der Flatbootmann. Amerikanische Erzählung.* Vienna: Markgraf, 1865; originally 1858.

―――. *Die Flußpiraten des Mississippi. Aus dem Waldleben Amerikas.* Jena: Costenoble, [1889]; originally 1848.

―――. *Der Freischütz. Scene aus dem Dresdner Leben.* Reprint Braunschweig: Graff, 1979; originally 1846.

―――. "Friedrich Gerstaecker in Arkansas. Selections from his *Streif- und Jagdzuege durch die Vereinigten Staate Nordamerikas.*" Translated by Clarence Evans and Liselotte Albrecht. *Arkansas Historical Quarterly* 5 (1946): 39–57.

―――. "Friedrich Gerstäckers Briefe an Hermann Costenoble." Edited by William H. McClain and Lieselotte E. Kurth-Voigt. *Archiv für Geschichte des Buchwesens* 14 (1974): cols. 1053–1210.

―――. *Fritz Waldau's Abenteuer zu Wasser und zu Lande.* Munich: Braun und Schneider, 1854. Reprinted Braunschweig: Friedrich-Gerstäcker-Gesellschaft, 1984.

―――. *Germelshausen.* Facsimile, edited by Thomas Ostwald. Braunschweig: Graff, 1975; originally 1859.

―――. *Gold! Ein Californisches Lebensbild aus dem Jahre 1849.* Jena: Costenoble, 1858.

―――. *Die Hazardspieler in Kalifornien.* Facsimile, edited by Thomas Ostwald. Braunschweig: Graff, 1976.

―――. *Herrn Maulhubers Reiseabenteuer.* Leipzig: Reclam, n.d.

―――. *Im Eckfenster. Roman.* Jena: Costenoble, 1872. Reprinted Braunschweig: Friedrich-Gerstäcker-Gesellschaft, 1981.

―――. *In Amerika. Amerikanisches Lebensbild aus neuerer Zeit. In Anschluß an "Nach Amerika."* 3rd ed. Jena: Costenoble, [1878]; originally 1872.

―――. *In the Arkansas Backwoods: Tales and Sketches.* Edited and translated by James William Miller. Columbia: University of Missouri Press, 1991.

―――. *Kleine Erzählungen und Nachgelassene Schriften.* Jena: Costenoble, [1879]. Reprinted Braunschweig: Friedrich-Gerstäcker-Gesellschaft, 1983.

―――. *Mein guter Herr von Cotta. Friedrich Gerstäckers Briefwechsel mit dem Stuttgarter Cotta Verlag.* Edited by Karl Jürgen Roth. Braunschweig: Friedrich-Gerstäcker-Gesellschaft, 1992.

―――. *Mein lieber Herzensfreund! Briefe an seinen Freund Adolph Hermann Schultz 1835–1854.* Edited by Thomas Ostwald. Braunschweig: Friedrich-Gerstäcker-Gesellschaft, 1982.

―――. *Mississippi-Bilder. Licht- und Schattenseiten transatlantischen Lebens.* Dresden: Arnold, 1847. Reprinted Braunschweig: Friedrich-Gerstäcker-Gesellschaft, 1985.

―――. *Nach Amerika! Ein Volksbuch.* Leipzig: Costenoble; Berlin: Gaertner, 1855.

―――. *Neue Reisen durch die Vereinigten Staaten, Mexiko, Ecuador, Westindien und Venezuela.* 2nd ed. Jena: Costenoble, 1876; originally 1868.

―――. *Ein Parcerie-Vertrag. Erzählung zur Warnung und Belehrung für Auswanderer und ihre Freunde.* Leipzig: Keil, 1869. Reprinted Braunschweig: Friedrich-Gerstäcker-Gesellschaft, 1984.

―――. *Pfarre und Schule. Eine Dorfgeschichte.* Leipzig: Wigand, 1849. Reprinted Braunschweig: Friedrich-Gerstäcker-Gesellschaft, 1983.

———. [Poems.] "Klänge aus den Tropen." In Augustin and Henle, eds., *Vom Old Shatterhand zum Sherlock Holmes*, pp. 147–52.
———. *Die Regulatoren in Arkansas. Aus dem Waldleben Amerikas*. Jena: Costenoble, [1889]; originally 1846.
———. *Reisen*. Stuttgart and Tübingen: Cotta, 1853–54. Reprinted Braunschweig: Friedrich-Gerstäcker-Gesellschaft, 1986.
———. *Streif- und Jagdzüge durch die vereinigten Staaten Nord-Amerikas*. Dresden and Leipzig: Arnold, 1844. Reprinted Braunschweig: Friedrich-Gerstäcker-Gesellschaft, 1981.
———. *Waidmanns Heil! Ein Buch für Jäger und Jagdfreunde*. Munich: Braun und Schneider, 1857. Reprint, edited by Thomas Ostwald and Egon Grieger. Cologne: Kettner, 1980.
———. *Wie ist es denn nun eigentlich in Amerika? Eine kurze Schilderung dessen, was der Auswanderer in Nordamerika zu thun und dafür zu hoffen und zu erwarten hat*. Leipzig: Wigand, 1849. Reprinted Braunschweig: Friedrich-Gerstäcker-Gesellschaft, 1983.
———, ed. J. Tyrwhitt-Brooks, *Vier Monate unter den Goldfindern in Obercalifornien*. Wyk: Verlag für Amerikanistik D. Kügler, 1984.
Braunsdorf, Lynn. "Gerstäcker at the California Gold Rush. Fact, Fiction, and a Translation." *Schatzkammer der deutschen Sprache, Dichtung und Geschichte* 21, nos. 1 and 2 (1995): 21–30.
Bukey, Evan Burr. "Friedrich Gerstaecker and Arkansas." *Arkansas Historical Quarterly* 6 (Winter 1947): 3–14.
Cobbs, Alfred L. "The Image of the Black in German Literature." In Phelps, ed., *The Harold Jantz Collection*, pp. 111–18.
Corkhill, Alan. *Antipodean Encounters: Australia and the German Literary Imagination*. Frankfurt am Main: Peter Lang, 1990.
———. "Friedrich Gerstäcker in Australia: An Appraisal of his Fictional Writings." *Outrider* 3, no. 2 (December 1986): 164–71.
———. "'Das unbekannte Südland'—Australien im deutschen Überseeroman des 19. Jahrhunderts." In Maler, ed., *Exotische Welt in populären Lektüren*, pp. 35–48.
Di Maio, Irene S. "Borders of Culture: The Native American in Friedrich Gerstäcker's North American Narratives." *Yearbook of German-American Studies* 28 (1993): 53–75.
Durzak, Manfred. "Nach Amerika. Gerstäckers Widerlegung der Lenau-Legende." In Bauschinger et al., eds., *Amerika in der deutschen Literatur*, pp. 135–53. Also in Durzak, *Das Amerika-Bild in der deutschen Gegenwartsliteratur*, pp. 38–58.
Evans, Clarence. "Friedrich Gerstäcker, Social Chronicler of the Arkansas Frontier." *Arkansas Historical Quarterly* 6 (1947): 440–49.
———. "Gerstaecker on the Konwells of White River Valley." *Arkansas Historical Quarterly* 10 (1951): 1–36.
Garzmann, Manfred R. W., Thomas Ostwald, and Wolf-Dieter Schuegraf. *Gerstäcker-Verzeichnis. Erstausgaben, Gesammelte Werke und Sekundärlite-

ratur mit Nachweis im Stadtarchiv und in der Stadtbibliothek Braunschweig. Braunschweig: [Stadtarchiv und Stadtbibliothek], 1986.

Hume, Amanda. "F. W. C. Gerstäcker: An Overlooked Informant on Language in Mid-19th Century Australia." *AUMLA* 66 (1986): 272–85.

Karsen, Sonja. "Friedrich Gerstäcker in South America." *Modern Language Studies* 5 (Fall 1975): 55–62.

Kolb, Alfred. "Friedrich Gerstäcker and the American Dream." *Modern Language Studies* 5 (Fall 1975): 103–8.

———. "Friedrich Gerstäcker and the American Frontier." Diss., Syracuse University, 1966.

Krumpelmann, John T. "Gerstaecker's 'Germelshausen' and Lerner's 'Brigadoon.'" *Monatshefte* 40 (1948): 396–400.

Kugler, Hartmut. "Rohe Wilde. Zur literarischen Topik des Barbarenbildes in Gerstäckers Roman 'Unter den Pehuenchen.'" In Maler, ed., *Exotische Welt in populären Lektüren*, pp. 149–63.

Landa, Bjarne Emil. "The American Scene in Friedrich Gerstäcker's Works of Fiction." Diss., University of Minnesota, 1952.

McClain, William H. "Die Gerstäcker-Briefe in der Kurrelmeyer-Sammlung." *Modern Language Notes* 82 (1967): 428–34.

Maler, Anselm. "Deutsche Südseebilder. Von der arkadischen Vision zum ethnographischen Realismus." In Maler and Schott, eds., *Galerie der Welt*, pp. 83–96.

Moltmann, Günter. "Überseeische Siedlungen und weltpolitische Spekulationen. Friedrich Gerstäcker und die Frankfurter Zentralgewalt 1849." In *Russland—Deutschland—Amerika. Russia—Germany—America. Festschrift für Fritz T. Epstein zum 80. Geburtstag*, edited by Alexander Fischer, Günter Moltmann, and Klaus Schwabe, pp. 56–72. Wiesbaden: Steiner, 1978.

Ockel, Jürgen. *Nach Amerika! Die Schilderung der Auswanderer-Problematik in den Werken Friedrich Gerstäckers*. Beiträge zur Friedrich Gerstäcker-Forschung, no. 3. Braunschweig: Friedrich Gerstäcker-Gesellschaft, 1983.

———. *"Wünsche wohl gespeist zu haben!" Eine Auswahl gastronomischer Schilderungen aus Friedrich Gerstäckers Werken*. Beiträge zur Friedrich Gerstäcker-Forschung, no. 5. Braunschweig: Friedrich Gerstäcker-Gesellschaft, 1986.

O'Donnell, George H. R. "Gerstäcker in America 1837–1843." *PMLA* 42 (1927): 1036–43.

Ostwald, Thomas. *Friedrich Gerstäcker. Leben und Werk*. Braunschweig: Graff, 1977.

———. "Friedrich Gerstäckers ethnographische Realien." In Maler and Schott, eds., *Galerie der Welt*, pp. 12–23.

———. "Zwanglose Betrachtung des Gesamtwerkes Friedrich Gerstäckers." *Mitteilungen der Friedrich-Gerstäcker-Gesellschaft*, no. 16 (1985): 19–23.

———, ed. *Das ecuadorianische Abenteuer. Friedrich Gerstäcker und die "Educador Land Company." Briefe und Dokumente.* Beiträge zur Friedrich Gerstäcker-Forschung, no. 4. Braunschweig: Friedrich Gerstäcker-Gesellschaft, 1991.
Pagni, Andrea. "Friedrich Gerstäckers 'Reisen' zwischen Ferne und Heimat. Überlegungen zum Reisebericht im literarischen Feld Deutschlands um 1850." In *Studien zur Literatur des Frührealismus*, edited by Günter Blumberger, Manfred Engel, and Monika Ritzer, pp. 276–88. Frankfurt am Main: Peter Lang, 1991.
Postma, Heiko. "Hagenmarkt und Mississippi. Der Erzähler Friedrich Gerstäcker." In *Literatur in Braunschweig zwischen Vormärz und Gründerzeit*, edited by Herbert Blume and Eberhard Rohse, pp. 215–30. Braunschweig: Stadtarchiv und Stadtbibliothek, 1993.
Prahl, A[ugustus] J. "America in the Works of Gerstäcker." *Modern Language Quarterly* 4 (1943): 213–24.
———. "Gerstäcker über zeitgenössische Schriftsteller." *Modern Language Notes* 49 (1934): 302–9.
———. "Seitenlichter auf den Charakter Gerstäckers." *Modern Language Notes* 49 (1934): 182–88.
[Rattermann, H. A.] "Zwei, in Europa verstorbene, ächte Deutsch-amerikanische Pioniere. 2. Friedrich Gerstäcker." *Der Deutsche Pionier. Monatsschrift für Erinnerungen aus dem deutschen Pionier-Leben* 6, no. 2 (April 1874): 42–49. Reprinted in *Mitteilungen der Friedrich-Gerstäcker-Gesellschaft* 6 (1981).
Roth, Karl Jürgen. *Die Darstellung der deutschen Auswanderung in den Schriften Friedrich Gerstäckers.* Braunschweig: Friedrich Gerstäcker-Gesellschaft, 1989.
———. "Friedrich Gerstäcker und Georg Herwegh. Anmerkungen zu zwei Gedichten." *Mitteilungen der Friedrich-Gerstäcker-Gesellschaft*, no. 6 (1981): 5–13.
———. "Gerstäckers 'Jugend- und Volksschriften' in einer Kritik des 19. Jahrhunderts." *Mitteilungen der Friedrich-Gerstäcker-Gesellschaft*, no. 16 (1985): 7–18.
———. "Herr von Sechingen auf Gerstäckers Spuren in Arkansas. Eine Erzählung und ihre Hintergründe." *Mitteilungen der Friedrich-Gerstäcker-Gesellschaft*, no. 14 (1984): 7–20.
———. "'Hrn. F. Gerstäcker's Buch ist ein ganz eigenthümliches...'— Gerstäckers Werke in der zeitgenössischen Literaturkritik." *Mitteilungen der Friedrich-Gerstäcker-Gesellschaft*, no. 19 (1990): 5–25.
Sammons, Jeffrey L. "Friedrich Gerstäcker: American Realities through German Eyes." In McCormick, ed., *Germans in America*, pp. 75–90.
———. "Friedrich Gerstäcker (1816–1872)." In *Dictionary of Literary Biography*, vol. 129, *Nineteenth-Century German Writers, 1841–1900*, edited by James Hardin and Siegfried Mews, pp. 110–19. Detroit: Gale Research, 1993.

———. "Friedrich Gerstäcker: German Realist of the American West." *Yale University Library Gazette* 70 (1995–96): 39–46.

Schutz, H. "Friedrich Gerstäcker's Image of the German Immigrant in America." In Ritter, ed., *Deutschlands literarisches Amerikabild*, pp. 319–37.

Seyfarth, Erich. *Friedrich Gerstäcker. Ein Beitrag zur Geschichte des exotischen Romans in Deutschland*. Freiburg im Breisgau: Waibel, 1930.

Steeves, Harrison R. "The First of the Westerns." *Southwest Review* 53 (1968): 74–84.

See also Doerry, "Three Versions of America"; Maler, *Der exotische Roman*; Schmidt-Dengler, "Die Ehre des Dampfschiffs," under Sealsfield, Charles; Woodson, *American Negro Slavery*.

Gerstner, Franz Anton Ritter von. *Die Innern Communicationen der Vereinigten Staaten von Nordamerika*. Vienna: Förster, 1842–43.

Gillespie County Historical Society. *Pioneers in God's Hills: A History of Fredericksburg and Gillespie County, People and Events*. Austin: von Boeckmann-Jones, 1960.

Gillhoff, Johannes. *Jürnjakob Swehn der Amerikafahrer*. Berlin: Verlag der Täglichen Rundschau, 1920; originally 1917.

Reppmann, Joachim. "Jürnjakob Swehn Symposium." *Society for German-American Studies Newsletter* 14, no. 3 (September 1993): 17.

Gladt, Karl. "'Es ist ein Land voll träumerischem Trug . . .' Kollektaneen zum Thema 'Nikolaus Lenau in Amerika.'" In *Lenau-Almanach 1979. Festschrift für Prof. Dr. Nikolaus Britz*, edited by Karl Gladt, pp. 63–82. Vienna: Braumüller, 1979.

Goebel, Julius. *Der Kampf um deutsche Kultur in Amerika*. Leipzig: Dürr, 1914.

Gong, Alfred, ed. *Interview mit Amerika. 50 deutschsprachige Autoren in der Neuen Welt*. Munich: Nymphenburger, 1962.

Graf, Oskar Maria. *Die Flucht ins Mittelmäßige. Ein New Yorker Roman*. Munich: Süddeutscher Verlag, 1957.

Grisson, Dr. Wilhelm. *Beiträge zur Charakteristik der Vereinigten Staaten von Nordamerika*. Hamburg: Perthes, Besser und Mauke, 1844.

Gruber, R[einhard] P. *Einmal Amerika und zurück*. Graz: Droschli, 1993.

Guthke, Karl S. *B. Traven. Biographie eines Rätsels*. Frankfurt am Main: Büchergilde Gutenberg, 1987.

Hammond, Theresa Mayer. *American Paradise: German Travel Literature from Duden to Kisch*. Heidelberg: Winter, 1980.

Handke, Peter. *Der kurze Brief zum langen Abschied*. Frankfurt am Main: Suhrkamp, 1972.

Nägele, Rainer. "Amerika als Fiktion und Wirklichkeit in Peter Handkes Roman *Der kurze Brief zum langen Abschied*." In Paulsen, ed., *Die USA und Deutschland*, pp. 110–15.

———. "Die vermittelte Welt. Reflexionen zum Verhältnis von Fiktion und Wirklichkeit in Peter Handkes Roman 'Der kurze Brief zum langen Abschied.'" *Jahrbuch der Deutschen Schillergesellschaft* 19 (1975): 389–418.

Harpprecht, Klaus. *Der fremde Freund. Amerika: Eine innere Geschichte.* Stuttgart: Deutsche Verlags-Anstalt, 1982.
Hausmann, Manfred. *Kleine Liebe zu Amerika. Ein junger Mann schlendert durch die Staaten.* Berlin: Fischer, 1931.
Heckmann, Herbert. *Das große Knock-out in sieben Runden.* Munich: Hanser, 1972.
Heilbut, Anthony. *Exiled in Paradise: German Refugees, Artists and Intellectuals in America from the 1930s to the Present.* Boston: Beacon Press, 1983.
Heine, Heinrich. *Historisch-kritische Gesamtausgabe der Werke.* Edited by Manfred Windfuhr. 15 vols. Hamburg: Hoffmann und Campe, 1973–97.
———. *Works.* Translated by Charles Godfrey Leland et al. London: Heinemann, 1892–1905.
Helbich, Wolfgang, ed. *"Amerika ist ein freies Land . . ." Auswanderer schreiben nach Deutschland.* Darmstadt: Luchterhand, 1985.
Hemingway, Ernest. *Islands in the Stream.* New York: Scribner's, 1970.
Hennigsen, Manfred. *Der Fall Amerika. Zur Sozial- und Bewußtseinsgeschichte einer Verdrängung. Das Amerika der Europäer.* Munich: List, 1974.
Hermand, Jost. "'Was ist des Deutschen Vaterland?' Börne contra Menzel." In *Ludwig Börne 1786–1837,* edited by Alfred Estermann, pp. 199–209. Frankfurt am Main: Buchhändler-Vereinigung, 1986.
Herwegh, Georg. *Werke.* Edited by Hermann Tardel. Berlin: Bong, [1909].
Hochhuth, Rolf. *Guerillas. Tragödie in fünf Akten.* Reinbek bei Hamburg: Rowohlt, 1970.
Hoehn, Matthew, ed. *Catholic Authors: Contemporary Biographical Sketches, 1930–1947.* Newark, N. J.: St. Mary's Abbey, 1958.
Hoffman, C[harles] F[enno]. *Wild Scenes in the Forest.* London: Bentley, [1839].
Barnes, Homer F. *Charles Fenno Hoffman.* New York: Columbia University Press, 1930.
Hoffmeister, Werner. "Rezeption und Demontage amerikanischer Mythen in der deutschen Gegenwartsliteratur." *Colloquia Germanica* 16 (1983 [1985]): 337–55.
Holitscher, Arthur. *Amerika heute und morgen. Reiseerlebnisse.* Berlin: Fischer, 1913.
Hollyday, G. T. *Anti-Americanism in the German Novel, 1841–1862.* Frankfurt am Main: Peter Lang, 1977.
Honour, Hugh. *The New Golden Land: European Images of America from the Discoveries to the Present Time.* New York: Pantheon, 1975.
Horsman, Reginald. *Race and Manifest Destiny: The Origins of American Racial Anglo-Saxonism.* Cambridge, Mass.: Harvard University Press, 1981.
Houben, Heinrich Hubert. *Zeitschriften des Jungen Deutschlands.* 2 vols. Berlin: Behr, 1906.
Imhoof, Walter. *Der "Europamüde" in der deutschen Erzählungsliteratur.* Horgen-Zurich: Münster, 1930.
Immermann, Karl. *Münchhausen. Eine Geschichte in Arabesken. Werke in fünf Bänden.* Vol. 3. Edited by Benno von Wiese. Frankfurt am Main: Athenäum, 1972.

Jantz, Harold. "Amerika im deutschen Dichten und Denken." In *Deutsche Philologie im Aufriß*, 2nd ed., edited by Wolfgang Stammler, 3:311. Berlin: Erich Schmidt, 1969.

―――. "The Myths about America: Origins and Extensions." *Jahrbuch für Amerikastudien* 7 (1962): 6–18.

Jefferson, Thomas. *Notes on the State of Virginia*. Edited by William Peden. Chapel Hill: University of North Carolina Press, 1955.

Johnson, Uwe. *Jahrestage. Aus dem Leben von Gesine Cresspahl*. 4 vols. Frankfurt am Main: Suhrkamp, 1970–83.

> Lennox, Sara. "History in Uwe Johnson's *Jahrestage*." *Germanic Review* 64 (1989): 31–41.
> 
> ―――. "Die *New York Times* in Johnsons *Jahrestagen*." In Paulsen, ed., *Die USA und Deutschland*, pp. 103–9.
> 
> See also Krätzer, *Studien zum Amerikabild*.

Jung, Werner. "Vom Bedürfnis anders zu werden: Die USA in der deutschen Literatur der siebziger und achtziger Jahre." *Monatshefte* 81 (1989): 312–26.

Jungk, Robert. *Die Zukunft hat schon begonnen. Amerikas Allmacht und Ohnmacht*. Stuttgart: Scherz und Goverts, 1954.

Katz, Jacob. *Jews and Freemasons in Europe, 1723–1939*. Cambridge, Mass.: Harvard University Press, 1970.

Keller, Gottfried. *Leben, Briefe und Tagebücher*. Edited by Emil Ermatinger. Stuttgart: Cotta, 1924–25.

Kennedy, John Pendleton. *Swallow Barn, or A Sojourn in the Old Dominion*. Philadelphia: Carey and Lea, 1832.

Kerr, Alfred. *Newyork und London. Stätten des Geschicks. Zwanzig Kapitel nach dem Weltkrieg*. Berlin: Fischer, 1923.

King, Irene Marschall. *John O. Meusebach: German Colonizer in Texas*. Austin: University of Texas Press, 1967.

Kisch, Egon Erwin. *Beehrt sich darzubieten: Paradies Amerika*. Berlin: Reiss, 1929.

> Lewis, Ward B. "'Egon Erwin Kisch beehrt sich darzubieten: *Paradies Amerika*.'" *German Studies Review* 23 (1990): 253–68.
> 
> See also Hammond, *American Paradise*.

Klotzbach, Kurt. *Die Solms-Papiere. Dokumente zur deutschen Kolonisation in Texas*. Wyk: Verlag der Amerikanistik, 1990.

Koeppen, Wolfgang. *Amerikafahrt*. Stuttgart: Goverts, 1959.

Kondert, Reinhart. *The Germans of Colonial Louisiana, 1720–1803*. Stuttgart: Heinz, 1990.

Krätzer, Anita. *Studien zum Amerikabild in der neueren deutschen Literatur. Max Frisch—Uwe Johnson—Hans Magnus Enzensberger and das "Kursbuch."* Frankfurt am Main: Peter Lang, 1982.

Krampikowski, Frank, ed. *Amerikanisches Deutschlandbild und deutsches Amerikabild*. Baltmannsweiler: Pädagogischer Verlag Burgbücherei Schneider, 1990.

Kriegleder, Wynfrid. "Die 'Prosa unserer Union' und die 'Poesie des deutschen Gemüthes.' Amerikabilder bei Charles Sealsfield, Ernst Willkomm und Ferdinand Kürnberger." *Jahrbuch des Wiener Goethe-Vereins* 97–98 (1993–94): 94–111. Reprinted in *Schriftenreihe der Charles-Sealsfield-Gesellschaft* 8 (1995).

Krobb, Florian. *Die schöne Jüdin. Jüdische Frauengestalten in der deutschsprachigen Erzählliteratur vom 17. Jahrhundert bis zum Ersten Weltkrieg.* Tübingen: Niemeyer, 1993.
Kroes, Rob, and Maarten van Rossem, eds. *Anti-Americanism in Europe.* Amsterdam: Free University Press, 1986.
Kürnberger, Ferdinand. *Der Amerika-Müde. Amerikanisches Kulturbild.* Frankfurt am Main: Meidinger, 1855.
———. *Der Amerikamüde.* Edited by Friedemann Berger. Weimar: Kiepenheuer, n.d.
———. *Briefe eines politischen Flüchtlings.* Edited by Otto Erich Deutsch. Leipzig: Tal, 1920.
———. *Feuilletons.* Edited by Karl Riha. Frankfurt am Main: Insel, 1967.
———. "Die Last des Schweigens." In *Österreichische Erzählungen des 19. Jahrhunderts*, edited by Alois Brandstetter, pp. 149–73. Salzburg: Residenz, 1986.
———. *Literarische Herzenssachen. Reflexionen und Kritiken. Neue wesentlich vermehrte Ausgabe. Gesammelte Werke*, edited by Otto Erich Deutsch, vol. 2. Munich: Georg Müller, 1911.
———. *Novellen.* Berlin: Hertz, 1878.
———. *Das Schloß der Frevel.* Munich: Georg Müller, 1912.
———. *Siegelringe. Eine Sammlung politischer und kirchlicher Feuilletons. Neue wesentlich vermehrte Ausgabe.* In *Gesammelte Werke*, edited by O. E. Deutsch, vol. 1. Munich: Georg Müller, 1910.
Bailey, L. H. "Ferdinand Kürnberger, Friedrich Schlögl and the Feuilleton in *Gründerzeit* Vienna." *Forum for Modern Language Studies* 13 (1977): 155–67.
Durzak, Manfred. "Traumbild und Trugbild Amerika. Zur literarischen Geschichte einer Utopie. Am Beispiel von Willkomms 'Europamüden' und Kürnbergers 'Amerika-Müden.'" In Durzak, *Das Amerika-Bild in der deutschen Gegenwartsliteratur*, pp. 16–37.
Ederer, Hannelore. *Die literarische Mimesis entfremdeter Sprache. Zur sprachkritischen Literatur von Heinrich Heine bis Karl Kraus.* Cologne: Pahl-Rugenstein, 1979.
Kühnel, Wolf-Dieter. *Ferdinand Kürnberger als Literaturtheoretiker im Zeitalter des Realismus.* Göppingen: Kümmerle, 1970.
Lang, Hans Joachim. "Ferdinand Kürnberger One Hundred Years Later." In Phelps, ed., *The Harold Jantz Collection*, pp. 51–70.
Lengauer, Hubert. *Ästhetik und liberale Opposition. Zur Rollenproblematik des Schriftstellers in der österreichischen Literatur um 1848.* Vienna: Böhlau, 1989.
Müller, Paul. "Ferdinand Kürnbergers Siegelringe. Ein Beitrag zur Geschichte der politischen Publizistik im Zeitalter des deutschen Liberalismus in Österreich." *Mitteilungen des Österreichischen Instituts für Geschichtsforschung* 52 (1938): 331–54.
Mulfinger, George A. *Ferdinand Kürnberger's Roman "Der Amerikamüde," dessen Quellen und Verhältnis zu Lenaus Amerikareise.* Philadelphia: "German American Annals" Press, 1903.

Pütz, Manfred. "Max Webers und Ferdinand Kürnbergers Auseinandersetzung mit Benjamin Franklin. Zum Verhältnis von Quellenverfälschung und Fehlinterpretation." *Amerikastudien/American Studies* 29 (1984): 297–310.
Sammons, Jeffrey L. "The Lorenzo Da Ponte Episode in Ferdinand Kürnberger's 'Der Amerikamüde.'" *Journal of German-American Studies* 15, no. 2 (June, 1980): 48–56. Republished with a postscript in Sammons, *Imagination and History*, pp. 237–47.
Scheichl, Sigurd Paul. "Franz Grillparzer zwischen Judenfeindschaft und Josephinismus." In *Conditio Judaica: Judentum, Antisemitismus und deutschsprachige Literatur vom 18. Jahrhundert bis zum Ersten Weltkrieg. Erster Teil*, edited by Hans Otto Horch and Horst Denkler, pp. 131–48. Tübingen: Niemeyer, 1988.
Stenger, Karl Ludwig. "Ferdinand Kürnberger (1821–1879)." In *Dictionary of Literary Biography*, vol. 129, *Nineteenth-Century German Writers, 1841–1900*, edited by James Hardin and Siegfried Mews, pp. 182–88. Detroit: Gale Research, 1993.
Zeisig, Adolf. Review of *Der Amerika-Müde*. *Blätter für literarische Unterhaltung*, no. 36 (September 4, 1856): 660–61. Reprinted in *Literaturkritik. Eine Textdokumentation zur Geschichte einer literarischen Gattung*, edited by Alfred Estermann, vol. 4, *1848–1870*, edited by Peter Uwe Hohendahl, pp. 371–74. Vaduz: Topos, 1984.
See also Kriegleder, "Die 'Prosa unserer Union.'"
Kunert, Günter. *Der andere Planet. Ansichten von Amerika*. Munich: Hanser, 1975.
Futterknecht, Franz. "Noch einmal: *Der andere Planet*—Zu Günter Kunerts *Ansichten von Amerika*." In *Günter Kunert. Beiträge zu seinem Werk*, ed. Manfred Durzak and Hartmut Steinecke, pp. 235–51. Munich: Hanser, 1992.
Osterle, Heinz D. "Ansichten von Amerika. Gespräch mit Günter Kunert." *Germanic Review* 60 (1985): 107–15.
Lacour-Gayet, Robert. *Everyday Life in the United States before the Civil War, 1830–1860*. New York: Ungar, 1969.
Lamprecht, Karl. *Americana. Reiseeindrücke, Betrachtungen, Geschichtliche Gesamtansicht*. Freiburg im Breisgau: Heyfelder, 1906.
Lang, Barbara. *The Process of Immigration in German-American Literature from 1850 to 1900*. Munich: Fink, 1988.
Lange, Friedrich. *Briefe aus Amerika von neuester Zeit, besonders für Auswanderungslustige. Aus der Brieftasche eines dorthin gewanderten Deutschen*. Ilmenau: Voigt, 1834.
Larkin, Jack. *The Reshaping of Everyday Life, 1790–1860*. New York: Harper and Row, 1988.
Lettau, Reinhard. *Täglicher Faschismus. Amerikanische Evidenz aus 6 Monaten*. Munich: Hanser, 1971.
Lich, Glen E., Günter Moltmann, and T. Michael Womack. "'New Crowns to Old Glory': Archives of the German *Adelsverein*." *Yale University Library Gazette* 63 (1988–89): 145–57.

Lindemann, Beate, ed. *Amerika in uns. Deutschamerikanische Erfahrungen und Visionen*. Mainz: v. Hase und Koehler, 1995.
McCormick, E. Allen, ed. *Germans in America: Aspects of German-American Relations in the Nineteenth Century*. New York: Brooklyn College Press, 1983.
Märtin, Ralf-Peter. *Wunschpotentiale. Geschichte und Gesellschaft in Abenteuerromanen von Retcliffe, Armand, May*. Königstein/Ts.: Hain, 1983.
Maler, Anselm. *Der exotische Roman. Bürgerliche Gesellschaftsflucht und Gesellschaftskritik zwischen Romantik und Realismus. Eine Auswahl mit Einleitung und Kommentar*. Stuttgart: Klett, 1975.
———, ed. *Exotische Welt in populären Lektüren*. Tübingen: Niemeyer, 1990.
Maler, Anselm, and Sabine Schott, eds. *Galerie der Welt. Ethnographisches Erzählen im 19. Jahrhundert*. Stuttgart: Belser, 1988.
Mandel, Siegfried, ed. *Group 47: The Reflected Intellect*. Carbondale: Southern Illinois University Press, 1973.
Markham, Sara. *Workers, Women, and Afro-Americans: Images of the United States in German Travel Literature from 1923 to 1933*. Frankfurt am Main: Peter Lang, 1986.
Matthias, L. L. *Die Kehrseite der USA*. Reinbek bei Hamburg: Rowohlt, 1964.
May, Karl. *Collected Works*. Edited by Erwin J. Haeberle. Translated by Michael Shaw. 6 vols. in 3. New York: Seabury, 1977.
———. *Freiburger Erstausgaben*. Edited by Roland Schmidt. 33 vols. Bamberg: Karl-May-Verlag, 1982–84.
———. *Mein Leben und Streben*. Edited by Hainer Plaul. Hildesheim: Olms, 1975.
———. *Der Pfahlmann*. Edited by L. J. Russum. New York: Oxford University Press, 1936.
——— *The Treasures of Nugget Mountain*. Adapted by Marion Ames Taggart. New York: Benziger, 1898.
———. *Winnetou*. Edited by Stanley L. Sharp and Alfred P. Donhauser. Englewood Cliffs, N. J.: Prentice-Hall, 1968.
——— *Winnetou, the Apache Knight*. Adapted by Marion Ames Taggart. New York: Benziger, 1898.
Anon. "Karl der Deutsche." *Der Spiegel* 16, no. 37 (September 12, 1962): 54–56, 59–60, 63–69, 71, 73–74.
Arnold, Heinz Ludwig, ed. *Karl May*. Munich: Text + Kritik, 1987.
Ashliman, D. L. "The American Indian in German Travel Narratives and Literature." *Journal of Popular Culture* 10 (Spring 1977): 833–39.
Augstein, Rudolf. "Weiter Weg zu Winnetou." *Der Spiegel* 49, no. 18 (May 1, 1995): 130–35, 138, 140–42, 144.
Augustin, Siegfried. "Old Shatterhands Kampf mit der 'Brennenden Blume.' Dokumentation eines Zweikampfs." In Augustin and Henle, eds., *Vom Old Shatterhand zum Sherlock Holmes*, pp. 47–69.
Berman, Nina Auguste. "Orientalismus, Kolonialismus und Moderne: Zum Bild des Orients in der deutschen Literatur um 1900." Diss., University of California at Berkeley, 1994.

Bloch, Ernst. "Die Silberbüchse Winnetous." In Bloch, *Erbschaft der Zeit*, pp. 169–73. Frankfurt am Main: Suhrkamp, 1962.
Bröning, Ingrid. *Die Reiseerzählungen Karl Mays als literaturpädagogisches Problem*. Ratingen, Kastellaun, and Düsseldorf: Henn, 1973.
Cook, Colleen. "Germany's Wild West Author: A Researcher's Guide to Karl May." *German Studies Review* 5 (1982): 67–86.
Cracroft, Richard H. "The American West of Karl May." *American Quarterly* 19 (1967): 249–58.
———. "The American West of Karl May." Master's thesis, University of Utah, 1963.
Doerry, Karl W. "Karl May (1842–1912)." In *Dictionary of Literary Biography*, vol. 129, *Nineteenth-Century German Writers, 1841–1900*, edited by James Hardin and Siegfried Mews, pp. 241–51. Detroit and London: Gale Research, 1993.
Feilitzsch, Heribert Frhr. v. "Karl May: The 'Wild West' as Seen in Germany." *Journal of Popular Culture* 27, no. 3 (Winter 1993): 173–89.
Frigge, Reinhold. *Das erwartbare Abenteuer. Massenrezeption und literarisches Interesse am Beispiel der Reiseerzählungen von Karl May*. Bonn: Bouvier, 1984.
Gerber, Margy. "Old Shatterhand Rides Again! The Rehabilitation of Karl May in the GDR." In *Studies in GDR Culture and Society*, vol. 5, edited by Margy Gerber et al., pp. 237–50. Lanham, Md.: University Press of America, 1985.
Graf, Andreas. "'Habe gedacht, Alles Schwindel!' Balduin Möllhausen und Karl May. Beispiele literarischer Adaption und Variation." *Jahrbuch der Karl-May-Gesellschaft* (1991): 324–63.
Heermann, Christian. *Der Mann, der Old Shatterhand war. Eine Karl-May-Biographie*. Berlin: Verlag der Nation, 1988.
———, ed. *Old Shatterhand läßt grüßen. Literarische Reverenzen für Karl May*. Berlin: Neues Leben, 1992.
Heinemann, Erich, ed. *Dichtung als Wunscherfüllung. Aussprüche über Karl May*. Ubstadt: Verlag Heimat- und Volkskunde, 1992.
———, ed. *Über Karl May. Aussprüche namhafter Persönlichkeiten*. Materialien zur Karl-May-Forschung, vol. 5. Ubstadt: KMG-Presse, 1989.
Henisch, Peter. *Vom Wunsch, Indianer zu werden. Wie Franz Kafka Karl May traf und trotzdem nicht in Amerika landete*. Salzburg: Residenz, 1994.
Hohendahl, Peter Uwe. "Von der Rothaut zum Edelmenschen. Karl Mays Amerikaromane." In Bauschinger et al., eds., *Amerika in der deutschen Literatur*, pp. 229–45.
Howard, James H. "The Native American Image in Western Europe." *American Indian Quarterly* 4 (1978): 33–56.
Ilmer, Walter, and Christoph F. Lorenz, eds. *Exemplarisches zu Karl May*. Frankfurt am Main: Peter Lang, 1993.
Jeglin, Rainer. "Karl May und der antisemitische Zeitgeist." *Jahrbuch der Karl-May-Gesellschaft* (1990): 107–31.

Klussmeier, Gerhard. "Karl May: Schriftsteller—kein Psychopath." In Augustin and Henle, eds., *Vom Old Shatterhand zum Sherlock Holmes*, pp. 71–112.

Köppen, Manuel, and Rüdiger Steinlein. "Karl May: Der Verlorene Sohn oder Der Fürst des Elends (1883–1885). Soziale Phantasie zwischen Vertröstung und Rebellion." In *Romane und Erzählungen des Bürgerlichen Realismus. Neue Interpretationen*, edited by Horst Denkler, pp. 274–92. Stuttgart: Reclam, 1980.

Kremer, Manfred E. "Edle Wilde im 'Dritten Reich'? Zur Rezeption der Indianer-Romane Karl Mays und Fritz Steubens." In *Begegnung mit dem 'Fremden.' Grenzen—Traditionen—Vergleiche. Akten des VIII. Internationalen Germanisten-Kongresses Tokyo 1990*, edited by Eijirō Iwasaki, 7: 443–50. Munich: iudicium, 1991.

Lorenz, Christoph F. "Von der Vaterfigur zum Indianermythos. Charles Sealsfields Tokeah als literarischer Ahnherr von Karl Mays Winnetou." In Brancaforte, ed., *The Life and Works of Charles Sealsfield*, pp. 291–302.

Lowsky, Martin. *Karl May*. Sammlung Metzler, M 231. Stuttgart: Metzler, 1987.

Mann, Klaus. "Karl May: Hitler's Literary Mentor." *Kenyon Review* 2 (1940): 391–400. Reprinted as "Cowboy Mentor of the Führer." *Living Age* 359 (1940–41): 217–22.

Melk, Ulrich. *Das Werte- und Normensystem in Karl Mays Winnetou-Trilogie*. Paderborn: Igel, 1991.

Mosse, George L. "Was die Deutschen wirklich lasen. Marlitt, May, Ganghofer." In *Popularität und Trivialität*, Fourth Wisconsin Workshop, edited by Reinhold Grimm and Jost Hermand, pp. 101–20. Frankfurt am Main: Athenäum, 1974.

Oel-Willenborg. *See* Willenborg.

Read, Helen Appleton. "Karl May: Germany's James Fenimore Cooper." *American-German Review* 2, no. 4 (June 1936): 4–6.

Schmidt, Arno. "Old Shatterhand und die Seinen. Eine Darstellung vom Leben und Werk Karl Mays." In Schmidt, *Das essayistische Werk zur deutschen Literatur in 4 Bänden*, 4:153–73. Zurich: Haffmanns, 1988.

———. "Vom neuen Grossmystiker (Karl May)." In Schmidt, *Das essayistische Werk zur deutschen Literatur in 4 Bänden*, 4:99–124. Zurich: Haffmanns, 1988.

Schmiedt, Helmut. "Die anhaltende Nähe des Fernen. Zur Editionsgeschichte von Karl Mays 'Winnetou I.'" In Maler, ed., *Exotische Welt in populären Lektüren*, pp. 137–47.

———. *Karl May. Studien zu Leben, Werk und Wirkung eines Erfolgsschriftstellers*. Königstein/Ts.: Hain, 1979.

Scholdt, Günter. "Hitler, Karl May und die Emigranten." *Jahrbuch der Karl-May-Gesellschaft* (1989): 60–91.

Stadler, Ernst A. "Karl May: The Wild West under the German Umlaut." *Missouri Historical Society Bulletin* 21 (1964–65): 295–307.

Stolte, Heinz. "Auf den Spuren Nathans des Weisen. Zur Rezeption der Toleranzidee Lessings bei Karl May." *Jahrbuch der Karl-May-Gesellschaft* (1977): 17–57.
Sudhoff, Dieter, and Hartmut Vollmer, eds. *Karl Mays "Winnetou." Studien zu einem Mythos.* Frankfurt am Main: Suhrkamp, 1989.
Ueding, Gert, and Reinhard Tschapke, eds. *Karl-May-Handbuch.* Stuttgart: Kröner, 1987.
Unucka, Christian, ed. *Karl May im Film. Eine Bilddokumentation.* Dachau: Franke, 1980.
Walker, Ralph S. "The Wonderful West of Karl May." *American West* 10, no. 6 (November 1973): 28–33.
Wechsberg, Joseph. "Winnetou of der Wild West." *Saturday Review*, October 20, 1962, pp. 52–53, 60–61. Reprinted *American West* 1, no. 3 (Summer 1964): 32–39.
Willenborg, Gertrud. *Von deutschen Helden. Eine Inhaltsanalyse der Karl-May-Romane.* Diss., University of Cologne, 1967. Republished under the name of Gertrud Oel-Willenborg. Basel: Beltz, 1973.
Wohlgschaft, Hermann. *Große Karl May Biographie. Leben und Werk.* Paderborn: Igel, 1994.
Wolf, Bobi. "Karl May." *Pacific Historian* 24 (1980): 301–11.
Wollschläger, Hans. *Karl May. Eine philologische Streitschrift.* Nördlingen: Greno, 1988.
———. *Karl May: Grundriß eines gebrochenen Lebens. Interpretation zu Persönlichkeit und Werk.* Dresden: VEB Verlag der Kunst, 1989.
———. *Karl May in Selbstzeugnissen und Bilddokumenten.* Reinbek bei Hamburg: Rowohlt, 1965.
See also Doerry, "Three Versions of America"; Märtin, *Wunschpotentiale*; Schmiedt, "Balduin Möllhausen und Karl May," under Möllhausen, Balduin.
Mechtel, Angelika. *Gott und die Liedermacherin.* Munich: List, 1983.
Meinig, D. W. *The Shaping of America: A Geographical Perspective on 500 Years of History.* Vol. 2, *Continental America, 1800–1867.* New Haven: Yale University Press, 1993.
Mesenhöller, Peter. *Mundus Novus. Amerika oder die Entdeckung des Bekannten. Das Bild der neuen Welt im Spiegel der Druckmedien vom 16. bis zum frühen 20. Jahrhundert.* Essen: Klartext, 1992.
Michelsen, Peter. "Americanism and Anti-Americanism in German Novels of the XIXth Century." *Arcadia* 11 (1976): 272–87.
Mikoletzky, Juliane. *Die deutsche Amerika-Auswanderung des 19. Jahrhunderts in der zeitgenössischen fiktionalen Literatur.* Tübingen: Niemeyer, 1988.
Möllhausen, Balduin. *Der Halbindianer. Erzählung aus dem westlichen Nordamerika.* Leipzig: Costenoble, 1861.
———. *Der Mayordomo. Erzählung aus dem südlichen Kalifornien und Neu-Mexiko; im Anschluß an den "Halbindianer" und "Flüchtling."* Leipzig: Costenoble, 1863.

———. *Palmblätter und Schneeflocken. Erzählungen aus dem fernen Westen.* Leipzig: Costenoble, 1863.

———. *Reisen in die Felsengebirge Nord-Amerikas bis zum Hoch-Plateau von New-Mexico, unternommen als Mitglied der im Auftrage der Regierung der Vereinigten Staaten ausgesandten Colorado-Expedition.* Leipzig: Purfürst, n.d.

———. *Tagebuch einer Reise vom Mississippi nach den Küsten der Südsee. Eingeführt von Alexander von Humboldt. Mit Illustrationen in Oelfarben- und Tondruck, mit Holzschnitten und einer Spezialkarte.* Leipzig: Mendelssohn, 1858.

Ashliman, D. L. "The Image of Utah and the Mormons in Nineteenth-Century Germany." *Utah Historical Quarterly* 35 (1967): 209–27.

Barba, Preston Albert. *Balduin Möllhausen: The German Cooper.* Philadelphia: University of Pennsylvania, 1914.

Dinckelacker, Horst. *Amerika zwischen Traum und Desillusionierung im Leben und Werk des Erfolgschriftstellers Balduin Möllhausen (1825–1905).* Frankfurt am Main: Peter Lang, 1990.

———. "Balduin Möllhausen (1825–1905)." In *Dictionary of Literary Biography*, vol. 129, *Nineteenth-Century German Writers, 1841–1900*, edited by James Hardin and Siegfried Mews, pp. 270–78. Detroit: Gale Research, 1993.

Graf, Andreas. *Abenteuer und Geheimnis. Die Romane Balduin Möllhausens.* Freiburg: Rombach, 1993.

———. *Der Tod der Wölfe. Das abenteuerliche und das bürgerliche Leben des Romanschriftstellers und Amerikareisenden Balduin Möllhausen (1825–1905).* Berlin: Duncker und Humblot, 1991.

Hartmann, Horst. *George Catlin und Balduin Möllhausen. Interpreten der Indianer und des Alten Westens.* Berlin: Reiner, 1963.

Miller, David Henry. "Balduin Möllhausen, a Prussian's Image of the American West." Diss., University of New Mexico, 1970.

Schegk, Friedrich. "Balduin Möllhausen. Vorstudien zu einer Monographie." In Augustin and Henle, eds., *Vom Old Shatterhand zum Sherlock Holmes*, pp. 113–46.

Schmiedt, Helmut. "Balduin Möllhausen und Karl May: Reiseziel St. Louis." In Arnold, ed., *Karl May*, pp. 127–45.

See also Graf "'Habe gedacht, Alles Schwindel!,'" under May, Karl.

Moellhausen, Henry. *Die in Texas und Virginien gelegenen, der Londoner allgemeinen Auswanderungs- und Colonisations-Gesellschaft gehörigen Ländereien.* Berlin: Schneider, 1850.

Moltmann, Günter, et al., eds. *Deutsche Amerikaauswanderung im 19. Jahrhundert. Sozialgeschichtliche Beiträge.* Stuttgart: Metzler, 1976.

Mundt, Theodor. *Geschichte der Literatur der Gegenwart.* Berlin: Simion, 1842.

Neitzel, Sarah C., and Terry K. Cargill. "'Stay at Home and Live with Integrity': Advice to German Emigrants to the United States from the Journeyman's Father." *Yearbook of German-American Studies* 26 (1991): 63–75.

Neuhaus, Volker. *Der zeitgeschichtliche Sensationsroman in Deutschland 1855–1878. "Sir John Rectliffe" und seine Schule.* Berlin: Erich Schmidt, 1980.

Nirenberg, Morton. *The Reception of American Literature in German Periodicals, 1820–1850.* Heidelberg: Winter, 1970.
Noether, Emiliana P. "As Others Saw Us: Italian Views on the United States during the Nineteenth Century." *Transactions of the Connecticut Academy of Arts and Sciences* 50 (1990): 119–50.
Osterle, Heinz D. "The Lost Utopia: New Images of America in German Literature." *German Quarterly* 54 (1981): 427–46.
———, ed. *Amerika! New Images in German Literature.* Frankfurt am Main: Peter Lang, 1989.
———, ed. *Bilder von Amerika. Gespräche mit Schriftstellern.* Münster: Englisch Amerikanische Studien, 1987.
Osterweis, Rollin G. *Romanticism and Nationalism in the Old South.* Gloucester, Mass.: Peter Smith, 1964.
Ott, Ulrich. *Amerika ist anders. Studien zum Amerika-Bild in deutschen Reiseberichten des 20. Jahrhunderts.* Frankfurt am Main: Peter Lang, 1991.
Palmer, R. R. *The Age of the Democratic Revolution: A Political History of Europe and America, 1760–1800. The Challenge.* Princeton: Princeton University Press, 1959.
Pattie, James O. *The Personal Narrative of James O. Pattie.* Edited by Timothy Flint. Cincinnati: Wood, 1831.
Paulding, James Kirke. *The Dutchman's Fireside: A Tale.* New York: Harper, 1831.
———. *Westward Ho! A Tale.* New York: Harper, 1832.
 Reynolds, Larry J. *James Kirke Paulding.* Boston: Twayne, 1984.
Paulsen, Wolfgang, ed. *Die USA und Deutschland. Wechselseitige Spiegelungen in der Literatur der Gegenwart.* Bern: Francke, 1976.
Penniger, Robert, ed. *Fest-Ausgabe zum 50-jährigen Jubiläum der Gründung der Stadt Friedrichsburg. Eine kurzgefaßte Entwickelungs-Geschichte der vom Mainzer Adelsverein gegründeten deutschen Kolonie in Texas, nebst Chronik der Stadt Friedrichsburg.* Friedrichsburg: n.p., 1896.
Pessen, Edward. *Jacksonian America: Society, Personality, and Politics.* Urbana: University of Illinois Press, 1978.
Pfanner, Helmut F. *Exile in New York: German and Austrian Writers after 1933.* Detroit: Wayne State University Press, 1983.
———, ed. *Kulturelle Wechselbeziehungen im Exil—Exile across Cultures.* Bonn: Bouvier, 1986.
Phelps, Leland R., ed. *The Harold Jantz Collection.* Durham: Duke University Center for International Studies, 1981.
Postl, Carl. *See* Sealsfield, Charles.
Price, Lawrence Marsden. *The Reception of United States Literature in Germany.* University of North Carolina Studies in Comparative Literature, 39. Chapel Hill: University of North Carolina Press, 1966.
Raabe, Wilhelm. *Alte Nester; Die Leute aus dem Walde.* In Raabe, *Sämtliche Werke,* vols. 14, 5. Edited by Karl Hoppe at al. Göttingen: Vandenhoeck und Ruprecht, 1960–94.
 Sammons, Jeffrey L. *Wilhelm Raabe: The Fiction of the Alternative Community.* Princeton: Princeton University Press, 1987.

Rahv, Philip. "Paleface and Redskin." *Kenyon Review* 1 (1939): 251–56.
Reitzel, Robert. *Adventures of a Greenhorn: An Autobiographical Novel.* Translated by Jacob Erhardt. Frankfurt am Main: Peter Lang, 1992.
Remini, Robert V. *The Legacy of Andrew Jackson: Essays on Democracy, Indian Removal, and Slavery.* Baton Rouge: Louisiana State University Press, 1988.
———. *The Life of Andrew Jackson.* New York: Harper and Row, 1988.
Richards, Donald Ray. *The German Bestseller in the 20th Century: A Complete Bibliography and Analysis, 1915–1940.* Bern: Herbert Lang, 1969.
Richter, Hans Werner. *Die Geschlagenen.* Munich: Desch, 1949.
Richter, Hans Werner, with Walter Mannzen, eds. *Almanach der Gruppe 47 1947–1962.* Reinbek bei Hamburg: Rowohlt, 1962.
Riedl, Joachim. *Leere Räume, laute Stimmen. Reportagen und Bilder aus den USA.* Munich: Kindler, 1994.
Rippley, La Vern J. *The German-Americans.* Boston: Twayne, 1976.
Ritter, Alexander, ed. *Deutschlands literarisches Amerikabild. Neuere Forschungen zur Amerikarezeption der deutschen Literatur.* Hildesheim: Olms, 1977.
Robin, Ron. *The Barbed-Wire College: Reeducating the German POWs in the United States during World War II.* Princeton: Princeton University Press, 1995.
Robinson, Therese Albertine Luise von Jakob. *See* Talvj.
Ross, Colin. *Amerikas Schicksalstunde. Die Vereinigten Staaten zwischen Demokratie und Diktatur.* Leipzig: Brockhaus, 1935.
———. *Unser Amerika. Der deutsche Anteil an den Vereinigten Staaten.* Leipzig: Brockhaus, 1936.
———. *USA.* Kolmar: Alsatia, 1943.
    Beck, Earl R. "Colin Ross in South America, 1919–1920." *Americas* 17 (1960–61): 53–63.
    Symington, Rodney. "Eine deutsch-amerikanische literarische Freundschaft: Else Seel und Ezra Pound." *Yearbook of German-American Studies* 21 (1986): 13–37.
Rossbacher, Karl Heinz. *Lederstrumpf in Deutschland. Zur Rezeption James Fenimore Coopers beim Leser der Restaurationszeit.* Munich: Fink, 1972.
Roth, Gerhard. *Der große Horizont.* Frankfurt am Main: Suhrkamp, 1974.
Rozwenc, Edwin C., ed. *The Meaning of Jacksonian Democracy.* Boston: Heath, 1963.
Ruland, Richard. *America in Modern European Literature: From Image to Metaphor.* New York: New York University Press, 1976.
Ruppius, Otto. *Der Pedlar. Roman aus dem amerikanische Leben.* New York: New Yorker Staatszeitung, 1857.
———. *Das Vermächtnis des Pedlars. Roman aus dem amerikanischen Leben. Folge des Romans: Der Pedlar.* Berlin: Duncker, 1859.
    Graevert, Theodor. *Otto Ruppius und der Amerikaroman.* Diss., Berlin, 1935.
    Hering, Christoph. "Otto Ruppius, der Amerikafahrer." In Bauschinger et al., eds., *Amerika in der deutschen Literatur,* pp. 124–34.
    *See also* Woodson, *American Negro Slavery*
Sammons, Jeffrey L. "The German Image of America: Is There Any There

There?" Harold Jantz Memorial Lecture. Pamphlet. Oberlin: Oberlin College, 1995.

———. "Germans Assessing America: Some New Acquisitions." *Yale University Library Gazette* 58 (1983–84): 40–50.

———. *Imagination and History: Selected Papers on Nineteenth-Century German Literature*. Frankfurt am Main: Peter Lang, 1988.

———. "Land of Limited Possibilities: America in the Nineteenth-Century German Novel." *Yale Review* 68 (1978–79): 35–52. Republished in Sammons, *Imagination and History*, pp. 217–36.

———. *Literary Sociology and Practical Criticism: An Inquiry*. Bloomington: Indiana University Press, 1977.

———. "The Schiller Centennial: 1859. Some Themes and Motifs." *University of Dayton Review* 20, no. 3 (Fall 1990): 5–13.

———. "Zu den Grundlagen des Antiamerikanismus in der deutschen Literatur." In *Alte Welten—neue Welten. Akten des IX. Internationalen Germanisten-Kongresses Vancouver 1995*, vol. 1, *Plenarvorträge*, edited by Michael S. Batts, pp. 33–47. Tübingen: Niemeyer, 1996.

Scharang, Michael. *Auf nach Amerika*. Hamburg and Zurich: Luchterhand, 1991.

Schlesinger, Arthur M. *The Age of Jackson*. Boston: Little, Brown, 1946.

Schleucher, Kurt. *Das Leben der Amalia Schoppe und Johanna Schopenhauer*. Darmstadt: Turris, 1978.

Schmitt, Albert R. *Herder und Amerika*. The Hague: Mouton, 1967.

Schuchalter, Jerry. "Literature, Representation, and the Negotiation of Cultural Lacunae." In *Lacunology: Studies in Intercultural Communication*, edited by Hartmut Schröder, Jerry Schuchalter, and Brett Dellinger, pp. 26–47. Vaasa: Vaasan Yliopisto, 1995.

———. "'Mein Eden, lieber Sigismund, öffnet seine Pforten nicht in Amerika': Dissenting Jewish Images in German Popular Fiction." *Nordisk judaistik/Scandinavian Jewish Studies* 13, no. 2 (1991): 100–15.

———. "Power and Fable across Textual and Cultural Borders: Gustav Freytag's Rewriting of the Frontier Narrative in *Soll und Haben*." In *Interdependence and Interaction: English in Contact with Other Languages and Cultures*, edited by Jerry Schuchalter, pp. 153–77. Vaasa: Vaasan Yliopisto, 1995.

Schwab-Felisch, Hans, ed. *Der Ruf. Eine deutsche Nachkriegszeitschrift*. Munich: Deutscher Taschenbuch Verlag, 1962.

Sealsfield, Charles. "Die Erzählung des Obersten Morse." In *Deutsche Erzähler*, edited by Hugo von Hofmannsthal, 3:363–511. Leipzig: Insel, 1912.

———. *Gesamtausgabe der Amerikanischen Romane*. Edited by Franz Riederer. 5 vols. Meersburg am Bodensee and Leipzig: Hendel, n.d. [1937].

———. *Das Kajütenbuch oder Nationale Charakteristiken*. Edited by Alexander Ritter. Stuttgart: Reclam, 1982.

———. *Der Legitime und die Republikaner*. Edited by Klaus Walther. Rudolstadt: Greifen, 1989.

———. *Morton oder die große Tour; Das Kajütenbuch oder Nationale Charakteristiken*. Edited by Klaus Walther. Rudolstadt: Greifen, 1989.

---. "Die Prärie am Jacinto." In *Österreichische Erzählungen des 19. Jahrhunderts*, edited by Alois Brandstetter, pp. 51–74. Salzburg and Vienna: Residenz, 1986.

---. *Sämtliche Werke*. Edited by Karl J. R. Arndt et al. 24 vols. Hildesheim and New York: Olms, 1972–91.

---. *The United States of North America as They Are; The Americans as They Are*. London: Simpkin and Marshall, 1828; Hurst, Chance, 1828. Photographic reprint with an introduction by William E. Wright. New York: Johnson Reprint, 1970.

Allerdissen, Rolf. "'Judenbuche' und 'Patriarch.' Der Baum des Gerichts bei Annette von Droste-Hülshoff und Charles Sealsfield." In *Herkommen und Erneuerung. Essays für Oskar Seidlin*, edited by Gerald Gillespie and Edgar Lohner, pp. 201–24. Tübingen: Niemeyer, 1976.

Arndt, Karl J. R. "Charles Sealsfield and the *Courrier des Etats-Unis*." *PMLA* 68 (1953): 170–88. Reprinted in *Sämtliche Werke*, ed. Arndt, 24: 61–79.

---. "Charles Sealsfield in America." *Zeitschrift für deutsche Philologie* 72 (1953): 169–82. Reprinted in *Sämtliche Werke*, ed. Arndt, 24:81–94.

---. "The Cooper-Sealsfield Exchange of Criticism." *American Literature* 15 (1943): 16–24. Reprinted in *Sämtliche Werke*, ed. Arndt, 24:32–40.

---. "*Early Impressions*: An Unknown Work by Sealsfield." *Journal of English and Germanic Philology* 55 (1956): 100–16. Reprinted in *Sämtliche Werke*, ed. Arndt, 24:15–31.

---. "The Louisiana Passport of Pennsylvania's Charles Sealsfield." *Pennsylvania Folklife* 33 (1984): 134–37.

---. "Newly Discovered Sealsfield Relationships Documented." *Modern Language Notes* 87 (1972): 450–64.

---. "Plagiarism: Sealsfield or Simms?" *Modern Language Notes* 69 (1954): 577–81.

---. "Recent Sealsfield Discoveries." *Journal of English and Germanic Philology* 52 (1954): 160–71. Reprinted in *German-American Literature*, edited by Don Heinrich Tolzmann, pp. 128–40. Metuchen, N. J.: Scarecrow Press, 1977.

---. "Sealsfield and Strubberg at Vera Cruz." *Monatshefte* 44 (1953): 225–28.

---. "Sealsfield-Postl als amerikanischer Dichter." *Schriftenreihe der Charles-Sealsfield-Gesellschaft* 4 (1989): 49–69.

---. "Sealsfield's Command of the English Language." *Modern Language Notes* 67 (1952): 310–13.

---. "Sealsfield's Early Reception in England and America." *Germanic Review* 18 (1943): 176–95. Reprinted in *Sämtliche Werke*, ed. Arndt, 24: 41–61.

---. "Sealsfield's Relation to David Warden, United States Consul in Paris, France." *Yearbook of German-American Studies* 18 (1983): 113–23.

Ashby, Nanette M. *Charles Sealsfield: "The Greatest American Author." A*

Study of Literary Piracy and Promotion in the 19th Century. Diss., Stanford University, 1939. Republished Stuttgart: Charles Sealsfield-Gesellschaft, 1980.

Benesch, Kurt. *Die vielen Leben des Mister Sealsfield*. Vienna and Munich: Österreichischer Bundesverlag für Unterricht, Wissenschaft und Kunst, 1966.

Bornemann, Felix, and Hans Freising, eds. *Sealsfield-Bibliographie 1945–1965*. Stuttgart: Charles Sealsfield-Gesellschaft, 1966.

Brancaforte, Charlotte L., ed. *The Life and Works of Charles Sealsfield (Karl Postl), 1793–1864*. Madison: Max Kade Institute for German-American Studies, University of Wisconsin–Madison, 1993.

Castle, Eduard. *Das Geheimnis des grossen Unbekannten. Charles Sealsfield—Carl Postl. Die Quellenschriften mit Einleitung, Bildnis, Handschriftproben und ausführlichem Register*. Vienna: Wiener Bibliophilen-Gesellschaft, 1943.

———. *Der große Unbekannte. Das Leben von Charles Sealsfield (Karl Postl)*. Vienna and Munich: Manutius, 1952. Republished as *Sämtliche Werke. Supplementreihe*, edited by Alexander Ritter. Vol. 25. Hildesheim: Olms, 1993.

———. *Der große Unbekannte. Das Leben von Charles Sealsfield (Karl Postl). Briefe und Aktenstücke*. Vienna: Werner, 1955.

Castle, Reinhild. *Die Sealsfield-Sammlung in der Bibliothek von Univ. Professor Dr. Eduard Castle in Wien*. Stuttgart: Charles Sealsfield-Gesellschaft, 1979.

Clavadetscher, Claudia. "Elise Meyer." *Schaffhauser Beiträge zur Geschichte* 58 (1981): 152–62.

Dallmann, William Paul. *The Spirit of America as Interpreted in the Works of Charles Sealsfield*. Diss., Washington University, 1935.

Djordjević, Miloš. "Charles Sealsfield als Moralist." In *Dichtung, Sprache Gesellschaft. Akten des IV. Internationalen Germanisten-Kongresses 1970 in Princeton*, edited by Victor Lange and Hans-Gert Roloff, pp. 419–24. Frankfurt am Main: Athenäum, 1971.

Emmel, Hildegard. "Recht oder Unrecht in der Neuen Welt. Zu Charles Sealsfields Roman 'Der Legitime und die Republikaner.'" In Bauschinger et al., eds., *Amerika in der deutschen Literatur*, pp. 75–80. Republished in Emmel, *Kritische Intelligenz als Methode. Alte und neue Aufsätze über sieben Jahrhunderte deutscher Literatur*, edited by Christiane Zehl Romero, pp. 109–16. Bern: Francke, 1981.

———. "Vision und Reise bei Charles Sealsfield." *Journal of German-American Studies* 15, no. 2 (June 1980): 39–47. Republished in Emmel, *Kritische Intelligenz als Methode*, pp. 117–23.

Faust, Albert B. *Charles Sealsfield (Carl Postl), Materials for a Biography: A Study of His Style; His Influence upon American Literature*. Baltimore: Friedenwald, 1892.

Fischer, Bernd. "Baumwolle und Indianer. Zu Charles Sealsfields *Der*

*Legitime und die Republikaner." Journal of German-American Studies* 19 (1984): 85–96.

———. "Form und Geschichtsphilosophie in Charles Sealsfields *Lebensbildern aus der westlichen Hemisphäre*." *German Studies Review* 9 (1986): 233–56.

Friesen, Gerhard. *The German Panoramic Novel of the 19th Century*. Bern: Herbert Lang, 1972.

———. "'Sealsfield's Unrealistic Mexico': A Reevaluation." *Seminar* 28 (1992): 159–67.

Fritz, Hubert. *Die Erzählweise in den Romanen Charles Sealsfields und Jeremias Gotthelfs. Zur Rhetoriktradition im Biedermeier*. Bern: Herbert Lang; Frankfurt am Main: Peter Lang, 1974.

Fuerst, Norbert. *The Victorian Age in German Literature*. University Park: Pennsylvania State University Press, 1966.

Grünzweig, Walter. *Charles Sealsfield*. Boise State University Western Writers Series, 71. Boise: Boise State University, 1985.

———. *Das demokratische Kanaan: Charles Sealsfields Amerika im Kontext amerikanischer Literatur und Ideologie*. Munich: Fink, 1987.

———. "'The Italian Sky in the Republic of Letters.' Charles Sealsfield and Timothy Flint as Early Writers of the American West." *Yearbook of German-American Studies* 17 (1982): 1–20.

———. "Der lüsterne Sklavenhalter: Charles Sealsfields Amerika dekonstruiert." *Jahrbuch des Wiener Goethe-Vereins* 97–98 (1993–94): 113–20. Reprinted in *Schriftenreihe der Charles-Sealsfield-Gesellschaft* 8 (1995).

———. "'Niemals verging sein deutsches Herz.' Charles Sealsfield in der Literaturkritik der NS-Zeit." *Österreichische Geschichte und Literatur mit Geographie* 30 (1986): 40–61.

———. "'Where Millions of Happy People Might Live Peacefully': Jacksons Westen in Charles Sealsfields *Tokeah; or the White Rose*." *Amerikastudien/American Studies* 28 (1983): 219–36.

Grünzweig, Walter, and Vivianne N'Diaye. "Voodoo im Biedermeier—Charles Sealsfields '*Pflanzerleben*' aus afroamerikanischer Sicht." *Schriftenreihe der Charles-Sealsfield-Gesellschaft* 4 (1989): 147–66.

Hartley, Paul Duncan. "Society and Politics in Europe and America in the Works of Charles Sealsfield." Diss., University of Leeds, 1986.

Heller, Otto. *The Language of Charles Sealsfield: A Study in Atypical Usage*. St. Louis: Washington University, 1941.

———. "Some Sources of Sealsfield." *Modern Philology* 7 (1909–10): 587–92.

Heller, Otto, and Theodor H. Leon. *Charles Sealsfield: Bibliography of His Writings Together with a Classified and Annotated Catalogue of Literature Relating to His Works and His Life*. St. Louis: Washington University, 1939.

Jahnel, Beate. *Charles Sealsfield und die Bildende Kunst. Die Landschaftsbilder in den Romanen Charles Sealsfields und ihre Parallelen in der amerikanischen und englischen Malerei des 19. Jahrhunderts*. Stuttgart: Charles Sealsfield-Gesellschaft, 1985.

Jantz, Harold. "Charles Sealsfield's Letter to Joel R. Poinsett." *Germanic Review* 27 (1952): 155–84.

Koepke, Wulf. "Charles Sealsfield's Place in Literary History." *South Central Review* 1, nos. 1 and 2 (Spring–Summer 1984): 52–66.

Krauss, Peter. "Kontinuität und Verflechtung der Motive bei Sealsfield." *Mitteilungen der Charles-Sealsfield-Gesellschaft*, ser. 2 (July 1983): 3–8.

———. "Sealsfields politischer Standort," *Mitteilungen der Charles-Sealsfield-Gesellschaft*, ser. 3 (October 1984): 6–12.

Kresse, Albert. *Erläutender Katalog meiner Sealsfield-Sammlung. Stand am 1. September 1960*. Edited by Felix Bornemann. Stuttgart: Charles-Sealsfield-Gesellschaft, 1974.

Krumpelmann, John T. "Charles Sealsfield and Weimar." In Friesen and Schatzberg, eds., *The German Contribution to the Building of the Americas*, pp. 173–86.

———. "Charles Sealsfield's Americanisms." *American Speech* 16 (1941): 26–31, 104–11; 19 (1944): 196–99.

———. "Sealsfield and Sources." *Monatshefte* 43 (1951): 324–26.

———. "Sealsfield's China Trees." *Monatshefte* 43 (1951): 44–45.

———. "Sealsfield's Inebriated Robins." *Monatshefte* 43 (1951): 225–26.

———. "Sealsfield Vindicated." *Monatshefte* 50 (1958): 257–59.

———. "A Source for Local Color in Sealsfield's *Cajütenbuch*." *Journal of English and German Philology* 43 (1944): 429–33.

Kucher, Primus-Heinz. "Charles Sealsfields *Austria as it is*. Ein Literaturrätsel und Reisebericht mit europäischer Rezeption im 19. Jahrhundert." *Zagreber germanistische Beiträge* 2 (1993): 37–50.

Leibrock, Felix. *"Wie geht es drüben?" Eine Ausstellung zu Leben und Werk von Charles Sealsfield (1793–1864)*. Solothurn: Zentralbibliothek, 1988.

Lich, Glen E. "Sealsfield's Texan: Metaphor, Experience, and History." *Yearbook of German-American Studies* 22 (1987): 71–79.

Magris, Claudio. "Der Abenteurer und der Eigentümer. Charles Sealsfields 'Prärie am Jacinto.'" In *Austriaca: Beiträge zur österreichischen Literatur. Festschrift für Heinz Politzer zum 65. Geburtstag*, edited by Winfried Kudszus and Hinrich C. Seeba with Richard Brinkmann, pp. 151–70. Tübingen: Niemeyer, 1975.

Nirenberg, Morton. "Review Essay: The Works of Charles Sealsfield." *German Quarterly* 52 (1979): 81–87.

Ostwald, Thomas, ed. *Charles Sealsfield—Leben und Werk. Biographie aufgrund zeitgenössischer Presseberichte, ergänzt durch Buchauszüge aus Literaturgeschichten*. Braunschweig: Graff, 1976.

Peter, Andreas. *Charles Sealsfields Mexiko-Romane. Zur raum-zeitlichen Strukturierung und Bedeutung der Reisemotivik*. Stuttgart: Charles Sealsfield-Gesellschaft, 1983.

Renner, Rolf Günter. "Arbiträre Zeichen. Das Eigene und das Fremde bei Charles Sealsfield (Karl Postl)." In *Begegnung mit dem 'Fremden.' Gren-*

zen—Traditionen—Vergleiche. Akten des VIII. Internationalen Germanisten-Kongresses Tokyo 1990, edited by Eijiro Iwasaki, 10:89–98. Munich: iudicium, 1991.

———. "Transatlantische Landschaften. Zum Bild der Neuen Welt bei Charles Sealsfield." *Schriftenreihe der Charles-Sealsfield-Gesellschaft* 1 (1986): 7–49.

Ritter, Alexander. "Charles Sealsfield (Karl Postl)—Die Deutung seines Werkes zwischen Positivismus und Funktionalität, europäischer Geistesgeschichte und amerikanischer Literaturgeschichte." *Literatur in Wissenschaft und Unterricht*, 4 (1971): 270-89. Reprinted as Jahresgabe der Charles Sealsfield-Gesellschaft, 1972.

———. "Charles Sealsfield: Politischer Emigrant, freier Schriftsteller und die Doppelkrise von Amerika-Utopie und Gesellschaft im 19. Jahrhundert." *Freiburger Universitätsblätter*, no. 75 (April 1982): 43–63.

———. "Charles Sealsfield (1793–1864): German and American Novelist of the Nineteenth Century." *Mississippi Quarterly* 47 (1994): 633–44.

———. "Charles Sealsfields gesellschaftspolitische Vorstellungen und ihre dichterische Gestaltung als Romanzyklus." *Jahrbuch der Deutschen Schillergesellschaft* 17 (1973): 395–414.

———. "Charles Sealsfields 'Madonnas of(f) the Trails' im Roman *Das Kajütenbuch*. Oder: Zur epischen Zähmung der Frauen als Stereotype in der amerikanischen Südstaatenepik zwischen 1820 und 1850." *Yearbook of German-American Studies* 18 (1983): 91–112.

———. *Darstellung und Funktion der Landschaft in den Amerika-Romanen von Charles Sealsfield (Karl Postl). Eine Studie zum Prosa-Roman der deutschen und amerikanischen Literatur in der ersten Hälfte des 19. Jahrhunderts.* Stuttgart: Charles Sealsfield-Gesellschaft, [1970].

———. "Geschichten aus Geschichte—Charles Sealsfields erzählerischer Umgang mit dem Historischen am Beispiel des Romans 'Das Kajütenbuch.'" *Schriftenreihe der Charles-Sealsfield-Gesellschaft* 4 (1989): 127–45.

———. "Restaurative Weltsicht und monologes Verbreiten der politischen Botschaft. Zu einem zentralen Strukturmerkmal der pragmatischen Romane Charles Sealsfields." *Jahrbuch des Wiener Goethe-Vereins* 97-98 (1993–94): 87–97. Reprinted in *Schriftenreihe der Charles-Sealsfield-Gesellschaft* 8 (1995).

———. *Sealsfield-Bibliographie 1966–1975. Mit einem Kommentar von Karl J. R. Arndt zum Publikationsstand der "Sämtlichen Werke."* Stuttgart: Charles Sealsfield-Gesellschaft, 1976.

———. "Sealsfield-Bibliographie 1976–1986." *Schriftenreihe der Charles-Sealsfield-Gesellschaft* 1 (1986): 50–65.

———. "Sealsfields Erzählformel seiner Amerika-Romane: Raum und Zeit als Welt und Geschichte. Anmerkungen zur Erzähltheorie am Beispiel des Romans *Kajütenbuch*." In Friesen and Schatzberg, eds., *The German Contribution to the Building of the Americas*, pp. 187–216.

———. "Die Stadt Natchez (Miss./USA) in der erzählenden Literatur vom Ende des 18. bis zur Mitte des 20. Jahrhunderts: René Chateaubriand, Charles Sealsfield, Eudora Welty und die Variationen eines literarischen Regionalismus." *Schriftenreihe der Charles-Sealsfield-Gesellschaft* 6 (1991 [1994]): 23–61.

———. "Die texanische Revolution und ihre Umdeutung ins Utopische: Zum gesellschaftspolitischen Gegenentwurf im Roman 'Das Cajütenbuch' von Charles Sealsfield." *Schriftenreihe der Charles-Sealsfield-Gesellschaft* 6 (1991 [1994]): 83–107.

Sammons, Jeffrey L. "Charles Sealsfield: A Case of Non-Canonicity." In *Autoren damals und heute. Literaturgeschichtliche Beispiele veränderter Wirkungshorizonte*, edited by Gerhard P. Knapp, pp. 155–72. Amsterdam and Atlanta: Rodopi, 1991.

———. "Charles Sealsfield (Carl Postl) (1793–1854)." In *Dictionary of Literary Biography*, vol. 133, *Nineteenth-Century German Writers to 1840*, edited by James Hardin and Siegfried Mews, pp. 248–56. Detroit: Gale Research, 1993.

———. "Charles Sealsfield: Innovation or Intertextuality?" In *Traditions of Experiment from the Enlightenment to the Present: Essays in Honor of Peter Demetz*, edited by Nancy Kaiser and David E. Wellbery, pp. 127–46. Ann Arbor: University of Michigan Press, 1992.

———. "Charles Sealsfields 'Deutsch-amerikanische Wahlverwandtschaften.' Ein Versuch." In Maler, ed., *Exotische Welt in populären Lektüren*, pp. 49–62.

———. "Charles Sealsfield's *Images of Life from Both Hemispheres*: A New Acquisition." *Yale University Library Gazette* 64 (1989–90): 66–72.

———. "The Shape of Freedom in Charles Sealsfield's Plantation Novels." *Schatzkammer der deutschen Sprache, Dichtung und Geschichte* 21, nos. 1 and 2 (1995): 1–20.

Schmidt, Max L. *Amerikanismen bei Charles Sealsfield*. Diss., University of Bonn, 1937.

Schmidt-Dengler, Wendelin. "Charles Sealsfield: Das Kajütenbuch (1841)." In *Romane und Erzählungen zwischen Romantik und Realismus. Neue Interpretationen*, edited by Paul Michael Lützeler, pp. 314–34. Stuttgart: Reclam, 1983.

———. "Die Ehre des Dampfschiffs. Zur Funktion der Technik im deutschen Amerikaroman des 19. Jahrhunderts." In *Jahrbuch der Grillparzer-Gesellschaft*, 3rd ser., 12 (1976): 277–89.

Schnitzler, Günter. *Erfahrung und Bild. Die dichterische Wirklichkeit des Charles Sealsfield (Karl Postl)*. Freiburg: Rombach, 1988.

———. "Erfahrung und Erfindung. Zum Romanwerk Charles Sealsfields (Karl Postls)." *Schriftenreihe der Charles-Sealsfield-Gesellschaft* 6 (1991 [1994]): 7–21.

———. "Karl Postl—Charles Sealsfield: Herkunft und dichterische Wirklichkeit." *Schriftenreihe der Charles-Sealsfield-Gesellschaft* 4 (1989): 31–48.

———. "Sealsfield und die bildende Kunst." *Jahrbuch des Wiener Goethe-Vereins* 97–98 (1993–94): 65–86. Reprinted in *Schriftenreihe der Charles-Sealsfield-Gesellschaft* 8 (1995).

Schroeder, Adolf E. "A Century of Sealsfield Scholarship." *Society for the History of the Germans in Maryland Annual Report* 32 (1966): 13–23.
Schuchalter, Jerry. "Charles Sealsfield's 'Fable of the Republic.'" *Yearbook of German-American Studies* 24 (1989): 11–26.
———. *Frontier and Utopia in the Fiction of Charles Sealsfield*. Frankfurt am Main: Peter Lang, 1986.
———. "*Geld* and *Geist* in the Writings of Gottfried Duden, Nikolaus Lenau, and Charles Sealsfield: A Study of Competing America-Paradigms." *Yearbook of German-American Studies* 27 (1992): 49–73.
Schüppen, Franz [B.]. "'Der Amerikaner lebt in und durch Stürme': Zur moralisch-didaktischen Dimension von Sealsfields Bild des Nordamerikaners." *Schriftenreihe der Charles-Sealsfield-Gesellschaft* 4 (1989): 71–126.
———. "Charles Sealsfield." In *Zur Literatur der Restaurationsepoche 1815–1848*, edited by Jost Hermand and Manfred Windfuhr, pp. 285–348. Stuttgart: Metzler, 1970.
———. *Charles Sealsfield, Karl Postl. Ein österreichischer Erzähler der Biedermeierzeit im Spannungsfeld von Alter und Neuer Welt*. Frankfurt am Main: Peter Lang, 1981.
———. *Paradigmawechsel im Werk Theodor Fontanes. Von Goethes Italien- und Sealsfields Amerika-Idee zum preußischen Alltag*. Schriftenreihe der Charles-Sealsfield-Gesellschaft 5 (1990 [1993]).
———. "Wirtschaftlicher Optimismus aus der Neuen Welt. Zu Voraussetzungen und Erscheinungsformen amerikanischer Ökonomie in Pennsylvanien, Philadelphia und bei Charles Sealsfield." *Schriftenreihe der Charles-Sealsfield-Gesellschaft* 6 (1991 [1994]): 109–39.
———, ed. *Neue Sealsfield-Studien. Amerika und Europa in der Biedermeierzeit*. Stuttgart: M[etzler] und P[oeschel], 1995.
Sebald, W. G. "Ansichten aus der Neuen Welt—Über Charles Sealsfield." In Sebald, *Unheimliche Heimat. Essays zur österreichischen Literatur*, pp. 17–39. Salzburg and Vienna: Residenz, 1991.
Sehm, Gunter G. *Charles Sealsfields Kajütenbuch im Kontext der literarischen Tradition und der revolutionär-restaurativen Epoche des 19. Jahrhunderts*. Stuttgart: Charles Sealsfield-Gesellschaft, 1981.
———. *Charles Sealsfields Sprache im "Kajütenbuch." Eine linguistische Studie*. Stuttgart: Charles Sealsfield-Gesellschaft, 1975.
Sengle, Friedrich. "Karl Postl/Charles Sealsfield." In Sengle, *Biedermeierzeit. Deutsche Literatur im Spannungsfeld zwischen Restauration und Revolution 1818–1848*, vol. 3, *Die Dichter*, pp. 752–814. Stuttgart: Metzler, 1980.
Shears, L. A. "Storm and Sealsfield." *Germanic Review* 8 (1933): 178–82.
Spaude, Edelgard. "Das Foucaultsche Pendel des Charles Sealsfield. Über Macht und Geheimnis im Morton-Roman." *Schriftenreihe der Charles-Sealsfield-Gesellschaft* 6 (1991 [1994]): 63–82.
Spiess, Reinhard F. *Charles Sealsfields Werke im Spiegel der literarischen Kri-*

*tik. Eine Sammlung zeitgenössischer Rezensionen*. Stuttgart: Charles Sealsfield-Gesellschaft, 1977.

Steinecke, Hartmut. "Charles Sealsfield and the Novel as a Means of Enlightenment." In *The Austrian Enlightenment and Its Aftermath*, edited by Ritchie Robertson and Edward Timms. Austrian Studies 2:132–44. Edinburgh: Edinburgh University Press, 1991.

———. "Literatur als 'Aufklärungsmittel': Zur Neubestimmung der Werke Charles Sealsfields zwischen Österreich, Deutschland und Amerika." In *Die österreichische Literatur. Ihr Profil im 19. Jahrhundert (1830–1880)*, ed. Herbert Zeman, pp. 399–422. Graz: Akademische Druck- und Verlagsanstalt, 1982.

———. *Romanpoetik von Goethe bis Thomas Mann. Entwicklungen und Probleme der "demokratischen Kunstform" in Deutschland*. Munich: Fink, 1987.

Steinmann, Denise. *Katalog der Sealsfieldiana in der Zentralbibliothek Solothurn*. In *Sämtliche Werke*, ed. Arndt, vol. 27. Hildesheim: Olms, 1990.

Strelka, Joseph P. "Österreichische Perspektiven Amerikas. Charles Sealsfields 'Prärie am Jacinto.' Zwischen Wirklichkeit und Traum." In Strelka, *Das Wesen des Österreichischen in der Literatur*, pp. 95–112. Tübingen and Basel: Francke, 1994.

Uhlendorf, B. A. *Charles Sealsfield: Ethnic Elements and National Problems in His Works*. Chicago: Deutsch-Amerikanische Historische Gesellschaft von Illinois, 1920–21.

Walther, Klaus. "Carl Postls mährische Kindheitslandschaft." *Schriftenreihe der Charles-Sealsfield-Gesellschaft* 4 (1989): 25–30.

Weiss, Walter. "Der Zusammenhang zwischen Amerika-Thematik und Erzählkunst bei Charles Sealsfield (Karl Postl). Ein Beitrag zum Verhältnis von Dichtung und Politik im 19. Jahrhundert." *Literaturwissenschaftliches Jahrbuch*, n.s., 8 (1967): 95–117. Reprinted in Ritter, ed., *Deutschlands literarisches Amerikabild*, pp. 272–94.

Wesseley, Herbert. "Charles Sealsfields Jugendland an der Thaya—in Wort und Bild." *Schriftenreihe der Charles-Sealsfield-Gesellschaft* 4 (1989): 7–23.

Zeman, Herbert. "Ein Mitteleuropäer sieht Amerika—die Genrebilder der frühen Erzählungen Charles Sealsfields." *Jahrbuch des Wiener Goethe-Vereins* 97–98 (1993–94): 57–63. Reprinted in *Schriftenreihe der Charles-Sealsfield-Gesellschaft* 8 (1995).

Zettl, Walter. "Pater Postl und Doktor Sealsfield oder die Suche nach dem Land der Freiheit." *Jahrbuch des Wiener Goethe-Vereins* 97–98 (1993–94): 47–56. Reproduced in *Schriftenreihe der Charles-Sealsfield-Gesellschaft* 8 (1995).

*See also* Doerry, "Three Versions of America"; Kriegleder, "Die 'Prosa unserer Union'"; Schuchalter, "Literature, Representation, and the Negotiation of Cultural Lacunae"; Schuchalter, "'Mein Eden, lieber Sigismund.'"

Sellers, Charles. *The Market Revolution: Jacksonian America, 1815–1846*. New York: Oxford University Press, 1991.

Semmingsen, Ingrid. *Norway to America: A History of the Migration.* Translated by Einar Haugen. Minneapolis: University of Minnesota Press, 1978.
Seyppel, Joachim. *Columbus Bluejeans oder Das Reich der falschen Bilder.* Munich: Rütten und Loening, 1965.
Simms, W[illiam] Gilmore. *Woodcraft; or, Hawks about the Dovecoat.* New York: Redfield, 1854.
———. *The Yemassee: A Romance of Carolina.* New York: Harper, 1835.
Ridgley, J. V. *William Gilmore Simms.* New York: Twayne, 1962.
Solger, Reinhold. *Anton in Amerika. Novelle aus dem deutsch-amerikanischen Leben.* 2 vols. New York: Steiger, 1872.
———. "Aus Hanns von Katzenfingen und seine Frau Tante, geb. F. v. K. Naturwüchsiges Helden-Gedicht." *Deutsch-amerikanische Monatshefte* 1, no. 1 (1864): 138–52.
———. *Der Reichstagsprofessor.* In *Der deutsche Michel. Revolutionskomödien der Achtundvierziger,* edited by Horst Denkler, pp. 389–429. Stuttgart: Reclam, 1971.
———. "Der Untergang. Bruchstück aus einer Elegie." *Deutsch-amerikanische Monatshefte* 3, No. 1 (1866): 242–43.
Denkler, Horst. "Die Schule des Kapitalismus. Reinhold Solgers deutschamerikanisches 'Seitenstück' zu Gustav Freytags 'Soll und Haben.'" In Bauschinger et al., eds., *Amerika in der deutschen Literatur,* pp. 108–23.
Dickie, Milton Allan. "Reinhold Solger." Diss., University of Pittsburgh, 1930.
Kapp, Friedrich. "Reinhold Solger." In Kapp, *Aus und über Amerika. Thatsachen und Erlebnisse,* 1:356–80. Berlin: Springer, 1876.
Schuchalter, Jerry. "Reinhold Solger's *Bildungsreise* to the New World: The Immigrant Intellectual on Trial in America." In *Crossing Scholarly Borders: Interdisciplinary Studies of Language and Literature,* edited by Rolf Lindholm, pp. 9–51. Vaasa: Vaasan Yliopisto, 1993.
Spahn, Raymond Jürgen. "German Accounts of Early Nineteenth-Century Life in Illinois." *Papers on Language and Literature* 14 (1978): 473–88.
Spiel, Hilde. *Lisas Zimmer.* Munich: Nymphenburger, 1965.
Spoerri, William T. *The Old World and the New: A Synopsis of Current European Views on American Civilization.* Zurich and Leipzig: Niehans, n.d. [ca. 1936].
Spuler, Richard. *"Germanistik" in America: The Reception of German Classicism, 1870–1905.* Stuttgart: Heinz, 1982.
Steinbrink, Bernd. *Abenteuerliteratur des 19. Jahrhunderts in Deutschland. Studien zu einer vernachlässigten Gattung.* Tübingen: Niemeyer, 1983.
Steinecke, Hartmut. *Romanpoetik von Goethe bis Thomas Mann. Entwicklungen und Probleme der "demokratischen Kunstform" in Deutschland.* Munich: Fink, 1987.
Stern, J. Peter. "Language Consciousness and Nationalism in the Age of Bernard Bolzano." In *Crisis and Culture in Post-Enlightenment Germany: Essays in Honour of Peter Heller,* edited by Hans Schulte and David Richards, pp. 129–54. Lanham, Md.: University Press of America, 1993.
Strubberg, Friedrich Armand. *Alte und neue Heimath.* Breslau: Trewendt, 1859.

———. *Amerikanische Jagd- und Reiseabenteuer aus meinem Leben in den westlichen Indianergebieten.* Stuttgart and Augsburg: Cotta, 1858.

———. *Bis in die Wildniss.* 2nd ed. Breslau: Trewendt, 1863.

———. *Friedrichsburg, die Colonie des deutschen Fürsten-Vereins in Texas.* 2 vols. Leipzig: Fleischer, 1867.

———. *Scenen aus den Kämpfen der Mexicaner und Nordamerikaner.* Breslau: Trewendt, 1859.

Barba, Preston Albert. *The Life and Works of Friedrich Armand Strubberg.* Philadelphia: University of Pennsylvania, 1913.

Huber, Armin O. "Frederic Armand Strubberg, Alias Dr. Shubbert, Town-Builder, Physician and Adventurer, 1806–1889." *West Texas Historical Association Yearbook* 38 (1962): 37–71.

See also Arndt, "Sealsfield and Strubberg," under Sealsfield, Charles; Gillespie County Historical Society, *Pioneers in God's Hills*; King, John O. *Meusebach*; Klotzbach, *Die Solms-Papiere*; Lich, Moltmann, and Womack, "'New Crowns to Old Glory'"; Märtin, *Wunschpotentiale*; Penniger, ed., *Fest-Ausgabe*; Woodson, *American Negro Slavery*.

Stuecher, Dorothea Diver. *Twice Removed: The Experience of German-American Women Writers in the 19th Century.* Frankfurt am Main: Peter Lang, 1990.

Suleiman, Susan Rubin. *Authoritarian Fiction: The Ideological Novel as a Literary Genre.* New York: Columbia University Press, 1983.

Sullivan, Walter. *In Praise of Blood Sports and Other Essays.* Baton Rouge: Louisiana State University Press, 1990.

Sutherland, Daniel E. *The Expansion of Everyday Life, 1860–1976.* New York: Harper and Row, 1990.

Talvj (Talvi). *The Exiles: A Tale.* New York: Putnam, 1853.

———. *Geschichte der Colonisation von New England. Von den ersten Niederlassungen daselbst im Jahre 1607 bis zur Einführung der Provinzialverfassung von Massachusetts im Jahre 1692.* Leipzig: Brockhaus, 1847.

———. *Historical View of the Languages and Literatures of the Slavic Nations; with a Sketch of Their Popular Poetry.* New York: Putnam, 1850.

Milović, Jevto M. *Talvjs erste Übertragungen für Goethe und ihre Briefe an Kopitar.* Nendeln: Kraus Reprint, 1968; originally 1941.

Wallach, Martha Kaarsberg. "Der Einfluß der Klassik in Talvjs Werken." In *Begegnung mit dem 'Fremden.' Grenzen—Traditionen—Vergleiche. Akten des VIII. Internationalen Germanisten-Kongresses Tokyo 1990*, edited by Eijirō Iwasaki, 7:89–96. Munich: iudicium, 1991.

———. "Die Erfahrung der Fremde in Talvjs Leben und Werk." In Maler, ed., *E otische Welt in populären Lektüren*, pp. 81–92.

———. "Talvj: Lebenserfahrung und Gesellschaftkritik der frühen Erzählungen." In *Autoren damals und heute. Literaturgeschichtliche Beispiele veränderter Wirkungshorizonte*, edited by Gerhard P. Knapp, pp. 211–30. Amsterdam and Atlanta: Rodopi, 1991.

———. "Talvj (Therese Albertine Luise von Jakob Robinson) (1797–1870)." In *Dictionary of Literary Biography*, vol. 133, *Nineteenth-Century German Writers to 1840*, edited by James Hardin and Siegfried Mews, pp. 280–88. Detroit: Gale Research, 1993.

———. "Women of German-American Fiction: Therese Robinson, Mathilde Anneke, and Fernande Richter." In Trommler and McVeigh, eds., *America and the Germans*, 1:331–42.
Tatum, John Hargrove. *The Reception of German Literature in U.S. German Texts, 1864–1918*. Frankfurt am Main: Peter Lang, 1988.
Taylor, William R. *Cavalier and Yankee: The Old South and American National Character*. New York: Braziller, 1961.
Thran, Jakob. *Meine Auswanderung nach Texas unter dem Schutze des Mainzer Vereins. Ein Warnungs-Beispiel für Auswanderungslustige*. Berlin: Krause, 1848.
Tocqueville, Alexis de. *Democracy in America*. Edited by Philipps Bradley. Revised by Francis Bowen. Translated by Henry Reeve. New York: Vintage, 1945.
Trefousse, Hans L. "Friedrich Hecker and Carl Schurz." *Yearbook of German-American Studies* 26 (1991): 33–41.
———. *Germany and America: Essays on Problems of International Relations and Immigration*. New York: Brooklyn College Press, 1980.
Trommler, Frank. "Inventing the Enemy: German-American Cultural Relations, 1900–1917." In *Confrontation and Cooperation: Germany and the United States in the Era of World War I, 1900–1924*, edited by Hans-Jürgen Schröder, pp. 99–125. Providence, R. I.: Berg, 1993.
Trommler, Frank, and Joseph McVeigh, eds. *America and the Germans: An Assessment of a Three-Hundred-Year History*. Vol. 1, *Immigration, Language, Ethnicity*. Vol. 2, *The Relationship in the Twentieth Century*. Philadelphia: University of Pennsylvania Press, 1985.
Urzidil, Johannes. *Das Große Hallelujah*. Munich: Langen-Müller, 1959.
Schwarz, Egon. "Urzidil und Amerika." *German Quarterly* 58 (1985): 223–37.
Victory, Beatrice Marguerite. *Benjamin Franklin and Germany*. Diss., University of Pennsylvania, 1915.
Vizetelly, Henry. *Glances Back through Seventy Years: Autobiographical and Other Reminiscences*. London: Paul, Trench, Trübner, 1893.
Wagner, Maria, ed. *Was die Deutschen aus Amerika berichteten 1828–1865*. Stuttgart: Heinz, 1985.
Wagner, Wolfgang. "The Europeans' Image of America." In *America and Western Europe: Problems and Prospects*, edited by Karl Kaiser and Hans-Peter Schwarz, pp. 19–32. Lexington, Mass.: Heath, 1977.
Wagnleiter, Reinhold. *Coca-Colonisation und Kalter Krieg. Die Kulturmission der USA in Österreich nach dem Zweiten Weltkrieg*. Vienna: Verlag für Gesellschaftskritik, 1991.
Walker, Mack. *Germany and the Emigration, 1816–1885*. Cambridge, Mass.: Harvard University Press, 1964.
Walser, Martin. *Brandung*. Frankfurt am Main: Suhrkamp, 1985.
Ward, John William. *Andrew Jackson: Symbol for an Age*. New York: Oxford University Press, 1962.
Weber, Paul C. *America in Imaginative German Literature in the First Half of the Nineteenth Century*. New York: Columbia University Press, 1926.
Wehdeking, Volker Christian. *Der Nullpunkt. Über die Konstituierung der deut-*

*schen Nachkriegsliteratur (1945–1948) in den amerikanischen Kriegsgefangenenlagern.* Stuttgart: Metzler, 1971.

Wettberg, Gabriela. *Das Amerika-Bild und seine negativen Konstanten in der deutschen Nachkriegsliteratur.* Heidelberg: Winter, 1987.

Winter, Eduard. *Die Sozial- und Ethnoethik Bernard Bolzanos: Humanistischer Patriotismus oder romantischer Nationalismus im vormärzlichen Österreich. Bernard Bolzano contra Friedrich Schlegel.* Österreichische Akademie der Wissenschaften Philosophisch-historische Klasse Sitzungsberichte, vol. 316. Vienna: Österreichische Akademie der Wissenschaften, 1977.

Winter, Rolf. *Ami go home. Plädoyer für den Abschied von einem gewalttätigen Land.* Hamburg: Rasch und Röhring, 1989.

———. *Gottes eigenes Land? Werte, Ziele und Realitäten der Vereinigten Staaten von Amerika.* Hamburg: Rasch und Röhring, 1991.

Wolzogen, Ernst von. *Der Dichter in Dollarica. Blumen-, Frucht- und Dornenstücke aus dem Märchenland der unbedingten Gegenwart.* 3rd ed. Berlin: Fontane, 1912.

Woodward, C. Vann. *The Old World's New World.* New York: Oxford University Press, 1991.

Woodson, Leroy Henry. *American Negro Slavery in the Works of Friedrich Strubberg, Friedrich Gerstäcker and Otto Ruppius.* Washington, D.C.: Catholic University of America, 1949.

Zantop, Susanne. "Dialectics and Colonialism: The Underside of the Enlightenment." In *Impure Reason: Dialectic of Enlightenment in Germany*, edited by W. Daniel Wilson and Robert C. Holub, pp. 301–21. Detroit: Wayne State University Press.

Zipser, Richard A. *Edward Bulwer-Lytton and Germany.* Frankfurt am Main: Peter Lang, 1974.

Zschokke, Heinrich. *Die Prinzessin von Wolfenbüttel. Novellen und Dichtungen*, vol. 7. New York: Radde, 1859–65.

    Oppel, Horst. "Die deutsche Siedlung in Louisiana im Spiegel des Amerika-Romans der Goethezeit. Heinrich Zschokkes *Prinzessin von Wolfenbüttel.*" In *Studies in German Literature*, edited by Carl Hammer Jr., pp. 18–38. Baton Rouge: Louisiana State University Press, 1963.

# Index

Adams, Abigail, 29
Adams, John, 29, 35
Adams, John Quincy, 12, 24, 29, 30, 35, 71, 77
*Adelsverein*, 101, 102, 103–4, 108–9, 120
Adler, Renata, 249
Adorno, Theodor W., 213
Albert (prince consort of England), 104
Alexandrine (princess of Baden; duchess of Saxe-Coburg-Gotha), 123
Alexis, Willibald, 14
Andersch, Alfred, 264
André, John, 35
Anneke, Mathilde, 259
Armand. *See* Strubberg, Friedrich Armand
Arndt, Karl, 38, 61
Arnold, Benedict, 35
Assing, Ottilie, 152, 259, 287 (n. 11)
Auerbach, Berthold, 24, 37, 216, 258–59
Austin, Stephen, 64

Bahr, Hermann, 213
Baird, Spencer F., 93
Bakunin, Mikhail Aleksandrovich, 219
Balzac, Honoré de, 5
Barba, Preston, 101
Barker, Lex, 249
Bentham, Jeremy, 56
Bernhard (duke of Weimar), 173
Biddle, Nicholas, 203
Billington, Ray Allen, 90–91, 148, 231, 250
Bismarck, Otto von, 169, 238, 241, 255
Blériot, Louis, 243
Bloch, Ernst, 235, 250
Blum, Robert, 168
Bodmer, Karl, 94
Böhm (partner of Gerstäcker), 165–66
Börne, Ludwig, 34, 211
Bolzano, Bernard, 3, 10, 55–57
Bonaparte, Joseph, 5, 12
Boone, Daniel, 6, 17
Borch, Herbert von, 300 (n. 40)
Borge, Tomás, 250–51

Brecht, Bertolt, 262
Brehm, Alfred, 123
Brenner, Peter, 100, 141, 153, 169
Brice, Pierre, 249
Brod, Max, 236
Bromme, Traugott, 115
Bryant, William Cullen, 208
Buchanan, James, 94, 99
Bülow, Dietrich von, 201
Buffon, George Louis Leclerc, Comte de, 201
Bulwer-Lytton, Edward, 18, 49, 84–85, 129, 200, 220
Burr, Aaron, 213
Byron, George Gordon, Lord, 219

Calhoun, John C., 30, 86
Carey, Henry Charles, 11
Carey, Mathew, 11
Carlyle, Thomas, 220
Castle, Eduard, 11–12
Catlin, George, 94
Chandler, Raymond, 268
Charbonneau, Baptiste, 91–92
Child, Lydia Maria, 16
Clark, William, 92
Clay, Henry, 65, 110, 170
Cody, Iron Eyes, 248–49
Conrad, Joseph, 89, 287 (n. 9)
Cooper, James Fenimore, 8, 16, 26, 62, 84, 90, 94, 96, 97, 107, 130–66 passim, 200, 230–31, 244, 251, 258, 263
Costenoble, Hermann, 95, 125, 129, 157–58, 177, 192
Cotta, Johann Friedrich von, 18, 24
Cotta, Johann Georg von, 115, 123, 126, 134, 157, 187
Coughlin, Charles E., 262
Cramer, Karl Gottlob, 95
Crockett, Davy, 115

Dalla Costa, Juan Bautiste (president of Guyana [Bolívar, Venezuela]), 173
Da Ponte, Lorenzo (father), 212–13

337

Da Ponte, Lorenzo (son), 212
Darwin, Charles, 147, 238, 239
Davis, Jefferson, 93
Defoe, Daniel, 129, 200
Denkler, Horst, 222
Dickens, Charles, 49, 95, 128, 129, 158, 211, 220, 221
Di Maio, Irene S., 148, 150
Disney, Walt, 286 (n. 14)
Doré, Gustave, 216
Dostoyevsky, Fedor Mikhailovich, 217
Douglas, Stephen A., 43
Doyle, Arthur Conan, Sir, 90, 229–30, 232
Draper, John William, 212
Droste-Hülshoff, Annette von, 162
Duden, Gottfried, 166, 210, 211
Dumas, Alexandre, 244
Durzak, Manfred, 169, 177

Eberle, Josef, 264
Ebner-Eschenbach, Marie von, 214
Eggebrecht, Harald, 253
Eichendorff, Joseph von, 100, 129
Einstein, Albert, 250
Elliott, William, 139–40
Emerson, Ralph Waldo, 220
Ernst II (duke of Saxe-Coburg-Gotha), 104, 123, 138, 173

Faubus, Orval, 115
Faulkner, William, 140–41
Federspiel, Jürg, 267–68
Feuerbach, Ludwig, 219
Fielding, Henry, 17
Fillmore, Millard, 277 (n. 45)
Fischer, Bernd, 88
Flint, Timothy, 16, 17, 50, 51, 54
Follen, Eliza Lee, 202
Follen, Karl, 202
Fontane, Emilie, 96
Fontane, Theodor, 96, 174, 258, 299 (n. 15)
Ford, John, 266
Franklin, Benjamin, 64, 210, 258–59
Fredrik I (landgrave of Hesse, king of Sweden), 101
Freiligrath, Ferdinand, 181
Frémont, John C., 95
Freud, Sigmund, 250
Freytag, Gustav, 99, 177, 219, 220–21, 223, 240

Friedrich I (king of Württemberg), 91
Friedrich II (king of Prussia), 31, 86
Friedrich III (Kaiser), 101
Friedrich Karl (prince of Prussia), 101
Friedrich Wilhelm (prince of Prussia). *See* Friedrich III
Friedrich Wilhelm IV (king of Prussia), 91, 93, 101, 220
Frint, Jakob, 55
Frisch, Max, 265
Fuerst, Norbert, 20
Fuller, Margaret, 202

Ganilh, Anthony, 16, 54
Gass, William H., 250
Gentz, Friedrich, 70–71
Gerstäcker, Anna Aurora, 123, 163
Gerstäcker, Friedrich (father), 113
Gerstäcker, Friedrich (son), xi, 61, 62, 69, 91–110 passim, 111–200, 211, 219, 221, 233, 234, 236, 243, 244, 246, 253, 254, 255, 257, 260, 263, 267
Gerstäcker, Luise Friederike, 113, 115, 160
Gerstäcker, Marie Louise, 124
Gerstner, Franz Anton Ritter von, 259
Gillhoff, Johannes, 260–61
Girard, Stephen, 12, 13
Goebel, Julius, 255
Goedsche, Herrmann, 127
Goethe, Johann Wolfgang von, 14, 68, 83–84, 113, 129, 133, 163, 202, 208, 211, 214, 218, 244
Goldsmith, Oliver, 211
Gotthelf, Jeremias, 14
Graf, Andreas, 96
Graf, Oskar Maria, 236, 262–63
Grant, Ulysses S., 196
Grey, Zane, 251
Grillparzer, Franz, 16, 214, 216, 218
Grünzweig, Walter, 14, 16, 24, 48, 77, 79
Grund, Francis, 288 (n. 22), 289 (n. 6)
*Gruppe 47*, 263–64
Gutzkow, Karl, 15

Haeckel, Ernst, 239
Haliburton, Thomas Charles, 212
Hamilton, Alexander, 35
Handke, Peter, 266–67
Harpprecht, Klaus, 300 (n. 40)
Harrison, William Henry, 169–70

Harte, Bret, 258
Hartmann, Moritz, 216
Hausmann, Manfred, 236, 261
Hawthorne, Nathaniel, 16, 208
Haydn, Franz Josef, 125
Hebbel, Friedrich, 259
Heckmann, Herbert, 268
Hegel, Georg Wilhelm Friedrich, 219, 224
Heine, Heinrich, 83, 88, 100, 101, 102, 103, 126, 129, 181, 208, 214, 216, 224, 277 (n. 45), 296 (n. 5)
Heinse, Wilhelm, 218
Heissenbüttel, Helmut, 236
Hemingway, Ernest, 248, 264
Henisch, Peter, 236
Henry, O. (William Sydney Porter), 136
Henry, Patrick, 41, 42, 65
Herder, Johann Gottfried, 259
Herwegh, Georg, 124–25, 219
Herzen, Aleksandr Ivanovich, 219
Herzog, Roman, 229
Hesse, Hermann, 247
Hitler, Adolf, 250–51, 262
Hochhuth, Rolf, 269
Hoffman, Charles Fenno, 139
Hoffmann, Ernst Theodor Amadeus, 128
Hofmannsthal, Hugo von, 7
Hohendahl, Peter Uwe, 251
Holitscher, Arthur, 265–66
Hollyday, Guy, 174, 208
Holthusen, Hans Egon, 236
Homer, 214
Hortense (queen of Holland), 5
Hosemann, Theodor, 177
Huch, Ricarda, 236
Huch, Rudolf, 236
Hugo, Victor, 125, 129, 214
Humboldt, Alexander von, 93, 94, 95

Immermann, Karl Lebrecht, 6, 222
Irving, Washington, 8, 16, 85, 94, 129, 131, 202
Ives, Joseph Christmas, 93–94, 95, 97–98

Jackson, Andrew, 12, 19, 24–36, 37, 38, 44, 47, 56, 60–78 passim, 86, 87, 88, 155, 170, 203
Jackson, Rachel, 65–66
Jahn, Gustav, 158
Jakob, Auguste von, 202

Jakob, Ludwig Heinrich von, 202, 206
Jay, John, 64
Jean Paul, 214
Jefferson, Thomas, 31–32, 38, 40, 41, 42, 68, 75, 211
Johann (archduke of Austria), 138
Johnson, Andrew, 193–94, 212
Johnson, Uwe, 267
Jung-Stilling, Johann Heinrich, 208
Jungk, Robert, 264–65

Kästner, Erich, 236
Kafka, Franz, 236, 265–66, 294 (n. 3)
Kapp, Friedrich, 220
Keats, John, 211
Keller, Gottfried, 214, 218
Kennedy, John Pendleton, 16, 17, 39, 46
Kerr, Alfred, 261
King, Martin Luther, Jr., 268, 269
Kipling, Rudyard, 238
Kisch, Egon Erwin, 261
Königstein (companion of Strubberg), 102
Koeppen, Wolfgang, 265
Kolb, Gustav, 126
Kompert, Leopold, 215–16
Kraus, Karl, 213, 250, 262
Kriegleder, Wynfrid, 34
Kürnberger, Ferdinand, 83, 208–19, 221, 223, 246, 257, 259
Kunert, Günter, 265

Lafitte, Jean, 25, 28, 32, 63
Lamennais, Félicité de, 55
Lamprecht, Karl, 259–60
Landa, Bjarne Emil, 153
Lang, Hans-Joachim, 213
Laqueur, Walter, 248
Laube, Heinrich, 15
Leland, Charles Godfrey, 277 (n. 45)
Lenau, Nikolaus, 210–11, 288 (n. 33)
Lerner, Alan Jay, 128
Lessing, Gotthold Ephraim, 239
Lewald, August, 216
Lewis, Meriwether, 92
Lewis, Sinclair, 234
Lichtenstein, Hinrich Martin, 93
Lincoln, Abraham, 38, 43, 194, 195, 220, 255, 258, 262
Loewe, Frederick, 128
*Lone Ranger, The*, 251–52

Longfellow, Henry Wadsworth, 208
Lorrain, Claude, 20
Louis-Philippe (king of the French), 33–34
Lover, Samuel, 16, 271 (n. 10)
Lowsky, Martin, 238, 239

Maass, Joachim, 262
Macpherson, James, 202
Madison, James, 35, 75
Magris, Claudio, 68
Mann, Klaus, 250, 252
Markham, Sara, 270
Marryat, Frederick, 130
Marx, Karl, 175
Mather, Cotton, 204
Matthias, L. L., 269
Maximilian (emperor of Mexico), 194
May, Heinrich August, 232
May, Karl, x, xi, 96, 105, 106, 109, 117, 139, 141, 146, 149, 227–56, 257, 263, 266, 270
May, Klara, 237, 239, 252, 254
Mays, Carl, 248
Mechtel, Angelika, 268
Melville, Herman, 16, 116, 123, 130, 157, 200
Menzel, Wolfgang, 84
Metternich, Clemens Lothar Wenzel (prince), 10, 11, 13, 24, 34, 55, 70, 80
Meusebach, John O., 103
Mikoletzky, Juliane, 257
Miller, James, 122, 126, 158, 164, 200
Milton, John, 63
Mitchell, Margaret, 203
Möllhausen, Balduin, 91–101, 105, 106, 107, 108, 110, 113, 129, 159, 219, 221, 236, 244, 246, 257, 258, 259, 275 (n. 1), 288 (n. 32)
Möllhausen, Caroline, 93
Möllhausen, Elisabeth (Baroness von Falkenstein), 91
Moellhausen, Henry, 91
Monroe, James, 75, 212
Montesquieu, Charles Louis de Secondat, Baron de, 57
Moore, Benjamin, 212
Moore, Clement, 212
Moore, Thomas, 129
Morton, Frederic, 246
Mosse, George L., 238
Mozart, Wolfgang Amadeus, 68, 212

Müller, Max, 216
Mundt, Theodor, 8, 15

Napoleon I, 15
Napoleon III, 5
Nietzsche, Friedrich, 217
Nolan, Philip, 6

Oppenheimer, J. Robert, 265
Ossian. *See* Macpherson, James
Ostwald, Thomas, 192
Ott, Ulrich, 269–70

Paine, Thomas, 262
Panizza, Oskar, 236
Parker, Theodore, 258
Pattie, James O., 17
Paulding, James Kirke, 16, 17, 46–47, 84, 85–86
Paul Wilhelm (duke of Württemberg), 91–92, 94
Pauw, Cornelius de, 33, 201
Plöhn, Richard, 239
Poe, Edgar Allan, 9, 16, 90
Poinsett, Joel, 10, 12
Polk, James, 170
Postl, Carl. *See* Sealsfield, Charles
Postl, Juliane, 3

Raabe, Wilhelm, 99, 128, 234, 240, 258
Rahv, Philip, 17
Randolph, John, 46–47
Reinhardt, Carl, 131, 177
Reitzel, Robert, 122
Retcliffe, John, Sir. *See* Goedsche, Herrmann
Richter, Hans Werner, 264
Richter, Jean Paul Friedrich. *See* Jean Paul
Ritter, Alexander, 18, 20, 36, 88
Robinson, Edward, 202
Robinson, Therese Albertine Luise von Jakob. *See* Talvj
Roebling, John, 198
Roosevelt, Franklin Delano, 262
Rosa, Salvator, 20
Rosas, Juan Manuel de (president of Argentina), 173
Rosas, Manuelita de, 173
Ross, Colin, 210, 261–62
Roth, Gerhard, 268

Rousseau, Jean-Jacques, 145
Ruge, Arnold, 219
Ruppius, Otto, 257

Saar, Ferdinand von, 214
Sacajawea, 92
Sacher-Masoch, Leopold von, 214
Scharang, Michael, 267
Schiller, Friedrich, 129, 165, 195, 201, 208, 214, 218, 220, 223, 244, 258
Schlegel, Friedrich, 8, 201, 218
Schlesinger, Arthur, 19
Schlieben, Erwin, 216–17
Schmidt, Arno, 232, 235–36, 251
Schmidt, Julian, 223
Schmiedt, Helmut, 240–41, 255
Schneider, Sascha, 243
Schnitzler, Günter, 14, 20
Schopenhauer, Arthur, 217
Schoppe, Amalie, 114, 259
Schubbert, Dr. *See* Strubberg, Friedrich Armand
Schuchalter, Jerry, 18, 20, 21, 45, 49, 71–72, 76, 222–23
Schüppen, Franz, 16, 55, 56
Schütz, Eduard, 113
Schultz, Hermann, 114, 115, 129, 131, 133, 134, 157, 160, 163, 173, 200
Schweitzer, Albert, 250
Scott, Sir Walter, 5, 14–15, 49, 84, 131, 202
Scott, Winfield, 102, 103
Sealsfield, Charles, xi, 1–89, 90, 98–99, 102, 103, 110, 128–29, 149–76 passim, 193, 199, 212, 221, 222, 239, 244, 246, 255, 259, 267, 291 (n. 15)
Sedgewick, Catherine Maria, 16
Seifert, Caroline. *See* Möllhausen, Caroline
Sengle, Friedrich, 13, 14
Seyppel, Joachim, 266
Shakespeare, William, 16, 63
Sherman, William Tecumseh, 124, 146, 148, 193, 195
Shubbert, Dr. *See* Strubberg, Friedrich Armand
Simms, William Gilmore, 16, 17–18, 47–48, 153
Slick, Sam. *See* Haliburton, Thomas Charles
Smith, Joseph, 159

Solger, Karl Wilhelm Ferdinand, 219
Solger, Reinhold, 138, 219–25, 246
Sophie (princess of Thurn and Taxis, duchess of Württemberg), 91
Spiel, Hilde, 263
Spiess, Christian Hinrich, 95
Staël, Germaine de, 18
Steinbrink, Bernd, 237
Stifter, Adalbert, 218
Stowe, Harriet Beecher, 47, 97, 106, 107, 153
Strubberg, Antoinette, 102
Strubberg, Emilie, 102
Strubberg, Friedrich Armand, 91, 97, 101–10, 113, 119, 138, 144, 154, 163, 211, 221, 246, 257
Strubberg, Heinrich Friedrich, 101
Sturt, Charles, 143
Sue, Eugène, 15, 105, 129, 218
Sullivan, Walter, 139
Sutter, John, 187, 188
Swehn, Jörnjakob. *See* Gillhoff, Johannes

Taggart, Marion Ames, 247
Talvj, 201–8, 221, 246
Tholuck, Friedrich August, 204
Thoreau, Henry, 145
Tocqueville, Alexis de, 33, 40, 43, 57, 63, 172, 176, 207
Traven, B., 21–22
Treitschke, Heinrich von, 254
Tucker, George, 16
Turgenyev, Ivan Sergeyevich, 214
Turner, Frederick Jackson, 71–72, 78
Turner, Nat, 43, 45
Tyler, John, 170
Tyrwhitt-Brooks, J. *See* Vizetelly, Henry

Urzidil, Johannes, 263

Van Buren, Martin, 10, 19, 77, 86, 169, 211
Varnhagen von Ense, Karl August, 152, 259
Victoria (queen of England), 104
Viertel, Berthold, 262
Vizetelly, Henry, 188
Voltaire, 214

Wallach, Martha Kaarsberg, 201, 205
Walser, Martin, 268

Walsh, Mike, 86
Washington, George, 41, 42, 64, 269
Wayne, John, 248
Weber, Max, 210, 213
Weiss, Walter, 66
Wellington, duke of (Arthur Wellesley), 34
Werner, Alfred, 262
Whipple, Amiel Weeks, 93
Whitman, Walt, 16
Whittier, John Greenleaf, 208
Wilhelm I (king of Prussia; Kaiser), 104, 214
Wilhelm II (Kaiser), 236, 238
Willkomm, Ernst, 209
Willrich, Georg, 203
Wilson, Woodrow, 261
Winchester, Jonas, 9
Winter, Rolf, 269
Wister, Owen, 251
Wittgenstein, Ludwig, 213
Wolzogen, Ernst von, 260
Woodward, C. Vann, 41
Wright, Fanny, 70
Wright, Orville, 243
Wright, Wilbur, 243

Zschokke, Heinrich, 257–58
Zuckmayer, Carl, 263, 265

www.ingramcontent.com/pod-product-compliance
Lightning Source LLC
Chambersburg PA
CBHW021800220426
43662CB00006B/132